Beyond the Crossroads

Beyond the Crossroads

THE DEVIL & THE BLUES TRADITION

Adam Gussow

The University of North Carolina Press
CHAPEL HILL

Cover illustration inspired by a still from the film *Crossroads*,
    directed by Walter Hill (1986).

Library of Congress Cataloging-in-Publication Data
Names: Gussow, Adam, author.
Title: Beyond the crossroads : the devil and the blues tradition /
    Adam Gussow.
Other titles: New directions in southern studies.
Description: Chapel Hill : The University of North Carolina Press, [2017]
Series: New directions in southern studies | Includes bibliographical
    references and index.
Identifiers: LCCN 2017002264 | ISBN 9781469633657 (cloth : alk. paper) |
    ISBN 9781469633664 (pbk : alk. paper) | ISBN 9781469633671 (ebook)
Subjects: LCSH: Blues (Music)—Southern States—History and criticism. |
    Blues (Music)—Religious aspects. | Devil in music. | Johnson, Robert,
    1911–1938.
Classification: LCC ML3521 .G94 2017 | DDC 781.6430976—dc23 LC record
    available at https://lccn.loc.gov/2017002264

The blues is nothing but the devil.
—JAMES "SON" THOMAS

Contents

Illustrations

Beyond the Crossroads

INTRODUCTION

The blues is like the devil . . . it comes on you like a spell
The blues is like the devil . . . it comes on you like a spell
Blues will leave your heart full of trouble . . . and your
    poor mind full of hell

—LONNIE JOHNSON, "Devil's Got the Blues" (1938)

BROADENING THE CONVERSATION

This book offers a series of explorations into the role played by the devil figure within an evolving blues tradition. It is primarily a thematic study, one that pays particular attention to the lyrics of recorded blues songs; but it is also a cultural study, one that seeks to tell a story about blues-invested southern lives, black and white, by mining an extensive array of sources, including government documents, church archives, telephone directories, and personal interviews. Although aspiring to the comprehensiveness of a true survey, I have chosen to emphasize certain themes at the expense of others. The first four chapters of this study investigate, in sequence, the origins and import of the phrase "the devil's music" within black southern communities; the devil as a toastmaster and pimp who both empowers and haunts migrant black blueswomen in the urban North of the Jazz Age; the devil as a symbol of Jim Crow and an icon for black southern bluesmen entrapped by that system; and the devil as a shape-shifting troublemaker within blues songs lamenting failed romantic relationships. The fifth and final chapter is an extended, three-part meditation on the myth-encrusted figure of Robert Johnson. It offers, in turn, a new interpretation of his life and musical artistry under the sign of his mentor, Ike Zimmerman; a reading of Walter Hill's *Crossroads* (1986) that aligns the film with the racial anxieties of modern blues culture; and a narrative history detailing the way the townspeople of Clarksdale, Mississippi, transformed a pair of unimportant side streets into "the crossroads" over a sixty-year period, rebranding their town as the devil's territory and Johnson's chosen haunt, a mecca for blues tourism in the contemporary Delta.

One of my chief desires, as this list suggests, is to broaden the conversation about the devil and the blues, rescuing it from the pronounced narrowing that has taken place in recent decades. As an Internet search of the words "devil blues" makes clear, crossroads legendry—Robert Johnson selling his soul to the devil at midnight at an imagined Mississippi Delta intersection—has come to dominate both popular understandings and more substantial studies, the latter of which generally critique the former. This impoverishment of our idea-set about the devil and the blues has occurred for several reasons, and not just because Johnson's legend-propagators and revisionists have run the table.

One reason is simply the loss of cultural memory incurred by the passage of time. With the arguable exception of Jon Michael Spencer's pioneering study *Blues and Evil* (1993), the full extent of the blues lyric tradition devoted to songs that name, petition, identify with, celebrate, and denigrate the devil and his hellish home is unknown to even the most dedicated aficionados and academics. Although the devil was a figure of considerable interest to African American blues singers, songwriters, and audiences between the 1920s and the 1960s, that period has passed, as have many of the specific social concerns that made the devil such an adaptable and effective lyric instrument for saying what needed to be said. This study, which began with the author's attempt to compile a comprehensive list of blues recordings invoking the devil and hell, recuperates both the lyric archive—roughly 125 recordings between 1924 and 1999—and the concerns that animated it.[1]

A second reason for the narrowness of contemporary understandings of the devil-blues tradition is the progressive whitening of the blues audience since the folk revival of the early 1960s, so that baby boomers and their desire to establish a workable genealogy for blues-rock have come to predominate. The elevation of Johnson and his mythology, mediated through a handful of his recordings and the awed testimony of Eric Clapton and other aging stars, has been vital to this process.[2] In 1986, shortly after Johnson was inducted into the Rock and Roll Hall of Fame as an "early influence," the first known photo of him was published in *Rolling Stone* magazine; that same year, Johnson's fictive transaction with the devil, revisited by his surviving black partner, Willie Brown (Joe Seneca), and Brown's youthful white apprentice, Eugene Martone (Ralph Macchio), was brought to the screen in *Crossroads*, the first and only Hollywood feature about the blues to be filmed on location in Mississippi. The combined effect of those investments, along with the unexpectedly popular release of Johnson's *Complete Recordings* (1990) on CD, was to reinforce sensationalist understandings of the devil's role in the blues. A stream of crossroads pilgrims soon found their way to Mississippi and, with the help of a state-sponsored "Every Crossroads Has a Story" ad campaign (1997), laid the groundwork for the emergence of that state's blues tourism industry at the turn of the millennium.

A third reason for the narrowness of the devil-blues conversation, paradoxically, is the Afrocentric turn in our understanding of crossroads mythology. The popular conception of Johnson as a spirit-conducting prodigy has been reinforced by African American scholars such as Julio Finn (*The Bluesman*, 1986) and Samuel Floyd (*The Power of Black Music*, 1995), who insist on framing his celebrated transaction not as a tragic Faustian bargain but as an empowering ritual interchange with Eshu-Elegbara (variously referred to as Eshu, Esu, or Legba), a Dahomean/Yoruban crossroads deity who, they argue, survived the Middle Passage and reappeared after Emancipation with his trickster's disruptiveness intact. "The tradition of making a pact at the crossroads in order to attain supernatural blues prowess," insists Finn, "is neither a creation of the Afro-American nor an invention of blues lore, but originated in Africa and is a ritual of Voodoo worship. It is doubtful whether Johnson could have written the lyrics of his songs without having been initiated into the cult."[3] "This new incarnation of Esu as the Devil," agrees Floyd, speaking of the Yoruban trickster spirit at large in the American South, "took hold as he emerged at the crossroads sometime in the late nineteenth century to deliver superior creative skills to black songsters, and exerted a powerful influence on the development of the blues."[4] Rejecting the characterization of blues as "evil" offered by scholars Paul Oliver and Paul Garon, demanding that we see the devil/Legba figure as an emblem of productive disorder rather than wholesale malevolence, these scholars certainly broaden the conversation—but only by reinforcing the popular overvaluation of the spirit-haunted crossroads within contemporary blues mythologies. Doing so, they make it hard for us to grasp just how much of the devil-blues tradition lies *beyond* the crossroads, outside the charmed circle.[5]

I have no desire to pick a fight with my African Americanist peers and elders. Quite the opposite: this study owes a great deal to Spencer, whose *Blues and Evil* offered both an invaluable road map and a bounty of useable evidence, not to mention a philosophical inclination to read lyric evocations of the devil in sociohistorical terms. That last interpretive strategy—to read the devil of certain blues songs, for example, as a figure for evil southern whiteness, as I do in chapter 3—can sometimes prove controversial, especially to those who are disinclined to view blues performance as a scene of virtuosic signifying. The objection was summed up by blues scholar David Evans in response to an early version of this manuscript:

> If someone says openly that someone or something is "the devil," then that's what is meant—the devil as archfiend and enemy of God and everything good—and *possibly* some secondary meaning as well. The devil can stand for a mistreater of the opposite sex or a mistreating white person or mistreating whites in general, and it can incorporate elements of African spiritual beings and belief systems, but for the most part the devil is the devil! This fact, uncomfortable as it may be to many modern scholars, must be faced.[6]

For the most part the devil is the devil: well, yes. And for the most part the bluesman's "baby," the one who mistreats him, is his woman. But sometimes, as Willie Foster and other black southern musicians have insisted and as Evans would surely concede, the bluesman sings about his baby mistreating him when he is filled with rage at his bossman.[7] Blues song can be a black performer's way of saying one thing openly—the permitted thing—but meaning another: "signifying and getting his revenge through songs," as Memphis Slim put it.[8] On a Deep South social landscape where black male expressive license was shadowed by apocalyptic white violence, signifying opened a space within which forbidden thoughts could be communicated while plausible deniability was maintained. It is possible, for example, that the bluesman who sings of being mistreated by his baby is singing about *both* his black wife and his white bossman—especially if, as I discuss in chapter 4, the bossman (or some other white man) is extracting sexual favors from his wife. The torturous racial and sexual politics of Jim Crow placed a premium on skillful signifying; the surreality of daily life under such circumstances demanded expressive tools adequate to the task, including the ability to enable unobjectionable and subversive meanings at the same time. In this respect, if not in all others, blues song borrowed from slave-era spirituals. As a method for interpreting blues songs, in other words, dogged literalism has its limits. That is especially true when the subject is the devil: a shape-shifter by definition, one who works behind the scenes and below the surface.

The early modern South, a fervently evangelical region in which the great majority of African American blues singers indexed by this study came of age, was indeed a world, as Evans suggests, where the devil was the devil, at least for those who hewed to "that old-time religion" evoked by the hymn of that name. This devil was the Bible's Satan, God's perennial antagonist, a figure against whose insidious temptations young people were warned daily, at home and in church, by parents, grandparents, and preachers. A remarkable number of blues performers, as I detail in chapter 1, including John Lee Hooker and Bessie Smith, grew up in households presided over by a man of the cloth. Many others were chastened by fervently churched parents. They absorbed the declamatory language and epigrammatic wisdom of the Bible; they preached the blues, warned against sin, and, on occasion, condemned wayward lovers in fiercely judgmental language, as Smith does in "Devil's Gonna Get You" (1928), repurposing religion to serve secular ends. The devil-blues tradition I investigate certainly draws on traditional folk beliefs about the devil, material that Spencer terms "devil-lore." Nature's uneven workings, for example, are attributed to the devil in Maggie Jones's "Thunderstorm Blues" (1924) and Charley Patton's "Devil Sent the Rain Blues" (1930). When Lonnie Johnson castigates his woman in "She's Making Whoopee in Hell Tonight" (1930) by singing, "Devil's got ninety thousand women, he needs just one more," he's endorsing a familiar condemnatory view of the devil as supreme tempter. But on other occasions, as young people with modern sensibilities, southern-born blues performers ironize, shrug off, or openly reject the Manichean certainties of their parents and preachers, including ideas about the devil and devil's music. "He told me that was devil music," sneered Snooky Pryor, a Delta blues harmonica player speaking of his father in terms echoed widely by his peers. "It wasn't no devil's music then, it ain't no devil's music now."[9]

Still, in one respect that remains important for this study, the blues-playing children shared an attitudinal orientation with their elders and slavery-era ancestors, drawing on and updating a long-standing pattern of imagery found in the spirituals: the southern white man, understood as the symbol of an oppressive social structure, was the devil, or could be covertly represented as one. The master, overseer, slave-catcher, and patroller of an earlier time had been supplanted, in the post-Reconstruction period, by the bossman, prison-farm captain, and sheriff; whips and chains had been redeployed in the context of a reconfigured prison-agricultural complex that coexisted with a putative freedom. But the white man was still in control, and the power wielded by the system he headed—absolute, arbitrary, consigning black victims to punishments that ranged from heightened anxiety to burning at the stake—made him a "Mr. Devil" indeed to Big Bill Broonzy, Lightnin' Hopkins, and other bluesmen who mocked him in signifying song. The South over which he ruled was, correspondingly, a kind of hell: a place from which one might, if lucky, escape "upward" to a northern Promised Land. The devil of the blues tradition, in other words, is sometimes more than *just* the devil, because ideas about good and evil in the segregated South were embedded in a racial binary with juridical backing, one that made whiteness "all right," in the words of Broonzy's parodic "Black, Brown, and White" (1946), while blacks were expected to "get back, get back, get back." As a result—or so I argue—the blues-devil, at least prior to the civil rights movement, is shadowed at certain moments by oppressive histories and the rebellious impulses those histories engendered. This study highlights those shadows, probes those histories, teases out traces of rebellion where such interpretations seem justified. If white southerners' ideas about black people had long been shaped, as Spencer and others have argued, by a conception of blackness-as-evil, then black blues singers used signifying language to subvert such aspersions, either by claiming a devilish "bad nigger" persona—rootless, promiscuous, unruly—as a source of strength rather than stigma, or by configuring spaces governed by malefic white power, in symbolic terms, as the devil's territory. I explore both expressive strategies in chapter 3.

AFRICAN SURVIVALS AND "EVIL" BLUES

One of the most vexed issues facing any investigator of the devil and the blues tradition is adjudicating the degree to which African American ideas about the devil, when they show up in connection with blues music, are sourced in an African cultural inheritance—rather than, for example, in European folk cultural beliefs and the Bible, both of which were clearly absorbed during the long acculturation process of slavery. A related issue, equally vexed, concerns the question of whether, and from whose perspective, the blues are "evil." Spencer's *Blues and Evil* is heavily invested in both questions; it begins with a full frontal attack on white blues scholars, including Oliver, Garon, and Evans, who, as "outsiders to the culture that produced the blues, have failed to capture the music's pervading ethos—its religious nature!"[10] The music's putative basis in African survivals, which I'll return to momentarily, plays a part in Spencer's critique, but even more important is his claim that Oliver and Garon have mistaken the part for the whole, taking the familiar condemnation of the blues as "devil's music" by black ministers and congregations as an accurate description rather than a slanderous, self-interested brief for the prosecution. In *Blues Fell This Morning* (1960), for example, Oliver argues that "for the most part the blues is strictly secular in content," adding that "in its bare realism the blues is somewhat bereft of spiritual values" and calling it "primarily the song of those who turned their backs on religion."[11] In *Blues and the Poetic Spirit* (1975), Garon takes an even harder line, insisting that "[the blues] . . . enters the fray wholeheartedly *on the side of Evil*. The 'devil's music' is the denunciation of everything religion stands for and the glorification of everything religion condemns. . . . The blues is uncompromisingly atheistic."[12] Yet Oliver, in the very act of making his claim, supplies lyrical evidence from "Fool's Blues" by J. T. "Funny Paper" Smith (1931) that undercuts both his own position and Garon's, showing a "fallen" bluesman who is seeking forgiveness through prayer but remains tormented by Jesus's nonresponsiveness:

> Y'know until six months ago I hadn't prayed a prayer since God
> knows when
> Until six months ago, people, I hadn't prayed a prayer since God
> knows when
> Now I'm asking God every day to please forgive me for my sins
>
> You know it must be the devil I'm servin', I know it can't be Jesus Christ,
> You know it must be the devil I'm servin', I know it can't be Jesus Christ,
> 'Cause I ask him to save me and look like he tryin' to take my life.[13]

Spencer is right to view blues songs of this sort as evidence not for blues' fundamentally secular nature, much less the singer's thoroughgoing identification with the devil and "evil," but rather for a category of real but troubled faith that, borrowing from sociologist Andrew Greeley, he terms "somewhat religious" and locates between "quite religious" and "rather unreligious."[14]

This study offers plenty of evidence in support of Spencer's thesis. Although many black southern blues performers were openly antagonistic to organized religion, mocking preachers for greed, lechery, and hypocrisy and, like Snooky Pryor, vigorously disputing the church's demonization of their music, they also sometimes expressed the frustration of true believers who felt themselves, as forcible excommunicants, to have been treated unjustly. "I didn quit church," insisted Texas songster Mance Lipscomb. "Church quit me. Cause they didn't want me ta play my music. An they say I was a sinner. I'm not a sinner. I been converted. An I'm got religion."[15] "I was a good old Baptist, singing in church," Muddy Waters told an interviewer. "I got all my good moaning and trembling going on for me right out of church. Used to be in church every Sunday."[16] Some of the strongest testimony rebutting Garon's claim about the blues locating itself squarely on the side of Evil are those moments in the lyric tradition when blues artists invoke the devil's name in ways that uncannily mirror an evangelical Christian perspective, as though acknowledging, or voicing, a parent's stern warning about the wages of sin. "I want all you women to listen to my tale of woe," sings Sara Martin of her life of promiscuity, drug use, and alcoholism in "Death Sting Me Blues" (1928). "I've got consumption of the heart, I feel myself sinking slow / Oh my heart is aching and the blues are all around my room / Blues is like the devil, they'll have me hellbound soon." [17] "Well the devil has got power, and don't you think he has," agrees Sunnyland Slim. "Boy if you ain't mighty careful, he will lead you to your grave." [18] In "Hell Bound Man" (1993), Big Wheeler begins by claiming, "I'm a hellbound man and I don't even care," but he ends with a stern, almost preacherly warning: "You hard headed mens and women, hear what I'm telling you / Don't let Satan get you, or you will be hellbound too." [19] Although a fair number of blues artists spoke against the practice of mixing sacred and blues material ("You can't serve the Lord and the Devil, too," insisted James "Son" Thomas), many others such as Rev. Gary Davis, Josephine Miles, Rev. Robert Wilkins, Charley Patton, Blind Lemon Jefferson, Rev. Rube Lacy, Arnold "Gatemouth" Moore, Ishmon Bracey, and Skip James spent portions of their lives as preachers, and many of them recorded both sorts of material—including, in Davis's case, "Don't Let the Devil Ride," a song later covered by Precious Bryant and James Peterson.[20] Bessie Smith's "Moan, You Moaners" (1930) is a straight-up call to repentance addressed to an imagined congregation and couched in ministerial language. "Just bend your head way down and pray / to have the devil chased away / come let your souls be saved today." [21]

If blues singers and their songs are, as Spencer maintains, neither bereft of spiritual values nor wholeheartedly on the side of evil, then it would be a mistake to claim that every single devil reference in the blues is grounded in some version of religious faith. A central premise of *Beyond the Crossroads* is that the devil figure was an extraordinarily useful icon for helping black southerners navigate the challenges of post-Reconstruction blues life precisely because its creole origins (African, European/folk, and biblical), complex racial valences (celebrating "bad" black assertiveness, bemoaning and/or castigating black sinfulness, signifying on evil whiteness), and immediate applicability to troubled romantic relationships allowed it to signify simultaneously in several dimensions, and in ways that sometimes defy easy ideological or theological parsing. The devil is often a carrier for whatever needs carrying; even seemingly transparent or inconsequential invocations of the devil, as a result, can disclose unexpected meanings.[22]

A good example is Bessie Smith's "Black Mountain Blues" (1930), authored by J. C. Johnson, a professional songwriter who crafted several of Smith's best-known songs, including "Empty Bed Blues":

Back in Black Mountain . . . a child will smack your face (2x)
Babies crying for liquor . . . and all the birds sing bass

Black Mountain people . . . are bad as they can be (2x)
They uses gunpowder . . . just to sweeten their tea

On this Black Mountain . . . can't keep a man in jail (2x)
If the jury finds them guilty . . . the judge'll go their bail

Had a man in Black Mountain . . . sweetest man in town (2x)
He met a city gal . . . and he throwed me down

I'm bound for Black Mountain . . . me and my razor and my gun
Lord I'm bound for Black Mountain . . . me and my razor and gun
I'm going to shoot him if he stands still . . . and cut him if he run

Down in Black Mountain . . . they all shoots quick and straight (2x)
The bullet'll get you . . . if you starts a-dodging too late

Got the devil in my soul . . . and I'm full of bad booze (2x)
I'm out here for trouble . . . I've got the Black Mountain blues[23]

With only one devil reference, and that in the final stanza, this composition might seem at first glance somewhat tangential to the tradition under consideration. Yet as Smith performs it, the first "devil" in that stanza is the highest note in the song: a belted D flat, from which Smith immediately drops a full octave, on "soul," to the tonal center below. The effect of that pitch-generated emphasis is to transform the devil into the carrier of all the rebellious and conflicting energies generated by the song to that point. The titular Black Mountain, mentioned in every stanza, is a symbolic location both geographically and ethically distinct: an unusual fusion of white hillbilly degeneracy (including moonshine-swilling children) and black badman violence, the latter voiced and claimed by the singer herself. It is also a place with plausible real-world referents: there are several Black Mountains scattered across the South, including one only eighty miles northeast of Smith's hometown of Chattanooga, Tennessee. The phrase "down in Black Mountain" configures the singer as a southern migrant brooding about a down-home community located at a considerable remove from her current northern (and perhaps urban) posting—New York City, for example, where Smith actually recorded the song. Black Mountain, as that "down" location suggests, is a violent, lawless hell, not to mention the home of Smith's cheating lover; but it's also a kind of utopia, a mountain world apart where (black) folks, including a "sweetest man," control their own destinies, for better or worse, thanks to a criminal justice system incapable of immobilizing and punishing anybody. It is "bad," in other words, in both senses that African American culture ascribes to that word: as admirable as it is dangerous. A narrative of romantic disrepair emerges from, and fuses with, an evocation of a benighted but self-determined black southern community. And the devil in Smith's soul, as she voices it in the final stanza, encompasses all that.

The reading I've offered here illustrates the general interpretive strategy of *Beyond the Crossroads*, one grounded in the idea that the devil, shapeshifter extraordinaire, is the blues' most malleable, dynamic, and important personage: not just an actor skilled enough to play many roles with many accents, but the *only* actor, apart from the blues singer himself, who is also an icon for the music as a whole. (Mr. Blues, an infrequent but similarly iconic figure, is sometimes a stand-in for the white man in his devil's guise.) Not surprisingly, some blues performers, a small but important cohort, have sought to identify themselves in various ways with the devil, rather than merely singing songs about him. Peetie Wheatstraw, Robert Johnson, and Tommy Johnson are the best known of these; I discuss the first two at length, but I also write about Cousin Leroy Rozier ("Crossroads"), Bo Chatmon ("I Am the Devil"), Stovepipe Johnson ("Devilish Blues"), Bill Gaither ("If I Was the Devil"), and Sylvester Weaver ("Can't Be Trusted Blues"). Several of these artists are associated with crossroads mythology; most are not. But all of them except Rozier, I argue, partake of the disruptive, uncontainable, good-and-evil phallicism of Legba—which is to say, all of them draw power, as signifying artists but also as cultural figures apprehended by their publics, from a specific portion of the blues' African cultural inheritance. This claim, which I have adapted from Spencer in line with ideas about African survivals dating back to Melville Herskovits's *The Myth of the Negro Past* (1941), has recently become controversial. Both Evans ("African Elements in the Blues," 2007) and Gerhard Kubik (*Africa and the Blues*, 1999) question whether Legba and his Yoruban equivalent, Esu, can be said to have "survived" in the American South in a way that enables them legitimately to be claimed as a source for the devil figure in the blues.[24]

Kubik, who has traveled widely in Africa and spent many decades researching the music there, disparages what he terms "the Nigerianization of

African-American studies" in the aftermath of Henry Louis Gates's *The Signifying Monkey* (1988). "African-American studies," he writes, "seem often to pass through a stage in which the cognitive worlds of several distinctive African cultures are mixed up and grossly reinterpreted by the authors, with the Guinea Coast and particularly Nigeria providing the most easily accessible materials."[25] After noting that Esu and Legba were indeed, as Herskovits argues, targeted by Christians in both Africa and the U.S. South as "devils," Kubik then offers several examples of Christians demonizing African religious ephemera, especially masks from Angola, Malawi, and Zambia. "Probably no one," he writes,

> will suggest that all those African religious traditions, variously stigmatized by Christians as "devil's things," must have survived in the back of the mind of blues singers. But why then also pick Esu and Legba, who incorporate religious ideas from just one delineated culture area of West Africa? Surely Yoruba and [Fon] religious ideas have had notable extensions in the Caribbean and Brazil, but little nineteenth-century presence in the United States.[26]

Why indeed pick Esu/Legba as a key antecedent of the blues-devil? There is no extant recording, at least until our own post-*Roots* age, of an African American blues singer referring to Legba, nor is that deity mentioned in blues interviews and autobiographies. Still, the theory of religious syncretism is premised on the concept of a conquered people's gods surviving by relinquishing their original names and strategically sequestering themselves within the conqueror's gods, hiding out beneath the surface while continuing in some fashion to serve the conquered people's needs. Blues singers don't need to have had Legba in mind, at least not in so many words, for the outlines of the deity, his cultural potentialities or energies of action (Keith Cartwright's term), to have persisted, especially in fusion with a Christian devil.[27] One of the principal arguments against syncretism in the American South in comparison with Catholic countries such as Brazil, after all, is that evangelical Christianity in the former region offered a much smaller pantheon of gods and saints than Catholicism in the latter—which is to say, only God and the devil. "The stringent minimalism of North American Protestantism," in hoodoo scholar Katrina Hazzard-Donald's words, "provided few points for syncretic transfer of African deity."[28] Another way of phrasing this is that the Christian devil was uniquely available for syncretic fusion with Legba—an African deity that had, so to speak, already been presyncretized with the devil by Christian missionaries prior to the Middle

Passage. Indeed, it has long been a truism of African American religious and folklore studies, most notably in the work of Herskovits and Zora Neale Hurston, that the devil of American black folk simply isn't the same devil as the biblical devil, nor do they relate to him in precisely the same way as their white southern neighbors.[29] He's more benign, less to be feared; a figure of uneasy comedy in some cases, even an intimate with whom one might do business. "So different is this tricksterlike creature from Satan as generally conceived, indeed, that he is almost a different being."[30] He was heavily admixed with Legba, in short: that was Herskovits's claim.

None of this is sufficient to rebut Kubik, but fortunately he undercuts his own claims. One reason why we might deem Esu and Legba to be formative influences on the American blues-devil, even though they reflect the religious ideas of "just one delineated culture area of West Africa," is offered by Kubik himself when he argues that "culture is not necessarily transmitted in proportion to people's numbers. *One* charismatic personality will suffice to release a chain reaction. *One* virtuoso musician can end up being imitated by hundreds. This fact has often been neglected by researchers proceeding from a collectivistic perception of culture."[31] Which is to say, the fact that Esu/Legba hails from one delineated culture area of Africa is largely irrelevant—although it *is* relevant that the part of Africa in question, the Bight of Benin, supplied almost 30 percent of Louisiana's African-born population between 1760 and 1800.[32] Beyond the basic and demonstrable claim that some relevant culture-bearers were on location, the numbers don't particularly matter. What matters is the cultural utility of the concept as embodied by its most charismatic practitioners—in this case, the idea of a highly phallic, highly mobile, devil-affiliated, good-and-bad culture hero associated with the crossroads.

As I discuss in chapter 5, black folk conceptions of crossroads rituals involving the devil, especially those collected by folklorists Harry Middleton Hyatt and Newbell Niles Puckett, are an uneven fusion of narrative and thematic motifs, some of which are clearly drawn from European folk culture but others of which make no sense unless viewed as African survivals, offering prima facie grounding for claims about Legba's continuing presence and utility.[33] More important for this study, however, is Spencer's claim that "it was specifically the personality of Legba, an emulative model of heroic action, that the blues person embodied . . . a being of synchronous duplicity. . . . He is both malevolent and benevolent, disruptive and reconciliatory, profane and sacred, and yet the predominant attitude towards him is affection rather than fear."[34] I reorient Spencer's claim in chapters 3 and

4 to suggest that Peetie Wheatstraw, Big Bill Broonzy, and other charismatic bluesmen incarnated Legba by undercutting and displacing the white devil with a phallic panache and signifying audacity that black blues audiences, most of them southerners or migrants from the South, found compelling. Legba, in Robert Pelton's formulation, "destroys normal communication to bring men outside ordinary discourse, to speak a new word and to disclose a deeper grammar to them."[35] If the devil is understood, in certain contexts, as the white man, then the devil's son-in-law, as Wheatstraw styled himself, is the man who makes love to the white man's daughter: an audacious claim indeed! But Wheatstraw walked his signifying talk, flaunting his white woman on the streets of East Saint Louis along with his "little white dog" on a chain.[36] He acted the devil, in other words, to undercut the white devil: a particularly potent form of synchronous duplicity, one with a deeper grammar we are just beginning to decode. Blues culture made a space for this kind of performer, and this kind of performative daring, not just because the cultural framework for apprehending Legba's enactment had persisted through the slavery period and beyond, however dimly, enabling audience recognition, but also because the harsh realities of Jim Crow life made a particular kind of culture hero supremely attractive.

SOUL SELLING AND CIVIC BRANDING

Important as Legba is to a fully rounded genealogy of the blues-devil, that phallus-wielding African crossroads guide is merely one aspect of a more encompassing phenomenon. This becomes evident the moment one makes gender a part of the conversation. Women, including blues singers, have no place at the crossroads; the mythology excludes them. Yet it was a black female blues singer who established the devil-blues tradition on record: Clara Smith's "Done Sold My Soul to the Devil" (1924), a composition by Porter Grainger remade by three other blues artists (John D. Twitty, Casey Bill Weldon, and Merline Johnson) and one Western swing group (Dave Edwards and His Alabama Boys) in 1937. In chapter 2, I probe the meanings of Smith's song, contextualizing it with reference to the respectability movement among African American club women and public anxiety about sexual immorality among young black female migrants to the urban North. In line with Ann Douglas's writings about "mongrel Manhattan" in the 1920s, I read the devil of the early blues as part of a continuum of transracial misbehavior that included jazz investments (Fats Waller's "There's Gonna Be the Devil to Pay," 1935), drinking culture, and fast nightlife, including "taxi girls" who hired themselves out as dance partners in New York's dance halls. In songs such as "Devil Dance Blues" (1925) and "Hellish Rag" (1927), blues singers such as Sippie Wallace and Ma Rainey evoked the pleasures and perils awaiting the southern-born black female migrant at large in the big city, contesting but also sometimes echoing the stern warnings offered by Christian ministers, black and white.

Robert Johnson is a special case. *Beyond the Crossroads* saves most of what it has to say about him for the final chapter, precisely because he and his accompanying mythology so completely dominate contemporary conversation about the blues-devil that a radical decentering was required. There is, for all that, something new to be said about Johnson. The portrait I offer is notably at odds with the idea of Johnson as a haggard, devil-haunted soul offered by Evans—but it also rejects the thoroughgoing skepticism about Johnson's investments in crossroads mythology offered by Barry Lee Pearson and Bill McCulloch, Elijah Wald, and other revisionists. I argue instead for Johnson as fearless young modernist who deliberately constructed his songs to offend uptight religionists and attract feminine attentions, signifying on crossroads mythology with ironic intent. Enabling this argument is the extraordinary detective work of folklorist Bruce Conforth, who recently located and interviewed the daughter and grandson of Ike Zimmerman, Robert Johnson's mentor, in the southern Mississippi town of Beauregard. Johnson lived with the family for "a long time," according to Zimmerman's daughter, "protected" by her father (the definition of a protégé) while he absorbed Ike's teachings. Zimmerman's spook-'em-up orientation toward his own wife and children, I argue—the "haints" he jokingly claimed he'd encountered while practicing guitar in a graveyard across the street from the family home—provides the template for Johnson's attitude toward his peers and his calculated invocations of devil-lore in his three best known devil-associated songs: "Cross Road Blues" (1936), "Hell Hound on My Trail" (1937), and "Me and the Devil Blues" (1937).

Johnson's long and unlikely afterlife in popular culture, the result of a staggering array of financial and imaginative investments, is explored in the remainder of chapter 5. Walter Hill's *Crossroads* (1986) gives Johnson only a few minutes of screen time, but that film, more than any other single cultural artifact, is responsible for engendering renewed popular interest in the blues mythology of soul-selling at a Deep South crossroads. This interest was generated by several factors, including the film's Mississippi setting, the interracial buddy plot featuring Joe Seneca and Ralph Macchio, and memorable dramatizations of the devil and his Mephistophelian assistant by African American actors Robert Judd and Joe Morton, respectively. But *Crossroads*, much maligned by reviewers and academics, is important for another reason, I argue: in staging its climactic scene as a battle between two young white blues guitarists, one of whom the film certifies as the legitimate inheritor of the blues by abjecting the other as a blues-metal poseur, the film refracts white anxieties about a mid-1980s moment when guitarist Stevie Ray Vaughan had suddenly become the first white blues performer to win major blues awards, defeating veteran black performers in the process. I interview the author of the film's screenplay, John Fusco, and the associate musical director, Arlen Roth, both of whom offer insights about Hill's directorial process—including, most notably, the fact that the screenplay and rough cut originally featured a *black* blues guitarist being defeated in the battle sequence, a scene Hill edited out of the final theatrical release.

The third and final section of chapter 5 is an extended narrative history of "the crossroads" in Clarksdale, Mississippi: the most important contemporary staging area, I argue, for what remains of the devil-blues tradition. Many are familiar with the guitar-encrusted monument that beckons tourists from that location, but few know the name of the sculptor (Vic Barbieri, a pedal-steel guitarist and retired shop teacher in the local schools) and fewer still are aware of the intersection's long and curious history as the site of two significant conflicts between the city of Clarksdale and the Mississippi Department of Transportation over a sixty-year period. This section begins by surveying the way Clarksdale's civic and cultural elites, including the Delta Blues Museum, have profited by blurring the lines between Johnson's mythology and Clarksdale's civic history, enabling them to merchandize the crossroads brand to business investors and blues tourists alike. Recuperating the actual history of the crossroads location in the 1930s with the help of Sanborn maps, newspaper accounts, and Department of Transportation blueprints, I show how it was transformed over a five-year period from a nondescript T-junction on the margins of the urban grid into the intersection of two freshly routed and paved state highways—but only over the objection of Clarksdale's white elites, who bitterly resisted the state's decision to locate the crossroads on the edge of town. Very quickly, however, Clarksdalians made a virtue of necessity. A bronze plaque erected in 1938 at "cross-roads," as the location was called, proudly spelled out the town's civic brand: library, churches, schools, and long-staple cotton. Over the next sixty years, that brand would be radically retooled. Spurred by *Crossroads* and the reissue of Robert Johnson's *Complete Recordings* on CD, Clarksdale became ground zero for Mississippi's nascent crossroads tourism industry, a phenomenon I explore through interviews with a half dozen scholar/aficionados who served as guides. Finally, with the erection of Barbieri's sculpture in 1999, the city cashed in on the factitious mythology that others had, over time, imposed on it—but only after the city attorney had crafted legislation, for the governor's eventual signature, in which Johnson's legendary deal with the devil was given the imprimatur of the city and state government. At that moment, I argue, Clarksdale decisively rebranded itself in the international blues touristic imaginary, breathing fresh life into the blues-devil for the twenty-first century even as it consolidated its position, the following year, with the Ground Zero Blues Club and an expanded, relocated Delta Blues Museum. As Mayor Bill Luckett, Ground Zero's coowner, proudly proclaimed on the Headline News Network in 2013, "Robert Johnson sold his soul to the devil to play blues guitar at our crossroads, our intersections of 49 and 61 Highways."

Although the year 2000 is the effective end date for this study, I offer some provisional thoughts in the conclusion about the blues-devil's flight path in the first decade and a half of the new millennium. Most notable, perhaps, is a surge of interest in the devil theme among white blues performers: not just redeployments of crossroads mythology in ways that gesture at Johnson as icon, but a broader imaginative investment in the devil as a way of exploring the evils and paradoxes of addiction, terrorism, and romantic misbehavior. Here, as in earlier years on the other side of town, the devil has proved to be a powerful ally.

1 , HEAVEN & HELL PARTIES
Southern Religion and the Devil's Music

My daddy, he was a preacher . . . my mother,
   she was sanctified
You know my daddy, he was a preacher . . . and my
   mother, she was sanctified
Well now you know I must've been born the devil . . .
   because I didn't want to be baptized

—LITTLE SON JACKSON, "Evil Blues" (1949)

PRIMAL SCENES, PREACHERS' BLUES

Any researcher seeking to understand the role played by the devil in the history and mythology of the blues stumbles repeatedly upon two primal scenes. Both are set in the harsh pastoral of a premodern Mississippi Delta, and both involve young black men determined to realize their destinies as creative artists. The first primal scene has become, arguably, the most visible contemporary manifestation of Southern Gothic: Robert Johnson at the crossroads, selling his soul to the devil—often figured as a larger, older black man—in exchange for supernatural skill on the guitar. The second primal scene, the obverse of the first, also involves a negotiation with larger, older figures who enact retribution on the mortal body of the bluesman-in-training. The figures in this second case are parents, grandparents, "old folks," who threaten and sometimes whip the disobedient son for daring to manifest an interest in "the devil's music."

If the first primal scene, recapitulated in novels, films, documentaries, the visual arts, touristic literature, and countless reviews of *The Complete Recordings of Robert Johnson* (1990), has become a staple of American pop culture, then the second primal scene has become a staple of the blues interview—"the bluesman's story," to invoke the subtitle of Barry Lee Pearson's trenchant study *"Sounds So Good to Me."* Pearson wisely cautions us that blues performers, evolving their life narratives through repeated contact with credulous journalists and audiences, may heighten the family conflict in their retellings as a way of subtly aggrandizing themselves, shaping their self-representations as determined freethinkers.[1] One recurring element of the bluesman's story, an outgrowth of this second primal scene, is an insistence that the blues is *not* the devil's music, regardless of what disapproving parents, ministers, and "church people" may say. Born in 1909 in the Delta town of Shelby, Mississippi, Henry Townsend offers a representative defense of his craft:

> When you use the term "blues," [a lot of people] say that's the devil's music. Well, it's just as good as gospel. The only difference is the gospel people singing about biblical days and what they done, but I'm not at biblical times. I'm of this age as of now. They can certainly discard the idea that blues will send you anyplace different from gospel, because as long as it's the truth, one truth is no greater than the other. So I just stick to the truth, and if you can condemn the truth, then I haven't got a chance, because that's all I'm telling. And the "devil's music"—I don't think the devil cares much for the truth.[2]

The "anyplace" referenced by Townsend—the pit into which blues-playing will surely send you—is of course hell, the final destination of all sinners. Rejecting this charge, Townsend depicts himself as a truthteller who is also, and crucially, a modernist. Although gospel music was itself a new and controversial art form in the 1920s and 1930s, one that provoked considerable dissension when it was introduced into mainline black churches in the urban North, Townsend represents it (and, by implication, the spirituals and other church music) as yesterday's news, a recapitulation of "biblical days." The blues, by contrast, locates itself squarely in "this age" and inoculates itself against the devil's-music charge, in Townsend's eyes, precisely to the extent that it tells the truth about its contemporary moment and milieu.

For those who inveighed against the "devil's music," however, a chief provocation *was* the truth, the contemporary social evidence, as they saw it: the worldly, "sinful" behaviors and attitudes exhibited by the young folk who produced and consumed the blues. Blues culture in Townsend's youth was marked by, if not defined by, violence, promiscuity, profanity, and alcoholism—this during Prohibition, when the presence of alcohol meant that the law was being broken as well.[3] Blues culture was a dynamic, disputatious, disreputable subculture. It excited young people, especially those in the restless working class trapped by plantation sharecropping. It animated the imaginations of young musicians in particular with an intoxicating promise of financial gain, artistic self-realization, social status, and sexual pleasure. For precisely the same reasons, blues culture alarmed black elders—parents and grandparents charged with juvenile discipline; ministers charged not just with safeguarding their congregants' virtue but also with increasing their flocks and their collections in a time of restless migration; educators and other middle-class guardians of respectability who hewed to an ideology of behavioral and economic uplift that viewed the spendthrift denizens of the jukes as a negative ideal. This alarm expressed itself within the family circle as threats, whippings, and warnings about the hellish provenance of the blues. Bluesmen evoke this primal scene with a vibrancy that conveys its shaping impact. Disobedience was catastrophic; yet disobedience was required if the music's call was to be honored. A minister's son born in Lambert, Mississippi, in 1921, harmonica player Snooky Pryor told an interviewer about the first time he played a house party on a plantation in the town of Vance, ten miles away:

> At that time I wasn't allowed to go out there, and that's when James Scott used to steal me out of the house, and then had to get back in there before everybody woke up and got up. If I didn't I'd be on the killin' floor!
>
> You couldn't miss gettin' back in. No. If one of us had got caught, you wouldn't be able to be interviewin' me today. No, there wouldn't have been no Snooky. 'Cause my old man would have killed me. I know he would have. 'Cause he hated that kind of music anyway, you know what I mean. . . . He told me that was devil music. It wasn't no devil's music then, it ain't no devil's music now. I wished he was alive now so he could see what the devil's music has did for me and is doin' for me."[4]

Pryor left home in 1936 at the age of fifteen and worked his way north through Arkansas, Missouri, and Cairo, Illinois, before arriving in Chicago in 1940. It was in 1936 that Robert Johnson, a decade older than Pryor and just as restless, recorded "Sweet Home Chicago," "Rambling on my Mind," and "Cross Road Blues." Johnson's stepfather, Dusty Willis, was no minister, merely a hardworking Delta sharecropper who disliked the blues, warned young Robert to stay out of the local juke joints, and beat him for his unwillingness to labor in the fields during the decade (1919–29) in which Robert lived with him. "His mother and stepfather didn't like for him to go out to those Saturday night balls," Son House claimed, "because the guys were so rough. He didn't care anything about working in the fields, and his [step]father was so tight on him about slipping out and coming where we were, so he just got the idea he'd run away from home."[5]

The same motifs—a restless prodigal son grasping at forbidden musical fruit, a violent and beckoning nightlife, moralistic and repressive parental figures—show up with remarkable frequency in the lives of bluesmen who came of age during the 1920s and 1930s, when the blues were emergent in the southern jukes and the devil's music was suddenly a commodified form of entertainment. The association of African American secular music with the devil and "sinfulness" has a long prehistory, of course, one that considerably predates its usage in blues contexts. As I'll explore in a moment, it is impossible to speak coherently about the association between the devil and the blues without discussing the transformations wrought on African American slaves and their fiddle-driven frolics by the evangelical Christianity that swept across the South during the eighteenth and early nineteenth century. By the same token, something new happens—or rather, many historical developments converge and collide—during the period in question, and that newness is what interests me.

One historical development is the introduction of the inexpensive steel-string guitar, a novel iteration of a familiar instrument, into the scene of southern music-making; its association with a new generation of traveling musicians; and its almost immediate condemnation as a "devil's plaything" by an older generation of church-identified African Americans in the South. A second development is the explicit adoption of the devil as countercultural icon, a constituent element of the socially projected self, by performers such as Peetie Wheatstraw and Robert Johnson—a strategy that psychologist Erik Erikson has termed "foreclosure into a negative identity,"[6] although bluesmen deploy that identity with a greater sense of irony than the myth of hellhound-haunted crossroads pacts suggests. (I explore this aesthetic stance in chapters 3 and 5.) Standing just behind this latter development is a significant attitudinal divergence between the conservative, religious parental generation, which sociologist Louis Jones in his 1941–42 study of the Mississippi Delta called the "railroad generation," and a rootless, skeptical, irreverent younger cohort—a black southern version of the Lost Generation, hard-drinking and newly mobile, flouting parental and church-imposed strictures within the confines of Jim Crow segregation. Homegrown blues wasn't the only music this generation danced to; the jukeboxes in Clarksdale, Mississippi, featured the latest pop, swing, and jazz hits by national stars. But blues, especially in the Delta, was the native sound that focused regional ambition and anchored community musicianship. As such, it suffered the brunt of the devil's-music charge.

John Lee Hooker, native of Clarksdale and singer of lines such as "Ain't no heaven, ain't no burnin' hell," is a representative figure here, and nowhere is he more representative than in the fact that he is the blues-singing child of a Baptist minister, one who could only realize his artistic gifts by leaving his father's house. A partial list of southern-born blues and R & B performers whose fathers were disapproving ministers or deacons includes not just Hooker and Pryor but also Skip James, Bessie Smith, W. C. Handy, Sunnyland Slim, the blues-playing fathers of Honeyboy Edwards and Eddie Burns, Big Joe Duskin, Lillie Mae "Big Mama" Glover, John Cephas, Chief Ellis, H. Bomb Ferguson, Ida Goodson, Sterling "Mr. Satan" Magee, Johnny Ace, and Sam Cooke. To this list must be added blues singers (and the occasional jazzman) who, although not directly descended from men of the cloth, report being chastised by their families and churches for their secular musical involvements, including Muddy Waters, Mississippi Fred McDowell, Mance Lipscomb, Koko Taylor, Jessie Mae Hemphill, Cedell Davis, Pops Staples, Eddy Clearwater, Jack Owens, Nappy Brown, Nat D. Williams, Lonnie Pitchford, and Mary Johnson. As the musicians later recount, the chastisements invariably failed to achieve their desired goal. "My grandmother . . . told me that devil music would surely bring about my downfall," Jelly Roll Morton told Alan Lomax, "but I just couldn't put it behind me."[7]

The tension between black Christianity and the devil's music took on unprecedented weight during the decades of the blues' ascendance, however, not just because the conflict was frequently situated within the primal scene of a family romance but also because the black southern ministers whose condemnation of the blues underwrote parental admonitions were themselves struggling with a range of profound challenges. This was especially true in the Mississippi Delta of the 1920s and 1930s, with its restless, rootless, notably youthful population. "Young people have begun to look down on the old-fashioned Negro preacher," wrote sociologist Gunnar Myrdal in 1944, summarizing his investigations of the previous five years. "Lately the problem seems to have become as serious in rural areas as in cities."[8] The claim I intend to explore in this chapter begins with that youthful disdain but quickly broadens: black southern preachers who condemned blues as the devil's music did so, I believe, because they were suffering from a multiply sourced anxiety, a kind of ministerial blues, that led them to see blues performers as their direct competitors for social status, money, audiences, and erotic attachments. Mocked as greedy and concupiscent by the bluesmen, derided by skeptical youth, viewed as superstitious by some in the rising black middle class, and—especially in the Delta—frustrated and financially distressed by the decimation of their congregations and collections as parishioners streamed north during the Great Migration, black southern preachers responded by blaming the blues: the dances it provoked, the passions and dissipations it engendered, the fallen souls it condemned to hell. The wounds they suffered and projected onto the music became, unexpectedly, a part of what the music was about. At the same time, some preachers struggled to adapt to the vagaries of their young parishioners and the beckoning presence of a newly commodified public sphere, relaxing their proscriptions on "devilish" entertainment and, in one notable case, recording a sermon that defended blues singing on biblical grounds.

GRIOTS, GODS, AND *GOJE* MUSIC

Seeking the "roots of the blues" in Africa has been a familiar gesture of blues scholarship since the publication of Paul Oliver's *Savannah Syncopators: African Retentions in the Blues* (1970), and scholarly due diligence requires that we ask whether there are any plausible African precedents for the figure who haunts this study, the guitar-toting bluesman who purveys "sinful" music. To what extent, more specifically, does the idea of the blues as devil's music—rather than strictly musical elements such as syncopation, call-and-response, and microtonal melodic nuance—trace back to the world from which enslaved Africans were forcibly exiled to America?

One possible precedent suggested by Oliver and others is the griots of Senegambia and Mali, regions from which the slave trade drew heavily. A caste of professional musician/storytellers attached to royal courts who traveled widely as young men to study with master musicians, griots (or *jeliw*) played the kora, a stringed instrument resembling a cross between a lute and a harp. Respected for their musicianship and verbal skills, griots were also regarded with some uneasiness by their fellow townspeople as being in communication with evil spirits; Wolof griots, notes Keith Cartwright, were "traditionally . . . buried inside the trunks of large hollow baobab trees at the margins of the bush, rather than in the cemetery."[9] To anybody familiar with Robert Johnson's "Me and the Devil Blues," with its insouciant final verse ("You may bury my body down by the highway side . . . So that my old evil spirit can catch a Greyhound bus and ride"), the griot theory might seem a productive line of inquiry. Blues musicians *were* sometimes viewed as unredeemed prodigal sons and, at burial time, held at arm's length by disapproving ministers and their congregations. The problem with the griot theory is an inconvenient fact: no definitive evidence exists for any griot ever having been brought to America as part of the antebellum slave trade.[10] Lucy Duran, a historian of African music, acknowledges the evidentiary gap only to insist that it doesn't matter. "Even if griots themselves were never enslaved," she argues, "there is plenty of evidence to suggest that timbres and musical instruments from West African griot traditions were recreated by slave communities across the Atlantic." But the absence of boots on the ground remains a problem—the result, it would appear, of the wily opportunism of a griot caste whose members, if their patrons were killed and enslavement seemed imminent, would change allegiance to the new rulers, rather than be enslaved. Even as some contemporary Malian musicians such as kora player Toumani Diabate (b. 1965, of the *jeli* caste) and guitarist Ali Farka Touré (1939–2006) present themselves as living incarnations of the blues' African roots, it is a caste-wide point of pride to have evaded the slave trade. "The non-enslavement of *jeliw*," Duran concedes, "has been cited to me by virtually every *jeli* I have spoken to."[11] Given historians' inability to place griots in the antebellum South and the categorical denial by their descendants that they were ever there, claims for the griot as the source of the devil concept in the blues seem shaky at best.

A second African precedent for the idea of blues as devil's music, as I noted in the introduction, is a pair of related trickster gods from West Africa associated with crossroads, Esu and Legba. Esu/Legba managed to survive the Atlantic crossing and the depredations of white Christian evangelists—who dismissed any remnants of African religion among the slaves as superstition and fetishism—only to reappear in the black folklore of the post-Reconstruction South, unevenly hybridized with Faustian ideas about devil-pacts, as an intimidating figure associated with crossroads encounters and the conferring of boons, including skill at card tricks and prowess on banjo, violin, accordion, and guitar. The issue at hand, however, isn't whether Esu/Legba lives on in the idea of a crossroad-devil but whether black southern religionists who condemned the blues as the devil's music had crossroads mythology in mind when they did so. There is little tangible evidence to support this last proposition. Some blues performers, as I note later in this study, configured themselves as conjurors of a sort, conversant with hoodoo practices in a way that would have drawn Christian disapprobation and placed them in plausible symbolic proximity to the "dark" workings of crossroads spirituality. But the majority did not—and the devil's-music charge was leveled at them and their juke-joint followers regardless.

Before dismissing the African-roots-of-devil's-music idea altogether, however, a third idea deserves airing. In *Africa and the Blues* (1999), ethnomusicologist Gerhard Kubik argues that the devil concept of the blues traces back to early Christianity and Islam and was carried into sub-Saharan Africa by wandering minstrels following the North African trade routes (the "Arab-Sudanic influence"), where it manifests among the present-day Hausa of Nigeria as a proscription on certain kinds of music-making. "The muslim scholar, macho and mosque head never plays an instrument or sings secular music or dance. They consider many kinds of Hausa music to be wicked, particularly *goje* music which is called the music of the devil." In West Africa, Kubik concludes, "*this* is the much more likely background to the idea of blues as a 'devil's music,' not religious concepts associated with *Esu* or *Legba*."[12]

Is Kubik right? The argument he sketches here, which leaps across the centuries and places a heavy cultural burden on one specific African musical tradition, is both productive and problematic. The *goje* is a one-string bowed lute, part of an extensive African fiddling tradition explored by Theresa Jenoure and Jacqueline Cogdell DjeDje in scholarship that seeks, among other things, to understand why the fiddle was so dominant among slave musicians in the antebellum South.[13] The music of the *goje* has long been associated with prostitutes—it is played in "harlots' houses, hotels, and in gambling places"—and in this respect it stands at the opposite extreme from the sanctified vocal music of the Islamic clerics who condemn it.[14] (Performances with musical instruments, notes ethnomusicologist David Ames, are "notable for their absence from Islamic rites and mosques," and "the exceedingly low rank assigned to professional [Hausa] musicians appears to stem, in part at least, from the influence of Islam.")[15] Historian Michael Gomez reminds us when and where this sort of condemnatory attitude originates: "To live as a Muslim in eighteenth- and nineteenth-century West Africa was to live in an increasingly intolerant society. This was the period of the *jihad*, of the establishment of Muslim theocracies, of self-purification and separation from practices and beliefs that were seen as antithetical to Islam."[16] Resonating most powerfully with the stigmatized juke joint milieu of the American South, perhaps, is Ames's observation that among the Hausa, "the social context of music was often more reprehensible to the censurers than was the music itself. . . . Music performed where alcoholic beverages were consumed was deemed wicked; and . . . the musicians . . . who performed regularly for harlots . . . were held in especially low esteem."[17]

Alcohol, sexually available women, male musicians tickling the strings, and uptight religionists gazing down with disdain: a promising origin-point indeed for blues as devil's music. Kubik's theory falters when we seek to connect the ethnographic situation he invokes—the demonization of Hausa fiddlers and their music by Islamic clerics—with the practical mechanics of cultural transmission on American soil. Although the Atlantic slave trade exported a significant number of Hausa through the Bight of Benin, the great majority of enslaved Hausa were transported to destinations other than North America, especially Brazil and Cuba. Although African survivals in African American culture don't stand in a strictly proportionate relationship to the number of enslaved culture-bearers, *some* culture-bearers in the relevant category are required; this particular "background" to the blues has almost none.[18] But perhaps this objection is overliteral, and misses Kubik's broader point. According to Gomez's estimates, 40 to 50 percent of the Africans imported to North America during the slave trade came from areas influenced by Islam to varying degrees—including, it is reasonable to presume, a sampling of musicians from the various, and variously stigmatized, fiddling traditions. African Muslims themselves, Gomez concludes, "may have come to America by the thousands, if not tens of thousands," bringing with them a complex of ideas about instrumental music and spiritual impurity.[19] What we have, in other words, is the sociological foundation for a broadly sourced conflict, one arising from a fundamentalist impulse to demonize music made outside established sacred spaces, on the one hand, and, on the other hand, the musicians' insistence on preserving performance traditions and ministering to their chosen constituencies. This background may well linger somewhere in African American cultural memory, one of several tributaries feeding into the twentieth-century concept of the blues as devil's music.

An accurate genealogy of the devil's-music idea in the American South, in sum, must acknowledge the possibility of African antecedents. But it must pay even closer attention to the economic incentives and existential challenges confronting both slave musicians and their successors in the decades after Emancipation. Ultimately the evidence suggests that the demonization of the blues is best understood not (or not primarily) as an African survival but rather as a racially inflected modern instance of an enduring conflict: fundamentalist religion, with its constricted behavioral protocols, pronouncing on a younger generation's yearning for pleasure, freedom, and moral license. Which brings us to one of this chapter's key claims: *The prelude to the blues' castigation as the devil's music is the stigmatizing—or attempted stigmatizing—of the black slave fiddler by fervent Christian converts in the aftermath of the Great Awakening.*

FIDDLES, FROLICS, CLERICS, AND DEVIL SONGS

The slave fiddler first becomes visible as a troubling figure, an instigator of licentious merriment, long before those mass conversions take place. In the early 1690s in Accomac, Virginia, a woman named Elizabeth Parker borrowed a "negro boy" from her sister and brought him along on a social visit to the daughter of the Reverend Thomas Teakle, one of the wealthiest clergymen in the state. Teakle was a man of "strict notions," according to his daughter, and "it occurred to the little company that it would be pleasant in the opportune absence of the clergyman to have a dance." The slave fiddler, doing their bidding, kept the dancers circling from Saturday night until late the next morning. When Teakle returned and was informed of the desecration that had occurred on the Sabbath, he brought court proceedings against Parker and her husband.[20]

We know nothing about this slave fiddler except the chain of custody— he was passed from sister to sister—and the fact that his spirited fiddling, bringing joy to white dancers on a Sunday morning, scandalized a Christian clergyman in colonial Virginia. We know nothing of his origins (was he African born or American born?) and thus nothing of his cultural patrimony: whether he brought to his appointed task personal memories, or transmitted familial memories, of having played a very different sort of music on a very different kind of fiddle, in a performance context that, like this one, serviced an important constituency even while courting disfavor from the authorities. But we might, if we are so inclined, view this early episode of slave musicking as a symbolic moment when two "sinful" folk fiddling traditions first come into conjunction on New World soil: a broadly based African tradition framed by Islamic judgmentalism and a European tradition mingling biblical proscriptions with pagan superstitions.

"The fiddle has often been regarded as the devil's own instrument," writes Barbara Allen Woods in her study of European devil legends, and those who wielded the fiddle in that part of the world partook of the devil's ability to entrance through dance; they became part of a disreputable brotherhood and gained a certain mystique.[21] In the Middle Ages, according to historian

Maximilian Rudwin, the devil was said to own a violin that "could set whole cities, grandparents and grandchildren, men and women, girls and boys, to dancing . . . until they fell dead from sheer exhaustion."[22] In Sweden and Norway, the *nåcken* was a male water spirit who played enchanted song on the fiddle, drawing women and children to their death in lakes and streams; he was willing to pass along his sorcerer's tricks if students showed up with the proper offering.[23] In 1711 Jonathan Swift famously declared that a certain Englishman accused of rape must be guilty because "he was a fiddler, and consequently a rogue."[24] Musicologist Maiko Kawabata notes in a study of Niccolò Paganini (1782–1840), the most infamous of devil-branded violinists, that "fiddlers were considered morally suspect" because their music was associated with the beer hall and "provided an incentive to dancing."[25] The colonial American world in which Elizabeth Parker's borrowed Negro boy sought to make his way with fiddle in hand, in other words, was a world primed to see him, and the frolic he incited, as trouble. And his African cultural patrimony, whatever its precise configuration, may well have primed him to expect this sort of thing. But he and others like him were soon buffeted with even greater force by the winds of spiritual upheaval.

Both the Great Awakening of the mid-eighteenth century and a second wave of revivalist fervor in the decades before the Civil War saw southern fiddlers, black and white alike, denigrated as sinners within Christian evangelical circles for their role in such frolics. "One can hardly overstate the importance of conversion to Christianity in the acculturation of blacks in the New World," insists Dena Epstein in her study of slave music, *Sinful Tunes and Spirituals* (1977), and a new insistence on distinguishing between sanctified and secular music (and dance) was one of the key markers for those who had found God.[26] Without the emergence of Afro-Christianity as a core element of black culture and the accompanying demonization of the fiddle, it is impossible to imagine blues emerging as "devil's music," a secular focus of religious condemnation, in anything like the fashion it did. Yet counterposed with this important cultural dynamic was another, even more powerful development: the emergence of the slave fiddler as the South's most charismatic and ubiquitous performer, a centerpiece of plantation frolics whose talents were valued by slaves and masters alike. "By the 1800s," notes Jenoure, "the black fiddler had become a celebrated figure, essential to the success of social events. . . . In spite of the valuable status of the fiddle, its association with dancing evoked condemnation among the religiously strict, evangelical sects, both black and white. Among some, fiddling was a skill of which only Satan was capable, hence its playing implied some level of communication with the Devil."[27] These two dynam-ics coexisted in uncomfortable proximity. While many southerners, black and white, simply ignored the religionists and took their pleasure in the fiddler's Saturday night ministrations, others felt the sting of condemna-tion and the pull of conscience, throwing down the devil's instrument and declaring themselves reborn.

Whites led the way here, following the trail blazed by English evangelist George Whitefield, who described in his journal how on New Year's Day 1740, while staying at a tavern in South Carolina,

> several of the neighbors were met together to divert themselves by dancing country dances . . . a woman was dancing a jig. . . . I endeavored to shew the folly of such entertainments, and to convince her how well pleased the devil was at every step she took. For some time she endeav-ored to outbrave me; neither the fiddler nor she desisted; but at last she gave over, and the musician laid aside his instrument.[28]

It's not clear from this account whether the fiddler is black or white, but the evangelizing impulse didn't much care: the fiddle was the devil's play-thing and the dance was a journey toward hell. For white Baptist firebrand Philip Mulkey, the prelude to his own conversion in the mid-1700s was the vision he had, after playing the fiddle at a dance in the Carolinas, of "the Devil grinning at him . . . with fiery eyes." He fainted, then revived and grew even more frightened, "thinking the Devil would be permitted to take him bodily."[29] Reverend John Todd of Hanover County, Virginia, wrote during the same period of his success in steering hundreds of his slave parishioners away from fiddle-driven dissipation and toward God's word: "The sacred hours of the Sabbath, that used to be spent in frolicking, dancing, and other profane courses, are now employed in . . . learning to read at home, or in praying together, and singing the praises of God and the Lamb."[30] A number of African American slaves took such proscriptions to heart, censuring retrograde behavior within the slave community and, on some occasions, silencing themselves after conversion. In 1899, Jeannette Robinson Murphy wrote that slaves on her family's antebellum Kentucky plantation were "often turned out of church for . . . singing a 'fiddle sing,' which is a secular song."[31] "I was always wild and played for dances," con-fessed Willis Winn of Texas (b. 1822), a former slave, "but . . . after I mar-ried I quieted down. When I joined the church, I burned my fiddle up."[32] A black slave fiddler from the South Carolina Piedmont named Griffin left home for a camp meeting up in the hills "in jolly, good humour," joking with one of his friends, "I don't mind camp meetin' ef day des let me play my fiddle." Several hours later he was picked up at the foot of a nearby mountain, unconscious, missing an ear. When he came to, he declared "Dis is de judgement ob de Lord; I'll nuver tech dat fiddle ag'in."[33]

The evangelical crackdown on slave fiddling was an uneven process, and less than a success: a quixotic attempt to demonize an established southern tradition that gave too much pleasure to too many people on both sides of the color line. The North, earlier to evangelize, was less forgiving, perhaps because fiddlers there didn't enjoy the same measure of goodwill bred by the ritual of the southern plantation frolic; black fiddlers in the North, according to Epstein, "were regarded as marginal vagabonds outside the bounds of respectable society."[34] Solomon Northup, a free Negro violinist from New York, seems to have derived a marginal benefit from the ritual purpose his talents granted him after he was kidnapped in 1841 and sold into southern slavery; rescued from a cotton plantation in Louisiana in 1853, he insisted that his skill as a fiddler had saved his life. "It introduced me to great houses—relieved me of many days' labor in the field—supplied me with conveniences for my cabin—with pipes and tobacco, and extra pairs of shoes, and oftentimes led me away from the presence of a hard master. . . . It heralded my name round the country—made me friends, who, otherwise would not have noticed me—gave me an honored seat at the yearly feasts, and secured the loudest and heartiest welcome of them all at the Christmas dance."[35] Fiddlers like Northup played for slave gatherings as well as the master's guests; "secular parties" were held at jails, sugar refineries, barns, and open-air spaces on the plantation.[36] As evangelism made converts within the plantation slave communities, these same locations were sometimes claimed for religious gatherings, leading to the audible beginning of a conflict, or at least a distinction, between sacred and secular music. Ex-slave Harry Smith of Kentucky (b. 1815) wrote that after dinner on his plantation, one could hear "preaching and prayer meetings by some of the old folks in some of the cabins, and in others fiddles would ring out. . . . old Christians sing and pray until four in the morning, while at the other cabins many would be patting, singing and dancing."[37]

As a distinction between sacred and secular music began to emerge within slave culture on the heels of mass conversions, slaves strove to distinguish legitimate (i.e., religious) dancing from more troublesome forms of frolic. The former included the circling, shuffling collective step known as the ring-shout or "shouting"; the latter could be recognized most plainly by the forbidden practice of foot-crossing. "Us 'longed to de church, all right," explained one Louisiana slave, "but dancin' ain't sinful iffen de foots ain't crossed. Us danced at de arbor meetin's but us sho' didn't have us foots crossed."[38] The evangelization of slave culture proceeded unevenly, with significant local and regional variations; plantation preachers themselves sometimes fiddled for parties in the quarters, even as local white missionary organizations decried what they called the "amusements" of the Negroes.[39] The chief amusement, according to the Association for the Religious Instruction of the Negroes in Liberty County Georgia in 1848,

> and that to which they become passionately fond is *dancing*. No one will deny that it is an amusement of the world, and not of the Church. Fiddlers and dancers are not sober and devout persons; neither are those, whatever be their professions, who encourage them. . . . Their dances are not only protracted to unseasonable hours, but too frequently become the resort of the most dissolute and abandoned and for the vilest purposes.[40]

It is impossible to know whether the complaint leveled here is based on a clear-sighted appraisal of African American cultural practices or, to the contrary, a cross-cultural (or racist) misunderstanding of an all-night "shout," of the sort described by Harry Smith. The mass of converted slaves, in any case, eventually embraced and upheld a distinction between sacred and secular that placed fiddle-driven breakdowns squarely on the side of illegitimate diversions: the devil's music, in short, although that specific phrase doesn't enter the conversation until the advent of blues and jazz. The preferred devil-imbued modifiers of the preblues era are "sinful," "wicked," and "worldly."

The demonizing dynamic I am sketching here, real and impactful as it was, was also far less comprehensive within the slave community than some might assume. Historians estimate that at least 75 percent of slaves remained unconverted at the dawn of the Civil War, in part because many of them disliked the version of Christianity being pitched to them by anxious masters in the late antebellum decades, one revolving around the catechism, "Slaves, obey your masters as in the Lord!"[41] Ex-fugitive slave Henry Bibb of Kentucky testified that "the Sabbath is not regarded by a large number of the slaves as a day of rest," and he noted that those who made "no profession of religion, resort to the woods in large numbers on that day to gamble, fight, get drunk, and break the Sabbath," a practice encouraged by slaveholders in search of amusement.[42] Certain regions of the South, especially coastal Georgia and South Carolina and the mouth of the Chesapeake Bay, were more thoroughly evangelized than others. In *Slave Songs of the United States*

(1867), for example, folklorists William Allen, Charles Ware, and Lucy Garrison noted the absence of secular songs and musical instruments among the Sea Islands freedmen. According to their ex-slave informants, "The last violin, owned by a 'worldly man,' disappeared from Coffin's Point 'de year gun shoot at Bay Pint' [that is, 1861, when Admiral Dupont took Hilton Head Island]."[43] Yet successful as evangelical religion was at demonizing the fiddle, first among whites and then among blacks, that success was never more than partial: a pitched battle for the Lord waged on many fronts, but a crusade that never enjoyed thoroughgoing success. Although some black fiddlers did indeed call it quits, during the antebellum years and beyond, an even greater number did not.[44] Having earned the status of what historian Paul A. Cimbala has termed a "folk elite" on southern plantations, fiddlers, banjoists, and other black instrumentalists continued to function in their traditional roles as repositories of folk culture and anchors of community identity during the postbellum decades—playing the fish fries, house parties, and picnics that had supplanted the antebellum frolics, and passing along their skills to successive generations of younger musicians.[45] The black fiddling tradition, as Tony Thomas and others have conclusively established, endured well into the middle of the twentieth century, making its mark on the blues through ensembles and performers such as the Mississippi Sheiks, Lonnie Johnson, Sid Hemphill, and Henry "Son" Sims, even while being rendered all but invisible on the "hillbilly" side of the white/black divide in the process implemented by recording companies and archived by cultural historian Karl Hagstrom Miller in *Segregating Sound: Inventing Folk and Pop Music in the Age of Jim Crow* (2010).[46]

Still, by the dawn of the new century, an important precedent had been established, one that critically impacts the history of the blues. The fiddle, for better or worse, had been tarred in the minds of a significant number of black southern Christians as the devil's instrument. It was a symbol of plantation frivolity, spendthrift dissipation, and—especially for a black middle class determined to forge uplift through religious probity—the "heathenism" so many wished to leave behind. The violin per se wasn't the problem; properly contextualized in classical orchestras, church recitals, and the like, the violin could be an acceptable engine of cultural uplift, especially in the urban North. The problem, in black Christian minds, was what happened when the violin went rogue, kicking off its shoes in a fit of Saturday night syncopation and conjuring up the ghosts of a ragged and uncivilized past. A new entrant, in any case, was about to displace the fiddle as the black South's most popular dance-inciting instrument. During the same period that the black church was struggling to extend and consolidate its reach as black America's preeminent independent institution, a new figure of disrepute was emerging on the southern horizon: the guitar-toting "musicianer," a son of the black church gone bad with the blues.

DEVIL'S PLAYTHINGS

In 1890, roughly 90 percent of African Americans still lived in the South, and 80 percent lived in the rural "black belt" counties.[47] Black southern life during the postbellum decades was marked by the rapid growth of independent black religious denominations, primarily the Baptists and Methodists, with Holiness and Pentecostal sects blossoming rapidly after the turn of the century. Congregations of like-minded black citizens, slave-born and free-born, had the power to police their own behavioral boundaries, discipline stragglers, and cast aspersions on the unchurched. Although church historian Michael Battle has argued with some justification that "white evangelism to slaves after the Second Great Awakening grew an antiworldly black spirituality that left the world to the devil," clearing a philosophical space for the blues, it is equally true that black southern religion in its institutional aspect became an increasingly worldly project after freedom dawned: an expanding material base of church buildings, land, and foreign missions supported by the Sunday morning collection plate; an evolving institutional hierarchy, foregrounded at annual conventions, within which black preacherly ambition could flourish.[48] The devil of the black southern church was, among other things, whatever or whomever interfered with this developmental process. Between 1890 and 1906, the number of black Baptist ministers increased from 5,500 to more than 17,000.[49] Seconded by their expanding (and largely female) base of parishioners, these are the men—and they were all men—who underwrote the demonization of the blues.

The considerable evidence for this claim, which I'll elaborate in the remainder of this chapter, is both anecdotal and circumstantial, but it includes virtually nothing in the way of published or recorded sermons by black southern preachers. Robert Sacré touches on this surprising lacuna when he notes that "if some religious songs point out that liars, murderers, cheaters, robbers, gamblers and other sinners need not expect mercy on Judgment Day and won't get on board the 'Gospel Train' to Heaven, blues singers or blues singing are rarely, if ever, mentioned in that list."[50] The one recorded sermon that does mention the blues by name, in fact, offers a pointed defense of the music, even as it substantiates my claim.

In "Is There Harm in Singing the Blues?" (1930), Rev. Emmett Dickinson, a Baptist preacher on Chicago's East Side, begins by declaring, "It's no harm to sing the blues," then denigrates and contradicts "the so-called preachers all over this land [who] are talking about the man or woman who sing the blues," insisting that his self-styled peers "don't know the meaning of the blues."[51] "Talking about" plainly means "criticizing," and yet direct evidence from the hands and mouths of those so-called preachers castigating the blues remains curiously absent from the historical record. Zora Neale Hurston offers one of the few examples: a sermon she transcribed in Eau Gallie, Florida (1929), in which the Reverend C. C. Lovelace, preaching on the wounds of Jesus, insists that "the blues we play in our homes is a club to beat up Jesus," although he makes only this one reference to the blues and doesn't associate the music with the devil.[52] Langston Hughes offers a related anecdote in "My Adventures as a Social Poet," a very brief essay in which he describes reading for the congregation of a black church in Atlantic City, New Jersey, some blues poems about "hard luck and hard work" shortly after his first book, *The Weary Blues* (1926), had been published. The preacher approached the pulpit with a note: "Do not read any more blues in my pulpit."[53] Disapproval, yes, but not outright demonization. Despite this lack, black preacherly and parental castigations of "the devil's music" wax large in the lore of the blues. This is partly because condemnatory preachers and disapproving fathers were so often the same individual, but also because the blues interview and blues autobiography—the prodigal son's confessions—have provided us with most of what we know on the subject.

W. C. Handy's *Father of the Blues* (1941) is a foundational text in this regard, as important for the way it anticipates the tradition as for the way it stands slightly oblique from it. Handy, born in 1873, came of age in a post-Reconstruction South animated by the expanding world of preblues secular entertainment: minstrel shows, marching bands, and, notably, a disreputable but virtuosic young black dance band violinist named Jim Turner who showed up Florence, Alabama, in the mid-1880s. "The drunker he was, the better he played," Handy remembered. "He planted in my heart a seed of discontent, a yearning for Beale Street and the gay universe that it typified."[54] "One of the most celebrated folk fiddlers of the Tennessee Valley," according to Handy's biographer, Turner was a Memphis barroom musician who also played private parties for whites and the occasional traveling minstrel show. He became for Handy a kind of threshold guardian to a world that Handy's father, a prominent local African Methodist Episcopal minister, viewed as the most negative ideal.[55] "Musicians were idlers, dissipated characters, whisky drinkers and rounders," Handy reported, voicing his father's attitude. "My father was a preacher, and he was bent on shaping me for the ministry. Becoming a musician would be like selling my soul to the devil" (11–12).

Here, rendered as a preacher-father's stern advisory, and long before it became linked with Robert Johnson, is the blues' perennial Faustian story line. We should remember that half a century separates the composition of Handy's memoirs from the paternal attitudes being described—a period during which the devil had become explicitly identified with the blues in many and various ways, including Clara Smith's "Done Sold My Soul to the Devil" (1924), which was covered in four slightly different versions by Casey Bill Weldon, John D. Twitty, Merline Johnson, and Dave Edwards, all released in 1937. Since Handy dictated *Father of the Blues* in the late 1930s, it is possible that the specific language of soul-selling he deploys was inflected by those emergent meanings rather than being a verbatim representation of his father's condemnation. What is crucially important and often forgotten is that the music at issue here is not the blues, because the blues don't yet exist in the mid-1880s as a named musical idiom. Handy is ahead of the curve. He manages to anticipate the emergence of a certain kind of blues story, an oedipal struggle surcharged with the primal sin of idolatry, even as—or precisely because—he takes an aging autobiographer's retrospective view. Nowhere is this truer than in the dramatic scene that concludes his book's opening chapter. An enterprising boy of twelve, young William has saved his meager earnings from several part-time jobs and purchased a shiny guitar from a local music store. He now carries it home and displays it proudly to his parents:

> I waited in vain for the expected congratulations. Instead of being pleased, my father was outraged.
>
> "A box," he gasped, while my mother stood frozen. "A guitar! One of the devil's playthings. Take it away. Take it away, I tell you. Get it out of your hands. Whatever possessed you to bring a sinful thing like that into our Christian home? Take it back where it came from. You hear? Get!"
>
> I was stunned. The words dim and far away like words spoken in a dream. A devil's plaything. I wanted to dispute the charge, but I knew that argument would mean nothing. My father's mind was fixed. Brought up to regard guitars and other stringed instruments as devices of Satan, he could scarcely believe that a son of his could have the audacity to bring one of them into his house. (10)

Handy's father, Charles, a former slave, was "brought up" by his own preacher-father, William Wise Handy, a literate ex-slave who became an ordained Methodist minister in 1865. What we're witnessing here is a collision between the paternal line, heavily invested in Christian prohibitions on worldly amusements, and a wayward son following his creative muse. Handy's choice of instrument, however, is anomalous, anticipatory: in 1885, when this scene takes place, the guitar was still relatively rare in the South, according to David Evans: "If [the guitar] occurs in folk music at all, either during the slavery period (up to 1865) or in the quarter century following Emancipation, it almost always exemplifies penetration of the folk music tradition by the genteel, cultivated urban guitar tradition. Then suddenly, during the period 1890 to 1910, the guitar is everywhere in the rural South, especially in black music and especially in the Deep South." Along with the piano, harmonica, and horns, the guitar—specifically, the mass-produced, mail-ordered, steel-string guitar—became popular among younger black musicians for a range of reasons, most of them having to do with connotations of modernity and social progress:

> These instruments held prestige for their players and listeners because they were new, because they were paid for with cash [rather than being homemade], and because they carried an aura of urbanity, gentility, social status, and upward mobility, precisely because they were not rural and traditional. For blacks in particular the guitar also lacked any residual associations with slavery, minstrel music and its demeaning stereotypes, or even with the South. It was something novel with very little cultural baggage other than symbolic associations that seemed to conform to notions of progress and success.[56]

Evans's claims, although sound in broad outlines, must be refined in light of recent scholarship. The gut-string classical or "parlor" guitar in the hands of freed and middle-class women had been a part of African American social life since before the Civil War.[57] Lynn Abbott and Doug Seroff document the parlor guitar's presence in a wide range of northern black venues in the early 1890s: an Odd Fellows lodge, a bicycle club stag party, a temperance club, a Baptist Church recital, a "refined and elevated" minstrel show. In 1893, George L. Knox, the editor of the *Indianapolis Freeman*, a black entertainment newspaper, suggested that the black guitarist had once been a "fad," enjoying a period of "grandeur, when every parlor was open to him"; the words "grandeur" and "parlor" support Evans's claim that what is being talked about is an earlier, tamer, considerably more respectable tradition of guitar playing, one absorbed and supplanted in black imaginations when the larger and louder steel-string guitar, thumped like a drum and wielded with phallic bravura, became the driving force in the southern juke continuum. At the 1891 commencement exercises for historically black New Orleans University, for example, nobody seemed to have been scandalized when a Miss Eloise Bibb performed "Sebastopol," a ubiquitous Spanish-flavored light classical piece emblematic of the parlor style.[58]

But perhaps some black southern religionists *were* scandalized even by such tame guitar stylings, and before the dawn of the blues; Handy's recollections of his father suggest as much. If the steel-string guitar became an emblem of racial modernity for the southern-born bluesmen whose destiny soon became intertwined with the future Father of the Blues, then for Handy's own preacher-father and other black southern Christians, the guitar had a more invidious set of symbolic associations. It was the fiddle all over again, but shiny and store-bought: the devil's plaything 2.0. (Big Bill Broonzy, a fiddler-turned-blues-guitarist, embodies this transition: early in his career, he claims, his uncle demanded that he choose either preaching or fiddling rather than "straddling the fence.")[59] Within the godly, established, respectable family circle the Handys occupied, the guitar was a glittering lure on the path toward downward mobility, devilish precisely because it threatened young William's presumptive future as a minister, inheritor of the paternal mantle. Alan Lomax has argued that the guitar—and especially blues guitar in performance—was disapproved of by church folk because the (male) performer who wields it is seen as a sexual shaman of sorts, an upsetter. "The guitar is butted against the hips . . . and handled in a masturbatory way. Meanwhile, the strings are choked down close to the sound hole, and plucked, stroked, frailed, as if female erotic parts were being played with, while the instrument itself emits orgiastic-like sounds."[60] This element of sexual temptation plays no evident role in the condemnatory response of Handy's father, but it is indisputably a part of the associational complex that soon envelops the blues, so that the guitar comes to symbolize all the worldly, nocturnal, pleasure-centered dissipations that transpire in and around the southern juke joint: dancing, drinking, smoking, cursing, fighting, and fornication. The guitar is what accompanies and provokes these activities, all of which are proscribed by Baptists, Methodists, and the Holiness and Pentecostal sects—although the Methodists, it is true, don't officially ban dancing until 1919.[61] In the 1940s, according to Ted Gioia, "B. B. King found that many Delta churches would cancel the performance of his gospel-singing group when they learned that the vocalists relied on guitar accompaniment—the six-string instrument had been so tainted by its association with the blues that many ministers could not bear seeing it inside the House of God."[62]

Before indexing the evidence for the "tainting" of the guitar and the demonization of the blues, we should pause to note an important exception to the general rule: the Church of God in Christ, or COGIC. Founded in 1897 by disaffected black Baptists, the Church of God in Christ, as I discuss later, did indeed view the blues as devil's music, and its members hewed to stricter codes of dress and behavior than did the Baptists. But they also interpreted scripture in a way that encouraged congregants to "shout" their faith—singing, dancing, moving, and playing—using a wide range of instruments, including tambourines, washtubs, drums, trumpets, trombones, and guitars. Where other Protestant denominations, according to Gayle Wald, biographer of star COGIC guitarist Sister Rosetta Tharpe, "set strict limits on rhythmic music, or anything that might stir the body to movement, COGIC admitted into its musical repertory elements of blues, work songs, and ragtime, cross-fertilizing these in a glorious hybrid with slave spirituals and traditional hymns."[63] The "blues" element of COGIC musicking was occulted, to be sure; blues lyrics were strictly forbidden and the juke-joint environment with its multiple temptations was off limits. But steel-string guitars, played in the Lord's service, were just fine. This radically distinguished COGIC from the Baptists, at least in the minds of black southern blues performers. "If you were in the Baptist church," B. B. King told folklorist William Ferris, "they didn't want you to bring a guitar in. . . . You can imagine what church I belonged to and enjoyed most—the Sanctified church, of course. They didn't care what instrument you played. If you were able to buy one and bring it in and play spirituals on it, it was OK."[64] Tharpe, who transformed gospel guitar playing into the engine of her own stardom, got into trouble regardless, first by recording what many viewed as an overly suggestive version of "Rock Me" with Lucky Millinder's orchestra in 1938, then by bringing her gospel show to Harlem's Cotton Club. "When she sang gospel on a secular stage," wrote one scholar of African American religion, "she scandalized the sanctified church. They never forgave her. Religious folk opposed singing in cabarets; it was synonymous with the Devil, God's enemy."[65]

If COGIC offered black southern guitarists a sanctified outlet for blues-musical impulses, then for Baptists and other mainstream black denominations, according to gospel historian Jerma A. Jackson, "the instruments used to generate the music assumed extraordinary importance," and the blues-identified guitar was clearly the leading offender in the eyes of parents, ministers, and parishioners.[66] John Lee Hooker (b. 1917) elegantly summarizes the charge: "My dad was a minister and he didn't want a guitar in his house. He said it was the devil's."[67] Like Hooker, Roebuck "Pops" Staples (b. 1914) grew up near Clarksdale; like W. C. Handy, his creative muse brought him into conflict with his father, a Baptist, at the dawn of his teen years, although the rural blues culture that called to him was something that didn't exist in Handy's youth. "My daddy thought the blues was the devil's music," Staples remembered. "Wouldn't even let me play the guitar, said that was the instrument of the devil, too. So I'd sneak out of the house, and that's how I saw Charley [Patton] and [Howlin' Wolf], when I was 12 or 13. It would be where someone had a big house, and on Saturday night they'd organize a dance. Ladies would be cooking chicken and chitlins in the kitchen, and they'd have a room for gambling, playing cards, drinking bootleg liquor, and a big room out in front where they'd play and dance."[68] Muddy Waters (b. 1913) grew up on Stovall Plantation, ten miles from Clarksdale, a blues-rich region that was also, during that period, remarkably dense with churches. In 1941, sociologist Lewis Jones wrote, "There are perhaps more churches than stores and schools combined."[69] Those churches were the spirited centers of antiblues propaganda, and the family was the chief instrument of indoctrination. "My grandmother told me when I first picked that harmonica up," said Waters, "she said, 'Son, you're sinning. You're playing for the devil. Devil's gonna get you."[70] In his youth, pianist Sunnyland Slim (b. 1907), the son of a Delta pastor, found two older generations aligned against the music he would go on to master. "My peoples didn't go for blues. My father was a Christian. Grandfather and grandmother were Christians—didn't go for that. . . . That was around 1912."[71] Guitarist Johnny Shines (b. 1915), who grew up in Memphis, just north of the Delta, saw the blues and church music as parallel streams in the same river, but he realized that church folk saw things differently. "Many people felt that if you sang the blues you were going to Hell and burn, burn, burn," he told an interviewer in 1973.[72] Some Delta bluesmen agreed. When folklorist Alan Lomax asked David "Honeyboy" Edwards (b. 1915), "If you were playing guitar at a dance and drinking and someone was to shoot you dead, you'd just go to hell?," Edwards replied, "I *believe* I would."[73] Others denied the charge, or tried to. Profiled in the *Chicago Defender* in 1955 at the height of his popularity, Waters offered a contorted defense of blues guitar playing, insisting that it was his God-given way of combating, rather than conjuring up, the devil:

Trouble ain't nothin' but the devil operating. And as long as there's a God in the skies—a God merciful enough to give you a prayerbook or a hymn, or a banjo or a guitar with which to express yourself and defy the devil, there's no sense in getting lost in a corner and giving the devil a victory.

I can hear some of my friends right now. "Muddy," they'll say, "How you gonna connect God up with a guitar—with jazz—with playing in a night club or cutting a blues record?" All I've got to answer is that the devil put everything on earth that is destructive and God gave us everything possible to be Christian in the way you do whatever you do. The devil can quote scripture, they say, so I guess it's fair for good people to take the devil's tools and use them to live a good and decent life.[74]

Is his guitar a gift from God or one of the devil's tools? Waters blurs this crucial issue. Regardless of his instrument's provenance, he insists on his ability to deploy it in a sanctified way, playing good music that purges bad feelings and routs the devil.

Defending his choice of vocation may have been easier for Waters, a Delta migrant to Chicago, than it was for his peers who'd remained down home. Guitarist Jack Owens (1904–97), a longtime resident of Bentonia, Mississippi, who recorded several blues with devil-themes, was viewed with suspicion by his churchgoing contemporaries, and his guitar was as much to blame as his repertoire. "Folks has a tendency to get Jack's music mixed up as to who he was," insisted Jimmy "Duck" Holmes, a younger local bluesman. "It doesn't mean he's playin' the music of the devil. Not meanin' Jack himself was devilish. And a lot of people thought, well, a man of that age playin' a guitar, they look at that as bein' Satanism. Folks'd say, 'Jack's playin' that guitar, he oughta be goin' to church.'"[75] Like Waters, Owens defended his blues playing with a trickster's rhetorical flair, reframing the issue in a way that undercut the narrow-minded dualism of his Christian neighbors. "Well," he acknowledged, "that's what they called it all the time, the devil's music, but I have heard 'em make notes on the guitar, and the preacher take that note and start off with it in the church behind the pulpit. And go on and preach. . . . That was a blues note."[76]

Owens's claim foregrounds a key element of the devil's-music dispute, a kind of sibling rivalry, in musical terms, where the "righteous" sibling, God's music, refuses to acknowledge its near-twin, the blues, *as* a sibling, insisting instead that the sinful relative is a stepchild or foundling, a wholly other. "If distinguishing clearly between sacred and profane is philosophically important, indeed critical, to African American fundamentalist Christians," writes ethnomusicologist Therese Smith, " . . . the reality of blurred boundaries and frequent interchanges between the sacred and profane remain at the heart of African American music making. . . . The saved may be invested in a clear opposition of their music (emanating from and iconic of their lifestyle) to 'devil's music,' but that opposition is not consistently played out either socially or in musical sound."[77] Forced to navigate this unstable situation, blues musicians often found themselves voicing the reality principle in ways that deliberately undercut fundamentalist fantasies of self-evident good and evil. Mance Lipscomb (1895–1976), an early Texas bluesman with a songster's broad repertoire, defended himself much as Owens did, blurring the boundaries erected by his churched neighbors and insisting on a basic continuity between sacred and "sinful" music. "No, I haven't played in church very often. See, they criticize me cause I'm a blues songster. You know what I am? Blues is in the church! I kin prove it ta you in one word: What is the blues? Blues is a feelin. If it's a feeling out in these nightclubs, it's a feelin in church. . . . It's a sad feelin, and a worried feelin." The blues interview becomes for Lipscomb, as for Owens and many others, a place in which to contest the devil's-music charge and reframe black communal censure in a way that allows the bluesman to assert his integrity. "I never woulda played music no mow," he told the compiler of his oral autobiography, Glen Alyn,

> but I had sumpn worthwhile: ta do my music playin cause they turnt me out the church. An they was sorry. Because I was a good songster, and I was a quiet man, an everbody like me. Couldn't give me no bad recommendation. So I got on, commence ta playin the gittah back, to and fro. Then I never did go back to the church.
>
> I didn quit church: church quit me. Cause they didn't want me ta play my music. An they say I was a sinner. I'm not a sinner. I been converted. An I'm got religion.[78]

Lipscomb seems to be telling a familiar story of a prodigal son's exile here, but then he reverses the terms. The bluesman suddenly becomes the rock, the moral center who is "quit" by the hypocritical church.

Although a certain number of blues performers do indeed play up their putative proximity to the devil in a way that justifies the devil's-music charge, a far greater number echo Lipscomb, Owens, and Waters, disputing the charge and, when seeing no other option, indicting those who indict them in a way that exposes a painful social breach. Where Lipscomb and Owens exiled themselves from church communities, North Mississippi blueswoman Jessie Mae Hemphill (1923–2006)—one of the few women guitarists in the down-home tradition—stubbornly chose to worship at the New Salem Baptist Church in Como after a 1993 stroke effectively ended her career as a blues performer:

> People look at me, you know, when I go to church. They think it's so terrible for me to go to church because I sing the blues. They say I ought not go to church. I say, "Well, I ain't doing no badder than nobody else." I said, "I ain't had no woman's husband and I ain't killed nobody. But somebody in here will be doing worse than me. Somebody in here now is going with some woman's husband, and that's just as bad as me playing blues." And I tell them, "God knows everything. God knows why I'm doing this. He know I needs to pay my bills." They say you can't serve the Devil and the Lord, too. But my belief about it is that God spared me and brought me this far.[79]

Hemphill's singing, rather than her guitar playing, is overtly at issue here, along with the familiar indictments (fornication, violence) that accrue to the blues. The fact that she levels a countercharge at her church sisters ("Somebody in here now is going with some woman's husband") highlights the social dynamics of the devil's-music campaign: fathers and ministers may have laid down the law, but women, often as not, were the enforcers. "When she was singin' them blues I told her—she was pavin' her way to Hell," said Emma Williams, the mother of St. Louis blues singer Mary Johnson (b. 1900).[80] (Williams may have had a point; between 1925 and 1930, her daughter was married to Lonnie Johnson, a guitarist/singer who went on to record more blues songs invoking the devil than Robert Johnson and Tommy Johnson put together.)[81] As a young man, guitarist Cedell Davis (b. 1926) moved back and forth between Helena, Arkansas, and the Mississippi Delta; his mother, he told an interviewer, "used to run me out of the house many a day because I was in there playing guitar. . . . She said if I kept on playing that guitar I was going to die and go to hell. My stepfather didn't believe in that, he say, 'He gonna die and go to hell if he don't have some money.' . . . Kept messing around there my mama told me say, 'Boy, you going to die and go to hell playing and fooling with that guitar singing 'Devil's songs.'"[82]

Blues performers, for the most part, have spoken loudly on their own behalf: representing themselves as the beleaguered young subjects they felt themselves to have been, engaged in a personal struggle with Christian believers that was also a traumatic struggle between familial generations.

Although the occasional supportive parent and stepparent shows up to significant effect, "older people," as a category, are the antagonists in this particular blues story. "Older people would tell you that was the devil's music—it was bad for ya," insisted Memphis DJ and Clarksdale native Dee Henderson (b. 1936), host of "Cap'n Pete's Blues Cruise," "and you had to have a strong mind to keep it in your mind like I did."[83] A strong backside was also a necessity; whippings were a rite of passage for future bluesmen. "We had a Victrola back then that played 78s," said Eddie "The Chief" Clearwater (b. 1935), a guitarist from Macon, Mississippi. "You'd put 'em on and wind it up and play the records. But if you played the blues on Sunday, you didn't dare let your parents hear. They say, 'Turn that off! That's the devil's music!' You'd get scolded and they might beat you if you played the blues. They might get a switch and whip you 'cause you were sinning against God."[84] Another pianist and minister's son, H. Bomb Ferguson (b. 1930) of Charleston, South Carolina, recalls his father's harsh discipline and hypocrisy with startling bitterness:

> Whenever he would catch me playin the piano, playin the boogie woogie, he hit me across my hand with a stick. Told me, "That's bad," you know, "That's the devil." I said, "One of these days I'm gonna play what I wanna play. . . . " 'Cause I really loved the blues. I wanted to play it—always did.
>
> Man, I think about things my momma went through, my father—he was a minister—and I tell anybody, he was alright, after I got older. He wasn't shit. He whipped your fuckin' ass, and get up in church, and everybody say, "Reverend Ferguson." When he died, I came when they was putting him in the grave. I meant to be late. What got me was he could get up in church and talk so nice and come home and kick your *ass*, buddy. I swear, I won't lie on it.[85]

The piano occupies a curious niche in the history of the devil's music. Unlike the fiddle, banjo, steel-string guitar, and other "boxes," pianos were considered polite parlor instruments in the early decades of the twentieth century, and both pianos and organs had an established place in black southern churches. But the piano was also firmly associated, thanks to sequential crazes for ragtime, barrelhouse blues, and boogie woogie, with sinful nightlife. A black southern household that possessed a piano—and ministers' families, a leg up economically, were more likely than most to possess one—was akin to a twenty-first-century household with a high-speed Internet connection: the devil was only a few clicks, or boogie-woogie riffs, away. Eternal vigilance was required on the part of the elders, since musically inclined sons and daughters were perpetually subject to temptation. Ferguson's story is exceptional for the rage it communicates, but his struggles are paralleled by the experiences of Ida Goodson (b. 1909), "Big Chief" Ellis (b. 1914), Big Joe Duskin (b. 1921), and Sterling "Mister Satan" Magee (b. 1936), all of whom were the piano-playing children of deep southern ministers or deacons.[86] The blues became forbidden fruit for these performers: a devilish eruption of good-time song into the home's sacred interior, conjured by the skilled fingers of the disobedient child as the father-minister hovered in the distance, ready to swoop down at any moment. The child's challenge, when discovered, was to modulate so instantaneously and seamlessly from blues-flavored riffs, grooves, and lyrics into their gospel equivalents that parental wrath would melt into praise for the child's sanctified sounds. Goodson, Duskin, and Magee all tell versions of this story, but Duskin's trials are distinguished by his Baptist father's violent, relentless, seemingly pathological determination to control his son—an obsession skillfully evoked in interviews conducted by blues scholars Steven C. Tracy and Barry Lee Pearson:

> It started with my father being a small town minister [in Birmingham, Alabama]. He sent me to music school to play the piano; church music, religious music. I played for the kids at Sunday school; and after Sunday school, everybody would go back upstairs and we would close the door, the kids and I. Then I got to playing the boogie-woogie until he caught me, and then he would crack me with whatever he put his hands on, belt, stick or what not. Tell me I'm gonna die and go to hell 'cause that's the Devil's music.
>
> I say, "I'm sorry, daddy, I ain't gonna play it no more." And every chance I would get I would play it.[87]

What follows, over the course of more than seven decades, is a tormented pas de deux between father and son, pursued from Birmingham up to Cincinnati, neighborhood to neighborhood, home to church to nightclub. "I . . . had hell in me," confesses young Joe, speaking of himself at age fifteen, explaining why he felt compelled to contravene his father's orders on seemingly every piano in town. His father's facility with a bullwhip waxes large in his telling. "Oh Lord, man, you talking about eating you up with that whip," he remembers. And: "He told me, said, 'If you ever let me catch you playing that devil's music I'm gonna skin you alive.'" And: "Don't bother that piano or let me catch you on it. Because if I do, I'll tear your ass to pieces"[88]:

When my dad got here to Cincinnati, never did want me to play the devil's music, and I used to be down on Hopkins Street, God, he'd bust my tail because I'd be just monkeying, didn't know what I was doin. When I finally got to church, you know. . . . I'd go to start playin. And so he come in one Sunday and he heard me playin on the piano and said to me, he said, "If I catch you playin' the devil's music again, I'm gonna take that bull whip and I'm gonna beat you almost to death with it." He said, "I don't want you playin no devil's music in this house." Say, "This is a house of prayer."[89]

Duskin refuses to psychologize his father, although the reader suspects that the family's half-dozen relocations in Cincinnati bespeak trouble of some sort; he comes to seem, in Duskin's telling, not merely un-Christian in his violence, but positively Satanic—a merciless Simon Legree rendered inhuman by his hatred of the blues:

The old man got a little piano [when we moved to Gorman Street] and brought it in. And he told me, says, "Don't ever play no devil's music on it!" So I could play church songs, too. So he had a minister and his wife come by. . . . And he told—the old couple come in and set down—and he said, "My son gonna entertain you." And he says, "I'll go get some pop and refreshments, cookies and stuff." Then while he was gone I played so many church songs, the old man asked me, say "Can you play anything other than church songs, son?" I said, "Yessir, I can." And he says, "Well, play some of it." I was beatin out some boogie-woogie when the old man come. God dog! The old man threw me down and started beatin me so bad with that bull whip. He stopped and they said, "Duskin! Wait a minute!" He said, "He didn't do that on his own, we asked him if he could play anything else, and he said Yeah." "HE SHOULD A TOLD YOU THAT I DON'T LOW THAT IN HERE!" And you know he chased those two old people out and they never did come back to the house no more.

Steve, that old man beat me so bad, Lord, man, I was praying for him to kill me, man. He was beatin me so bad with that bullwhip. And he actually brought blood out of it, out of my back and all that.[90]

The black humor of absurdist exaggeration can't mask the human tragedy of a father-son relationship gone terribly wrong. Yet the absurdity continues: when he is eighty-nine, Perry Duskin offers his son a compromise: Don't play the devil's music "until I'm dead in the grave" and then do what you want. The son agrees, convinced that he's gotten the better end of the deal.

The elder Duskin lives to be 105, forcing his son to shelve his career as a blues performer for sixteen years.

BURNIN' HELL?

The tragicomic drama of Perry and Big Joe Duskin, a violently judgmental and repressive father-minister and his rebellious, blues-besotted son, stands as a representative but extreme example of what I am arguing is one of the constitutive relationships of the blues—as important as the failed relationship between lovers or the signified-upon relationship between black bluesman and white bossman, each of these themes being the subject of a later chapter in this study. The devil is summoned by the blues tradition, including church people who unexpectedly became part of that tradition, to express the agonistic essence of each relationship: "the devil's music," "Devil Got My Woman," "Devil Jumped the Black Man." Although the devil played an important role in black secular music from the first Great Awakening through the 1890s—the fiddle was his instrument, the dance was his snare—the oedipal rages and resentments that percolate through the devil's-music dispute and the sheer volume of testimony from blues musicians whose lives were impacted by church and familial disapproval have no parallel in the preblues period. It is worth remembering that at the dawn of the twentieth century, as African American adults in the South suddenly found themselves victimized by the combined onslaught of lynching, segregation statutes, disenfranchisement, and slander in the press and popular culture, their churches and their households were two of the only areas over which they retained more or less complete control. The blues, competing with and mocking their ministers and seducing their children, threatened to undermine both domains. This fact alone helps account for much of the drama that accompanies the phrase "the devil's music."

The example of John Lee Hooker is significant in such a context; it represents an important counterpoint to the rage and powerlessness evidenced by H. Bomb Ferguson and Big Joe Duskin in the face of paternal/ministerial censure. Hooker's father, William Hooker, was a part-time preacher at a Baptist church near the family home in Clarksdale, Mississippi. Young John Lee wasn't merely brought up in the church: he was, as he described it, "a *great* gospel singer" by the age of nine or ten. "When I come into the church everybody look round, and when I started singin,' people start shoutin' and hollerin.'"[91] His churched youth was the rule rather than the exception among blues performers, especially those hailing from Mississippi; Robert Sacré lists B. B. King, Elmore James, Otis Spann, Sunnyland Slim, Bukka White, Magic Sam, and Mojo Buford in this connection, along with Texans such as Lightnin' Hopkins and T-Bone Walker.[92] When John Lee was still a preteen, an itinerant bluesman named Tony Hollins (b. circa 1900) began to court his sister Alice under the disapproving eye of Rev. Hooker. Hollins's repertoire, which included songs like "Crawling Kingsnake," "Married Woman Blues," and "Tease Me Over Blues," was guaranteed to raise the hackles of any daughter's father, much less a Delta minister with a reputation to protect, but Hollins went one step further: he gave John Lee a guitar. In contrast with W. C. Handy's minister father, William Hooker allowed his son to keep the guitar, but he refused to allow it in the house. "I had to keep it out in the barn," remembered John Lee. "All the time I was pluckin' on it, and my daddy called it the Devil. He said, 'You can't bring the Devil in this house.' They all feel like it Devil music back then," Hooker added. "They call blues and guitar and things the Devil's music. That was just the way they thought. Not only my father, everybody thought that. The white and the black ministers, they thought it was the Devil's music."[93]

Although his Christian rigidity in such matters was typical for his time, place, and station, Hooker's father exercised no violent discipline over his son, nor did the son violate his father's proscription, although things might have come to that pass had not an irresistible new opportunity presented itself. When John Lee was fourteen, his mother, Minnie Ramsey, left his father to move in with Will Moore, a popular local bluesman who performed with recording artists like Charley Patton and Blind Lemon Jefferson. All of Hooker's brothers and sisters stayed with their father. John Lee was welcome to stay, too, said Rev. Hooker, but not if he expected to play his guitar indoors. Rarely has a young bluesman-in-training been presented with a starker choice. Without apparent rancor against his birth father ("He loved the heck out of us, he would give his right arm for us"), John Lee nevertheless vacated the premises and moved in with his mother and Moore.[94] "Will Moore gave his new stepson his next guitar," writes Charles Shaar Murray, "an old mail-order Stella to replace Tony Hollins's battered gift. Moore became John Lee Hooker's spiritual and artistic father figure: the father who approved, the father who encouraged, the father who supported, the father who empowered."[95]

Moore did this by wholly supplanting Hooker's birth father, short-circuiting what might otherwise have become one more example of the primal scene I invoked at the beginning of this chapter: a disobedient son and disciplinarian father butting heads over the devil's music. Hooker's insurgency was plainly enabled by his mother's support as well. "My mother was open-hearted, very open," said Hooker. "She wanted me to do what I wanted to do best, because she felt that if I was forced to go to church, it wouldn't be for real. . . . So she said . . . 'If this is what you wanna do, you and Will go ahead and I won't object'" (32–33). Housed and nurtured by Delta-style freethinkers—rather than, for example, by willfully licentious jukehouse good-timers of a sort conjured by Baptist jeremiads—young John Lee was empowered not merely to sing and play the blues but to speak with a heretical boldness that directly repudiates his father's evangelical perspective. "The church has got 'em brainwashed to *death*, the ministers, the preachers," Hooker told Murray many years later. "I believe in a Supreme Being, don't get me wrong, but I don't believe that there's a hell that you're gonna be tortured in. I believed in all of that, then I grew up and realized, and I wrote the song: '*Ain't no heaven, ain't no burnin' hell / where you go when you die, nobody can tell*'" (32–33).

The song Hooker is referring to is one of his earliest recordings, "Burnin' Hell" (1949), and the line he references is one that shows up in an earlier recording by Son House (b. 1902), a Clarksdale-based bluesman of the prior generation who was also, and tormentedly, a Baptist preacher. The contrast between "Burnin' Hell" and House's "My Black Mama, Part 1" (1930), from which the provocative lines may have been adapted, is revealing. The thematic focus of House's song is his troubled relationship with his woman: something is "the matter" with her, she's a "jet black woman" who "will make a mule kick his stable down," she is a "milkcow" (lover) who has "been gone" for too long. In the context of this complaint, House's proclamation, "Yeah it ain't no heaven now, it ain't no burning hell / Said, where I'm going when I die can't nobody tell," suggests that the lover who hitches his happiness, his "heaven," to the mutable feelings and behaviors of a mortal woman is doomed to, but also gifted with, a perpetually deferred fate; he's never firmly consigned to the ranks of the saved or damned.[96] Hooker, by contrast, says nothing about the woman; she's no longer the point. He keeps the church-defying couplet, and makes it the germ of a driving, compulsive narrative of spiritual emergence, the shedding of faith's burden, using a one-chord groove that he'd learned from Will Moore:

Well everybody's talking 'bout that . . . burnin' hell

Ain't no heaven or . . . ain't no burnin' hell
Where I die, where I go . . . nobody tell, I said. . . .

Everybody talking . . . 'bout that . . . burnin' hell
Yeah
Yeah

Well mama told me . . . papa did too
"Go down to the church house, now son
Get on yo . . . bended knee
Ask Deacon Jones just to . . . pray for you
I said, ask Deacon Jones . . . oh Lordy, pray for you"

I bowed
I bo . . . bowed
I went to the church house . . . on my knees
Told Deacon Jones, I said, "Ah . . . pray for me"
Deacon Jones said, "Now, chillun, here's my hand
Yes now chillun now now now"
I'm going, "Yes yes
Pray for you, if I do never pray no more"

Yeah, Deacon Jones . . . he prayed that morning

[guitar and harmonica break]

Yes, I done prayed, I done sung
Did everything that a poor man sho could do
Now I . . . ain't gonna pray no more[97]

Blowing harmonica on the recording is Eddie Burns (b. 1928), a native of Belzoni, Mississippi, raised in Clarksdale by a guitar-playing father who was a deacon in the Baptist church and who supported his son's interest in the blues even as his fellow church members looked askance at his own musical commitments, which included performing at local houseparties.[98] "Burnin' Hell" is notable on several counts, not least the fact that it denies the existence of the devil by denying him a residence—a powerful way of making a point that Hooker reiterated forty years later in an interview with the *New York Times* and that Henry Townsend, Snooky Pryor, Muddy Waters, Jessie Mae Hemphill, and many other Mississippi blues performers clearly share: "The blues is no devil music."[99]

Like the opening scene of Hurston's novel *Their Eyes Were Watching God* (1937), in which a proud, self-actualized heroine walks back into the life of her small black southern town after a transformative journey and is greeted by a chorus of criticism, Hooker's song begins by evoking his community, headlined by his father and mother, as a scandalized collective whose demands must be navigated but also—if he is to remain true to himself—defended against. In denying heaven and God's hellish retribution, he has sinned in the eyes of this community and *will* be burned in the hell he denies unless he humbles himself and repents. Deacon Jones, whom Murray aptly calls "the folkloric archetype of the black divine," is, in my reading, the song's exemplar of a Manichean ideology that the singer is in the process of rejecting.[100] After uttering the heresies that lead "everybody" to rush him toward Deacon Jones for discipleship and salvation, young John Lee nevertheless allows himself to participate in the religious ritual, bowing and submitting to the Deacon's ministrations. And here, in the original recording, something astonishing happens. After Hooker says, "Yeah, Deacon Jones . . . he prayed that morning," words cease and the guitar and harp ride alone for the next eighteen seconds. The ritual space of fervent evangelical prayer has been reclaimed by, supplanted by, the rowdiest of blues dance grooves. The groove *is* the prayer. Hooker honors the church-based energies of his music and his performance style, even as he offers a stinging rebuke to those in the church who would reflexively parse the world into entirely distinct spheres of the saved (prayerful deacons) and the damned (guitar-wielding bluesmen). The stumbling final lines of the song—"Yes, I done prayed, I done sung / Did everything that a poor man sho could do / Now I . . . ain't gonna pray no more"—belong simultaneously to Deacon Jones (they're his confession of a ritual task completed, for better or worse) and to Hooker himself. Liberating himself by singing this song, he's rocked a new world into being.

DEACON JONES'S BLUES

What about the spiritual torment that confronted several generations of bluesmen who dared to reject that faith and sing songs that aligned them with the devil? What about Son House, torn between his preacherly vocation and his yearning to rule the juke house? What about Robert Johnson singing "Me and the Devil Blues" and being trailed by hellhounds to his early grave? "These men," wrote Greil Marcus, voicing this familiar view, "who had to renounce the blues to be sanctified, who often sneered at the preachers in their songs, were the ones who really believed in the devil; they feared the devil most because they knew him best."[101] The idea that bluesmen, especially Mississippi bluesmen, "knew" the devil in some particularly intimate and haunting way has been a core element of blues mythology at least since Rudy Blesh offered his imaginative evocation of Robert Johnson back in the 1940s ("full of evil, surcharged with the terror of one alone among the moving, unseen shapes of the night") based on a close listening to "Hell Hound on My Trail."[102] In recent years this overly romantic view has been critiqued by Jon Michael Spencer and Elijah Wald, among others. Dismayed by what he sees as the willingness of many scholars to take the reductive devil's-music slur at face value, Spencer invokes the term "synchronous duplicity" as a way of getting at the sacred-secular dialectic, a kind of DuBoisian double consciousness, that he sees as "characteriz[ing] the lives of these great musicians."[103] Certainly synchronous duplicity describes John Lee Hooker's achievement in "Burnin' Hell": blues grooves staking their claim on sacred consciousness, deconstructing rather than reinforcing evangelical certainties, above all the enduring slur on "sinful" music. Wald extends Spencer's attribution of double consciousness to the bluesman's community, both those who listened to the blues and those who preferred not to. "If one believes the world is caught in a Manichean battle between God and the Devil, good and evil, saved and damned," writes Wald, "it follows logically that the psalm singers go to heaven and the fiddlers go to hell. But assuming that Delta dwellers of the 1930s were humorlessly Manichean about such matters is condescending bullshit."[104]

Yet the truth is, some Delta dwellers of the 1930s—the preponderance of Baptist, Methodist, and Pentecostal preachers and many of their adult parishioners—*were* humorlessly Manichean about such matters, as were their peers across the South. This is precisely why the phrase "devil's music" had such currency, and why it was backed up by whippings. But a significant number of Delta dwellers, especially younger people and especially in cities like Clarksdale and, to the north, Memphis, were not humorlessly Manichean. Where religion was concerned, they were skeptical, mocking, playful. The loss of religious faith, the loss of respect for religious leaders, that black southern youth exhibited during this period was something noted with surprise by contemporary sociologists; the blues was the soundtrack to this generational rebellion against parental and ministerial rigidity. This is not to say that their elders' ritual condemnation of the blues as devil's music didn't engender a welter of negative feelings—the blues, in a word—in a younger generation of blues musicians. Quite the reverse: such condemnation, in a social environment dominated by the heavy hand of the black church, inevitably helped shape both the aesthetic contours of the music and the life journeys of those who chose to play it. But previous commentators have paid far too little attention to generational divergences in matters of black southern religious faith and to the notably destabilized social position of those black southern preachers who were demonizing the blues. They have ignored the fact that Deacon Jones *himself* had the worst kind of blues. He lashed out at the devil's music as a way of alleviating those feelings—and burying the competition.

Consider the familiar opposition of preacher and bluesman as articulated by anthropologist John Szwed in an influential article, "Musical Adaptation among Afro-Americans" (1969): "Unlike the stable, other-worldly, community-based image of the preacher (approved by Negro and white communities alike), the bluesman appears as a shadowy, sinful, aggressive, footloose wanderer, free to move between sexual partners and to pull up stakes as conditions call for it." [105] The first half of Szwed's formulation is profoundly mistaken, at least if what we're talking about is the Mississippi Delta between 1920 and 1940. Delta preachers, as a group, were radically *de*stabilized by the Great Migration and the disastrous diminishment it was wreaking on their membership rolls and collection plates. Struggling to deal with that loss in the context of the church hierarchy, they were relentlessly focused, in a distinctly this-worldly way, on their repeated failure to deliver the bottom-line numbers they'd been assigned. Although some preachers stuck it out on the home front, many pulled up stakes and fled to the North along with their parishioners, attempting to reconstitute in urban settings the down-home congregations that had fled out from under them. [106] The phrase "community-based" fails to describe such a desperate context. As for Szwed's claim about black southern preachers being "approved by Negro and white communities alike," this is no more than a half-truth, which is to say that half of it is flagrantly untrue. During the 1920s and 1930s, Deacon Jones was being mercilessly lampooned by blues singers, mocked by gospel singers, heatedly criticized by his own peers, and laughed at or ignored by many young black southerners, churched and unchurched. In some ways, and startlingly, Szwed's description of the bluesman—"a shadowy, sinful, aggressive, footloose wanderer, free to move between sexual partners and to pull up stakes as conditions call for it"—is an apt description of a certain kind of Delta preacher during this period. Certainly this is how he was represented in the black popular culture of the time.

Exhibit A is "He Calls That Religion" (1932), a recording by the Mississippi Sheiks. Arguably the most popular blues ensemble ever to come out of the state, the Sheiks were the Chatmon family band: Bo (b. 1893), Sam (b. 1897), and Lonnie Chatmon, all of them the sons of an ex-slave fiddler named Henderson Chatmon (1850–1934), along with vocalist/guitarist Walter Vinson. The Sheiks didn't just embody the transition from the preblues world of fiddle-driven string bands to the guitar-driven blues, but they fused the two styles in a distinctive way. One element of their attitudinal modernity was a series of sexually suggestive double-entendre recordings, including "Driving That Thing" (1930), "Cracking Them Things" (1930), "Loose Like That" (1930), and "The New Shake That Thing" (1930). In this respect the group took its cue from Bo, who under the pseudonym Bo Carter had a concurrent career as a solo recording artist (sometimes in duets with Vinson) with an even more outrageously suggestive repertoire: "She's Your Cook but She Burns My Bread Sometimes" (1930), "Pin in Your Cushion" (1931), "Banana in Your Fruit Basket" (1931), "Ram Rod Daddy" (1931), and "My Pencil Won't Write No More" (1931). Vinson, emerging from this sex-charged miasma, sings lead on "He Calls That Religion," and his cocky, declamatory lambasting of a lecherous preacher reveals no trace of spiritual torment. Nor does it attack religious hypocrisy from the standpoint of one who has aligned himself with the devil, or "evil." Quite the reverse: Vinson speaks as a disillusioned true believer, a blues-preacher who consigns Deacon Jones to the devil's precincts:

> Well the preacher used to preach to try to save souls
> But now he's preaching just to buy jellyroll
> Well he calls that religion
> Yes he calls that religion
> Well, he calls that religion, but I know he's going to hell when he dies
>
> Was at the church last night, happy as I could be
> The old preacher was trying to take my wife from me
> Well he calls that religion, etc.
>
> . . . .
>
> He will swear he's keeping God's commands
> Have women fussin' and fightin' all over the land
> Well he calls that religion, etc.
>
> The reason that people stop going to church
> They know that preacher was trying to do too much
> But still he calls that religion, etc.
>
> Old Deacon Jones, he was a preachin' king
> They caught him round the house trying to shake that thing
> Oh, he calls that religion, etc.
>
> Oh yes, he calls that religion[107]

Blues becomes devil's music here, from the perspective of institutionalized southern evangelicalism, *not* because it advocates on behalf of fornication, dirty dancing, fighting, and other sinful jukehouse behaviors, but because it accuses Deacon Jones of engaging in and fomenting those things. Its frontal assault on ministerial hypocrisy and malfeasance dares to claim the moral high ground that the church hierarchy itself hoped to monopolize, subverting public faith in preacherly authority. The bluesman speaks in the voice of sinned-upon monogamy! And the devil, he would have us believe, is waiting to claim Deacon Jones.

Given both the lascivious tenor of many of the Sheiks' and Bo Carter's other hits and the frankly sexual energies that it was the jukehouse performer's duty to summon in his audience, the charge of sexual misbehavior leveled by "He Calls That Religion" surely struck those clerics who heard it as the most devilish sort of double-speak. By the same token, the charge was true enough that it stung. Here the devil's-music dispute was driven, among other things, by a sense of competition—including erotic competition. "For black men of the Depression-era Delta whose intelligence, artistic ability, or simply wanderlust exceeded the norm," writes blues historian Mark Humphrey, "the roles of preacher or performer of social music were the primary options to agrarian indentured servitude."[108] Both social roles made one the focus of the erotic attentions of large numbers of women, single and attached. It was generally understood that both preachers and bluesmen acted on those attentions. But there was a crucial difference: bluesmen could flaunt that fact—flaunting it actually increased their charisma and earning power—while preachers were forced to dissemble and deny their concupiscence in line with biblical injunctions. West Coast R & B bandleader Johnny Otis (1921–2012), who saw no necessary conflict between his musical activities and his pastoral role at the head of the Landmark Community Church in Los Angeles, spoke of this competitive dynamic, framing it in terms of dollars and sex:

Many Black preachers carried on about what they called "the devil's music." Black churchgoers, especially the young, listened to the anti-blues sermons and went out and enjoyed themselves anyhow. They understood that the anti-blues preachers saw the music as competition. If members of the congregation partied with the blues all Saturday night, they probably wouldn't show up in church Sunday morning. They were always preaching against out-of-wedlock sex, too, weren't they. And anybody knew that they would jump over the Empire State Building to get one of those pretty, big-legged sisters in the choir.[109]

Or, as Delta bluesman James "Son" Thomas (b. 1926) put it, "You can't go by what the preacher say, because he and the bluesman looking for the same thing—some money, some chicken, and a nice-looking woman. That's all they looking for. He preaching the Bible but you can't go by that."[110]

Contemporary sociological evidence confirms this portrait, making clear that the mockery and skepticism expressed by blues performers toward their ministerial competitors was widely shared by younger African Americans, especially in the Mississippi Delta. In *After Freedom: A Cultural Study in the Deep South* (1939), sociologist Hortense Powdermaker reported on the striking lack of respect for religious leaders that she'd discovered among black youth during her fieldwork in Indianola between 1932 and 1934: "Old people complain that today the young join a church without having any real experience, that they do not know what true religion is. Young folks, they say, no longer take the minister's words seriously, or look up to him. . . . Young people snicker in church at the preacher's ungrammatical speech, and at home they openly jeer at him. His usual reputation for sexual looseness; the rumors, scandals, and jokes that circulate about his relations with various women in his congregation, do not improve his standing. When he sermonizes about adultery, they do not take him very seriously."[111] Sociologist Charles S. Johnson, probing the skeptical attitudes toward organized religion that he'd encountered among black youth across the entire Deep South in the late 1930s, noted that "the least favorable attitude toward the church [in the entire South] is found in Coahoma County, Mississippi," the rural plantation districts surrounding Clarksdale.[112] "A survey of black cultural production from the era," concurs religious historian Jonathan L. Walton, "reveals that intellectuals ranging from scholars to blues artists to kids cracking jokes on street corners found a myriad of ways to criticize the perceived sense of financial and sexual entitlement that had come to characterize African American clergy."[113] Given the degree to which this youthful disdain dovetailed with the audible mockery of blues recordings such as "He Calls That Religion," and considering the extent to which bluesmen were their (highly) visible erotic and economic competitors, how could Delta ministers *not* be tempted to project their anger and frustration, and the anxiety bred by their eroding social status, as righteous condemnation of the devil's music?

Bluesmen had an unexpected ally in exposing the malfeasance and hypocrisy of black southern preachers: at least one sanctified recording that agreed with them. "The Devil's Gonna Get You" (1941), by a jazzy, swinging quartet called The Gospeleers, playfully savages a morally bankrupt preacher, dovetailing attitudinally with the irreverent snickers and jeers reported by Powdermaker. He's a dandyish, fast-talking, Bible-toting extortionist:

> You better watch out, the devil's gonna get you one of these days
> You better watch out, the devil's gonna get you one of these days,
>   by and by
> He's a liar and a pretender too, if you ain't careful he'll conjure you
> You better watch out, the devil's gonna get you one of these days
>
> You done let your beard grow out, and I know what it's all about
> Keep that Bible out your hand, I know you're no preacher man
> You better watch out, the devil's gonna get you, etc.
>
> You got on your frock-tail coat, and a collar back around your throat
> A high silk hat and a walkin' cane, looks to me like you're going insane.
> You better watch out, the devil's gonna get you, etc.
>
> You better stop your gambling, and telling all your big lies
> Cause a lowdown hypocrite, I sure do despise
> You better watch out, the devil's gonna get you, etc.
>
> You can't preach and you can't pray, and I don't believe a word you say
> You've done got yourself in Dutch, cause you take up collection too much
> You better watch out, the devil's gonna get you, etc.[114]

"Ministers with a keen sense of status wrestled against the widespread suspicion that men of the cloth were hypocritical charlatans," writes religious historian Paul Harvey in his study of black (and white) southern Baptists between 1865 and 1925, and no issue was subject to more suspicion than the question of the collection plate.[115] In a monograph titled "The Afro-American Pulpit in Relation to Race Elevation" (1892), African American minister Francis J. Grimke complained that "greed for money" was one of the three key defining attributes of the post-Emancipation black church. "Everything seems to be arranged with reference to the collection. The great objective point seems to be to reach the pocketbooks of the people."[116] "Preacher in de pulpit preachin' might well," went an old folk saying, "But when he gits the money yo' kan go to hell."[117] Here, too, the blues musician scored both the moral advantage—since he frankly acknowledged his pecuniary self-interest rather than cloaking it in assertions about "doing the Lord's work"—and, arguably, the worldly advantage in profits actually accrued; neither fact endeared him to his ministerial competitor. The average black preacher in a rural or small-town church, according to one scholar, received an average salary of $250 to $350 a year by the dawn of the twentieth century.[118] Inflation would have raised this somewhat by the 1920s, although the Depression slashed much of that increase; one would expect baseline salaries in the Black Belt, by the same token, to lag. If we stipulate $400 as the average annual salary (or accrued collection-plate harvest) of a Delta preacher in 1932, that's a little more than a dollar a day.[119] In 1932, when Honeyboy Edwards (b. 1915) first began to travel with Big Joe Williams (b. 1903), he played a "good-timing house" in Greenwood, Mississippi, and raked in considerably more than a preacher's daily wages. "Man, we played. Women was flocking, giving us nickels and dimes and quarters, and we was keeping the house lively." Ministers enjoyed ancillary benefits, of course, including free meals from the parishioners they visited, but so did bluesmen. "I'd just switch around, go to all them little towns at different times, so I could make that money," remembered Honeyboy, describing an itinerant life that might see him shuttling between Clarksdale, Drew, Shaw, and Cleveland in the course of successive weekends. "That's how I made it. I didn't stay nowhere where I got old. 'I sure miss you.' 'Come back, man.' 'Where you been the last two weeks?' People treat you just like you was a preacher when you're playing the blues, 'Come on, go home with me. My wife will fix dinner.'"[120]

As Honeyboy makes clear, bluesmen were competing directly with preachers on multiple economic fronts: not just the Saturday night tips/Sunday morning collections axis, but as charismatic houseguests on whom "parishioners" might bestow indulgences. On rare occasions the competition was literally head-to-head. In 1967, Arthur Vinson of Rolling Fork, Mississippi, told folklorist William Ferris that the devil's-music dispute—which by that point also included rock and roll—could be traced to preacherly resentment in such cases: "I think that your highly religious people will brand musicians that play blues and rock and roll as being 'carriers of evil' for the simple reason that you can git your combo together—guitar, bass, and drums—and go out here and play. You can git up under the tree, anywhere, and the people will gather around, you see. In most cases you can draw more people out there where you're playing than the minister can draw in that church house because he's preaching and you're right across the street from him."[121]

If he happened to be pastoring in the Mississippi Delta of the 1920s, Deacon Jones's "bluesman blues" were greatly exacerbated by the damage being wrought on his and his fellow pastors' ministries by the Great Migration. At precisely the same moment that he was being publicly mocked by his blues competitors and disrespected by the young, his congregation was deserting him in record numbers to make a dash for the promised land of Chicago and other points north. "Since the typical small town or rural congregation numbered fewer than 100 members," writes historian Richard Sernett, "the loss of key individuals or several families was a serious matter."[122] Mississippi, which had almost a tenth of America's black population in the 1910 census, helped lead the northward charge. "In many places hundreds have gone within the last few months," wrote a Methodist Episcopal minister in 1923. "Many churches have depleted memberships because of the exodus. Seventy-five were counted that left one community within twenty-four hours."[123] This catastrophic loss of membership meant that some ministers no longer drew regular salaries; and since district superintendents were responsible for extracting mission contributions from the individual churches within their multicounty purviews, the failure to meet these quotas also linked Mississippi's ministers, superintendents, and ecclesiastical leaders in a troubled hierarchy, bruised—and bluesed—by decimated church rolls, depleted coffers, and seriously eroded influence in their national organizations.

One of the prime staging grounds for Deacon Jones's comeuppance was the annual meeting of the Upper Mississippi Conference of the Methodist Episcopal Church, a forum at which a series of district superintendents shared news of the past year's pastoral successes and challenges. The center of black Methodism in the Delta was the Clarksdale District, a territory comprising most of six counties with a population of roughly 190,000, two-thirds of whom were African American.[124] To read the annual reports delivered by Clarksdale's superintendent between 1917 and 1927 is to be brought face to face with confusion, anxiety, and chagrin as ministerial ambition is repeatedly blasted by facts on the ground, most of which are intimately bound up with the blues. In 1917, Rev. Norman R. Clay, the current superintendent and a recent relocatee to Clarksdale from the hill country town of Holly Springs to the east, reported that "the ravages of the boll weevil, and flood rains" had caused "the greatest unrest and emigration of our people known in years, to points in Arkansas, Oklahoma and the

North and West." He kept his eyes on the prize, regardless. "The delta, the garden spot of the state and the country, has a great future, in which our church ought to share in a large way if God wills it. . . . The fruitfulness of this growing country is abundant and the progress of our church for the next few years ought easily to double her rate of increase along all lines of church and membership activities."[125] Although this prophecy could hardly have been more mistaken, Clay struggled to put a positive spin on the bad news as it began to arrive. In his 1919 report he noted what he called "a restlessness on the part of labor" due to "lack of protection and just treatment"—a reference to the wave of lynching that was spreading through the Midwest and South during the "Red Summer." This restlessness, and the conditions that provoked it, he said, "keeps the church and mission peevish and nervous." Unless something was changed, he concluded, "labor will be lost to the delta and members to the churches."[126]

If peevishness and nervousness characterized the collective spirit of black Delta ministers in 1919, then 1920 was the watershed. Superintendent Clay showed up at that year's meeting with a litany of complaints that bespoke economic desperation and spiritual crisis. A catastrophe had overwhelmed his district's ministers, he told his Methodist brethren, binding them in a community of suffering with parishioners who had chosen to stay behind but also causing them to lose their parishioners' respect:

> The exodus has left, and is still leaving, many of the churches weak and ready to die . . . [and] this whole situation has burdened the conference. . . . The pastor sometimes finds the charge much weaker in membership than he was led to believe. Then he sets out to make his salary by doing other work. Almost without exception a supplementary job lessens his efficiency as a pastor, as it rapidly becomes his principal means of support. The psychological effect upon the membership is far from satisfactory. Ordinarily they cease to give him their full support and they finally lose interest in him and the welfare of the church. . . . Many of our pastors are cramped physically, mentally, and, I fear, spiritually, because of the small salary with a large family to care for and children to educate. . . . The people would have more respect for and look upon them with more reverence and their sermons would have greater weight if they were not often looked upon as objects of charity.[127]

Rev. N. R. Clay was, in his own way, as profound a singer of the Delta blues as the musicians who dominate the histories and mythologies of the region. He sings the plight of his people—above all, the impoverished, anxious, humiliated African American ministers who were trying to hold their broken lives and parishes together amid the wreckage wrought by the boll weevil, the sharecropping system, Jim Crow justice, and the epic dispersals of the Great Migration. Nothing could be further from the derisive, mocking portraits of ministerial misbehavior offered by the Mississippi Sheiks and the Gospeleers than the stark realities of Delta ministerial life rendered here. Yet these realities can help us understand the energies that drove the devil's-music dispute from the preachers' side: not just a competitor's jealousy of the bluesman's claimed erotic license, but economic desperation and a keen sense of status anxiety. When times are desperate, scapegoats serve useful communal functions. The words "blues" and "devil's music" never surface in the Clarksdale District superintendent's reports, but in his 1921 address, after delivering another round of bad news, Rev. Clay shunts some of the blame for his and his fellow ministers' failures to meet financial goals onto a familiar target:

> This is a year of the greatest unrest among the people I have witnessed. They move from landlord to landlord, and many move to town from the farm, to Memphis; St. Louis; Chicago; Detroit; Cleveland and the north generally. This largely accounts for our decrease in membership. We plead with them, we offer them solutions for their domestic and financial problems, but to no avail: The moving spirit is in the air. They seem to think moving is a panacea for all their ills, thus breaking up some of our most substantially organized churches and circuits. This condition embarrasses the district superintendent and pastors in putting over a program handed down by the church. . . .
>
> *The Cause*——There are many elements entering into the cause of this disaffection and dissatisfaction. Yet it seems to me these are some of the causes: The drop in the price of cotton; the lack of food stuffs; the failure to make a crop of any kind in some places and a lack of settlement, in some places, all contribute to the cause. Some of these, I say, make no more cotton, and off to town they go. There to be preyed upon by the many slick devices and destructive diseases and unsanitary conditions known in the slums of a town and city life.[128]

"The moving spirit is in the air": One could hardly ask for a more succinct definition of the blues, especially when that spirit is an intractable restlessness composed of equal parts disaffection, dissatisfaction, and ambition. Robert Johnson sang, "I got to keep movin', I got to keep movin', blues falling down like hail," and "Come on, baby don't you want to go."

Honeyboy Edwards said, "The blues is something that leads you, that lays on your mind. You got to go where it leads you."[129] The blues evoked in Clay's report—the restless feelings driving black folk in the Delta to abandon plantations in the rural districts and resettle in the town of Clarksdale or flee to the urban North—are literally destroying, "breaking up," the Delta's black Methodist congregations. The "program handed down by the church" is essentially a failed business plan: the restless condition of the people has made it impossible for Clay and his pastors to raise their expected annual contribution to the statewide church's missionary activities out of their Sunday collections and tithes, much less grow their congregations and expand their pastoral outreach. "This condition embarrasses the district superintendent" is Clay's way of confessing his own humiliation.

"The moving spirit is in the air": It was blues musicians, far more than any other cultural agents, who voiced the moving spirit bemoaned by Clay, transforming it into poetry and entertainment. And it was blues musicians, performers such as Charley Patton, Son House, and Sunnyland Slim, who provided the entertainment in the barrelhouses and juke houses of Clarksdale's disreputable "New World" district that Clay indicts, albeit somewhat obliquely, in the final line of his lament. W. C. Handy described the New World, which he worked with his band between 1903 and 1907, as a place of "shuttered houses" filled with "soft cream-colored fancy gals from Mississippi" and "boogie-house music." The oldest and most respectable Negro families, according to Handy, lived not far from the New World; "on their way to the Baptist and Methodist churches," he said, "they were required to pass before the latticed houses of prostitution."[130] Clarksdale bluesman Will Moore, John Lee Hooker's stepfather, described the typical Delta barrelhouse of the 1920s as a place where folks "shoot the craps, dance, and drink whiskey."[131] When Superintendent Clay, Clarksdale's voice of black Methodist probity, indicts the "slick devices and destructive diseases and unsanitary conditions" that prey upon the migrant parishioners who have vanished from the membership rolls in his district, he is indicting that blues milieu: gambling, drinking, fast women, and sinful music. Devil's music. Part of a contemporary whirlwind of restlessness, immorality, and youthful irreverence that was destroying the black church and its ministers in the Delta. "Many of the churches have lost from one-third to one-half of their membership," reported the new superintendent of the Clarksdale District, J. M. Marsh, at the 1923 meeting of Mississippi's Methodist Episcopal clergy.[132] N. R. Clay had stepped down, or been replaced.

It is analytically unsound for any study of the blues to imagine that the devil's-music dispute can be summed up by the trials of one minister from one specific faith tradition overseeing one six-county Mississippi Delta purview. If this chapter has circled inward as it proceeds, it has also, I hope, circled outward to suggest the range of spiritual, psychological, aesthetic, and economic investments that helped make the phrase "devil's music" such an indelible part of black southern life in the first half of the twentieth century. That being said, I believe that Clarksdale and the surrounding Delta, including Memphis to the north, are particularly germane to the current discussion. This is true not just because the preponderance of available evidence comes from blues performers associated with those areas, but because the devil's-music dispute was a generational conflict—modern black youth rejecting the strictures of conservative black elders—and because the sociology of the Delta was uniquely conducive to such a breach.

This is not to say that the conflict didn't materialize elsewhere. Many commentators have remarked on the cynicism of black youth, northern and southern, in the decades between the world wars. Sociologist Gunnar Myrdal identified a clear point of attitudinal divergence in the late 1930s between African Americans young and old over the question of church-endorsed behavioral proscriptions:

> The denominations to which Negroes predominantly belong—Baptist and Methodist—attempt to exercise strict control over morals, and have a rather broad definition of morals. For want of a better term, we may say that they have "puritanical" standards of behavior. . . . The practices of gambling, drinking, drug-taking, smoking, snuff-dipping, card-playing, dancing and other minor "vices" are condemned. . . . These injunctions seem to have an effect on middle class Negroes, especially those who are ready to settle down. . . . The bulk of the lower class, and the youth of all classes, seems to pay little attention to them.[133]

The attitudinal alignment between the black lower class (which includes, presumably, both the working class and the criminal underclass) and black youth is intriguing, suggesting as it does that blues culture, and the behavioral freedoms it endorsed, was also a kind of youth culture during this period. Myrdal's finding is supplemented by the testimony of Leila Holmes, a Holiness preacher in South Carolina interviewed by the Federal

Writers Project in 1939, who thought pop culture—commodified songs and dances—was the devil's way of claiming the young. "The younger generation in Columbia is just ruined. The songs they sing are plumb outlandish. They dance somethin' scandalous, day and night, by these nickelos [jukeboxes]. Instead of being in school tryin' to learn how to be decent, they out cuttin' the buck day in and day out, steppin' in every trap the devils got set for 'em."[134]

Jukeboxes came to the Mississippi Delta in the 1930s, and their presence bespoke a secular, urbane modernity—since they played the latest hits by Louis Jordan, Fats Waller, and others—that was as alluring to the young as it was unnerving to their parents. If the prewar Delta was not, as it has sometimes been depicted in blues mythologies, a premodern backwater suffocated by white sadism and veiled by hoodoo moons, neither was it quite as swimmingly up-to-date as Harlem, Chicago, and other urban centers, although the currents of attitude and feeling carried by pop music helped narrow the difference. This gradient helps explain some of the passion that drove the Great Migration, a hunger not merely to escape oppression but to embrace what was already half-known from evidence that had percolated into the Delta: sheet music and recordings, pop songs (such as "St. Louis Blues") covered by wandering guitarists, but also a more generalized attitude of youthful rebellion and devil-may-care sophistication propagated by both the white bohemians of the Lost Generation and the black bohemians known as New Negroes. Many of the latter—Langston Hughes, Zora Neale Hurston, Wallace Thurman—were themselves migrants from the hinterlands, but so too were Ernest Hemingway and F. Scott Fitzgerald. As I argue in chapter 2, young black and white urbanites of the 1920s had their own notable investment in devil-themed blues, one that can't wholly be distinguished from the devil's-music dispute in Mississippi and elsewhere in the South. Cultural currents flowed both ways, and black youth who remained in the Delta were not immune to the siren song of modernity. Modernity just took a little longer to arrive down home.

The most detailed and insightful survey of African American life in the northern Mississippi Delta during this period is the Fisk University–Library of Congress Coahoma County Study made in 1941 and 1942, a collaborative effort that brought folklorist Alan Lomax together with a trio of black academics: musicologist John W. Work, sociologist Lewis Wade Jones, and Samuel C. Adams Jr., a doctoral student in sociology. It was a vexed partnership in certain ways; Lomax's role as the study's official (white) figurehead remains a point of scholarly debate. But the study, parts of which show up in Lomax's memoir, *The Land Where the Blues Began* (1993) and the bulk of which shows up in the manuscripts by Work, Jones, and Adams collected in *Lost Delta Found* (2005), goes a long way toward dispersing the gothic mists that seem to shroud discussions of the prewar Delta, particularly when the devil and the blues are the subject at hand. Most notably, all four men agree on the rough outlines of a four-generation schematic that helps explain why the devil's-music dispute took such a potent form in the region. Adapting Jones's terms, I'll call these generations "the river generation," "the railroad generation," "the automobile generation," and "the young moderns."

The river generation, according to Jones, were those who, by the early 1940s, had lived into their seventies and eighties. They were the pioneers who cleared and settled the Delta. They drained swamps, cut down trees, hauled out stumps, and built levees. They were men, most of them, and they had a pioneer vitality and rough-hewn, secular tastes. Lomax interviewed an eighty-six-year-old fiddler named Alec Robertson, a survivor from this period. He had "fiddled for the devil for fifty-seven years," he told Lomax, before suddenly getting religion with the help of his Holiness ladyfriend at the age of seventy-five. "The devil had his hands on me principally," he admitted. "I'd do anything a person could do—dip snuff, chew tobacco, drink whiskey, cuss, and run around. . . . I used to be rough, but, since I got religion, it changed all them old habits."[135]

The men of the river generation were tamed and supplanted by the railroad generation, the men and women who came onto the scene after the country had been opened up. "They are people, now between the ages of fifty and seventy," writes Jones, "who found the frontier pushed back, the river dwindling in importance, and the era of the railroad beginning":

People belonging to this second generation [of black Delta residents] are now old, but they are still strong and vigorous. Having come with the first orderly regimes established after the frontier, they still represent order. They frown alike on the violence of the pioneer life they found and the disorderly life of the present. Mrs. Reed, referring to one of the pioneer heroes, remarked, "I just couldn't stand him. He was the kinda man didn't have no respect for nobody—for himself and nobody else. He was a devil." The present, in contrast to the orderly past which she helped to develop, seems confused and disorderly to her as well as to her contemporaries. Their world reached its flowering around the First World War and suffered a collapse later which has never been quite understood. . . . In the active lives of the second generation the church became the dominant institution of the community.[136]

This second generation might just as well have been called the church generation—or the blues-is-the-devil's-music generation, since it was churchgoing people of this age who leveled that charge at the songs and guitars favored by the generation that followed, and who whipped their blues-struck children into line. Rev. William Hooker, John Lee's father, is one of these. So, too, is Muddy Waters's grandmother Della (b. 1881), who told Muddy, when he first picked up a harmonica, "You're playing for the devil. Devil's gonna get you." This was the generation that built Baptist and Methodist churches throughout the Delta, then watched their membership rolls dissolve as the Great Migration swept through in the aftermath of the Great War. This generation demonized the blues, transforming the restless, good-timing music into symbol of all that was wrong with the modern world.

The third generation in the black Delta was the blues-inventing generation, the generation that built the juke joints. Born between 1890 and 1910, Charley Patton, Son House, Tommy Johnson, Willie Brown, and Skip James were members of this cohort. Like their Lost Generation peers in the big cities, the young people of this generation lived in a rapidly changing world that had been liberated by the automobile—in their case, the paving of Mississippi's highways in the 1930s—and, in the war's aftermath, a sense that many of the old rules were no longer in effect. "They have no pleasant memories of the isolation and stabilization before motor transportation arrived," writes Jones. "They have enjoyed the freedom of movement the 'good road' brought as they rattled about in the second-hand cars their cotton money bought. . . . Electric lights in the church and electricity to make their nickels bring music out of 'Seeburgs' [jukeboxes] and radios are their pride." Although their parents might see the church and the devil's music as incommensurable, this generation wasn't quite so sure: Patton, House, and James each found different ways of preaching the blues, reconciling (or merely alternating) the roles of preacher and bluesman.[137]

The fourth generation, the young moderns, consisted of black Delta residents born later than 1910: the thirty-and-under crowd. These are the familiar superstars of the Delta blues, many of whom ended up in Chicago as part of the second Great Migration after World War II: Howlin' Wolf (b. 1910 but coming into his own slightly late), Robert Johnson (b. 1911), Muddy Waters and Sonny Boy Williamson (1913), Willie Dixon (1915), Elmore James (1918), John Lee Hooker (1920), B. B. King (1925). To list those names now is to be confronted with a pantheon of blues elders, the "old school," so it comes as a shock to see them in social context as the teenagers and twenty-somethings they were when Louis Jones came to Coahoma County in 1941. "Youths and children," observed Jones, "try to get a grip on life in the midst of a disintegrating past and a fascinating present. . . . They pick cotton, play their games, follow their parents through a routine of living, and go to school. They sing the songs currently popular on the radio and the juke boxes and learn others as they hear them sung by older people at home and in the fields."[138] The younger bluesmen were perched, in attitudinal and behavioral terms, on the cutting edge of this generational cohort; they were style-setters among the young moderns. Not everybody was happy about the style they set. Samuel C. Adams interviewed an unnamed woman from the railroad generation who viewed Clarksdale and its young people as hopelessly fallen and the contemporary church as incapable of saving them:

> When I was a girl I didn't go into town and stay out all of the night. Mothers just not raising their girls right; allowing girls to smoke cigarettes, ride automobiles, drink, and do everything. And the church don't say nothing about it. These younger folks calling themselves having a good time. They drinks whiskey, they gambles, and they goes to town. . . . They want to go to town to raise all kind of devilment. And you know there ain't very much right in our cities now. There used to be special places to raise the devil, now the whole city. They got a class now that oughta be called the New Rising Devil Class.[139]

The New Rising Devil Class: a disturbing new generation of freethinking young people who are determined, in this pious old woman's judgmental eyes, to raise the devil every chance they get.

The King and Anderson Plantation, on which Adams conducted most of his research, was a huge enterprise located directly adjacent to Clarksdale, a town of 12,000, roughly 10,000 of whom were black. Clarksdale, which according to Adams had 9 Negro juke joints, 8 Negro churches, and 100 Negro ministers, was treated in his study as "the seat of urban influence" vis à vis the plantation. One of John Work's informants, an elderly male Sunday schoolteacher in Clarksdale and another member of the railroad generation, confirmed the unnamed woman's claim that young moderns in the town—and the Delta as a whole—were manifesting far too much independence of mind. The church itself had become so modern these days that it no longer tried to control young people by threatening them with the prospect of being cast into hell:

> The devil didn't seem to have much of a chance in the hills. . . . But now you take down here. . . . Mobility is very great, and the ordinary community controls that you find up in the Hills . . . well, you don't find them here. . . .
>
> Not so long ago I was teaching Sunday School to a group of these boys and girls around here, and we was talking about using one's talents. You know how God gave every man certain talents, and some used them wisely and others used them foolishly. . . .
>
> Then several inquisitive souls began to want to know if a person could use his talents successfully—and be a sinner? They talked about the gambler, the card shark, the policy operators, and finally they got settled down on Blues singers.
>
> They wanted to know if it was a greater sin to let one's talents lay aside or to use one's talents in the wrong way, yet share the profits with the church. You can see what sort of things these youngsters got on their minds. Yes sir! They're getting all modern. They talked about Ella Fitzgerald who makes her living singing the blues. Some thought that singing the blues was her talent and they couldn't see how that was wrong, especially if she shared her profits with the church.
>
> No, the church ain't like what it used to be—the days of eye-balls-a-drippin' and skulls-a-bilin'.[140]

A crucial point emerges from the testimony of these two members of the railroad generation: the devil was alive and well in the Delta in 1940, but he lived primarily as a rhetorical strategy deployed by the old folks to express their disapproval of young moderns—including the Delta bluesmen—who simply didn't take religion, much less hellfire-and-brimstone sermonizing, very seriously. To rhapsodize, as Greil Marcus famously did, that the blues singers "sang as if their understanding of the devil was strong enough to force a belief in God out of their lives," is to miss this point.[141] What the blues singers of the automobile generation and the young moderns who followed them understood was that their elders, struggling to maintain control, were determined to smear them—their music, their new freedoms, their comparative religious irreverence or indifference—with the devil's brush, including insults like "New Rising Devil Class." What they took very seriously indeed, virtually all of them, was the need to insist that blues was *not* the "devil's music," regardless of what their elders and religiously minded peers might say. A few, of course, decided to mock their elders not by fighting the charge but by embracing it, transforming it into a badge of honor, an emblem of insouciant modernity.

The word "irreverence" is particularly important in this context: it contradicts pretty much everything we have been taught to think about Delta religiosity and the Delta blues, the latter epitomized by the haunted figure of Robert Johnson. "He walked his road like a failed, orphaned Puritan," insists Marcus, ". . . framing his tales with old echoes of sin and damnation. There were demons in his songs—blues that walked like a man, the devil, or the two in league with each other."[142] Yet the contemporary evidence cuts sharply against this portrait, suggesting instead that Johnson's peers—his audience—had lightheartedly dismissed threats of hellfire that were the lingering inheritance of the Great Awakening. "The Christianity of these Negroes," writes Hortense Powdermaker of her Indianola subjects in the early 1930s, "is in essence quite different from that of the missionizing period, and of most local Whites today. Benevolent mercy rather than stern justice is the chief attribute of the Negro's God. . . . The accent has shifted from hell to heaven, from retribution to forgiveness, from fear to hope." Church affairs, she added, were characterized by "gusto and hilarity."[143]

Both John Work and Samuel Adams remark on a singular church event that took place in Clarksdale in the fall of 1941: a "Heaven and Hell" party given by the YMCA and YWCA Business Club of the St. John Baptist Church. "In addition to its being a concession to the demands of the younger people for greater secular activity," notes Work, "the 'heaven and hell' party represents temporarily at least a practical abandonment by the church of its former rigid community sanctions." The elder of the church, Deacon Jones[!], tells Adams that "all the deacons . . . are going to stay away from the party. We are going to let them younger folks, you understand, have their way." The party itself is described by a young female schoolteacher:

> Well, I'll tell you, it's costing a dime to get in. You buys a ticket, which tells you which way you'll be going—to Heaven, or to Hell. Now you can't go to both of them. You got to do what the ticket says. Well, if you gets a ticket to Heaven they serves you ice cream and cake, and you just sits around and talks, and maybe plays games. But if you gets a ticket to Hell they serves you hot cocoa and red hot spaghetti—and they dance, play cards, checks, and do most anything.[144]

If it's hard for us to imagine a Baptist church in Mississippi in 1941 allowing its young parishioners to carve a temporary party-space called "Hell" out of its sanctified interior and sell tickets to the shindig, then we don't know quite as much about the world that gave rise to the Delta blues as we thought we did. The aftermath of the devastation wrought on the Delta's churches by the Great Migration of the 1920s, plainly, was a new readiness on the part of church elders to adapt to the needs and desires of a youthful, playful clientele.

The spirit of youthful irreverence indexed by the "Heaven and Hell" party and the aging Clarksdale informants quoted earlier shows up at various points in the blues tradition, refiguring the devil and hell in ways that subvert the old folks' Manichean rigidities. "He Calls That Religion" (1932) is one example; it mischievously turns the tables on Deacon Jones, accusing him of the money-hunger and lust that were usually the bluesman's cross to bear and consigning him to hell with righteous indignation. Two additional examples will clarify my point. The first, Robert Johnson's "Me and the Devil Blues" (1937), has often been cited as Exhibit A in invocations of the bluesman's presumptive "closeness" to the devil and his implacable evil, and for obvious reasons:

> Early this morning . . . when you knocked upon my door
> Early this morning, ooh . . . when you knocked upon my door
> And I said hello Satan . . . I believe it's time to go
>
> Me and the devil . . . was walkin' side by side
> Me and the devil, whoo . . . was walkin' side by side
> And I'm going to beat my woman . . . until I get satisfied
>
> She said you don't see why . . . that you will dog me 'round
> [spoken] Now baby you know you ain't doin' me right, dontcha?
> She said you don't see why . . . ooooo . . . that you will dog me 'round
> It must-a be that old evil spirit . . . so deep down in the ground
>
> You may bury my body . . . down by the highway side
> [spoken] Baby I don't care where you bury my body when I'm dead
>   and gone
> You may bury my body . . . ooh . . . down by the highway side
> So my old evil spirit . . . can catch a Greyhound bus and ride[145]

Greil Marcus likens the opening stanza, with its "eerie resignation," to "that moment when Ahab goes over to the devil-worshipping Parsees he kept stowed away in the hold of the Pequod."[146] Russell Banks, in an essay titled "The Devil and Robert Johnson" (1991), psychologizes the bluesman and is profoundly disturbed by what he finds:

> This is the work of a disturbed male psyche telling its frightening and frightened secrets. No apology, no rationalization, no denial. Just the awful truth of the sick need to beat a woman. By switching abruptly in a single verse from the flirtatious, slightly heretical image of a man striding side-by-side with the devil to the image of that same man making the terrifying promise that he will beat his woman until he gets his satisfaction, Johnson imbues the figure of Satan with radical sexual complexity and power, and gives to his raw little narrative a chilling believability that utterly transforms the romantic convention of the male figure in thrall to the devil.[147]

Eerie, frightening, awful, sick, terrifying, raw, chilling, and in thrall to the devil: nothing playful here! Or is there? Elijah Wald has argued that "an unbiased reader, unaware of the Johnson legend, might see quite easily" that "as far as the lyrics go, this is meant to be a funny song," but much of the humor, I suggest, is contained in the two rapid-fire spoken asides.[148] Both of these asides are directed at the woman that the singer claims he's going to beat "until he gets satisfied"; their combined effect is to undercut the seriousness of his threat by establishing a kind of lighthearted, intimate bond with the woman over which his bravura self-projections hover rather than loom heavily. Eerie resignation? A frightened young man? Marcus and Banks have, I think, completely misread Johnson's tone, and they are not alone.

Any reading of the song must begin by framing it within the contexts I've elaborated in this chapter—above all, the emergence of the young moderns onto the stage of the black Delta, animated by a restless irreverence through which they distinguished themselves from the humorless religiosity of their elders. According to Michael Taft's concordance of prewar blues, "Me and the Devil Blues" is the only blues song in which the name "Satan" appears, although it's quite common in the spirituals ("Satan, Your Kingdom Must Come Down," etc.).[149] Johnson's opening stanza, in other words, establishes intimacy with a devil figure or devil principle in a startlingly bold way, one calculated to offend religious pieties and, not coincidentally, to accrue cool-points among young moderns. Since Johnson's generation was already being slandered as the Delta's "New Rising Devil Class," the entire song—with its invocation of the devil-as-comrade and its parading of the singer's "old evil spirit"—may be seen as a cocky declaration of guilty-as-charged. "I'm *bad*, baby," the singer laughs, "and I don't care who knows it."[150] The devil-may-care attitude toward burial expressed in the final stanza is a direct affront to churched elders, since they most definitely *did* expect to be buried in their churches' graveyards. The final line of the song again strikes a jarringly modern note, conflating spiritual concerns with a relatively new mode of interstate transportation, Greyhound buses, one that distinguished the restless young of Johnson's generation from the railroad generation and the stodgy Pullman coaches they aspired to.

Framed in this manner, "Me and the Devil Blues" begins to emerge not as the tortured romantic confession Marcus and Banks would have us believe but as something closer to a put-on: a flirtatious dialogue between the singer and his baby edged with braggadocio, complaint, and a modicum of tenderness, all of it enlarged in a slightly cartoonish way through the singer's calculated invocations of the devil. More precisely, the song seems determined to keep both readings—romantic confession and put-on—in dialectical tension. The "you" in the opening stanza is the singer's woman, knocking on his door after a presumptive late night out carousing, but it's also his long-simmering rage at her misbehavior that suddenly crests as he rises from his sleepless bed, prepared to slap her around. The devil is simply that rage, personified and claimed.[151] But the third stanza upends this reading. The tortured syntax of the A line, with its repeated "you," makes it unclear who is doing the dogging around and who is complaining about it—that is, who is to blame here—and the singer's spoken aside is a tender complaint rather than a furious threat. Truth be told, there *is* no rage in the song as Johnson sings it. Johnson is cool, playful, almost flippant toward the end: a trickster flown with the wind. He cares too little, not too much. The persona through which he speaks here is in thrall to nobody—not his baby, certainly not the devil—and couldn't care less about the religious folk his song is sure to offend. He is "evil" only in the sense of being contrary, self-directed, impossible to pin down. Like John Lee Hooker's "Burnin' Hell," "Me and the Devil Blues" is a young modern's declaration of spiritual independence, one that works its magic spell by deliberately scrambling the Manichean certainties of the elders who dominated the Delta's religious landscape.

The devil and woman-trouble both resurface in my final example, "Whitewash Station Blues" (1928) by The Memphis Jug Band, as does a fearless irreverence. Memphis, where cotton merchants presided, was often considered the northern terminus of the Mississippi Delta; in purely musical terms, the bouncy hokum stylings of "Whitewash Station Blues" have little in common with the recordings by Hooker and Johnson, but philosophically the three songs form a continuum of youthful modern skepticism. Surveying the King and Anderson Plantation in 1941, Samuel Adams noted the "growing disinterested attitudes of the [black] plantation youth toward things religious and sacred," highlighted by a "pervasive skepticism of the pretensiveness of the church."[152] As the Delta's nearest large urban center, Memphis—and the city's young musicians—helped encourage such attitudes:

> Build a Whitewash Station two mile to glory . . . so the jug band'll
>   have a chance (2x)
> You can toot your whistle, blow your horn
> The Memphis Jug Band done been here and gone
> Build a Whitewash Station two miles to glory . . . so the jug band'll
>   have a chance, I say, the jug band'll have a chance.
>
> Now if you want to get to heaven, I'll tell you what to do
> You put on a sock, a boot and a shoe
> You place a bottle of corn in your right hand
> That'll pass you right over in the Promised Land
> And if you meet the devil, he ask you how you do
> I'm on my way to heaven, don't you want to go too
> Know there's a place that do just as well
> They call Whitewash Station ten miles from hell
>
> Build a Whitewash Station two mile to glory . . . so the jug band'll
>   have a chance (2x)
> Lord mama, what's on your mind
> You keep me worried and bothered all the time
> Build a Whitewash Station two mile from glory . . . so the jug band'll
>   have a chance, I say, the jug band have a chance.[153]

White's Station, later White Station, was an independent township within greater Memphis, roughly ten miles east of Handy Park on Beale Street; it took its name from a small train station in that area. "Whitewash Station Blues" seems to be a play on that location and the Christian idea of a "train to glory," with a mischievous twist: musicians, as W. C. Handy's minister-father reminded us, are rounders, idlers, dissipated characters, and need to be spiritually cleansed—or, as a last resort, whitewashed—in order to pass over into the Promised Land. The song concerns itself with salvation solely for the purpose of mocking those who are truly concerned with such things. Chief among these were the local faithful of COGIC: the equivalent, for the Memphis Jug Band, of the Baptists and Methodists who demonized bluesmen in the Delta.

The Church of God in Christ, the largest Holiness-Pentecostal sect, was based in Memphis, held huge annual gatherings there (the "National Holy Convocation of Saints"), and had, in 1925, constructed its first National Tabernacle not far from Beale Street. The founder of COGIC, Rev. C. H. Mason, made the distinction between sacred and secular music "crystal clear," according to Rev. David Hall, Mason's pastoral successor at Temple COGIC, the "mother church" founded by Mason in 1907: "He said blues was the Devil's music."[154] The behavioral and spiritual ideal of COGIC members, as historian Anthea Butler has noted, was sanctification, a word which "meant [that] the Holy Spirit would work to cleanse the sin away from a person's life, and that cleansing produced visible signs that a believer's life was free from sin."[155] Plain, modest dress and a strict renunciation of alcohol were two keynotes of the sanctified life. The Official Manual of the Church of God in Christ, for example, calls on believers to wear "attractive and dignified attire."[156] In its second stanza, "Whitewash Station Blues" burlesques this sanctification process, counseling the would-be pilgrim to wear one sock and two mismatched pieces of footwear and to greet St. Peter with a bottle of corn liquor in hand. If the devil is encountered before St. Peter's gates are reached—well, bring him along on the Glory Train, too! Here, as in Robert Johnson's "Me and the Devil Blues," the blues singer invokes the devil in a way that seems calculated to offend religious sensibilities, allowing him a meaningful space in human life yet granting him no real power to claim the singer's soul.

The fruit of the devil's-music dispute, as these examples suggest, isn't just the pained witness borne by several generations of black southern blues players who were chastised and sometimes beaten by parents and ministers for their errant musical tastes. It is also the comic response offered by some of those musicians, particularly those I've termed the young moderns. Sometimes this comedy takes the form of harsh mockery of ministerial misbehavior and hypocrisy, as in "He Calls That Religion." Sometimes, as in "Me and the Devil Blues," it takes the form of playful asides that undercut religious (or demonic) high seriousness. Sometimes it finds comic, redemptive middle ground between godly and devilish things—as in "Whitewash Station Blues," which situates itself ten miles from hell and two miles from glory. All of these responses, along with Hooker's signal proclamation, "Ain't no heaven, ain't no burnin' hell," are consistent with a rising tide of religious skepticism that characterized black southern youth between 1920 and 1940, especially those hailing from the Mississippi Delta. "The sacred-secular dichotomizing resulting from Christian dualism," Jon Michael Spencer has argued, "does not permit the option of integrating a church upbringing with blues strivings," but the blues artists I've discussed here undermine the sacred-secular dichotomy with considerable success, refusing to accept the world into which they were born on the dualistic terms dictated by their Christian elders.[157] Offered heaven or hell by their ministers, they demanded a Heaven and Hell party, sold tickets, and enjoyed themselves mightily.

2 , SOLD IT TO THE DEVIL

The Great Migration, Lost Generations, and the Perils of the Urban Dance Hall

The road to hell is too often paved with jazz steps.

—JOHN R. MCMAHON, "Unspeakable Jazz Must Go!" (1921)

FEELING DEVILISH

This study is premised on the claim that the devil's presence in the blues has, in our own day, become overidentified with crossroads mythology and a fictive Deep South soul-selling location as a result of specific imaginative and financial investments in the figure of Robert Johnson. It may come as a surprise, then, when I suggest that the nation's metropolitan center, New York City, played a key role in thrusting both the blues-devil and the trope of soul-selling into the national imagination, and more than a decade before Johnson cut his first sides. Migrant southerners, black and white, helped drive this process, with black female blues singers taking the lead. The morals of newly urbanized youth were at stake—irreverent young moderns who paved the way for their peers in Mississippi, including Johnson. In 1923, an Indiana-born, Texas-and-Virginia-schooled preacher named John Roach Straton set up a radio station in the basement of Calvary Baptist Church in midtown Manhattan with the express purpose of fighting the devil that had been loosed by a Prohibition-flouting, jazz-dancing, flapper-driven Lost Generation. "I hope that our radio system will prove so efficient," he thundered, "that when I twist the Devil's tail in New York, his squawk will be heard across the continent. . . . The people will not get any doubts or negations or question marks from the Calvary pulpit. . . . I shall try to continue to do my part, as the Bible expresses it, in tearing down the strongholds of Satan."[1] The following year, a migrant blues singer from Spartanburg, South Carolina, named Clara Smith entered the studios of Columbia Records, only a mile from Straton's pulpit, and threw down the gauntlet in symbolic terms, recording the very first devil-themed blues, "Done Sold My Soul to the Devil" (1924).[2] The song spoke to the condition of migrant black women in the urban environment—some of whom had "fallen" and become prostitutes, others of whom were merely rejoicing in the freedom of after-work dance hall life, still others of whom (especially in Holiness and Pentecostal congregations) had become more religious when confronted with urban disarray and might well have heard the song as a scandalous but instructive example of the wages of sin. But the song resonated more broadly, enabled a wider range of identifications, than this invocation of a black female public suggests. And dance, not just song, was a pivotal issue.

Kathy Ogren has argued that jazz in the 1920s became "the specific symbol of rebellion" for a disillusioned younger generation, and the devil—as a trickster, a good-timer, an instigator of nighttime revels—haunts that generation's soundtrack, especially at the moment when white feet (and black and white feet intertwined in a black-and-tan bohemia) find themselves propelled by "hot" black rhythm and the urgings of black voices.[3] Smith's inaugural devil-blues becomes legible when framed within this larger tradition, a "discourse of disbelief," in Ann Douglas's words, that "became the only thoroughly accredited modern mode" for a Lost Generation striving to throw off Victorian repression.[4] The devil, along with his temptations and his unholy congregants, waltzes through "Devil Dance Blues" (1925), "Hellish Rag" (1927), "I'm Feelin' Devilish" (1930), "There's Going to Be the Devil to Pay" (1935), and "The Devil with the Devil" (1939). Blues and jazz were deeply intertwined during the 1920s—not just with each other, but as emergent forms subsumed within then-dominant pop styles. Bessie Smith, Ma Rainey, Lizzie Miles, and other soon-to-be-recorded blues stars toured the Mississippi Delta during the 1910s with black minstrel troupes and tent shows; billed as "Southern coon shouters" and "up-to-date coon shouters," they were far more likely to be backed by minstrel bands or jazz combos than barrelhouse pianists or rough-edged blues guitarists such as Charley Patton.[5] It is impossible to disentangle North and South, urban and rural, male and female, black and white, when constructing an accurate genealogy of the devil figure in the blues. He—or she—is an overdetermined presence haunting both the blues lyric tradition and the juke-continuum of concert halls, dance halls, cabarets, speakeasies, country juke joints, and other nocturnal gathering spaces in Atlanta, Chicago, Detroit, and Harlem as well as the rural South. To reduce the blues-devil to Legba at the crossroads, an African survival—as both the feature film *Crossroads* (1986) and African Americanists such as Julio Finn and Samuel Floyd do—is to miss these multiple investments, especially moments where cross-racial conversations are taking place.

Both the emergence of the black southern preacher as a focus of mockery and the tableau of a devilish soul-sale, for example, are anticipated by Tin Pan Alley in ways that help contextualize the blues tradition's embrace of those themes. "O Death, Where Is Thy Sting" (1918), composed by white songwriter Clarence A. Stout and published by W. C. Handy, became a pop hit for West Indian–born Bert Williams, arguably the highest-paid black performer of the era. A comic monologue delivered with dry wit rather than broad burlesque, it manages perfectly to encapsulate the spirit of modern irreverence that would become the era's mongrel keynote—as attractive to youthful white refugees from midwestern small towns fevered by the Temperance movement as to young African Americans breaking away from their southern church homes. The devil is a key player here, a fulcrum around which moral rebellion gleefully organizes itself. Mose Jackson, a black parishioner, not only fails to be terrified by the "fiery" thralldom of Hell evoked by Parson Brown but is positively entranced by the "vampire women" and booze that Brown warns him he'll find there:

Now, Parson Brown, one Sunday morn
    Was giving good advice,
He warn'd his congregation to
    Refrain from sin and vice,
He drew a fiery picture 'bout
    The devil down below,
And said folks, quit your sinnin'
    Or to him you're bound to go.
Why Hell is full of vampire women,
    Whiskey, gin, and dice,
Satan, tell him to get behind thee
    And prepare thou for Paradise.
Mose Jackson jump'd up from his chair,
    And said, "Parson, is that true?
That Hell is full of what you said
    Well then just let me say to you:
If what you say is positive truth,
    O Death, where is thy sting?
I don't care now 'bout those pearly gates,
    Or [to] hear the angels sing;
With booze and women down below,
    Mister devil and I will [just] put on a show,

Cause if what you say is the positive truth,
　　O Death, where is thy sting?"[6]

Songs that satirically mock black preachers as gluttonous and concupiscent hypocrites incapable of self-governance have a long prehistory in minstrelsy and the "coon song" tradition; this song, by contrast, mocks its preacher by dramatizing the failure of his righteous oratory to achieve its intended end.[7] The titular refrain, from Corinthians 15:55, inverts the meaning of Paul's sermon on the Victory delivered by Christ, suggesting that the presence of strong drink, lusty women, and hot dice can transform the threat of hellfire into a promise of epicurean satisfaction. "Mose Jackson" is a working-class black southern everyman, not an urban hipster, but his gleeful rejection of Parson Brown connects the two worlds.[8] Cultural historian Karen Sotiropoulos reads the devil-sponsored "show" he yearns toward as a marker of the era's emergent secular leisure culture, "complete with alcohol, gambling, and sexual temptation," and the way that culture challenged the black church's authority over public life in North and South alike.[9]

What is new here isn't an older generation's anxieties about a young generation going bad; Cotton Mather bemoans devil-snared American youth before America even exists. The new note is the presence of popular culture, "amusements" associated with the burgeoning urban scene, and an attitude of spiritual distraction and brazen irreverence that they encouraged. The devil becomes a particularly potent idea—a positive good, in fact, for youth seeking to sharpen the generational divide and align themselves with modernity. To be black and modern, in such a context, is an ideologically charged condition, one that seeks to throw off the "old Negro" of the plantation tradition in two very different ways. On one side stood those who preached respectability, uplift, "holiness," a self-determined claiming of the moral high ground that abjured popular culture and its voracious, salacious, criminalized images of blackness tracing back to antebellum minstrelsy. On the other side stood a significant cohort of black youth, including performers such as Handy, who saw popular culture as a promising field of action within which creativity could be explored, selfhood could be enlarged, and financial independence could be earned in ways that the cotton field and the service trades had long precluded. This cohort viewed the Victorian puritanism of its elders not as a justified response to white racism but as an oppressive retrenchment in the certainties of old-time religion. W. E. B. DuBois anticipates the coming generational divide in his 1897 essay "The Problem of Amusement":

I have heard sermon after sermon and essay after essay thunder warnings against the terrible results of pleasure and the awful end of those who are depraved enough to seek pleasure. I have heard a fusillade of "don'ts" thrown at our young people: don't dance, don't play cards, don't go to the theatre, don't drink, don't smoke, don't sing songs, don't play kissing games, don't play billiards, don't play football, don't go on excursions— that I have not been surprised, gentlemen and ladies, to find in the feverish life of a great city, hundreds of Negro boys and girls who have listened for a life-time to the warning, "Don't do this or you'll go to hell," and then have taken the bit between their teeth and said, "Well, let's go to hell."[10]

The jaunty irreverence that DuBois associates with black urban youth at the turn of the century becomes a transracial style during the 1920s. Perfectly exemplifying that spirit was Irving Berlin's "Pack Up Your Sins (and Go to the Devil)" (1922), a hit in the *Music Box Revue* on Broadway. "If you care to dwell where the weather is hot," went one section,

> H-E-double-L is a wonderful spot.
> If you need a rest and you're all out of sorts,
> Hades is the best of the winter resorts.
> Paradise doesn't compare;
> All the nice people are there.
> They come from ev'rywhere
> Just to revel with Mister Devil.
> Nothing on his mind but a couple of horns.
> Satan is waitin' with his jazz band.[11]

"An unexpected 'damn' or 'hell' uttered on the New York stage," wrote *Harper's* editor Frederick Lewis Allen in *Only Yesterday* (1931), his popular history of the Jazz Age, "was no longer a signal for the sudden sharp laughter of shocked surprise; such words were becoming the commonplace of everyday talk."[12] Casual, playful, and sometimes favorable invocations of the devil and hell in black popular music, including the blues, are of a piece with this larger cultural development, as is mockery directed at men of the cloth. Between 1930 and the early 1950s, religious themes in black popular music tended to emerge in the context of humor, parody, or satire. As musicologist Teresa Reed notes, Louis Jordan, the Dominoes, Little Esther Phillips, and others "recorded a whole repertoire of humorous 'deacon' tunes which highlighted the seedier facets of the black preacher's image."[13] "Who is it that's handsome and good looking?" Jordan asks his Tympani Five, preening as he mimics a self-satisfied cleric in "Deacon Jones" (1944). "Who is it that can smell a rooster cookin'?" Deacon songs are freedom songs: songs of liberation from the behavioral protocols imposed by uplift ideology that do their releasing work by nullifying men of the cloth as greedy, lust-driven hypocrites—or, as in the case of "O Death, Where Is Thy Sting," as stuffy, irrelevant hindrances to the having of a good time in the modern world.

Yet parody is a double-edged sword, and the condemnatory power of the black church, expressed through its language and its ritual forms, was not so easily evaded. As the euphoria of the Jazz Age faded after Black Friday into Depression-era doldrums, the figure of the African American preacher admonishing his errant flock was put to puckishly subversive use by Fats Waller in "There's Going to Be the Devil to Pay" (1935).

You can listen to temptation . . . you can even go astray
But if you listen to temptation . . . there's gonna be the devil to pay
You can wink your eye at morals . . . if you care to live that way
But if you wink your eye at morals . . . there's gonna be the devil to pay

All you sinners, you oughta know . . . Satan's waitin' for the gang and
    you down below

You can go to church on Sunday . . . even wash your sins away
But if you're only good on one day . . . there's gonna be the devil to pay

[spoken/preached:]
. . . Look out there. What! Oh no no no, don't tell me he's down here?
Daniel down here? Is Daniel here? Well alright then, tell him latch onto them
lions and turn 'em loose. I'm going. Yeah. Haha! Oh yes yes. What is this?

That sounds like one of the . . .

Bring it on out there, Mr. Johnson. Yes. Play it boy! I didn't know you was
down here. Oh, give it me! Yeah!

You can listen to temptation, you can even go astray, etc.

All you sinners . . . [scats] aw bye bye

Bring it on out there, Satan!

Go to church on Sunday . . . and wash your sins away
But don't be good on one day . . . 'cause there's gonna be the devil to pay.[14]

Waller, born and raised in New York City, was the son of Edward Waller, a southern-born Baptist migrant and Harlem street-corner preacher who brought his son out onto the sidewalks to play harmonium in the Lord's service. Composed by Robert Emmerich, a white songwriter and pianist who worked with Thomas Dorsey's orchestra, the song pretends to evoke a chastened after-the-party tableau in which the Lost Generation's "sinners," those who have "listen[ed] to temptation" and "wink[ed] . . . at morals," will be brought to judgment, but it substitutes the devil for God as a focus of energized attention—God is never mentioned—and uses Waller's euphoric spoken interlude to make it clear that the devil's party is still having all the fun. Hell is imaged as a sort of lowdown dance hall, a Lion's Den Café to which the gang's all invited and in which Daniel easily vanquishes his leonine antagonists. The gleeful informality with which Waller urges Satan to "bring it on out there" offers a precedent, arguably, for Robert Johnson's "Me and the Devil Blues" (1937), with its shockingly intimate greeting, "Hello Satan, I believe it's time to go." Waller was immensely popular in the Mississippi Delta; although the song wasn't one of Waller's big hits, Johnson could have encountered it, in the Delta or elsewhere. When sociologist Louis Jones investigated popular music tastes in Clarksdale in 1941, Waller was one of a handful of artists whose recordings showed up on the jukeboxes of all five black cafés in town. Muddy Waters told Alan Lomax that same year that Waller was his favorite radio star.[15] With swing maestro Waller, as with Handy, John Lee Hooker, and so many foundational figures of the blues, the devil and his hell-bent energies speak through an African American minister's prodigal performer-son. But there were prodigal daughters, too, who entered into the conversation, and ministers who struggled to beat back the demon that had been loosed in a generational tide.

DENS OF INFAMY AND SHAME

Who, or what, was the devil to whom a black female migrant from the South might sell herself after she arrived in the northern metropolis during the first several decades of the twentieth century? Was he a john, black or white, to whom she might prostitute herself? Was the devil her pimp? Was the devil any man, no matter how gentle and well intentioned, with whom she might consort out of wedlock? Or was he a well-known subset of such men: a bad man, a sweet man, a rounder, somebody "gracile and dangerous," as poet Robert Hayden wrote of Bessie Smith in "Homage to the Empress of the Blues," someone who beat her, took her money, smiled at her tears, and disappeared? Was the devil visible in the financial seductions of a job she might take as a hostess in a dance hall where the blues were sung? Or was the devil that confronted this poor woman a more comprehensive negative behavioral ideal: any of a dozen retrograde actions, from dressing unchastely to parading in public, that reflected a falling away from the code of spiritual purity, moral uprightness, and bourgeois (or working-class) respectability preached by the Baptists, Methodists, and above all the followers of the Memphis-based Church of God in Christ?

These questions together sketch the ideological context within which Clara Smith's 1924 hit recording, "Done Sold My Soul to the Devil" would have become meaningful for the African American audience that was its core constituency. Before discussing the song and the four variant versions (three blues and one hillbilly) that were issued in 1937, we would do well to acknowledge that the challenge posed by black female sexuality—how to control it, channel it, and express it; how to protect it from the depredations of white men, black pimps, and the hurtful Jezebel stereotype continually inscribed by popular culture—was a source of vivid interest and intense concern to many African Americans during this period, not least the mothers of daughters entranced by the siren song of show business.

The life of Lil Hardin (1898–1971), jazz pianist and future wife of Louis Armstrong, offers one example. Growing up in Memphis in the first two decades of the century, Hardin lived with her grandmother, a former slave on a Mississippi plantation, and her mother, Dempsey, a domestic. Like Edward Waller, Dempsey intended for her musically gifted child to play music in the Lord's service, but the Memphis environs—including W. C. Handy and his marching band—got in the way. "What Dempsey heard on Beale Street horrified her," writes Hardin's biographer James Dickerson,

> because she considered it the "devil's music." Those feelings had nothing to do with the way the music sounded. It had everything to do with the stories, true stories, she feared about the young girls that were lured to Beale Street by the bright lights and promises of pretty new clothes, only to discover that their only financial assets were their bodies. So many young women were flocking to Memphis at the turn of the last century that the city was forced to create a women's protection agency to deal with the problem associated with their arrival. . . .
>
> By the time Lil was nine, her skills on the organ were such that she landed a position as the organist for her Sunday school class at the Lebanon Baptist Church. Her favorite hymn was "Onward Christian Soldiers,"

and she played it at every opportunity. Unfortunately for her career as a church organist, she added jazz and blues riffs to the song. This rebellion delighted her classmates, but ultimately attracted the wrath of her pastor, who agreed with Dempsey that blues and jazz were the devil's music.[16]

Hardin's grandmother used to "run me away," Hardin claimed, when she'd linger on the back porch listening to a cousin who played guitar. "That's vulgar music," her grandmother would cry. "Get away!" And her mother, she remembered, "hated any form of popular music," beating Hardin with a broomstick when she discovered sheet music for Handy's "St. Louis Blues" among Lil's papers. Several years later, after mother and daughter moved to Chicago, an incorrigible nineteen-year-old Hardin hooked up with the New Orleans Creole Jazz Band, playing piano with them for three weeks before Dempsey found out. "A nasty, filthy, dirty cabaret?" her mother raged. "Oh, after all the money I've spent on you, sending you to school to make you a lady and you end up in a vulgar, no good cabaret! You'll quit tonight."[17]

Vulgar, dirty, and devilish: thus did the church and family strive to discipline youthful black female performers attracted to jazz and blues and the nocturnal demimonde in which the music thrived. What distinguishes Hardin's experience from that of her male peers in the Delta is the role played by urbanization—a southern regional process here, one drawing on the rural populations of Mississippi, Arkansas, and Tennessee, as well as the more familiar northward migration pattern—and the way that process imperils black female virtue. Hardin's experience is paralleled on both points by that of other female performers. Lillie Mae Glover (1906–85), aka Baby Ma Rainey, was the daughter of a Pentecostal minister in Middle Tennessee who ran off to join a medicine show when she was fourteen after an abortive first foray with a Nashville operation. Singing popular music was "the worst thing in the world" to her family, she said. "They was all church people. They came and got me off of the stage."[18] Like Big Mama Thornton and a number of black urban working women whose chosen milieu was made up of dance halls, bootleg joints, and gambling dens, Glover eased her path by dressing and acting like a man; she earned a reputation on Beale Street, according to historian Sharon Harley, as a "pretty tough boy," a "pistol-toting blues singer and hoodoo woman."[19] R & B singer Ruth Brown (1928–2006), whose father directed an AME church choir in Portsmouth, Virginia, ran away from home at seventeen, heading north to Washington, D.C., and then New York. In later life she insisted that her father had taken pride in her achievements, but only after considerable struggle. "It went against everything that he had stood for, because he had said, 'No, no, no—you're not going to sing outside the church.'. . . There were these awful untrue thoughts about people involved in show business, as the movies and radio and everything else depicted them—you know, you have visions of the ball-room girl or the 'hostess with the mostest'—and *no, I will not have my child be a part of that*. If you sang anything outside the church, it was truly the devil's music."[20] Even those black female performers who remained in the South and steered clear of the blues knew what disfavor loomed if the line were crossed. Georgia native Bernice Johnson Reagon (1942–), daughter of Baptist minister J. J. Johnson and a member of the SNCC Freedom Singers in the 1960s (as well as founder of the a cappella ensemble Sweet Honey in the Rock), agreed that "in [the] more rigid churches . . . if you sang the blues, you were sort of worshipping the devil almost."[21]

The devil's-music accusation was especially freighted in an ideological context where migration, prostitution, and the blues had come to be asso-ciated in various ways. In her pioneering study of women's blues, Daphne Duval Harrison notes that, by 1910, young black women emerging from "the [southern and small-town] churches, schools, and clubs where they had sung, recited, danced, or played" discovered that they could earn fifty dollars a week or more as entertainers in urban theaters or with traveling shows, while domestic work only paid eight to ten dollars a week.[22] Many aspirants went to the cities *as* domestics, in fact, hoping to leverage their new urban environs into stage careers. Even when things worked out as planned, migrants who became professional jazz and blues entertainers con-fronted the massed resistance of the black Baptist women who, in historian Evelyn Brooks Higginbotham's words, "[waged] war against gum chewing, loud talking, gaudy colors, the nickelodeon, jazz, littered yards, and a host of other perceived improprieties."[23] The 1922 Chicago Commission on Race Relations objected to one café because it tempted the young black women who performed there with "immoral enticements": jazz, suggestive dances, and interracial couples.[24] Detroit's black community leaders, according to historian Victoria Wolcott, "sounded warnings about the dangers of blues throughout the 1920s," insisting in one editorial that blues singing "only poisons the soul and dwarfs the intellect."[25]

Black female performers often paid a heavy price in their religious com-munities for daring to partake of forbidden pop-musical fruit, and the conflict was aggravated when southern religion migrated north and defined itself in opposition to sinful urban disarray. Clothing became a wedge issue: show business required of a female performer a level of sexual suggestiveness — or so it was presumed — that violated church-endorsed guidelines. "The dress code developed in the 1920s," according to religious historian Anthea Butler, "was designed to combat the vices of the city and to separate the sanctified women from outsiders."[26] Soul singer Maxine Brown (1939–) migrated from South Carolina to New York as a teenager; when her first single, "All in My Mind," became a hit in 1961, the members of her Pentecostal church were up in arms, in part because her concert appearances required that she dress the part of an R & B singer:

> My church condemned me! They heard I was wearing lipstick and short sleeves that you could see through! [Laughs.] And we're doing the "devil's music." And let me tell you, when you come from churches like that, they put such a guilt trip on you. Oh, my God! They could really give it to you. And all my life, that's one of the things that I just couldn't get away from. And we all[,] we *all* who come from this type of background, these parents are dead set against us doing the devil's music, and our pastors and what have you.[27]

The testimony offered by Ruth Brown and Maxine Brown speaks to the persistence of a social indictment that had its origins, as Lil Hardin's and Lillie Mae Glover's recollections suggest, in the anxieties of an earlier era. The devil's-music charge — and specifically the association of blues and jazz with dangerous, dissipatory, disrespectable nightlife — was one component of that anxiety; the moral perils of migration were another. Undergirding both anxieties was a more comprehensive desire to reclaim black female virtue, in the face of white stereotypes about African American licentiousness, through what Higginbotham has termed the politics of respectability. Middle-class and elite black women strove with mixed success to "win the black lower class's psychological allegiance to temperance, industriousness, thrift, refined manners, and Victorian sexual morals."[28] Black churches played an important role in this disciplining process from the 1890s onward, particularly the Church of God in Christ (along with other Holiness denominations) and the National Baptist Women's Convention, both of which prescribed a strict dress code for female members. "Preached about and sung about, dress became the foremost social marker of COGIC women for decades," notes Butler. "During the interwar and prohibition period, however, it was also a source of constant struggle."[29]

It is impossible to disentangle the critique leveled at the world of jazz and blues entertainment from the larger social phenomenon that Hazel Carby has aptly characterized as a series of moral panics between 1910 and the mid-1930s revolving around the figure of the vulnerable young African American female migrant, a fallen woman understood to be "sexually degenerate and, therefore, socially dangerous."[30] Prostitution was the devil here: youthful naïveté, economic need, spiritual disrepair, urban disorder, and the presence of sexual predators all combined, in the eyes of uplift's guardians, to terrible effect. The head of the National League for the Protection of Colored Women wrote in 1910 of the "swarm of Northern harpies and procuresses whose business it is to meet the incoming masses, and under pretense of assisting them to find homes and work, land them in dens of infamy and shame."[31] The situation was indeed grim, if more morally ambiguous than it might first appear. In *Love for Sale*, a study of prostitution in New York during the first half of the twentieth century, historian Elizabeth Alice Clement argues that "while white madams and pimps made headlines in the 1920s, black men and women increased their participation in all aspects of prostitution during the decade." This trend continued into the 1930s, and it was significantly inflected by racism: black women faced discrimination within the sex industry — they were forced to walk the streets instead of working out of hotels, were treated more harshly by the police, and suffered more exploitation by pimps — but they ended up doing sex work in the first place precisely because they were discriminated against within the broader urban economy, particularly after the crash of 1929. "The data suggests that black women's economic opportunities deteriorated so significantly during the Depression that they resorted to prostitution in numbers far greater than their proportion in the population."[32] Yet, according to Wolcott, black female migrants who were drawn into the sex trade, recognizing that they were in a double bind precipitated by a conflict between moral and economic imperatives under the sign of racism, finessed the question of respectability in a way that enabled them to maintain a sense of self-respect regardless of how others viewed their lives:

> By combining day work with prostitution, African American women [in Detroit] could earn a dependable income. . . . Indeed, day work and casual prostitution had some similarities: both were irregular forms of employment that offered flexibility. Women could pick day work or exchange sex for money when they needed to bring in extra income. The difference between the occupations was that wages for a full day's housework were equal to wages for one trick — between $1 and $3. [Some women] did not fit into the models of respectable and disreputable workers presented by reformers and civic leaders. [Day workers who occasionally turned tricks]

used available forms of employment to survive in the city without making stark distinctions between having a "respectable" identity as a domestic worker or having "fallen" as a prostitute.[33]

This discussion of the moral ambiguities of prostitution among young black urban women during the 1920s and 1930s may seem like a distraction from the putative subject of this chapter: the emergence of the devil as a central figure in the blues lyric tradition and an evolving mythology of the blues. In truth, it has brought us right to the devil's doorstep.

I DONE SOLD MY SOUL

In his influential study *Blues, Ideology, and Afro-American Literature: A Vernacular Theory* (1984), Houston A. Baker Jr. defines the "blues matrix" by offering a series of examples in which "personae, protagonists, autobiographical narrators," and others "successfully negotiate an obdurate 'economics of slavery' and achieve a resonant, improvisational, expressive dignity."[34] Money is the point: more specifically, the desire to reclaim and possess one's own body and soul in a political economy conditioned by the black subject's ruthless reduction to the status either of chattel—a material commodity—or, after Emancipation, "worthless" black flesh valuable solely as a source of exploitable labor power. What does it mean, in such a context, to claim that one has sold one's soul to the devil? Especially in post-Emancipation landscapes, the mere fact that one claims the *right* to engage in such a transaction, spiritually ill-advised as it might be, testifies to the still-novel fact of black freedom. You can't sell what you don't own; self-ownership is good and distinguishes one from a slave. By the same token, prostitution—the repeated sale of one's own flesh for the sexual pleasuring of the purchaser, with one's pimp spiriting away most of the profits—threatens to cast the black female subject into a new kind of slavery, depriving her of the resonant, improvisational, expressive dignity imaged by Baker. Yet might not a bold avowal of soul-selling have served as a way of accumulating cultural capital: an assertion of one's fearless urban modernity, one's decisive break with puritanical southern religiosity?

I view Clara Smith's 1924 recording "Done Sold My Soul to the Devil," authored by African American composer Porter Grainger under the pseudonym Harold Gray, as a text that positions its black female subject within this rich and contested ideological terrain.[35] Born in Spartanburg, South Carolina, in 1895, Smith served an apprenticeship on the southern black theater circuit before migrating to Harlem in 1923. By the time she waxed "Done Sold My Soul to the Devil"—the inaugural recording of the devil-blues tradition—she had twenty-five sides to her name, had just opened the Clara Smith Theatrical Club, and was well on her way to becoming the "Queen of the Moaners":

I was like a ship on the . . . stormy sea, 'cause my daddy put me back
Along comes the devil, sly as he could be . . . and grinning like an old
    chess cat
He said, I can make you happy, give you back your man
If you'll follow me in sin
I was so blue, I took him on, and look what a hole I'm in

[chorus]
I done sold my soul, sold it to the devil, and my heart done turned
    to stone
I've got a lot of gold, got it from the devil, but he won't let me alone
He trails me like a bloodhound, he's slicker than a snake
He follows right behind me, every crook and turn I make
Done sold my soul, sold it to the devil, and my heart done turned to stone

I done sold my soul, sold it to the devil, and my heart done turned
    to stone
I've got lots of gold, got it from the devil, but he won't let me alone
I'm stubborn and I'm hateful, I'd die before I'd run
I drink carbolic acid, and I totes a Gatling gun
I've done sold my soul, sold it to the devil, and my heart done turned
    to stone

I live down in the valley, right by a hornets' nest,
Where lions, bears, and tigers all comes to take their rest
I done sold my soul, sold it to the devil, and my heart done turned
    to stone.[36]

"Done Sold My Soul" signifies pointedly on prostitution: the song offers us a narrative of a lovelorn black female—a naïve migrant, it would seem, adrift in an urban wilderness—who has allowed herself to be seduced by a pimp's devilish promises and sold herself into the slavery of a streetwalker's life.[37] Here is the negative ideal conjured up by the National League for the Protection of Colored Women, a member of the incoming "masses" who has succumbed to the sex trade's depredations and ended up mired in "infamy and shame." Carbolic acid, according to the authors of a study titled *Brothels, Bordellos, and Bad Girls*, was "used by prostitutes to commit suicide; death was agonizing but quick."[38] (It was also used more generally in the blues demimonde to poison and disfigure rivals and mistreating partners.)[39] The reference to it here serves two functions: it suggests that prostitution is, in fact, what is being signified on, but it also helps represent the singer as a larger-than-life badwoman, someone who guzzles poison not to end her life but to affirm her indomitability. She's not a victim, or not merely a victim; she's a cold-hearted killer, too. Shame has been transmuted into defiance, infamy embraced as a source of identity. This is not to say that shame is erased. The singer is indeed in a "hole." She is a fallen woman, and knows it. The song is fascinating precisely because it stages a morality play in which the wages of sin are, up to a point, exactly what black southern evangelicalism and its northern adherents insisted they would be: misery, devil-hauntedness, a hardened (rather than charitable) heart, and earthbound riches that fail to console. One can easily imagine African American church mothers in Harlem or Detroit overhearing the song and finding in it explicit confirmation of their worldview, one that confronted the devils of secular urban modernity and unregulated, preyed-upon, travestied black female sexuality with the Victorian stringency of what theologian Katie Geneva Cannon has termed "lady-like, super-morality."[40] The song offers us, from this perspective, the chastening spectacle of a black woman gone bad in the worst possible way.

Yet even as it affirms the religious and behavioral premises on which the politics of respectability was based, "Done Sold My Soul to the Devil" offers its audience an indelible image of female shamelessness: a "bad" woman who is also bold, brave—and quintessentially modern. She drinks, for example, and brags about it. The carbolic acid she drinks may gesture toward her life as a prostitute, but the *fact* that she drinks signifies on the transracial phenomenon, widely noted during the 1920s, of young women boldly taking their place alongside men in Prohibition's covert but highly public drinking culture. (Drinking bathtub gin was always a potentially lethal gamble; a woman who *literally* drinks poison and suffers no harm is a serious drinker indeed.) In Harlem, according to historian Kathleen Drowne, a generational divide emerged during the Jazz Age as black southern migrants, male and female, "embraced drinking culture as one important component of the newfound social freedoms they were able to enjoy in the North," incurring the wrath of their elders, who saw bootlegging as a crime, alcoholism as a sin, and public inebriation as an incitement to white social disparagement.[41] A somewhat different dynamic was at work in black Detroit, argues Wolcott, where the advent of Prohibition helped blur the line between respectable and unrespectable female behavior by making women who drank into culture heroes:

> Illegal drinking establishments were ubiquitous in the city, particularly in the African American community, and in them men and women mixed freely. Female blues performers sang about the central place of blind pigs in African American urban culture and the role of female entrepreneurs in establishing them. . . . Performers often began their careers in small jook joints . . . where drinking was a central activity. Some performers, such as Bessie Smith, became known for their heavy drinking. . . . The blues-women's songs about running speakeasies and drinking alcohol linked the image of the glamorous female urban resident with illicit behavior.[42]

Across town, and sometimes side by side in black-and-tan cabarets, white women were claiming their own place at the bar. In *The Night Club Era* (1933), an informal history, Stanley Walker jokes that "soon after 1920 great, ravening hordes of women began to discover what their less respectable sisters had known for years—that it was a lot of fun, if you liked it, to get soused. All over New York these up and coming females piled out of their hideaways, rang the bells of speakeasies, wheedled drugstores into selling them gin and rye, and even in establishments of great decorum begged their escorts for a nip from a hip flask."[43] Walker's phrase "less respectable sisters" nods at working-class whites, especially the Irish, but it also includes the African American women with whom white middle- and upper-class flappers, urged on by the provocations of the blues queens and the jazz bands that backed them, now suddenly felt an attitudinal kinship—albeit one that coexisted with casual racism and primitivist condescension.

"Done Sold My Soul to the Devil" manages to evoke both the transgressive irreverence of this emergent behavioral ideal and the sadness that comes from the loss of moral anchoring, a loss that defines modernity. The blues diva, notes Ann Douglas, was "a different figure from the Negro suffragist and club woman. . . . Unlike the [Victorian] matriarch, she doesn't hold herself or anyone else to conventional moral standards, for she considers them inadequate or irrelevant to her own needs; and her needs, which may well include giving vast pleasure to multitudes via her art, are her paramount concern."[44] Smith's song voices the ne plus ultra of modern womanly defiance—conceding the harsh judgment of conventional morality before slapping it away with a brash snarl. In a December 1921 jeremiad titled "Unspeakable Jazz Must Go!," the editor of the *Ladies Home Journal*, John R. McMahon, might have been anticipating Smith's thralldom to the devil when he declared that "the road to hell is too often paved with jazz steps"; he clearly sensed the generational shift in behavioral ideals that would help Smith's shockingly frank confession find an audience when he decried the fact that the young woman of the day "drinks, swears, smokes, toddles and chatters stories that once belonged to the men's smoke room."[45] Looking back on the decade in *Only Yesterday* (1931), Frederick Lewis Allen acknowledged that "an upheaval in values" had taken place. "Women no longer wanted to be 'ladylike' or could appeal to their daughters to be 'wholesome'; it was to widely suspected that the old-fashioned lady had been a sham and that the 'wholesome' girl was merely inhibiting a nasty mind and would come to no good end. . . . It was better to be modern,— everybody wanted to be modern,—and sophisticated, and smart, to smash the conventions and to be devastatingly frank. And with a cocktail glass in one's hand it was easy at least to be frank."[46]

Clara Smith's devil-blues, one of the decade's representative texts, epitomizes this sort of convention-smashing frankness. It crystallizes the discourse of disbelief that Douglas credits as "the only thoroughly accredited modern mode," yet it refuses to break entirely with black southern evangelicalism. The devil that Smith summons up, even as he underpins her flamboyantly "bad" persona, is no friend. He is looming, entrapping, omnipresent. Attentive to such paradoxes, Hazel Carby has noted the way black female blues singers "acted creatively to vocalize the contradictions and tensions of the terrain of sexual politics in the relation of black working-class culture to the culture of the emergent black middle class."[47] Yet as Higginbotham has argued, it's a mistake to assume that the black working class during the blues era consisted entirely of Prohibition-flouting good-timers looking to scandalize their uptight social betters. Especially in northern cities shaped by migration, the Bible was integral to the life of the working poor; rising numbers of Holiness, Pentecostal, and store-front Baptist churches testified to this fact. The devil of Smith's song acknowledges both the fear-driven judgmentalism of black working-class evangelicals (epitomized by the Reverend A. W. Nix's popular recorded sermon "Black Diamond Express to Hell," 1927) and the uplift ideology of the black middle class, which would have been inclined to see Smith's devil as a pimp, a pool-hall hustler, one of the no-good men spawned by the pleasure-centered life of the modern urban scene. "Done Sold My Soul to the Devil" proclaims the same bad news as these guardians of public morality, then shocks by making its bold proclamation into the grounds of a new identity—a conversion to the devil's party—rather than the prelude to repentance and rebirth in Jesus.

SELLING IT AGAIN: BLACK SPIDER DUMPLING
AND THE YAS YAS GIRL

Porter Grainger's composition, a hit for Clara Smith, has a curious after-life. Soon after the song's initial release, it shows up in folklorist Lawrence Gellert's collection of black southern field recordings, identified as "Done Sold My Soul," as well as in Howard W. Odum's and Guy B. Johnson's study of black folk music, *Negro Workaday Songs* (1926), in a chapter titled "Woman's Song of Man." "It is here," write Odum and Johnson, "that one finds the closest relation between folk songs and the formal blues."[48] Collected in the field from an unnamed (and presumably female) informant, the song is titled "I Done Sol' My Soul to de Devil." A footnote clarifies: "Very similar to phonographic piece, *Done Sold My Soul to the Devil*." The only difference between Smith's version and the folk version is the dialect voice in which Odum and Johnson have couched the latter:

> I done sol' my soul,
> Done sol it to de devil,
> An' my heart done turned to stone.
> I got a lot 'o gol'
> Got it from de devil,
> Because he won't let me alone.

This oral version and Gellert's are significant because their existence suggests that the recording was popular enough to have spawned such folk replicas. Odum invokes the song again, without naming it, in *Wings on My Feet: Black Ulysses at the Wars* (1929), the second volume in his trilogy of semifictionalized memoirs narrated in the voice of "Left Wing" Gordon, an itinerant black construction worker Odum had befriended in Chapel Hill. Odum's Gordon recounts a story about an Atlantic crossing in a military transport boat that encounters bad weather and only narrowly escapes disaster. After the worst has passed, a YMCA song leader tries unsuccessfully to get the troops to sing, then calls out to Gordon, "Well, my good man, you soldiers have not yet come to appreciate high quality of singing which I give you." Gordon's response is dismissive: "'Hell, who's good man,'

I says. 'Not me. I'm bad man, bad as Hell, I know. An' don't be callin' me yo' good man; I done sold my soul to the devil an' my heart done turned back to stone.' By this I was signifyin' I want him to leave me alone.'"[49] Here, notably, a gender switch occurs: the soul-selling confession of Smith's badwoman protagonist has been transformed into roughneck masculine assertiveness. Whether the agent of the gender switch was Gordon himself or Odum putting words in Gordon's mouth is impossible to determine.

The subsequent history of "Done Sold My Soul to the Devil" confirms its importance to the devil-blues tradition, in part because of the ease with which it expands to encompass both genders and a range of lyric material. In 1937, four new versions of the song were suddenly issued by four different artists, three of them men. The remake that hews most closely to Smith's 1924 recording is the Western swing version by Dave Edwards and His Alabama Boys, a white ensemble led by the vocalist and fiddler Guy "Cotton" Thompson.[50] To the extent that the devil-blues tradition—and the conceit of soul-selling in particular—has been embraced by white performers and audiences in recent decades, Thompson's twangy cover provides that cultural development with an unexpected ancestry. Of the four later recordings, his is the only one to include Smith's prelude, which sources the singer's devil-haunted misery in the grief inflicted by an absconding lover. The lover's sex has been changed: Smith's "daddy" and "man" becomes Thompson's "baby" and "gal":

> I'm just like a ship on the stormy seas, since my baby quit me flat
> Along comes the devil, as high as he can see . . . and treats me like an
>   old house cat
> He says, I can make you happy, give you back your gal
> And all your needed friends
> I was so blue, I took him up, so look what a hole I'm in[51]

The other three remakes, all recorded by African American blues performers between March and June 1937, eliminate the lover, the devil's gold, and the devil-as-bloodhound image, adding new material (in boldface below) that emphasizes the singer's violent indomitability. Casey Bill Weldon (1901–72) was first into the studio with "Sold My Soul to the Devil":

> I done sold my soul, sold it to the devil, and he won't let me alone
> I done sold my soul, sold it to the devil, my heart has turned to stone
> I live down in the jungle, right by a hornet's nest, where lambs, lions,
>   and tigers all come and take their rest

I done sold my soul, sold it to the devil, and he won't let me alone
Done sold my soul to the devil, my heart has turned to stone

Well I'm stubborn and I'm hateful, I'd die before I'd run
I'd drink carbolic acid, I'd tote a Gatling gun.
I done sold my soul, etc.

I walked into town with my razor and Gatling gun.
I'll cut you if you stand, and shoot you if you run
I done sold my soul, etc.

Well I eat black widow spider dumplings for my dessert
I go to a boiler shop, have 'em to make my shirt
I done sold my soul, etc.

Well well I went to a place . . . that I know so well
I've taken a few shots . . . at the devil in hell
All the little devils, they all jumped on the wall
Said Catch him papa, or he's gonna kill us all
I done sold my soul, etc.[52]

Weldon, often confused with Will Weldon (c. 1904–34) of the Memphis Jug Band, was a slide guitarist and composer—the author, most notably, of "I'm Gonna Move to the Outskirts of Town"—who enjoyed a brief, productive recording career in the late 1930s before dropping out of view.[53] His remake of the song is the most pugnacious of all the versions, with its repeated invocation of the Gatling gun and its reprisal against the devil in hell, a key motif in the "Stagger Lee" cycle. The oppressive sense of devil-hauntedness that freights Smith's original has eased here as the subject's opportunities for effective action have multiplied. The cluster of images that constitutes a critical portrait of prostitution in the earlier recording—a broken-hearted woman who has sold herself for "lots of gold" into the thralldom of a sweet-talking, two-faced, ever-surveillant pimp—has disappeared. The striking figure of a singer who "eat[s] black widow spider dumplings for . . . dessert" animates a sexual persona very different from Smith's: a voracious destroyer of femmes fatales. Weldon's version of the song paints a portrait of a devil-sponsored, multiweaponed badman.

Although Weldon recorded his version in March 1937, it is John D. Twitty, aka "Black Spider Dumpling," who is usually associated with the black spider image. Twitty's version of the song, recorded in May and titled "Sold It to the Devil," simplifies the shooting-the-devil-in-hell sequence and adds several traditional couplets, one of which radically unsettles the song's meaning:

> I've sold my soul, sold it to the devil, and my heart done turned to stone
> I've sold my soul, sold it to the devil, but he won't let me alone
> Said I'm hateful and I'm evil, I carries a Gatling gun
> I drink carbolic acid, be darned if I will run
> But I've sold it, I have sold it, sold it to the devil, and my heart done
>   turned to stone
>
> I done sold my soul, sold it to the devil, but he won't let me alone
> **I got a little baker shop right downtown**
> **Everything I bake, it is nice and brown**
> But I sold it, etc.
>
> I sold it, I sold it, sold it to the devil, but he won't let me be 'lone
> **My life it is unhappy, it won't last me long**
> **Everything I do, seem like I do's it wrong**
> But I sold it, etc.
>
> I sold my soul, sold it to the devil, but he won't let me be 'lone
> **I eat black spider dumplings for my dessert**
> **Go to the blacksmith, let him make my shirt**
> But I sold it, etc.
>
> I've sold my soul, sold it to the devil, but he won't let me be 'lone
> I live down in the valley, by a hornet's nest
> Where the bears, lions, and tigers, they come to take their rest
> But I sold it, etc.
>
> I done sold my soul, sold it to the devil, but he won't let me be 'lone
> **I went to a place that I knew so well**
> **I shot that Devil right in Hell**
> But I sold it, etc.[54]

Apart from this recording, Twitty was an inconsequential artist, most likely born in Birmingham, Alabama, and residing in Chicago, who had only eight sides to his name. What is striking about his version of the song is the second verse: a conventional bit of sexual signifying when found in women's blues but given a strange new twist—queered, one might say—when voiced by a man. One way of hearing the song is as a pimp's lament: his "baker shop . . . downtown" is his urban stable of black female ("nice and brown") prostitutes and the devil is the unending stream of johns whose cash payments have reduced the remorseful singer, in his own eyes, to a soul-starved and vengeful procurer. A second, less obvious way of hearing the song is as the lament of a gay male prostitute whose sales pitch has suddenly turned to ashes in his mouth. Both scripts resonate with what we know of the urban sex trade during the period, according to Clement's study of prostitution in New York City. "The 1920s marked a period of expansion of black women's involvement in brothels as both prostitutes and madams and of black men's participation as prostitutes, pimps, and what investigators called 'male madams.'. . . By the late 1930s, the majority of black women in the sex trade walked the streets, suffered the most at the hands of the police, and profited least from their labor."[55] Twitty's version of the song subordinates braggadocio to despair with the help of the chorus's reiterated "but," as though the devilish soul-sale, evidenced by his chronic trafficking in flesh, has hopelessly compromised every possible avenue of escape. Even shooting the devil doesn't seem to help much.

Only a month after Twitty recorded the song, in June 1937, Merline Johnson recorded a substantially identical version, also titled "Sold It to the Devil"; it duplicates the earlier recording's brisk stride piano and melismatic vocal flourishes, although it lacks the "black spider dumpling" verse:

> I sold my soul, sold it to the devil and my heart have turned to stone
> I sold my soul, sold it to the devil, and he won't let me alone
> I'm hateful and I'm evil, I carries a Gatling gun
> I drink carbolic acid, be darned if I will run
> But I sold it, I have sold it
> Sold it to the devil and my heart have turned to stone.
>
> I've sold my soul, sold it to the devil, and he won't let me alone
> I live down in the valley, by a hornet's nest . . . where the bears, lions,
>   and tigers, they come to take their rest
> But I have sold it, etc.
>
> I have sold my soul, sold it to the devil, and he won't let me alone
> **I've got a little baker shop, right downtown**
> **And everything I bake, I bakes it nice and brown**
> But I have sold it, etc.
>
> [spoken over piano solo] Yes, I done sold my soul. I've sold it to the
>   devil, too.

I sold my soul, sold it to the devil, and he won't let me alone
My life it is unhappy, it won't last me long
And everything I do seem like I do's it wrong
But I have sold it, etc.

I sold my soul, sold it to the devil, and he won't let me alone
I went to a place I knew so well
I shot the devil right . . . down in Hell
But I had sold it, I had sold it, sold it to the devil, and my heart had turned
to stone, oh yeah . . . heart had turned to stone[56]

Johnson is a representative figure for this study: a black female blues star, southern-born and northward-bound, who navigated Baker's "economics of slavery" during the Swing Era by forsaking respectability for prideful self-assertion grounded in heightened sexuality and mediated, in this case, by invocations of the devil. Stage-named "The Yas Yas Girl"—a bawdy moniker that today might translate as "the girl with the junk in the trunk"—Johnson was reportedly born in Mississippi in 1912, which would make her the same age as Robert Johnson (b. 1911). Migrating to Chicago, she was one of the most popular blueswomen of the late 1930s, recording almost a hundred sides between 1937 and 1947. (Her accompanists included Casey Bill Weldon, Big Bill Broonzy, and Lonnie Johnson, who collectively issued a total of ten devil-blues recordings.) "Sold It to the Devil," her seventh recording and first release as "The Yas Yas Girl," helped launch her, as it helped launch Clara Smith thirteen years earlier.[57] Although Johnson's version of the song tracks Twitty's quite closely, a series of small differences—including a slightly brisker tempo and the plucky, brazen vocal aside over the piano solo—combine to shift the song's tenor, so that despair is brought back into a tensed relationship with indomitability.

The vivid, profane, stone-hearted protagonist evoked by Merline Johnson is softened by a lingering sense of regret, of lost innocence—a lost innocence that Johnson's song, the era's song, struggles repeatedly to throw off but ends up merely holding at bay. Again we might ask, Who, or what, is the devil Johnson's protagonist shoots at the end of her song? Is he her pimp? Her john? Is the murdered devil a way of naming and exorcising the chronic despair bred by a soul-destroying life of whoredom? Or is the devil who haunts this restless, rebellious lament a way of acknowledging the cost of becoming modern: a guilty nod, as it were, to the stern judgmentalism of the fathers and mothers back down home?

For many Christians in the 1920s and 1930s, black and white alike, the devil's hand was visible not just in prostitution but in the sinful activity that provoked a wide spectrum of sexual misbehavior: dancing, and specifically couples dancing in public to jazz and blues. Dance halls and juke joints, in this view, were the devil's lair. Katrina Hazzard-Gordon has written eloquently of the "jook continuum," theorizing the emergence of African American social dance forms in the post-Reconstruction South and mapping their northward spread in subsequent decades.[58] During the Jazz Age, however, sepia-hued dance steps were transformed from black folk culture into mainstream pop culture; they became a commodified crossover sensation thanks to the recording industry and an explosion of urban dance halls. The self-appointed defenders of virtue, especially white virtue, were moved to fight back in highly public ways. In a book titled *The Devil's Ball or the Modern Dance* (1920), for example, Rev. Melvin G. Morris of Baltimore delivered a lengthy indictment underscored with capitalized epigrams at the bottom of each page: "The Dance Hall Is Hell's Ante-Room!" "Would Jesus be Guilty of the 'Bunny-Hug' of 'Jazz'?"[59] The jook continuum—and especially its named dances with their devilish, animalistic associations— became the scene of a pitched battle between Christian evangelists and young urban moderns, including composers and performers who mocked or ignored the evangelists' criticisms but occasionally also acknowledged a rueful ambivalence.

Sippie Wallace's "Devil Dance Blues" (1925), the singer's own composition, is central to this discussion. Wallace (b. 1898), the daughter of a Baptist deacon, was raised in Houston and sang and played piano in her father's church. Her parents, according to blues scholar Daphne Duval Harrison, "like most good Baptists, would not countenance the 'devil's music' in their home and punished their children if they were caught listening to it or playing it."[60] Wallace discovered tent-shows early on, and by the age of seventeen she had run away to New Orleans, ending up later in Chicago, where she began her recording career in 1923. "Devil Dance Blues," recorded in New York City, is both a spiritual confession and an ethnographic miniature, a text that evokes the powerful ambivalences of a creative artist who has been caught up in the seductions of the era's dance-maddened urban nightlife:

I had a dream last night . . . and it filled me full of fright
I had a dream last night . . . it filled me full of fright
I dreamed I was in the dance hall where the devil danced at night

I saw the sweet Mrs. Devil dancing in her hall
I saw the sweet Mrs. Devil dancing in her hall
She was out with the devil where he was giving a ball

He had on a robe that was made of gold
He had on a robe that was made of gold
I never seen no devil look so sweet before

It was a dream . . . a dream I've never had before
It was a dream . . . a dream I've never had before
I dreamed we all were dancing and put on a great big show[61]

Dream-narratives featuring the devil are not uncommon in the blues tradition; examples include Sylvester Weaver's "Devil Blues" (1927), Bessie Smith's "Blue Spirit Blues" (1929), Louisiana Red's "Too Poor to Die" (1975), Long John Hunter's "Dream about the Devil" (1992), and Watermelon Slim's "Devil's Cadillac" (2006). Their origins lie in the black church of the slave era: the testimonies given by the newly converted, often following a dark night of the soul in which the devil-as-tempter has materialized and been wrestled to the ground. In *Religious Folk-Songs of the Southern Negroes* (1909), Howard Odum offers a bit of lyric testimony that "was composed by a negro man after he had recently 'come through.' He always loved to talk of what he had seen, what he knew would happen and how he could get out of difficulties." Odum quotes two verses:

The devil come down to the worl' one day
An' I heard him holler, hoo-ray, hoo-ray!
Come out, I'm havin' a holiday

That was the word I heard him say,
But I knowed if I danced to his holiday,
There'd be something doing an' the devil to play[62]

Odum's black southern informant presumably meant "pay," not "play," in line with the familiar soul-selling script. The informant's testimony, imaging the devil's temptation as an urging toward licentiousness expressed specifically as dancing, offers us insight into Wallace's composition. Where Clara Smith had sung the year before (1924) of getting "lots of gold" from the devil, the gold robe in "Devil Dance Blues" is part of the devil's uniform, an element of his impossibly seductive appearance. Literal prostitution—female sexual virtue—isn't at issue for Wallace; what haunts her is the glittery, spiritually vapid, wholly secular life into which her career as an entertainer has cast her. She images an urban dance hall as the hell into which she has fallen. The honorific "Mrs. Devil" has, I suggest, a racial cast, configuring the African American subject as a troubled, subordinated participant in a black-and-tan bacchanal, a "great big show" orchestrated by a devilish white Gatsby for his wife and friends. Wallace sketches a self-portrait of a blues diva who hungers for secular success but is haunted—and awakened to her own plight—by a church-installed conscience.

"Devil Dance Blues" reflects much more than the singer's private spiritual struggle, however. Echoing loudly here is the era's ongoing public debate, a culture war that was swirling around the urban scene and its "devil dance dens." That specific term was the title of an article by journalist John B. Kennedy that appeared in *Collier's* in 1925, the same year as Sippie Wallace's song. Kennedy's focus was the social phenomenon of the "taxi" girl—essentially a partner-for-hire at ten cents a dance—and the environs in which she made her living. "Dancing," wrote Kennedy, "was once a diversion. Now it is a trade. . . . In its recent and most widespread development it has enrolled thousands of girls who sell the social favor of their time and company. . . . The trade of the taxi girl is plied in the bright-light centers, where jazz bands smite the air."[63] According to a survey conducted by *Social Forces* magazine that year, "over 14% of the men in Manhattan and 10% of its women attended dance halls and cabarets three times weekly," and the number of "dance palaces" had increased in just a few years.[64] By 1927, according to one historian, taxi-dance halls had been licensed in all corners of America; by 1931, almost 100 taxi-dance halls were operating in New York City alone, staffed by more than 8,000 licensed dance hostesses who serviced roughly 40,000 men a week.[65] Despite the sensationalistic title of his article, Kennedy's language was mild in comparison with the condemnations of social dancing issued by white and black evangelicals—condemnations that proved powerless against the cultural tide. In *The Devil's Ball* (1920), Rev. Morris conflated prewar, juke-joint-spawned dances such as the Grizzly Bear, Bunny Hug, and Texas Tommy with contemporary fads such as the Foxtrot and Shimmy and called them "Devil-conceived [and] Hell-born."[66] To that list might be added the Itch, the Fish Tail, the Grind, the Mooche, the Fanny Bump, Ballin' the Jack, and the Funky Butt, along with the blues-drenched slow drag. All these dances were evolved by, and popular with, the black working class, and many of them crossed the color-line during this period; with their "skirt-lifting, body-caressing, and thrusting pelvic movements," according to cultural historian Tera Hunter, "[they] conveyed amorous messages that offended moral reformers."[67]

"Offended" is putting it mildly. The words "devil," "evil," and "hell" run through the era's commentary. In "Does Jazz Put the Sin in Syncopation?" (1921), her infamous broadside in the *Ladies' Home Journal*, Anne Shaw Faulkner decried jazz music and its "evil influence on the young people of today. . . . Never before have such outrageous dances been permitted in private as well as public ballrooms, and never has there been used for the accompaniment of the dance such a strange combination of tone and rhythm as that produced by the dance orchestras of today."[68] Rev. Revels Alcorn Adams, an influential member of Mississippi's African Methodist Episcopal church, claimed in *The Social Dance* (1921) that "dance is the spur of lust, a circle of which the devil himself is the center." The devil-spawned dance he had in mind was the same upsurge of black working-class dynamism that Hunter contextualizes and defends in *To 'Joy My Freedom* (1997), a source of leisure-time pleasure and self-validation for the washerwomen and cooks of Jazz Age Atlanta. Where they took joy, Adams decried licentiousness. "Mixed dancing is bad enough," he thundered, "but the new tangles of legs and arms, the fancy dips and darts of the body, the opened unshamed [*sic*] hugging will go on to still more disgusting lengths. Let all Godly people denounce this muck-raking, maiden-murdering, man-destroying institution that we know as the dance hall."[69] Although it was an interior space, the urban dance hall was associated by black Baptist women of the National Baptist Convention with that catch-all villain, "the street," in part because it encouraged "perpetual promenading" and the "demoralizing habit of hanging out," and culminated—or so the argument went—in the wholesale conscription of black maidenhood into black prostitution, confirming white stereotypes.[70] "The poison generated by Jazz music and improper dancing," claimed one Baptist leader, "will completely demoralize the womanhood of today. The sure way to ruin is by way of the public dance hall."[71] Women of other Christian denominations agreed, arguing for an intimate connection between public behavior and individual spiritual health. Rosa B. Horn, a South Carolina–born evangelist who established the Pentecostal Faith Church in Harlem in 1926 and had a large following among southern migrants and working-class blacks, preached a sermon titled "What Is Holiness?" "After we have been converted we must be sanctified and set apart from the world of sin"—a world that included card playing, telling lies, and, of course, "dancing for the devil."[72] Ruth R. Dennis, a Wilberforce-trained theologian and AME evangelist, preached against the sexual menace of popular dance from her own Harlem pulpit, indicting parents for their failure to rein in modern youth. In a 1927 sermon titled "What Are We Going to Do with the Children?," she noted that

> children are considered by twentieth century parents too young to pray and receive religious instruction. "They don't understand what they are doing" is the excuse given for delinquency in religious activities. But they are not too young to understand dancing and having beaus— "that is cute." And everywhere may be seen babies in the cradle who can't talk (shame on parents of the race who encourage and teach their babies) but who can shake that thing and mess around. Children never seem too young to understand and sing the most vulgar suggestive songs that should be prohibited.[73]

"Shake That Thing" was the title of a dance hit recorded by both Charlie Jackson and Ethel Waters in 1925 and covered by half a dozen other artists in 1926; "Ev'rybody Mess Around" (1926) was another of Waters's hits. The complaint about energetic, animal-themed popular dances and urban dance halls leading young people to the devil was still being made a decade later when Works Progress Administration (WPA) interviewers caught up with a Holiness preacher in Chicago. "All they think about is doing some kind of dance where they draw up like a cold cricket. The people are going astray. The world has so many attractions. They have the Grand Terrace, the Savoy, and all kinds of entertainment. . . . They should be teaching them how to sit down and keep quiet."[74]

Faced with what felt like a culture-wide onslaught during the 1920s and 1930s, black and white Christians attacked popular dance not just from their pulpits but also in recordings and on the airwaves. Rev. A. W. Nix, a Birmingham, Alabama, native, heard the complaint of his female coevals when he attended the National Baptist Convention in Chicago on 1921 and resolved to strike a blow for the Lord. In 1927 he traveled to New York and recorded a two-part sermon titled "Black Diamond Express to Hell," a riveting performance in which he inveighs against a long string of sins, including drinking, gambling, stealing, and dancing, each of which he depicts as a way station on the road to perdition, with the devil as hell-bent conductor.[75] "The devil cries out, 'All aboard for hell!'" Nix shouts hoarsely, ventriloquizing God's antagonist. "First station! Is Drunkardsville. . . Next station! Is Dancing Hall Depot. Wait there, I have a lot of church members that get on down there. Some of you think you can sing in the choir on Sunday and Charleston on the ballroom floor on Monday. But you gotta go to hell on the Black Diamond train."[76] An African-sourced dance step that first emerged in South Carolina during the 1910s, the Charleston had become a crossover sensation in 1923, when it was featured in the Broadway production *Runnin' Wild* with lyrics by Cecil Mack and music by stride pianist James P. Johnson. Nix's invocation of the song is notable because the lyrics, in effect, had invoked *him*: puritanical Christianity as the repressive negative ideal. "If you ain't got religion in your feet," went the familiar lines, "You can do this prance and do it neat." A cultural battle was being waged here over the meaning of the devil's dance, with rebellious moderns intentionally seeking to shock their elders—and to profit from the transvaluation of values that had taken place in the aftermath of the Great War.

Anticipating and paralleling Nix's efforts was one of the most charismatic white evangelists of the age: Rev. John Roach Straton. Born in Indiana, schooled and saved in Georgia, case-hardened at Baylor University in Texas, Straton took the pulpit of Calvary Baptist Church in midtown Manhattan in 1918 and began a decade-long campaign filled by what his biographer, Ralph G. Giordano, has characterized as "savage attacks and condemnations" against social dancing and New York's commercial dance halls.[77] He began with a tract, *The Dance of Death: Should Christians Indulge?* (1921) and spread his message through the newspapers, telling an interviewer with the *Brooklyn Daily Eagle* in 1922 that "the very fires of Hell are raging right at them in the [dance] palaces and amusement centers of the city and . . . multitudes of young men and women are being swept away to eternal destruction."[78] The following year, 1923, as the Charleston's fancy footwork seized the popular imagination, Straton set up his own radio station, WQAO, in the basement of the church and announced that he was going to "twist the Devil's tail in New York" so that his "squawk [would] be heard across the continent."[79] Amused by the culture war that had broken out over jazz and social dancing, *American Mercury* editor H. L. Mencken gave journalist Gregory Mason a mischievous assignment early in 1924: "Visit as many New York City dance halls as possible and find Satan." Mason's article, "Satan in the Dance Hall," was published in June of that year. Despite the claims leveled by Straton, Nix, Adams, and their fellow evangelicals, Mason was unable to find Satan—although he did discover legions of dance hall censors, numerous municipal regulations, and a surprising amount of police oversight.[80]

One irony of the culture war, as the Charleston suggests, is that popular music and dance in the Jazz Age thrived in the face of evangelical condemnation not only by ignoring it, but also by incorporating and mocking it, transforming it into a naughty thrill that heightened the party atmosphere. If public dancing to jazz orchestras, their conductors, and their presiding blues queens was the devil's chosen purview—well then, let's all get devilish and go to hell! That was the irreverent spirit that animated Fats Waller's "There's Going to Be the Devil to Pay" (1935) and "I'm Feelin' Devilish" (1930) by Stanley "Fess" Williams, a Kentucky-born, Tuskegee-educated clarinetist and bandleader whose Royal Flush Orchestra held court at Harlem's Savoy Ballroom for most of the 1920s:

> Oh by golly, I'm feeling devilish . . . by golly, I'm feeling revelish
> By golly, I'm feeling devilish now
>
> You're the kind of gal I'm behaving for . . . the kind I've been saving for
> You're the kind my love I've been saving for and how
>
> Once you wait a while . . . like your style . . . now listen, you
>   little aggravator
> If I do, come on you . . . you'll just have to see me later
> Cause oh by golly, I'm feeling devilish . . . I mean I'm feeling revelish
> Oh by golly, I'm feeling devilish now
>
> [*instrumental break*]
>
> [spoken] Gwan, boy . . . when you play that cornet, you really makes me feel devilish. And you know, folks, when you're feeling devilish there's a kind of peculiar feeling that comes over you that's hard to explain.[81]

Williams's linking of "devilish" and "revelish" playfully revalues the same linkage evoked by Howard Odum's black respondent after his conversion, embracing rather than rejecting the euphoric "holiday" promised by the devil and attributing it to the awakened libido (marked by a "peculiar feeling") of a virtuous, virginal man—he's been "behaving" and "saving" himself until now—who has met the woman of his dreams and is being further incited by hot cornet playing. In "Hellish Rag" (1927), recorded in Chicago, Ma Rainey offers a festive counterpart to Sippie Wallace's fear-laced "Devil Dance Blues," one as untroubled by a sense of sin as the recordings of Waller and Williams. The devil dance den depicted by Rainey is literal, not figurative: a party in Hell given by the devil himself:

1 . . . They gave a holiday . . . there below
   And as I knew they played, everybody swayed
   To that tune they never heard before

   Now the devil he got full of whisky and gin
5 Everybody went straight up in the wind
   And old Jasper cried, and he heard him sigh.
   Mister, play it again

   Aw play that rag
   Miss Shuffle's shuffling
10 Play that rag
   Now that's the only tune I love to hear you play
   I's about to holler but Hey, Hey Hey
   Play that rag
   Miss Shuffle's shuffling
15 Play that rag
   Now the devil, he got happy, got way back
   Want everybody to ball that jack
   Can't you see I'm happy, I'm mighty happy
   I mean that hellish rag, oh babe
20 I mean that hellish rag

   Oh, play it . . . play it big boy[82]

Rainey's recording, like Waller's and Williams's, evokes a swinging, dance-oriented community, one loosely organized through call-and-response aesthetics and a sense of ritual purpose into a meaningful social whole. Rainey's devil is a heavy drinker "full of whisky and gin," which makes him a lawbreaking culture hero in a time of Prohibition, but he's more than that. What Rainey does (ll. 7–15 and 18–21), much like the Reverend Nix in *Black Diamond Express to Hell* but to diametrically opposed purpose, is ventriloquize the devil; here, rather than an implacable avenger, he's a garrulous jazz hound, a master of the revels who repeatedly cries, "Play that rag!" Rainey evokes herself, through the devil's euphoric urgings, as Miss Shuffle, a kind of unholy sand dancer, and that self-description might remind us, as Jacqui Malone points out in *Steppin' on the Blues: The Visible Rhythms of African American Dance*, that the classic women blues singers' "dance movements . . . were no less important than their actual singing."[83] A performer's dance helped dramatize the song, "putting it across" in contemporary parlance, but it also helped create community within black working-class circles by offering what Hunter calls "positive affirmations of cultural memories and racial heritage, and the envisioning of new possibilities and new racial realities."[84] Dance was the medium through which audience and performer engaged each other in a ritual communal ceremony, affirming both their hip modernity and their down-home sense of racial belonging. "Hellish Rag" images that ceremony, quite deliberately, as an ungodly scene—and a relaxed, pleasurable, life-bringing one, a slap in the face to Puritanism, especially the southern evangelical temper that had chased black migrants north crying, "The devil's gonna get you in that big city!" Ma Rainey's brazen reply is, "Done been got, and we're having a ball!"

In the ideologically charged cultural climate of the 1920s, the visible rhythms of black dance set to jazz and blues soundtracks became associated, for both dancers and dance-condemners, with the sinful life; what distinguished the dancers from their critics was a spirit of youthful modern irreverence that translated "sinful" as "wicked" or "naughty," both of which were synonyms for fun. For whites of the Lost Generation, such fun was edged with a frisson of racial disrepute, of rubbing shoulders with scandalous, sexually charged sepia nightlife, that increased its attraction. "Black music . . . earned a central place among white moderns," argues Sotiropoulos, "giving them a sense of themselves as up-to-date, not only as intellectual leaders, but as social progressives who discarded Victorian self-control for public exuberance and passion."[85] For African American moderns, especially young migrant women in northern and southern cities, the situation was more complicated. The devil they confronted, and evoked in their songs, had real social referents: he was a pimp, a john, a no-good man, a male sexual tempter on the road to spiritual and economic thralldom. He was a black man, or white man, who exercised power over you, demanding that you degrade your body, violate your spirit, and abdicate your godliness. He was, in some sense, exactly what the parents and ministers back down home, and the visible, vocal church people up north, said he was. This knowledge troubles songs such as "Done Sold My Soul to the Devil" and "Devil Dance Blues."

But the devil was also an emblem of urban modernity, a master of the revels in a postwar, Prohibition-flouting period of transracial cynicism about the meaning of the words "virtue" and "virtuous." As such, he was somebody with whom young black moderns could form a productive alliance. Embracing him was a way of telling sanctimonious moral crusaders, overprotective parents, and philandering ministers to go to hell. Here, the irreverent modern temper among New Negro youth partook of the general rejection of parental moral leadership, even while refusing to share their white peers' pessimism about the direction of world history. "The older generation had certainly pretty well ruined this world before passing it on to us," wrote a young white man in the *Atlantic Monthly* (1920) in a representative statement of Lost Generation ennui. "They gave us this thing, knocked to pieces, leaky, red-hot, threatening to blow up; and then they are surprised that we don't accept it with the same attitude of pretty, decorous enthusiasm with which they received it, way back in the eighties."[86] The youth of the Great Black Migration had a great deal to gain from the leaky, red-hot urban world of 1920s America, and the devil, along with his music and dance, became an icon of the time, helping to shape their indecorous enthusiasms. In this respect, singers like Clara Smith and Ma Rainey, along with bandleaders like Fats Waller and Fess Williams, helped pave the way for the delayed attitudinal modernity that swept through the Mississippi Delta with the introduction of jukeboxes in the mid-1930s. The Lost Generation, their bandleaders, and their blues queens are the unacknowledged precedent for that curious "Heaven and Hell" party staged by black teenagers at a Clarksdale church in 1941—neither approved of nor attended by the deacons but allowed to proceed nonetheless—and the iconoclasm of Robert Johnson's "Me and the Devil Blues" (1937).

By the time Johnson recorded that tune, Ma Rainey had left show business behind, returned home to Columbus, Georgia, and joined the Friendship Baptist Church, where her brother was a deacon. She never again performed the blues. (A retreat to the certainties of old-time religion, later in life, is part of the pattern of many blues lives.) But there were other black southern blues performers, many of them restless male migrants, who found in the devil, and hell, figures rich with signifying potential—a way of speaking back boldly but surreptitiously to the oppressive realities of life back down home.

3. I'M GOING TO MARRY THE DEVIL'S DAUGHTER

Blues Tricksters Signifying on Jim Crow

> There are, for example, many hidden references to the white
> man in the Negro's songs. This is an interesting field of research
> in which little has been done.
>
> —GUY B. JOHNSON, "Double Meaning in the Popular
>   Negro Blues" (1927)

THE LION'S DEN

The claim that the white man is the devil, by now a cliché of black su-
premacist politics, achieved early and notable mainstream exposure in Alex
Haley's 1963 interview with Malcolm X published in *Playboy* magazine.[1]
"The first time I heard the Honorable Elijah Muhammad's statement, 'The
white man is the devil,'" insisted his most charismatic disciple, "it just
clicked." The general sentiment, if not the precise statement, has a long history in African American political and religious thought. It surfaces in the
eighteenth century, as the first Great Awakening begins to evangelize slave
culture, and, as a series of coded indictments, it pervades the spirituals. As
overt condemnation, the equivalence of white man and devil traces back
at least as far as David Walker's *Appeal* (1829), where the author's outraged
screed led him to indict "the whites" as a group, down through history:
"We view them all over Europe, together with what were scattered about
in Asia and Africa, as heathens, and we seem them acting more like devils
than accountable men."[2] It was the slaveholding American South, however,
where Walker saw the deviltry of the former emerging most poisonously:
not just grievous physical mistreatment and economic exploitation of black
by white, but a comprehensive spiritual and intellectual deprivation, a denial
of the means for achieving "good sense and learning," that prevented black
slaves from becoming conscious—as he now was—of the burning injustice
of their degraded condition:

Do you suppose one man of good sense and learning would submit himself, his father, mother, wife and children, to be slaves to a wretched man like himself, who, instead of compensating him for his labours, chains, handcuffs and beats him and family almost to death, leaving life enough in them, however, to work for, and call him master? No! no! he would cut his devilish throat from ear to ear, and well do slaveholders know it.[3]

Walker was living far north of the Mason-Dixon line when he penned these lines, of course, as was Frederick Douglass when he wrote in his *Narrative* (1845) of the slave traders who swarmed over him in jail after his attempted escape in Easton, Maryland: "I felt myself surrounded by so many fiends from perdition. A band of pirates never looked more like their father, the devil."[4] The rhetoric of demonization cut both ways on America's racialized antebellum landscape: the "dissatisfied" slave, according to Douglass, "has the devil in him"—or so the slaveocracy insisted—"and it must be whipped out." Betsy Freeland, the mother of Douglass's then-master William Freeland, was so infuriated by Douglass's brazen play for freedom and the corrupting influence he'd had on her other slaves that she called him a devil, a yellow devil, and a long-legged mulatto devil, all in the space of four sentences—at least as he tells it.[5] As for Walker, the antipathy with which he and his abolitionist tract were viewed by southern whites is well known, and he did not test their forbearance in person. He may have *thought* that the white man was the devil during his youth in North and South Carolina, but that was not a sentiment one could utter publicly on southern soil during the antebellum period and remain alive, much less broadcast nationwide from that location. That was still residually true in 1963, when Malcolm X sat down for his *Playboy* interview in the relative safety of Harlem.

The post-Reconstruction and Lost Generation decades, a time in which the devil became pointedly associated with blues music, sit on the continuum that runs from Walker to Malcolm. As the whips and chains of chattel slavery were reconfigured into murderous vigilantism and the "slavery by another name" of peonage and convict leasing, the slavemaster-as-devil (along with his overseer and patroller allies) was supplanted in the black popular imagination by his successors: the white bossman, sheriff, and prison-farm warden, all of whom became ways of symbolizing an emergent prison-agricultural complex that Houston A. Baker Jr. has aptly termed the Deep South's "carceral network."[6] The blues lyric tradition, as I will argue below, updates the Satan figure of the spirituals—in his not infrequent guise as a stand-in for a white mistreater—as a response to the altered conditions of black life enforced by southern segregation. The blues-devil was many things, of course, not one thing. Evil whiteness was merely one referent, and a deliberately veiled one, in an array of potential meanings; on many occasions, as David Evans has insisted, the devil of the blues was "just" the devil: God's antagonist, a mind- and romance-troubling figure of evil with no overt racial contours. Yet there was indeed a Jim Crow devil, one whose presence in the blues deserves to be explored, and he is the subject of this chapter. When black bluesmen addressed him, they mocked and undercut him and the hell he presided over behind the veil of signifying song. But their response took another form as well. The bluesman's trickster persona — rootless, promiscuous, and untrustworthy — evolved, in part, as a way of contesting the physical threat, and ego-threat, that this devil's real-world equivalents embodied. Bluesmen *acted* the devil, one might say, in order to *oppose* and *displace* the white devil.[7] And the devil's daughter, a recurrent figure in the blues lyric tradition, played a role in that process. If the white man is the devil, then the black man who consorts with the devil's daughter is playing a dangerous game indeed.

The signifying drama that emerges from this superheated atmosphere offers a particularly vivid variation on what Jon Michael Spencer has called the synchronous duplicity of the blues: not the fusing of sacred and secular realms, as Spencer has argued, but rather a roguish libertinism that barely contains a slanderous racial insubordination.[8] The bluesman's psychological investment in the devil, in "bad behavior," coexists with a desire to evade, destabilize, and usurp the devilish prerogatives of white mastery. A fear of encirclement and containment permeates the lyric archive, as does a desire to burst free, to dance clear of subjection to the devil and his hellish, possessive designs. This celebration-of-escape motif is evident in the earlier spirituals, to be sure, as the material realities of slavery inflect long-standing Christian beliefs about spiritual thralldom: "Ole Satan thought he had me fas' / Broke his chain an' I'm free at las'."[9] But the desire to *supplant* the devil — to partake of his style, access his outsize powers, outdo him at his game — is new to the blues era, at least within the confines of African American culture. In his groundbreaking study of blackface minstrelsy, *Love and Theft* (1993), Eric Lott explores the unstable intermixtures of desire and mockery, fascination and derision, that condition nineteenth-century white theatrical burlesques of blackness, and some of that same instability marks black blues' coded invocations of white deviltry. The attitudinal ground out of which such invocations arise is the suffocating sense of disciplinary threat in a context of postslavery freedom, a double bind that stifled forthright expressions of dissatisfaction with Jim Crow by making them de facto lynching offenses. "White people may or may not be very conscious of this threatening atmosphere in which Negroes live," wrote sociologist John Dollard in 1937 after a Mississippi sojourn,

> but Negroes are extremely conscious of it and it is one of the major facts in the life of any Negro in Southerntown. I once asked a middle-class Negro how he felt about coming back down South. He said it was like walking into a lion's den; the lions are chained; but if they should become enraged, it is doubtful whether the chains would hold them; hence it is better to walk very carefully. . . . Every Negro in the South knows that he is under a kind of sentence of death; he does not know when his turn will come, it may never come, but it may also be at any time. This fear tends to intimidate the Negro man.[10]

The metaphor of southern life as a lion's den into which the bluesman has entered or in which he resides shows up frequently in blues song, but so do dramas in which the bluesman sallies forth in his trickster persona, insouciant and unintimidated, and mocks the devil, as he does in Lightnin' Hopkins's "The Devil Jumped the Black Man" (1962):

> The devil jumped the black man, he said, "Do you wanna race?"
> The black man looked at the devil, said, "Man, you know you out
>   your place."
> The devil jumped at him again, and he began to run
> That black man looked back at the devil, he said, "Ain't we havin'
>   lots of fun."
> He said, "Let's get it."
> You can't run.
> You can't run.
>
> The black man pulled off his hat, he said, "I'm goin', son."
> Looked back at the devil, he say, "You can't run."
> You just can't run.
>
> Lord you just can't run
>
> The devil said, "Oh boy, you sure bothered me."
> But the black man told the devil, "You just keep on following me,
>   you'll see.
> I ain't gonna give you a chance to . . . stick your pitchfork in me."
> . . . .

When I got home, my wife was as mad and she could be
I said, "That old devil tryin to stick his pitchfork in me."
He can't run
He sure can't run
I looked back at him and waved my hand, told him, I said,
    "You sure havin' a lot of fun."

He can't run.[11]

The deep cultural origins of Hopkins's recording are the slave trickster tales, especially those featuring contests of wits between the Master and John, a strong and wily slave, and, back beyond that, the African animal trickster tales that gave rise to Brer Rabbit. A similar contest dynamic is at work in Hopkins's song, which betrays its preblues origins by the fact that it takes the form of a lyricized folktale *about* a black man rather than employing the blues' distinctive first-person confessional mode—although the first-person voice emerges in the final stanza as the song's victorious protagonist suddenly shows up at home, supplanting the frame narrator and sidestepping his wife's anger. This confessional mode is itself one of the places where blues testimony owes an aesthetic debt to the spirituals. In *Slave Songs of the United States* (1867), William Allen, Charles Ware, and Lucy Garrison cite a relevant antecedent fragment: "I an' Satan had a race, Hallelu, hallelu, / I an' Satan had a race, Hallelu, hallelu."[12] The contest with the devil is ancient, but the spirituals, shaped by the material and social realities of slavery, know that this "race" is a life-and-death matter of a race-specific sort: a runaway black slave braving the wilderness with hellish hounds and a vengeful white master or overseer, or both, snapping at his heels.

"The Devil Jumped the Black Man" resonates most fully when we hear it as a cagey symbolic drama, one that draws on slave-era materials to signify on Jim Crow social relations in a way that earns its trickster protagonist a victory over the (white) devil. Hopkins modernizes his antebellum material by signifying wittily on the protocols of Jim Crow, beginning with the black man's dismissive retort to the devil, "Man, you know you out your place." The image of the devil jumping the black man is a coded invocation of white mastery violently asserting possession, but the word "place," supersaturated with a specific racial connotation on post-Reconstruction terrain, enables Hopkins to thumb his nose brazenly at Evil Whiteness, inverting Jim Crow's hierarchy by usurping the southern white man's jealously guarded right to mark such boundaries. He sasses and vanquishes his antagonist while maintaining a wide-ranging mobility that places him symbolically beyond the grasp of whoever would immobilize and imprison him. That sassing and escape is comical here—"fun," "run," and "son" create a sing-song rhyme—but the social reality on which they signify was anything but, as Dollard suggests. Sassing a white man could easily become a lynching offense; in 1895, Ida B. Wells-Barnett listed "insulting whites" as the pretext for several lynchings; a century later, Stewart Tolnay and E. F. Beck cited "arguing with white man," "being obnoxious," "demanding respect," "inflammatory language," "insulting white man," and "unruly remarks" in a list titled "The Reasons Given for Black Lynchings."[13] The devil's eagerness to pitchfork the black man, in such a freighted context, is a way of symbolizing the polymorphous tortures that accompanied lynching-as-spectacle and the instruments used to effect them: knives of every variety, poultry shears, sheep clippers, blowtorches, sledgehammers, crowbars, axes, and of course pitchforks. George Sharp, a white man of conscience, was seven years old in 1930 when two black men were lynched in Marion, Indiana, a state permeated by the resurgent Ku Klux Klan. "My great-grandfather told me he went down there and put a pitchfork through one of the guys hanging there. . . . His attitude was, There's no good niggers but dead ones. . . . Of course, he was from Florida."[14]

The idea of the Jim Crowed South as a kind of hell ruled by a malefic white devil wasn't just signified on by southern blues lyricists such as Hopkins; it was also bluntly evoked by the northern black press. Spencer describes a front-page cartoon in the *Chicago Defender* titled "Take My Seat, Mr. Dixie" (1927):

> a dark, horned devil was turning over his fiery throne to a white man representing "The South." The explanation, which appeared later on the editorial page, said: "His satanic majesty, the devil, has abdicated his throne in favor of the forces of Dixie. Even hell, with all its vaunted evil, with its instruments of torture, with its brimstone and sulphur, with its torturing imps, cannot compete with America's Dixie in barbarity, and the devil grudgingly abdicates his throne. . . . Dixie is hell. . . . Slavery was an institution of hell, founded upon the very principles by which that nether world is governed."[15]

Spencer views this editorial's overt identification of the devil with oppressive southern whiteness as a Jazz Age phenomenon, one associated with a politically engaged black metropolitanism and the waning of religious faith: educated migrants, skeptical of the fervent Deep South evangelicalism they'd left behind, were also now free to publicly demonize "the white courts, the white press, the Dixie whites, the white-clad Klan" whose clutches they'd escaped. No longer spooked (and kept in behavioral line) by the biblical devil with whom their down-home elders had chastised them, they put a familiar religious vocabulary to new and politically efficacious use. Without wholly disputing this view, I see attitudinal and expressive continuities where Spencer sees divergences. If the *Defender* editorial strategically conflates antebellum southern slavery and post-Reconstruction southern violence, evoking the latter's surpassing egregiousness only to fold it into a characterization of the South as an enduring hell, then an important truth lingers in the paradox: the violent, possessive domination of blacks by whites is the foundation of both racial slavery and Jim Crow segregation. Although the ritual tortures of the latter period arguably exceeded in brutality what had come before, the devil—an agent of evil presiding over his benighted realm—provided black folk with a symbolic language nuanced enough to communicate the specific challenges of each period while offering a through-line, as it were, of shared imagery.

OLE SATAN LIKE DAT HUNTING DOG

It should go without saying that the devil of the black South wasn't always and in every case envisioned as white. Quite the reverse: when imagined vividly, whether in conversion narratives or stories about crossroads encounters at midnight, he was far more likely to be depicted as a "big black man," consistent with European folk conceptions and evangelical tradition inherited during the long process of New World acculturation—and consistent with the discretion bred in slaves and their descendants by keen sense of self-preservation. By the same token, at least when the devil is being evoked in African American spirituals, folktales, and blues songs, the mark of evil whiteness often hovers like a virus in close proximity to the "strong sense" of evil that Spencer views as the devil's most recognizable attribute: not overtly activated, but *available* to be activated when contextual cues allow. This last claim, although it remains controversial, has been an important touchstone in African American scholarship for many decades, beginning with John Lovell's rejection in 1939 of the white folkloristic consensus that the spirituals were wholly focused on the spirit-world rather than gesturing, surreptitiously but pointedly, at the brutal terrestrial world in which slaves actually lived and suffered. "We cannot accept the pretty little platitudes to be found in such excellently written books as Odum and Johnson's *The*

Negro and His Songs. Satan is not a traditional Negro goblin; he is the people who beat and cheat the slave. . . . Hell is often being sold South."[16] "In freedom as in slavery," agreed Lawrence Levine in *Black Culture and Black Consciousness* (1977), "the devil—over whom blacks generally triumphed in their songs—often looked suspiciously like a surrogate for the white man."[17]

Under certain conditions, such as slave narratives dictated many decades after Emancipation, where white malfeasance was safely distanced and retribution therefore unlikely, cagey significations dissolved into frank declarations of absolute evil. "White folks was the devil in slavery times," insisted ex-slave Lizzie McCloud, speaking of the whipping she'd endured at the hands of her master. "I was scared to death of 'em." "Dey was de devil turned a-loose," recalled Appalachian ex-slave Callie Elder, speaking of the patrollers who'd chased her and her kin. Interviewed in Natchez, Mississippi, in 1937 at the age of 104, James Lucas remembered the period right after the war as "de wors' times" he'd ever seen: "Dem Ku Kluxes was de debbil. De niggers sho was scared of 'em, but dey was more after dem carpet-baggers dan de niggers. . . . Sometimes dey would go right in de fiel's an' take folks an' kill 'em. . . . Day is all dead and gone, but dey sho' was rabid den."[18] The devil of the blues draws key elements of his character from the devil-on-earth evoked by the slave informants above. He's a wide-ranging, doggedly pursuant shape-shifter whose cruel hands claim black bodies and souls. Like Douglass's arch-slavebreaker, Edward Covey, he's everywhere at once—stealthy, snakelike, surveillant. The real-world anchor for this figure was the violent, dominating, and ever-present white boss. In "Couldn't Find a Mule" (1973), Mississippi-born pianist Sunnyland Slim sung about that boss with rare candor, engendered perhaps by the geographic and chronological distance at which his Stockholm recording session placed him from the remembered southern scene he was evoking:

> Lord, I worked old Maude this morning, God knows I done worked
>   old Belle
> Oh, I worked old Maude, captain, you know I done worked old Belle
> I couldn't find a mule in that whole corral, Lord, that had its shoulder well
>
> I been kind of worried, I been thinkin' about what's been goin' on
> You know I been kind of worried, Lord, I been had my travelin' shoes on
> I seed the captain whip the water boy, and durn near bust his head
>
> Uumh, oh Lord, oh Lord, oh Lord, [spoken] get prayers in it
> Oh Lord, oh Lord, oh Lord, oh Lord

An' I though about what my mother and father said, it's never too late
  to pray [spoken] All right now

You know I told the captain that my mother was dead
Oh, I told the bossman early this morning, Lord, that my poor mother
  was dead
He said, Negro, if you don't go to work, you will soon be dead too

[spoken] Hear what I said
Uumh, Lord have mercy on my poor sinkin' soul
Ooooooh—have mercy on a poor man's sinkin' soul
The devil's got the badge of that white man, it's too late for him to try
  to pray [spoken] Sho' is, y'all[19]

Working the fields with a pair of lame mules, riddled with anxiety at thoughts of the (black) water boy's savage beating by his white boss, the bluesman surrenders to the Lord and turns in his final stanza to the figure of the devil—and possession by the devil, more specifically—as the best available way of symbolizing the boss's callous, murderous misuse of power. Perpetual vigilance is required, along with a prayerful reaffirmation of parental religion and "travelin' shoes," in the face of such unbounded maleficence, but none of those things may be enough to maintain the bluesman's freedom or save his life.

The devil that Sunnyland Slim sings of in "The Devil Is a Busy Man" (1954), by contrast, has no overt racial identifiers attached. But the deadly power he wields over the singer is consistent with the violent discipline inflicted by the white boss in "Couldn't Find a Mule":

Well, the devil is a busy man . . . whooo he stays right on my trail (2x)
No matter what I try to do . . . the devil gets in my way

I steal off to myself . . . whoo, I set down and begin to think
Well . . . steal off to myself . . . whoo, I set down and begin to think
No matter what I try . . . the devil gets right in my way

Alright

Well, the devil has got power . . . whoo, and don't you think he has (2x)
Boy, if you ain't mighty careful . . . he will lead you to your grave[20]

"The Devil Is a Busy Man" crystallizes the paradox explored by this chapter, evoking the devil in his tripled guise. Most obviously, he's the biblical tempter whose snares the singer warns against in language inherited from his churched elders; but he's also an ineludible, death-dealing presence, one with a shadowy white penumbra evoking a collective history of racial subjection; and he's a figure for the bluesman's own fickle nature—the wrong mind (rather than right mind) that urges him toward violence, addiction, promiscuity, rambling, and other reckless, unregulated behaviors that "gets in [the] way" of righteous living. The second and third devils are interlinked. The former, exerting malign power and control over the black subject, helps beget the latter: a black trickster who sometimes celebrates his own ungovernability and sometimes (as here) bemoans it. The devil is both his worst self—an Enemy he's in thrall to—*and* his freest, wildest self, beholden to no white man.

This devil-spawned ungovernability, as I'll explore in a moment, becomes a badge of pride in the blues tradition, expressed through masculine self-proclamations about having "ways like the devil." Hell, the devil's purview, takes on similarly doubled meanings: it's both the reviled land of Jim Crow and the low-down southern home-place where fun, frolic, and family—the secular community that nurtures the devil's music—all reside. Champion Jack Dupree evokes this paradox in "My Home's in Hell" (1968), although the former meaning somewhat obscures the latter:

> Walked all the way from New York City . . . way down to New Orleans
> [spoken] Boy that's a long walk, man
> Walked all the way from New York City . . . way down to New Orleans
> I'm goin' down to Louisiana . . . just to find my queen oh queen
>
> Well I know my baby, she'll be there to take me in
> Yes I know my baby, she will be there to take me in
> She'll have a big celebration, a celebration to welcome me in
> [spoken] Alright boy, play me some guitar, man
>
> Well the preacher said, "God made man . . . God made man out of mud"
> Preacher said, "God made man . . . God made man out of mud"
> But when the good Lord made me . . . I must of slipped out, slipped out
>   of the good Lord's hand
>
> Preacher said, "God don't like ugly" . . . my home must be down in hell
> Preacher said, "God don't like ugly" . . . my home must be down in hell
> Ain't nobody ever died . . . ain't nobody ever come back to tell[21]

Dupree represents himself here as a benighted soul, a resident of hell whom the Lord has dropped like a hot potato and the devil has presumably claimed, but he also incarnates the devil in the weak sense encompassed by the word "devilish": he's footloose, pridefully unrepentant, a man of the world carrying festive erotic energies back home to the community. The singer's geographical trajectory is notable: a doubled "down" that is simultaneously a voyage from the North into the South and a return "home" to hell. Is that home a place of ritual renewal or a scene of beleaguerment—a deadly place that no one returns *from*? Dupree's biography, juxtaposed with a second recording, offers reason to think that he's signifying here, albeit obscurely, on malignant southern whiteness.

A native of New Orleans, Dupree grew up in an orphanage after his parents died in a fire set by the Klan, and he lived an unusually peripatetic life even for a bluesman, including time in Chicago and Indianapolis, service as a cook in the Navy during World War II, two years as a prisoner of war in Japan ("Black people lived good [in the camp] because they weren't put with the whites," he claimed), a significant recording career in New York after his release, and then, in 1958, a three-decade expatriation to Europe that represented a repudiation of American racism.[22] "I found England was a heavenly place for me," he later told a British interviewer. "I don't care who else find it difficult, but to me it's heaven. When you leave from slavery and go into a place where you're free . . . I couldn't go back there, because anybody that spit on me, I'd kill them."[23] The words "heavenly" and "heaven" are striking here, evoking a promised land into which one has been delivered out of a latter-day slavery of racial mistreatment, a kind of hell. That Dupree associated this hell specifically with Dixie is made clear by "I'm Going to Write the Governor of Georgia," a blues song that he composed and recorded in 1946 in the immediate aftermath of a lynching but that remained unreleased during his lifetime:

Well I'm gonna write the governor, tell him about the Georgia state
Well I'm a write the governor, tell him about the Georgia state
Well I'm a tell him to do something, just before it is too late

When I was down in the Pacific, fightin' the Japanese
Well, when I was in the Pacific, fightin' the Japanese
I had to go back down in Georgia and bow down on my knees

I got people down in Georgia that I'm afraid to go and see
I got people down in Georgia that I'm afraid to go and see
Well I'm afraid that gang down there . . . 'cause they might lynch
    poor me

Now they taken out two men, and also their wives
Well they taken out two men, and also their wives
Well they taken them out in the woods, and they taken the people's lives

I'm going to write the governor, tell him 'bout the Georgia state
Well, I'm a write the governor, tell him 'bout the Georgia state
Well they better do something, just before it is too late[24]

The episode referred to here is the so-called Moore's Ford lynching, in which two young black couples—including George W. Dorsey, a five-year veteran of the Pacific War—were hung from a bridge in rural Georgia.[25] All the bad things in the song are located "down": not just in the Pacific theater of war, where a black man might at least battle his nation's enemy with a sense of masculine purpose, but in the violent down-South of America, a place of murderous intimidation that destroys black communal ties. The singer survives the hell of war and returns home only to be confronted with another battlefront, another demon-filled hell.

"I'm Going to Write the Governor of Georgia" is the urtext hovering behind "My Home's in Hell." Refusing the veil, the earlier song speaks with unusual frankness at a moment of heightened public feeling—so pointedly, in fact, that it might well have provoked violent southern reprisal had it been released at the time. The latter song, far more concerned with celebrating black communal bonhomie and acknowledging the singer's fallen nature than indicting the South for its racial sins, nevertheless places itself in symbolic proximity to such an indictment. It grants the singer plausible deniability as it does so: his home "down in hell" is, after all, a place to which he has been consigned by the (black) preacher and his own bad behavior, not by a white mob. Still, a walk "down to New Orleans" is aligned lyrically with a descent into hell. This is how the blues do their work under the sign of Jim Crow. Signifying protects the singer and creates an aesthetic space within which singer and audience are free to conjure—playfully, angrily, or both—with what everybody knows but nobody dares to say openly: the refuge where love and communal affirmation await may be located in a benighted land where death hovers, ready to strike. The South may be home, but that doesn't mean it's not hell.

The blues learned this double-voiced approach from the spirituals. It was an approach grounded, in James Cone's words, in "a history of servitude and resistance, of survival in the land of death." Racial slavery, understood not simply as a way of organizing labor relations but as the bodily possession of black by white enforced through violence, found an apt covert emblem in Satan and his hellish designs. "Black slaves," argues Cone,

> took the biblical description of Satan as the Evil One and applied it to their experience. Satan for them was a supernatural being who enslaves people in sin. Though less powerful than God, Satan was more powerful than people. . . . Just as God is present in the forces that make people human and enable them to struggle against the evils of slavery, so Satan is present in the dehumanizing forces that contribute to slavery. Satan's earthly representatives are slaveholders, slave catchers, and slave traders.[26]

Determined to represent the evil of their enslavers without courting reprisal, slaves were as circumspect in their antebellum spirituals as they were forthcoming in their post-Emancipation narratives, but the two streams of testimony share one striking quality: an intimacy, a desire to personalize their oppressor. The grammar of the spirituals, as exemplified in the following assortment of verses, underscores the direct personal encounter within a context of iniquitous power relations; the themes of surveillance, possession, fear, struggle, escape, mobility, and self-determination predominate. The dark night of the soul in which the spirit of the slave-singer wrestles with Satan is a mask, as often as not, for the primal encounter of slave and slave-catcher in the policed space beyond the plantation:

> Old satan tole me to my face,
> "I'll git you when a you leave this place;"
> O brother dat scere me to my heart,
> I was 'feared to walk a when it was dark.
>
> I started home but I did pray
> An' I met old satan on de way;
> Ole satan made a one grab at me,
> But he missed my soul an' I went free
>
> The Devil's mad and I'm glad,
> He lost the soul he thought he had
>
> I tell you brother you better not laugh,
> Ole satan'll run you down his path,
> If he runs you lak he run me,
> You'll be glad to fall upon yo' knee.

Ole Satan like dat hunting dog.
He hunt dem Christians home to God.

Ole Satan's mighty busy,
He follers me night an' day
An' every where I 'pinted
Dere's something in my way.

Old Satan is one busy ole man;
He rolls dem blocks all in my way
But Jesus is my bosom friend;
He rolls dem blocks away.[27]

To call Satan "busy" was a calculated understatement; a folksy, intimate rendering of the disciplinary apparatus that was simultaneously—from the slave's perspective—as abstract as the transatlantic slave trading network and as concrete as the chains and patrollers that bruised, shamed, and immobilized individual runaways. "Out of necessity," writes theologian Dwight N. Hopkins, "slaves developed a deceptive linguistic culture of survival to subvert white discovery of genuine slave thought. But when this spiritual burst forth from the prayerful lips of black folk in the 'Invisible Institution,' their own sacred political and cultural space, Satan distinctly and most definitely denoted slavery and the evils of white people. For the slaves Jesus, the bosom friend, ceaselessly and consistently destroyed the 'blocks' of the devilish slave system and thereby thwarted death and preserved black life."[28]

It was Jesus and God, twin figures of righteousness, who helped the slave singer of spirituals maintain the fiction of otherworldliness whenever the grammar of domination and resistance threatened to collapse the distance between "Ole Satan" and worldly white figures of authority. How could the slave master object to his slaves putting aside "heathenish" African customs to celebrate the power of the heavenly master and his son over the evil tempter? But the evidence from many of the slaves' own mouths—not coded in the spirituals but spoken plainly in moments of post-Emancipation candor—was clear: the white masters to whom they had been subjected, body and soul, *were* the devil. They were his living image, his incarnation. "If they ever was a living devil," one ex-slave insisted of his master, "that plantation was his home and the owner was it! . . . That man got so mean even the white folks was scared of him."[29] In Tallapoosa, Alabama, a slave owner named Gum Threat handled his slaves in the final years before Emancipation with "indifferent brutality," according to historian Douglas Blackmon, torturing at least one runaway by placing a hot coal in the middle of his back after having him strapped face down on the floor. "Iffen they ever was a devil on this earth it was Gum Threat," insisted one of his former slaves many years later. "He jest didn't have any regard to his slaves. . . . He beat them for everything they done and a lot they didn't."[30] George King, a former slave from South Carolina, called his former master's plantation "two-hundred acres of Hell," a place where he had been subjected to a "devil overseer" and a "she-devil Mistress."[31] Hell, for slaves, was both the earthly prison in which they found themselves under the dominion of such man-devils and the prophetic domain, "deep down in the ground," to which those man-devils would be forcibly returned, with appropriate perpetual punishments, after death.

The death of an unkind master or overseer, not surprisingly, often precipitated jubilation and dissembling among the slaves. After his former master's corpse was brought home, recalled ex-slave Jacob Stroyer, "all the slaves were allowed to stop at home that day to see the last of him, and to lament with mistress. After all the slaves who cared to do so had seen his face, they gathered in groups around mistress to comfort her; they shed false tears, saying 'Never mind, missus, massa gone home to heaven,'" even as others were saying, "Thank God, massa gone home to hell."[32] On rare occasions, slaves on antebellum plantations dropped the mask to speak—or sing—the truth unadorned. Ex-slave Martha Jackson described how the death of a hated overseer led the master to send "down in de woods and all over de plantation . . . lookin' fer de niggers to come to de Big House," and how the slaves came "a-shoutin' and a-clappin' de han's and a-holl'rin sumpin awful: 'Ole John Bell is de'd en gone / I hope he's gone to hell!'"[33] As late as World War II, according to historian Neal McMillan, black field hands in the Mississippi Delta were still singing a version of an old slave song, one that evidently retained contemporary relevance thanks to a felt continuity between exploitative labor arrangements in the sharecropping era and the earlier period:

> My ole mistress promised me
> Before she died she would set me free. . . .
> Now she's dead and gone to hell
> I hope the devil will burn her well.[34]

From an African American perspective, in short, the devil of the antebellum South was at once—when the racial subtext was activated—a covert way of symbolizing the figureheads of a white slaveocracy and an agent of retribution *against* those figureheads. This devil's home was in hell, not only the hell on earth he created for his (or her) slave subjects but also the hellish afterlife to which his slaves, dreaming of vengeance, consigned him as punishment for his sins. If "the downfall of the archfiend forms the principal topic of their anthems," as a Scottish trader described the spirituals he'd heard sung by slaves in Charleston, South Carolina, in 1830, then their emotional investment in this particular drama had worldly sources indeed.[35]

HELL AIN'T BUT A MILE AND A QUARTER

What happens to the white devil signified on by the spirituals when the Emancipation Proclamation loses him the black soul he thought he had? More precisely, how do that devil's real-world referents respond to that loss, and how does the blues lyric tradition evoke the new devil and new hell that emerge phoenix-like from the ashes of Emancipation? The antebellum couplet quoted earlier in this chapter suggests that the devil is mad and the slave-singer is glad when such losses occur, and the first part of that formulation—the white devil's anger—certainly carries forward into the brave new world of black freedom. "However these [white] men may have regarded the negro slave," wrote journalist Whitelaw Reid after visiting Mississippi in 1866, "they hated the negro freeman. . . . They were virulently vindictive against a property that escaped from their control."[36] "Too late to talk about the 'suppressed vote' now," cried a black Floridian in 1887 in the face of white violence. "We are in the hands of the devil."[37] The gladness evoked by the spiritual lasts, in symbolic terms, no longer than the brief moment in which Jubilee is celebrated. Then the devil's anger begins once again to tighten the figurative noose around black southern lives. This new slavery is a foundational component of the world that gave rise to the blues: an unevenly distributed but comprehensive set of disciplines comprised of vagrancy laws, lynch law, convict leasing, prison farms, and the protocols of Jim Crow, all of them driven by a deadly mixture of racial triumphalism—the white man must remain on top—and the profit motive. The devil and hell of the blues tradition are profoundly shaped by the confrontation between black southern blues singers and these material and attitudinal realities.

A considerable body of recent scholarship has clarified the price that black southerners, and black men in particular, have paid for the reconstruction and expansion of the laws, practices, and institutions that corralled and immobilized them in the post-Emancipation decades and beyond. The story is sketched in the titles of the studies themselves: *"Worse Than Slavery": Parchman Farm and the Ordeal of Jim Crow Justice*; *Slavery by Another Name: The Re-enslavement of Black Americans from the Civil War to World War II*; *Slavery Revisited: Blacks and the Southern Convict Lease System, 1865–1933*; *Dark Journey: Black Mississippians in the Age of Jim Crow*.[38] In "A Concluding Meditation on Plantations, Ships, and Black Modernism" (2001), Houston A. Baker Jr. traces a line from the slave ships and plantations of the Black Atlantic through the prison-agricultural and prison-industrial complex of the present day (especially Texas and Louisiana) to evoke "a carceral network that has continually held the black-South body in a state of 'suspended rights.'"[39] The middle term or "passage" in that history, he asserts, is southern convict lease labor, a brutal and profitable system that emerged in the 1870s and was slowly phased out after the turn of the century. Black men were arrested for vagrancy and other trumped-up charges, then turned over to white bosses who paid their "court costs" and other factitious fees before marching them off into the fields or mines and working them to death in a way that even slaves were rarely worked. The convict lease system was so brutal that an accumulation of bad publicity, lawsuits, and public disgust, abetted by muckraking journalism, ended up forcing southern legislatures to outlaw the practice. In 1888, for example, an investigative report titled "A Hell in Arkansas" surveyed the brutal conditions at the Coal Hill convict camp, an infamous coal mine in western Arkansas that drew official notice after an autopsy on a recently buried prisoner's corpse revealed "a broken spinal cord, crushed genitals, and eyes hanging out of their sockets."[40] Prison farms such as Parchman, Angola, and Sugarland evolved, astonishingly, as what was considered at the time to be a humane modern alternative to convict leasing. They, too, came under attack by reformers when their abuses were exposed. Sugarland was known as "the Hell-Hole of the Brazos," and Parchman was known to locals as "the Devil's Island of the Delta."[41]

Black southern blues singers found ways of speaking back to, and sometimes mocking, this network of imprisonments; the figure of the devil and his hell proved to be crucial props in this endeavor. The devil could be called out as loudly and pointedly as one wanted, yet the cover of piety could be maintained. "Blues men and women," as Cone notes, "would have to be very naïve to couch the blues in white categories of protest," and black southern blues singers were anything but naïve about the trouble that might rain down on those who openly flouted the protocols of Jim Crow.[42] Private conversations, of course, allowed for candor. "When some blacks talked about whites as the devil," B. B. King confessed in his autobiography, speaking about communal rage at the hanging of a black man in Lexington, Mississippi, in the 1930s for the crime of touching a white woman, "I could see the source of their wrath. I could still see the dead man outside the courthouse on the square."[43] But the highly public nature of blues recordings, together with a ludic tradition of sexual signifying in which double-voiced language—crawling king snakes, shaken peaches—said with a wink and a leer what obscenity laws prevented from being said directly, combined to foster a strain of insurrectionary indirection within the devil-blues tradition. Everybody but the white devil and his precious daughter got the joke.

An instructive example in this context is a 1938 recording by Big Bill Broonzy, "Hell Ain't but a Mile and a Quarter." Born and raised in a family of cotton sharecroppers near Pine Bluff, Arkansas, on the edge of the Arkansas Delta, Broonzy (1903–58) shared with Champion Jack Dupree both a familiarity with white racist violence that was an unexceptional element of black men's lives in that place and time and a willingness to speak candidly about such things in the aftermath of World War II, a period when African American expectations for equal treatment surged noticeably. Both men also confronted the problematics of such blunt talk. Like Dupree, whose "I'm Going to Write the Governor of Georgia" remained unreleased for many decades, Broonzy composed "Black, Brown, and White" in 1945 but encountered strong resistance from the recording industry. "I tried RCA, Victor, Columbia, Decca and a lot of little companies," he recalls in his autobiography, *Big Bill Blues* (1955), "but none of them would record it." When Broonzy protested that the long string of injustices cataloged by the song were all true, the industry's collective response, as he wittily dramatizes (or embroiders) it, was "Yes . . . and that is what's wrong with it. You see, Bill, when you write a song and want to record it with any company, it must keep the people guessing what the song means. Don't you say what it means when you're singing. And that song comes right to the point and the public won't like that."[44]

The irony here, as Broonzy surely knew, is that the industry had a point: although Lawrence Gellert, Irwin Silber, and other white urban leftists may have been thrilled to hear blues songs animated by overt protest, the black audience had historically shown its preference for witty double entendre.

Broonzy also knew the trouble that could descend on a black man who dared speak truth to white southern power. In 1946, while visiting New York, he sat down with his southern-born Chicago bandmates Memphis Slim and Sonny Boy Williamson at the instigation of folklorist Alan Lomax and spoke at length into Lomax's Presto disc recorder about the violence and indignities inflicted by Jim Crow. Broonzy talked of an uncle who had been lynched by a white mob; of the workings of chain gangs; of the murderous sexual jealousy of white men. He also talked, pointedly, about how black men who wanted to cuss out their white boss but to avoid a vicious beatdown would cuss out their mules instead—"signifying and getting revenge thru songs," as Memphis Slim put it. Lomax was overjoyed at the outpouring, which went far beyond the comparatively benign inventory of wrongs cataloged in "Black, Brown, and White." "Here, at last," he wrote later, "black working class men had talked frankly, sagaciously, and with deep resentment about the inequities of the Southern system." But Broonzy and the others, hearing their own voices played back to them, were suddenly terrified what that same system might do to them if the recording were made public. "You don't understand, Alan," they told Lomax, begging him to be discreet. "If these records came out on us, they'd take it out on our folks down home; they'd burn them out and Lord knows what else."[45]

"Hell Ain't but a Mile and a Quarter" is situated on the cusp of this postwar eruption of angry, anxious candor. A coded evocation of the Jim Crow South as segregated space policed by the devil and his henchmen, it gestures simultaneously at small-town and prison-farm life. It tells the truth, but it tells it slant, to paraphrase Emily Dickinson, and the fantasy with which it ends helps distance its insurrectionary tenor in a way that courts white amusement (not to mention black hilarity) rather than risk white reprisal:

I said hell . . . hell ain't but a mile and a quarter
I said hell . . . hell ain't but a mile and a quarter
And when you get there, they will give you brimstone for water

There is one place . . . that I really don't want to go
There is one place . . . that I really don't want to go
Hell ain't but a mile and a quarter . . . before you get there you will
    find [Poka-tola]

When you get there, you will have to obey the devil's orders
When you get there, you will have to obey the devil's orders
I just stopped by to tell you, y'all . . . that *hell* ain't but a mile and a quarter

The next thing I'm gone do . . . I'm going to marry the devil's daughter
The next thing I'm gone do . . . I'm going to marry the devil's daughter
You may think it's a long way, but *hell* ain't but a mile and a quarter

I'm gonna take her, I'm gonna put her up on the shelf
When I marry her I'm gonna take her . . . I'm gonna put her up on
    the shelf
Yeah, and I'm gone say from now on, Mr. Devil . . . I'm gone rule this
    hell myself[46]

Broonzy's song, as I read it, is an allegory of a black southern man's voyage across the tracks. In the first three stanzas, the singer sketches his descent from the relative safety of his own neighborhood into the hellish hostility of a Jim Crowed downtown rippling with behavioral protocols and alert to black male transgression. Hell, by this reading, is only a short walk away. When you get there, they'll "give you brimstone for water," which is a way of symbolizing the violent intimidation, the stone-hearted meanness, that often confronted black southern men in such public spaces—spaces, it should be noted, where segregated water fountains were one visible form through which a demeaning racial order was maintained. The second stanza expands on the first, inscribing the singer's reluctance to visit such a place, but it concludes with an obscure reference to a transit point that sounds in Broonzy's mouth like Poka-tola. Might he be suggesting that the road to hell runs through Ponchatoula, a small town roughly fifty miles north of New Orleans on the far side of Lake Pontchartrain? If so, why does that locale show up here? Again, speculation is required. Ponchatoula is associated with a horrendous act of racial violence. In 1900 there was a quadruple lynching in the town; four black men accused of robbery and the beating of a white woman were hung from a tree—a tree that whites later referred to as "The Christmas Tree," and that blacks avoided, claiming it was haunted.[47] Although there's no direct evidence that Broonzy knew of the lynching, the historical context in which he chose to record the song may lend credence to this line of speculation.

"Hell Ain't but a Mile and a Quarter" was composed not by Broonzy, as it happens, but by Red Mike Bailey (John McBailey), a blues pianist associated with the St. Louis scene that nurtured Peetie Wheatstraw and Henry Townsend in the 1930s. In *Big Bill Blues*, Broonzy recounts how a talent scout for several record companies in Chicago asked him to travel to East St. Louis and bring back Red Mike and a second blues singer, his half-brother Black Mike. Broonzy executes the mission and discovers that both men were born in Duck Hill, Mississippi—"not far from my home," he notes. "I also recorded one of Red Mike's songs," he adds, after mentioning the song by name. "This happened in 1937."[48] Broonzy's chronology is slightly in error—he recorded "Hell Ain't but a Mile and a Quarter" in November 1938, four months after Red Mike recorded it—but the conjunction of the place, date, and song is startling.[49] What happened in 1937 in Duck Hill was one of the most brutal lynchings in Mississippi's history. A pair of black moonshiners, Roosevelt Townes and "Bootjack" McDaniels, were arrested for the shotgun murder of a white storeowner, George Windham, whisked away to the state capital of Jackson, then returned a week later to the county seat. A waiting mob seized them and drove twelve miles back to Duck Hill before beating them with chains, gouging out Townes' eyes, torturing both men with a blowtorch, shooting McDaniels to death after he confessed, then dousing Townes with gasoline and burning him to death. The double lynching made the front page of national newspapers; *Life* magazine published a gruesome photo, as did at least one black newspaper. The NAACP issued a report titled "Lynching by Blow Torch." The Duck Hill outrage and another in Bainbridge, Georgia, spurred antilynching legislation, but southern senators filibustered for more than a month; one senator from Louisiana, according to Philip Dray, "[set] a new Senate record for continuous holding of the floor" by lecturing his colleagues "for twenty-seven hours and forty-five minutes on the inevitable 'mongrelization' of the white race that would occur if blacks were ever granted full social equality."[50]

There is no evidence that Red Mike specifically wrote "Hell Ain't but a Mile and a Quarter" in response to the 1937 Duck Hill lynching, or that Broonzy knew of the incident—although both men would quite likely have heard of it, given how widely it was publicized. The song sketches an enduring condition as much as a historically specific situation, maintaining plausible deniability at all costs. Whether the "brimstone" that "they" will give you when you get to hell signifies on this singular episode of blowtorch torture, or the more common lynching ritual of burning black men alive, or the routine southern experience of being a black man cast alone into inhospitable territory, is less important than the ability of the song simultaneously to enable all these possible meanings at a pressured historical moment when total candor was impossible. The year 1938 had been a bad one for lynchings in Mississippi, with one in June and two in July; one victim in Rolling Fork was shot and killed, then dragged for several miles and burned.[51] Broonzy's 1947 statement to Lomax about how verbalized complaints by him could see his "folks down home . . . burn[ed] . . . out" makes clear that he brooded on such things. By the early 1950s, when he began to write down the stories that Belgian journalist Yannick Bruynoghe eventually edited into *Big Bill Blues*, Broonzy was willing to speak openly. "When anybody asks me if I'm from Mississippi, I'll say yes, but I'm mad and don't like to talk about it, because I was born poor, had to work, and do what the white man told me to do, a lot of my people were mobbed, lynched, and beaten."[52] During his 1956 tour of Europe, Broonzy carried a cut-out newspaper article on the Emmett Till lynching in Money, Mississippi, showing it to his hosts and fans, in his biographer's words, as "a particularly egregious example of the treatment to which black southerners were often subjected"—not just the harshest sort of vigilante violence but also the active participation of local lawmen.[53]

Broonzy wasn't a Mississippi native, as we now know thanks to his biographer, Bob Riesman, but his youthful memories of life in Arkansas provided him with more than enough fuel for his accusations. In 1919, when Broonzy was a teenager, a black male veteran in nearby Pine Bluff named Clinton Briggs who refused the order of a white woman to "'get off the sidewalk' met his death at the hands of a mob who 'lashed him to a tree with tire chains and shot him forty times.'"[54] Broonzy's phrase "had to . . . do what the white man told me to do" illuminates both acts of violence—southern white men avenging a perceived dishonor to southern womanhood—and aligns precisely with the third stanza of "Hell Ain't but a Mile and a Quarter": "When you get there, you will have to obey the devil's orders / I just stopped by to tell you, y'all . . . that *hell* ain't but a mile and a quarter." The "devil's orders" are the behavioral protocols of Jim Crow; the word "hell," which Broonzy emphasizes here and in the verse that follows, suggests that a hellish time hovers closely over any black man who violates them—above all, the absolute proscription on physical contact with, or perceived disrespect toward, white women, a proscription responsible for the death of Briggs and Till.

Both the scenario evoked by the recording and Broonzy's statement about having to do "what the white man told me to do" are powerfully corroborated by the reminiscences of bluesmen Yank Rachell and Mance Lipscomb. "Back in them days, down South, the people wasn't right," complained Rachell, speaking about his hometown of Brownsville, Tennessee. "They do or done everything to you down there. Seven o'clock they blow you off the streets. . . . But, you know, a white lady come by wearin' shorts, you better not look at her. 'Nigger, what the hell you doin' lookin' at that white woman?' All that kind of stuff, you know . . . Colored folks catch hell all the time. They kill ya if they think ya outta line."[55] "I was scared ta go down the street," agrees Lipscomb, speaking of his hometown in the East Texas cotton country. "If I meet a white fella, he's down the street an he had his nice clothes on, I had ta give im the street. An dont touch up against a white lady. Do, you gonna git kilt, Nigra. . . . This town here is rotten with that!"[56] "It was forbidden for us to touch the white woman!" Johnny Shines told a Chicago journalist in 1990, remembering his life as a rambling musician in the Deep South at midcentury.[57] In "The Devil's Daughter" (1973), recorded in France, he signifies on that proscription, singing that the object of his desire has "hair like Mary" and "evil tempting ways." "You as pretty as an angel, but you don't do nothing that you ought to / When you walk down the street you look so sweet, but you still the devil's daughter." The final two stanzas of Broonzy's recording, in line with this theme, are a sly and hilarious rejoinder to the white man's murderously jealous protectorate over white southern womanhood. If the violent southern white man is, for many southern black men, the devil incarnate—and this chapter has broadly exampled that proposition—then the black southern bluesman who openly fantasizes about marrying the devil's daughter is flirting with apocalypse. Broonzy takes the perennial miscegenationist nightmare, encapsulated in the question, "Would you let your daughter marry one?," and ups the ante, in symbolic terms. He doesn't just marry the white man's daughter, but usurps the white man's place by putting her "up on the shelf"—an act that simultaneously reverences, immobilizes, and trivializes her. He burlesques white southern masculinity's need to romanticize the southern lady, then boots white southern masculinity out of the way, being sure to doff his hat with the sanctioned Jim Crow honorific, "Mr.," as he does so. As a cue to his black southern audience, Broonzy pauses a split-second before emphasizing the word "hell" in the penultimate verse. If you think hell is far from here, he warns his listeners, just try marrying the white man's—I mean the devil's—daughter. You'll see just how close by hell really is.[58]

Broonzy's own words and actions corroborate this reading of the song as veiled protest and psycho-sexual revenge. In real life Broonzy escaped the hell evoked in the song not by avoiding the devil's daughter, but by leaving the South and displacing his affections onto her white female surrogates, especially those with foreign accents. If his May 1952 interview with Alan Lomax in Paris is to be believed, he did so with something like malice aforethought. He had been in Paris for several months at that point—a follow-up to his inaugural European tour the previous year—and had fallen into a romance with a white French social worker named Jacqueline. "In describing [to Lomax] a black man moving from the South to the North and choosing to seek out a white woman," writes Broonzy's biographer,

> [Bill] zeroed in on [the man's] motivation: "Why he do it? Because he knows he's doing something to hurt the white man! That's why he do it! Because the white man don't want him to have a white woman, and he say, 'Well, I'll hurt this son of a gun. I couldn't hurt him in Mississippi, but I'll hurt him here.' . . . He just do that to hurt the white man, because that's the only get-back he can get back at him."[59]

In 1953, during his next trip to Paris, Broonzy wrote to Lomax that he was living with Jacqueline; a subsequent letter asked Lomax to bring him a pair of wedding bands. Several years later, Broonzy fell in love with a Dutch woman, Pim van Isveldt, and the couple had a son, Michael, although Broonzy remained married to his African American wife, Rose, back in Chicago. In *Big Bill Blues*, Broonzy plays down the vengeance motive under-girding interracial liaisons by insisting, with wide-eyed disingenuousness, that he personally meant no harm when he crossed the tracks. "When I went to the North," he admits, "I tried to be like him"—that is, the white man—

> and I got me a white woman and a big car. Some time I'd have no money to buy gas but I'd pawn my watch or my ring, so the other Negroes could see Big Bill's car and white woman. I did have the white woman because I wanted her, not to hurt anyone. I just wanted to be and act like a white man. I had a black wife at home, and in the South the white man had a white wife and a Negro woman, children by them both, and in no place he went had he to get back for nobody, and everybody like him. So that's the reason why I tried to play and do things like him. . . .
>
> Lots of times I would wonder why a white man would kill me if he'd seen me with a white woman. What is it she's got that my Negro woman ain't got? He has a white woman and he has a Negro woman, too. So I came to the North and tried it.[60]

This statement speaks with puckish partial candor about the issues that "Hell Ain't but a Mile and a Quarter" covertly burlesques: the mystification of the southern white lady, the sexual jealousy that drives the southern white man's violent assertion of racial privilege and exclusive access, and the black southern bluesman's determination to upend the hierarchy by occupying the white man's subject position as cock-of-the-walk. Broonzy references the "Negro woman" three times here; she plays no role in the earlier song, but her presence in this later confession helps Broonzy indict the white man for adultery and hypocrisy even while insisting, tongue firmly in cheek, that he "want[s] to be and act" just like him and can't understand why the white man is so bothered by that. To say that "everybody" likes the southern white man is a slyly mocking half-lie, one that deliberately obscures the pain inflicted on black southern men and women by the protocols of Jim Crow, including the white man's right to unrestricted sexual predation. Those protocols are the "devil's orders" that enable the southern white man to "get back for nobody" while forcing black folk, as Broonzy protests in "Black, Brown, and White," to "get back, get back, get back." Broonzy mutes his true feelings here for the sake of the genial folk-raconteur persona that he evolved with the help of his Belgian editor/amanuensis, one designed for the public consumption of folk-music aficionados. The discrepancy between the (seemingly) frank earlier interview and this exercise in partial candor highlights the interpretive challenge posed by black southern blues singers who choose to signify on charged and dangerous material.

THE DEVIL'S SON-IN-LAW

In the process of sketching this chapter's argument, I suggested earlier that the bluesman's trickster persona—rootless, promiscuous, and un- trustworthy—evolved, in part, as a response to the daily pressures of Jim Crow as embodied and administered by the devil's real-world equivalents. If the condition of disciplinary encirclement represented by vagrancy laws, lynch law, the behavioral protocols of Jim Crow, convict leasing, and the prison-farm system was imagined, in sum, as a kind of devil's snare presided over by white southern manhood, then black southern blues performers, I claimed, engaged in a potent symbolic drama, acting the devil in order to undercut and supplant the white devil in ways that they and their auditors would have found immensely satisfying. They did so in order to maintain masculine self-respect as free and empowered agents of their own des- tinies within a deterministic economic framework that viewed them as exploitable, disposable, politically neutered units of labor power. Acting the devil could take a variety of forms, from behaving like a fully entitled white man to adopting the shadiest of subterranean identities associated with what normative southern jurisprudence might call "Negroes of the criminal class." As the discussion of Big Bill Broonzy and "Hell Ain't but a Mile and a Quarter" should make clear, these performative orientations were not mutually exclusive, nor were they merely a matter of lyric pos- turing. Broonzy enacted in his own life the insurrectionary fantasy that he had sounded in his recording, displacing the white devil and claiming the affections of the devil's symbolic daughter—an act that, had it been committed in Mississippi rather than in Chicago or Europe, would have seen hell rain down on him, as he was the first to acknowledge.

Although this specific connection between the white southern devil and his black blues antagonist has not previously been noted, a number of commentators have remarked more generally on the way black southern bluesmen partake of a "devilish" identity that troubles the prevailing moral codes of the post-Reconstruction South. Peetie Wheatstraw, who styled himself as "the Devil's Son-in-Law" and "the High Sheriff from Hell," is the emblematic figure, along with the Robert Johnson of "Me and the Devil Blues" (1937), but the circle they subtend is spacious and includes Bo Chatmon ("I Am the Devil," 1934), Stovepipe Johnson ("Devilish Blues," 1928), Bill Gaither ("If I Was the Devil," 1938; "Mean Devil Blues," 1939), Sylvester Weaver ("Can't Be Trusted Blues," 1927), and many others. According to Jon Michael Spencer, this ne'er-do-well bluesman is a "supernatural trickster" who draws his energy from the African-sourced, pre-Christian world of conjure, including crossroads spirits such as Legba.[61] He's a "badman trickster," counters Ayana Smith: associated with violence, alcoholism, and addiction, he's "a real force of destruction for a society with strict moral codes."[62] He's sexually promiscuous and draws here, too, on his inheritance from Legba, a phallic deity par excellence. Spurning black Christians and others who would stigmatize him, this devilish bluesman, according to Melissa Richard, manifests a psychological orientation that Erik Erikson has called "foreclosure into a negative identity," embracing rather than rejecting their claim that he plays devil-sponsored music and thrilling the juke-joint crowd with his audacity. "The Devil, as a sign of Evil," argues Paul Garon, "couldn't help but conjure up a sympathetic feeling among those listeners who felt that as African Americans in a white world, they needed an *agent of opposition* to carry on through their lives."[63] Grounded in an Afrocentric holism, Spencer agrees with Smith, Richard, and Garon that the devil-identified bluesman serves an oppositional function, but he rejects, as ill-considered dualism, the idea that this bluesman is "evil," bad, or otherwise wholly implicated in the negative side of any cultural equation. "It was specifically the personality of Legba," Spencer argues,

> an emulative model of heroic action, that the blues person embodied. . . .
> Legba . . . is a being of synchronous duplicity, a duplicity like that in the

blues. He is both malevolent and benevolent, disruptive and reconciliatory, profane and sacred, and yet the predominant attitude toward him
is affection rather than fear. . . .

Legba's and the blues singer's "badman" qualities—trickiness, capriciousness, lawlessness, and rampant sexuality—have been, from the
Victorian or Eurocentric perspective, interpreted as demonic rather than
as holistic. These qualities have been perceived as causing anarchy rather
than as functioning to open up social and psychological boundaries, to
enlarge the scope of the human, and to turn repressive dead ends into
liberative crossroads.[64]

Although there is no evidence to suggest that black southern blues performers deliberately modeled themselves on Legba, or even knew who that
African deity was prior to his reclamation by the Black Arts Movement in
the late 1960s, Spencer's fundamental claim is sound: bluesmen who struck
a "devilish" pose were certainly doing more than advocating evil for its own
sake, and their signal purpose was indeed to turn "repressive dead ends into
liberative crossroads." The burdening presence of the prison-agricultural
complex that upheld Jim Crow was an engine that spurred their creativity.

The connection between white disciplinary containment and unruly
black behavior is manifest in Stovepipe Johnson's "Devilish Blues" (1928).
Little is known about Johnson; a pianist who yodeled, he recorded with
Ma Rainey and Georgia Tom, and he waxed several sides under his own
name, including this one, where the singer configures "these blues" less as
an emotional state than as a threat from which one yearns to escape:

[spoken]
Lord, Stovepipe done got devilish

I'm going to the river . . . we must see the water run
[moan] see the water run
Let me be your washstand, sweet Lord till your [dresser] comes

I'm going to do more for you baby . . . than the good Lord done
[moan] . . . than the good Lord's done
I'm going to buy you some hair . . . cause the Lord didn't give you none

My mama's dead, poor . . . papa's on the county farm
[moans] on the county farm
And I ain't got nobody to . . . teach me right from wrong

Oh, I wonder . . . where I can go
[moan] . . . where I can go
I'm going and hide someplace where these blues won't find me no more

Oh, there is something . . . it's rolling 'cross my mind
[moan] . . . rolling 'cross my mind
And every time I see my baby, make me want to [yodeling moan][65]

The narrative pretext for the singer's devilish behavioral orientation is
the parental abandonment he sketches in the third stanza: his mother is
dead and his "papa's on the county farm," leaving him with "nobody to . . .
teach me right from wrong."[66] The prison-agricultural network has, in effect, played the devil's role, destroying a family and sundering the moral
bond between father and son. The abandoned son responds by claiming
the devil's God-supplanting powers: he configures himself as a placeless,
amoral rogue who woos his female listener with talk of disposable cash
(he'll buy her the hair God failed to give her) even as he dreams of hiding
"someplace where these blues won't find me no more." I read Stovepipe's
blues, in line with Spencer's theory of synchronous duplicity, as a strained
spiritual condition that mingles a hunger for romantic solace—Honeyboy
Edwards spoke about "burying his soul" in his wife, Bessie—with an equally
strong desire to evade the ceaseless surveillance and immobility inflicted
by the carceral network.

As Edwards makes clear in his autobiography, those two blues zones
were linked, from the bluesman's perspective, because the principal actors
in each drama, the black woman and the white bossman, were enmeshed
in the plantation economy. The Mississippi Delta of the 1920s and 1930s
evoked by Edwards sees him cycling through an unending stream of short-
lived romantic associations with women who worked on plantations; he'd
"lay up" in their shacks all day, eat what they brought home from the white
folks' kitchen, go out for an evening walk, then drink and make love. But
he "didn't want to get hooked up to no plow" to support a woman, didn't
want to become indebted to—and thus subject to the control of—a white
boss, and so he inevitably decamped after a week or two. When he lingered
on a plantation, his after-hours visibility was matched by his invisibility
during the long working day, and both forms of self-presentation were
calculated to maximize his freedom in the face of a racially stratified system
that had repeatedly imprisoned him, in one way or another, and compelled
his unrecompensed labor:

In the South they had that vagrancy law, that hog law. I got pulled for that a number of times. That means better have a job or don't be seen on the streets. The police pick you up in the street during the day when everybody's working. "What you doing walkin' around here? Get in the car!" They carry you to jail and they give you four or five days, and that time was spent out in the fields, working the cotton. "Don't you know so-and-so out there, his cotton growed up with grass, and he can't get nobody to workin'? You could be out there workin'!" But he didn't want to give nobody but a dollar a day and nobody wanted to work all day in the hot sun for a dollar. The way to get by all that, stay in the house all day long. I was like a groundhog. Come six o'clock, I'd take a bath, come out like I been in the field. They don't know whether you been in the field or not then. That's the way I done.[67]

Edwards's statement is a late-life confession, not contemporaneous testimony of the sort offered by Broonzy in the 1946 Lomax interview, but it offers further evidence for my claim that black southern blues performers behaved "badly," in conventional Christian terms—drank, fought, gambled, slept around, rambled incessantly, skimmed whatever living they could from the world—as a form of existential infrapolitics, a way of maximizing their lived sense of freedom in the face of the imprisoning, exploitative unfairness of the Jim Crow system. "I wasn't going to work for nobody," Edwards declares repeatedly. "I was so fast, I went too fast to catch any root anywhere. I don't know why I was like that. I was always wanting to pull up and leave, go somewhere else" (173). Honeyboy's twenty-four-year marriage to Bessie was enabled by the fact that she, unlike the great majority of her peers from the Delta, was not bound to plantation work, "the white man's kitchen" (or fields), and was willing to align herself with his peripatetic lifestyle.

Although Edwards never describes himself in devil-identified terms or sings songs of that sort, the behavioral model he embraced is a familiar thematic within the devil-blues tradition, and the carceral network hovers behind it. In "I Am the Devil" (1934) by the Mississippi Sheiks, vocalist Walter Vinson gleefully embraces Christianity's negative ideal and finds the ne'er-do-well persona immensely empowering:

Yes, I'm the devil . . . oh and I don't care none (2x)
I say, Yeah I am the devil, I'm going to take souls as they come
. . . .

Goin' to town tonight, all across the city . . . the way I'm goin' out with
    them girls, you know it's a really pity
Yes, I'm the devil, etc.

Devil is a man, in your face he'll grin . . . all he want you to do is just a
    little of sin
Yes, I'm the devil, etc.

Stay in all day, don't get out until dark . . . night is the time I get my
    business right, mmm
Yes, I'm the devil, etc.

Some say at twelve, some say at two . . . when you come to this place,
    I know just what to do
Yes, I'm the devil, etc.[68]

A black man in the South who "stay[s] in all day" and "do[es]n't get out
until dark" is, as Honeyboy Edwards makes clear, a man who has found a
way of evading the dawn-to-dusk field labor that is the foundation of the
plantation economy. (The Mississippi Sheiks were arguably Mississippi's
most popular recording artists as well as live act during the period, and
a significant part of their audience was implicated in that economy.) The
devil-identified lyric persona bodied forth here is a self-satisfied and highly
mobile Lothario who finds several different ways of saying that sex, not
love, is what he's after. Where Stovepipe Johnson expresses regret that he's
been stripped of parental role models to teach him "right from wrong,"
Vinson betrays no such regrets; in fact, he conceives of his lived world as a
hell over which he presides—he's a brawler as well as a lover, and all who
"come down" to visit him are going to "catch some hell."

Sylvester Weaver works this same vein of aggressive sexuality in "Can't
Be Trusted Blues" (1927). The song contrasts sharply with his "Devil Blues"
(1927), which evokes a nightmarish dreamscape "way down below" where
the singer is tortured with a pitchfork, chased by hellhounds, burned, and
surrounded by devils:

Devil had me cornered . . . stuck me with his old pitchfork
Devil had me cornered . . . stuck me with his old pitchfork
And he put me in an oven . . . thought he had me for roast pork

Hellhounds start to chasin' me . . . and I was a running fool
Hellhounds start to chasin' me . . . and I was a running fool
My ankles caught on fire . . . couldn't keep my puppies cool

A thousand devils with long tails and sharp horns, Lordy
Saw a thousand devils with tails and sharp horns
Everyone wandering, tried to step on my corns

For miles around me, heard men scream and yell, Lord
For miles around me, heard men scream and yell
Couldn't see a woman, I said, Lord, ain't this hell[69]

"Can't Be Trusted Blues," however, inverts that power relationship, representing the bluesman, in an incongruously sweet croon, as a ravenous and implacable devil-on-earth who incarnates the black beast rapist of southern myth:

I don't love nobody . . . that's my policy
I don't love nobody . . . that's my policy
I'll tell the world that . . . nobody can get along with me

I can't be trusted . . . can't be satisfied
I can't be trusted . . . can't be satisfied
The men all know it . . . and pin their women to their side

I will sure backbite you . . . gnaw you to the bone
I will sure backbite you . . . gnaw you to the bone
I don't mean maybe . . . I can't let women alone

Pull down your windows . . . and lock up all your doors
Pull down your windows . . . lock up all your doors
Got ways like the devil . . . papa's skating on all fours[70]

The devil summoned up by Weaver in his opposed pair of songs is Hamlet's king of infinite space: he's either a bad dream of white southern mob vengeance or the hypermobile black beast spawned by, and disciplined by, that threat. Spencer has argued that Weaver, like Sam Collins in "Devil in the Lion's Den" (1927), is playing the hypersexual devil in order to voice "a suppressed side of the human personality that is a part of the 'truth of our being,'" rather than offering himself as an incarnation of "unbounded, inexplicable evil," a mistaken claim Spencer attributes to Oliver and other blues scholars.[71] Both views miss a specific political subtext: the way black masculinity draws on the devil figure in an effort to remain unbounded by the prison-agricultural complex that would enclose it. Collins's song begins by evoking the singer's abandonment in almost exactly the same terms used by Stovepipe Johnson in "Devilish Blues": "Now my mama's dead and my . . . papa can't be found / I ain't got me nobody . . . throw my arms around." The trope of paternal disappearance, in a black southern blues context, is always double-edged: men disappeared, dropped out of sight, for many reasons, but as Blackmon's study and others make clear, the unlocatable black man was a figure haunted by the depredations of the convict lease system, vagrancy laws, and prison farms.

The devil, in short, was a figure of useable power for many black southern blues musicians: a rakish, voracious, dangerous, unpredictable, unconstrained exemplum of masculine potency. These qualities made the devil a particularly attractive role model in a Jim Crowed South intent on emasculating and immobilizing African American men. Yet precisely these same qualities—with the arguable exception of rakishness—could be and were associated with *white* southern masculinity to the extent that it manifested as the combined infringements of Jim Crow. As W. Marvin Dulaney has noted, white southern masculinity has historically been implicated in the region's police power; part of what it meant to be a southern white man, even as slave patrols gave way to post-Emancipation police forces and ad hoc vigilantism, was to be charged, explicitly or implicitly, with the power to regulate the movement and behavior of black men in public space.[72] A black southern bluesman who courted the devil's power, the devil's pleasure-centered freedom, could easily find himself in thrall to precisely what he sought to evade. A song like Johnny Copeland's "Devil's Hand" (1982) registers the black male subject's powerlessness in the face of a devil that signifies, for those with ears to hear, on the white world's multiple disruptions, even as—within a conventional black Christian framework—it indexes his own failure to regulate his appetites:

> I woke up early one morning . . . and saw the devil play his hand (2x)
> You know he wrecked my life . . . just like a hurricane
>
> When you're playing with the devil . . . don't you know you're playing
>   a losing hand
> When you're playing with the devil . . . you're playing a losing hand
> 'Cause cheating is all that devil understands
>
> Please Mr. Devil . . . go back where you belong (2x)
> Get out of my life and leave poor me alone
>
> I made one mistake, I . . . I thought the devil wouldn't drop by here
> But believe me when I tell y'all the devil is everywhere

I woke up early one morning and saw the devil play his hand
You know he wrecked my life . . . just like a hurricane

That doggone devil
That no-good devil
That lowdown devil
That dirty devil
That doggone devil . . . wrecked my life like a hurricane[73]

"Devil's Hand" frames the singer's losing struggle with the devil as the pained confession of a bested card player, somebody who once was blind to the full extent of the devil's destructive prowess but now sees the truth of his situation. The "hand" played by the devil is the singer's way of acknowledging the wrecked life that his own unnamed nocturnal behaviors—gambling? juking? whoring?—have bequeathed to him while simultaneously denying responsibility for that outcome by attributing all agency to his doggone, no-good, lowdown antagonist. Yet "Devil's Hand" resonates equally compellingly in the context of disciplinary violence, white-sponsored "trouble": the devil it petitions (in the second person) and castigates (in the third person) is a malign authority figure who wields economic power to the black subject's disadvantage, like a plantation boss who says, "Take it or leave it" to the sharecropper as he settles up after the harvest.

Copeland, born in 1937, was the son of sharecroppers in Haynesville, Louisiana, a thoroughly Jim Crowed town where one of his fellow natives, the Reverend Frederick Douglass Kirkpatrick [1933–86], found his own tenant family turned upside down after the death of his mother led the white landowner to confiscate his family's livestock and order them off the property by nightfall.[74] The words "cheating," "lying," and "deceiving" signify on a world of social relations organized around precisely this sort of race-based economic subjection, a "losing hand" that is, the black subject suddenly realizes, all he'll ever be dealt. This devil—the honorific "Mr." is one that Jim Crow required of any black man addressing a white man—is kin to the white record executive Sturdyvant in August Wilson's play *Ma Rainey's Black Bottom* (1984) who shamelessly toys with the black trumpeter, Levee, encouraging his hopes of becoming a well-remunerated song composer before dashing them at the play's conclusion, playing his hand to devastating effect. If the successful blues subject, in Houston A. Baker's formulation, transcends "the economics of slavery" in moments of "resonant, improvisational, expressive dignity," then "Devil's Hand," like Wilson's play, evokes the blues subject's total and humiliating comeuppance.[75]

A full sounding of "Devil's Hand," in other words, requires that we make a space for both of these readings—the devil inciting black misbehavior and the devil symbolizing white exploitation. The devil evoked here is "just" the devil, which is to say the biblical antagonist thundered against every Sunday within the sanctuary of the black church; but he is also more than that. Nor are we wrong to hear, in the intimacy of the singer's petition to the devil and scope of his claim *about* the devil, an echo of the spirituals updated in a way that acknowledges the uniquely pressured individualism of black life during the Jim Crow decades. The antebellum spirituals, as I noted earlier, offer a great deal of first-person testimony about encounters between an imperiled black soul and Satan, but in virtually all cases the singer is reporting that encounter after the fact, sharing his struggle—and his victory—with an imagined community of fellow Christians. "I met old satan in my way; / He say, young man, you too young to pray."[76] The direct lyric address *to* Satan is unusual in the antebellum period; Lovell's monumental study offers only two examples: "Go 'way, Satan, I don't mind you" and "Stand back, Satan, let me come by."[77] In "Devil's Hand," by contrast, the spirit of resistance has been replaced by desolation; the community of faith has been supplanted by an imputed juke-joint audience, but no amount of lamentation seems to release the singer from the devil's burdensome presence. "Please, Mr. Devil . . . go back where you belong / Get out of my life and leave poor me alone." Copeland personalizes his relationship with the devil in a way that resonates not only with other devil-blues ("Me and the Devil Blues," "The Devil Jumped the Black Man") but also with the blues tradition as a whole, filled as it is with apostrophes to "Mr. Blues," "blues," and other oppressors, including the all-purpose "baby." The grammar of the blues, sourced in slavery and evolving under Jim Crow, dictates that any of those apostrophes is, at any given moment, potentially a calling-out of white injustice—one intended for black communal consumption and protected by the veil of signifying but also one that stages a strikingly solitary and intimate encounter, offering us an oppressor whose breath is warm, so to speak, but whose true face remains elusive.

In an earlier study, *Seems Like Murder Here: Southern Violence and the Blues Tradition* (2002), I speculated that this lyric strain in the blues could be traced to the efflorescence of spectacle lynching in the South during the late nineteenth- and early twentieth-century moment when blues music was emerging as a form of black public address. Black male subjectivity, I argued, found in the drama of the blues encounter a way of reconciling the paradox posed by new and unprecedented mobility, on the one hand—the traveling musician's, laborer's, and vagrant's right to hit the highway or hop a train—and, on the other, the tightening network of disciplines represented by vagrancy laws, convict leasing, prison farms, and, most hauntingly, public lynching spectacles. The oppressive "Mr. Blues" of Little Brother Montgomery's "The First Time I Met You" (1936) seems to emerge simultaneously from everywhere and nowhere, a spectral shadow that suddenly materializes on the doorstep as an in-your-face, ever-present opponent:

> Now my blues got at me, Lord, and run me from tree to tree (2x)
> You should have heard me begging Mr. Blues, don't murder me
>
> Good morning, blues, what are you doing here so soon? (2x)
> You be's with me every morning, Lord, and every night and noon

This named, often apostrophized presence was, I argued, the black male subject's way of symbolizing the unreal but palpable threat of the mob, a monster of sorts that could emerge from the social field with little warning to wreak punishments worse than death.[78] "Devil's Hand" offers evidence for this thesis as the devil's oppressive reach parallels the blues': "I made one mistake, I . . . I thought the devil wouldn't drop by here / But believe me when I tell y'all the devil is everywhere." There is nothing notable, in and of itself, about an evocation of the devil as a crafty and omnipresent opportunist who pounces on his victim. But that tableau takes on new meaning in a social context where the devil is indisputably, if unevenly, associated with white maleficence and where blues musicians, specifically associated with criminalized vagrancy, seek language to communicate their sense of being corralled and besieged. "We was hemmed up," is how Texas bluesman Mance Lipscomb put it. "You could go around a block [right here in Chicago]," insisted guitarist Otis Rush, a migrant from Philadelphia, Mississippi, speaking of the Klan's long geographical and temporal reach, "and you'll run into one of them. . . . They everywhere, man! Look at what they just did to this man in Texas—drag a man behind a pickup truck until he's dead." Willie Dixon, another migrant Chicagoan, remembered of his own Mississippi childhood in the 1920s that "the Ku Kluxers marched by our house, dragging some black guy up to the school, tarrin' and featherin' and all that kind of stuff. You couldn't do nothing about these things. The black man had to be a complete coward."[79]

But of course cowardice was not the only available response. Migration north—removing oneself from the scene of the white devil's crime—was an alternative, as the life arcs of Montgomery, Rush, Dixon, and countless other southern-born, Chicago-bound bluesmen bear witness. Indicting, mocking, and otherwise signifying on the white devil, adapting religious vocabulary to the purposes of veiled critique, was a second strategy. The third strategy was swallowing the devil whole: routing cowardice by insisting, in one's aggressively outsized, "bad" lyric persona, that the devil is right *here*, and everywhere, in the person of the black bluesman.

Peetie Wheatstraw, the self-styled "Devil's Son-in-Law" and "High Sheriff from Hell," may have been the first and is certainly the best-known blues performer to have deployed the third strategy. What commentators have missed is the degree to which Wheatstraw's devilish persona is a trickster's signifying performance that mocks the white devil even as it leverages his power in the direction of black collective liberation. Born William Bunch in Ripley, Tennessee (1904), fifty miles northeast of Memphis, Wheatstraw— as he would later name himself—moved with his family to a farm near Cotton Plant, Arkansas, sometime before 1920. Cotton Plant was a small, black-majority community in the Arkansas Delta, seventy-five miles northeast of Little Rock; gospel performer Sister Rosetta Tharpe (1915–73) was born there, and jump blues bandleader Louis Jordan (1908–75) hailed from nearby Brinkley. As was the case with so many other blues performers of his generation, Wheatstraw's father was a disapproving religionist—a deacon in the local church who, after his son's death, reluctantly allowed him to be buried in the church cemetery, but only in an auxiliary section out front, near the road, and without a headstone.[80] On the face of it, Wheatstraw's outsized, devil-associated persona seems a familiar tale of filial rebellion against paternal authority backed by evangelical condemnation. "The use of the nickname 'Devil's Son-in-Law' by Bunch," as Steven C. Tracy suggests, "seems to be a conscious effort on his part to mock religious attitudes towards blues music."[81] But the story is more complex than that.

Cotton Plant, although Jim Crowed, seems to have enjoyed relatively benign race relations during Wheatstraw's youth and beyond. When the performer, now a famous recording star, would visit the area in later years, according to one informant, the white owner of the plantation in McClelland where he'd play piano and guitar late into the night "was lenient with blacks [and] tried to let us have a good time," and Wheatstraw would hold court for a large and racially mixed crowd.[82] East St. Louis, Illinois, where Wheatstraw settled in the late 1920s after hoboing through the South, was another matter entirely. "Not noted for its hospitality to its black residents," according to Garon, the river town adjacent to St. Louis, especially the

"Valley" district, was wide-open morally—a haven for pimps, prostitutes, gamblers, bootleggers, and blues singers—but remained scarred by the 1917 race riot in which whites burned, shot, and lynched between 40 and 150 blacks after blacks shot and killed two police officers in self-defense. Many believed that both the police and the National Guard had assisted the white rioters; the Chamber of Commerce had called on the police chief to resign. "The same racism that precipitated the riot continued to manifest itself at the trials which followed," according to Garon, "and judges, juries and prosecutors again discriminated against blacks outrageously."[83]

The long tail of the East St. Louis riot, an African American grievance with second-class citizenship lingering behind that city's thriving entertainment underworld, is the racial gradient within which William Bunch's self-reinvention as Peetie Wheatstraw becomes comprehensible. Like many in the Valley, Wheatstraw found himself at the mercy of aggressive white policing. "He got arrested plenty," remembered his contemporary, Henry Townsend, a St. Louis blues pianist. "Being a musician, how could you avoid it? They cooked up something on him regardless of what he was doing."[84] Wheatstraw took his revenge in songs such as "Drinking Man Blues" (1936), which tells the story of a rowdy, booze-stoked bender that culminates in a violent attack on a neighborhood cop and—just as outrageous—the usurpation of his powers: "It [booze] made me hit the policeman, and knock him off his feet / Taken his pistol and his star, oooh, well, well, and walking up and down his beat."[85] But in "C and A Train Blues" (1934), Wheatstraw had already referred to himself in a spoken aside by both of the monikers that became closely associated with him, and these, too, may be read as forms of infrapolitical resistance: "Boys, when you ain't seen your girl in a long time, please do like Peetie Wheatstraw, the Devil's Son-in-Law, the High Sheriff from Hell. I'm gonna see her before the sun rise again."[86] Garon has argued that "these designations gave Peetie a sense of power, opposition, and resistance and it gave his listeners a figure of great majesty with whom they could identify," and he goes on to insist that Wheatstraw's "alliance with the Devil . . . as a sign of Evil, couldn't help but conjure up a sympathetic feeling among those listeners who felt that as African Americans in a white world, they needed an *agent of opposition* to carry on through their lives."[87] Spencer, as I noted earlier, concurs on the general question of Wheatstraw's oppositional identity—"[his] life itself embodied the mythology of the badman"—but interprets the devil-associated identity, like the "bad" in badman, within an Afrocentric, nondualistic context, reading Wheatstraw as a good-bad, troublesome-liberating incarnation of Legba, the phallic god of the crossroads.[88] Both readings are valid but incomplete. I view Wheatstraw's self-renaming as roguish signifying on the prerogatives of white male policing and white male mastery more generally. To say, as Garon does and many have suggested, that Wheatstraw's pair of monikers shows him to be "in alliance with the devil" is to miss the joke being told at the white man's expense.[89]

If the white man is the devil, then the black man who publicly identifies himself as the devil's son-in-law is claiming that he has married—and had sexual congress with; fucked—the white man's daughter. Any such "alliance with the devil" is in fact a brazen form of mockery and thus an *undercutting* of the white devil. Like boxer Jack Johnson before him, and anticipating Big Bill Broonzy, Wheatstraw dramatized his "badness" by violating the taboo against black men consorting with white women, and he did so in a way that heightened the symbolism of the gesture, staging his rebellion for an underworld community that couldn't help but savor the richness of the joke. "Peetie Wheatstraw lived in the red-light district [of East St. Louis]," recounted Honeyboy Edwards. "He had a white old lady and a little white dog, too! He was a big shot down there, got dressed up every day and walked that dog down the street on a little chain."[90] He walked the dog, not the woman, but the pairing, Honeyboy's testimony suggests, is what registered in the memory of his peers.

East St. Louis, it must be remembered, was a community given its feeling and tone by the presence of many recent black male migrants (including Wheatstraw and Honeyboy) from Arkansas, Mississippi, and other Deep South locales where the white woman, encountered on the street, was a death-dealing phantasm to be navigated with exquisite deferential care. East St. Louis and its sister city across the river, scarred by the events of 1917, were borderlands: neither wholly Jim Crowed nor as socially progressive as the "promised land" of Chicago, these were urban locales where black resistance against white domination was a daily struggle, one prosecuted through the sorts of hidden transcripts described by anthropologist James C. Scott. In "The Infrapolitics of Subordinate Groups," Scott offers a table that indexes three forms of domination—material, status, and ideological—and two ways, overt ("public declared") and covert ("disguised, low profile, undisclosed"), in which subordinate people resist "practices of domination." Overt resistance against status domination takes the form of "public assertion of worth by gesture, dress, speech, and/or open desecration of status symbols of the dominant." Covert resistance offers a "hidden transcript of anger, aggression, and disguised discourses of dignity e.g., rituals of aggression, tales of revenge, use of carnival symbolism, gossip, rumor, creation of autonomous social space for assertion of dignity."[91] Wheatstraw's ritualized daily cock-of-the-walk promenade, which substitutes the little white bitch-dog on a chain for the (sexed up, possessed, desecrated) white woman at home and makes him the master of both, responds both overtly and covertly to the status domination effected by the police, evoked by Henry Townsend, and defined by Scott as "humiliation, disprivilege, insults, assaults on dignity." One has to imagine Wheatstraw's self-dramatizations in social context, staged for the daily consumption of recent black male migrants from points south and their East St. Louis peers, many of them intimately familiar with the violent protocols of white male mastery. Here comes the Devil's Son-in-Law! There goes a bad, bad man—the High Sheriff from Hell! Sometimes a little white dog on a chain is just a pet. Sometimes, in symbolic terms, it's the black man's revenge and the white man's worst nightmare.

Wheatstraw's recordings worked in tandem with this public ritual to shape the bluesman's persona as a devil-associated, white-devil-antagonizing badman; they created an autonomous social space for the assertion of dignity, offering a hidden transcript revolving around gossip and rumor in a way that alloyed the badman with the ever-mobile, shape-shifting trickster. All but three of Wheatstraw's 164 issued recordings, according to Tracy, are sub-credited "The Devil's Son-in-Law," two of those three are instead subcredited "High Sheriff from Hell," and the remaining side, titled "Devil's Son-in-Law" (1931), was the first time in which he actually referred to himself on record by that moniker:[92]

1 I wonder would you acknowledge mama . . . baby, now you made my
    life a wreck
  And now, well, would you, baby, mmm . . . mama now you made my
    life a wreck
  Mama now I'd rather have a rattlesnake, honey now, wrapped a-round
    my neck

  When you used to love me, now little mama, mama, go clear down to
    my toes
5 When you used to love me, baby . . . now it would go clear down to
    my toes
  Well-well, the other way that I love you, mama . . . honey now don't
    nobody know

Now I've got eleven women, ummm . . . and I got one little
    Indian squaw
I say I got eleven women . . . and I got one little Indian squaw
Well-well, now the next time you see me . . . I'm liable to be the
    devil's son-in-law

. . . .

10   Baby, you will never catch special deliveries, mama . . . honey, directed
        to my chest
    Tell you now you will never get . . . (special deliveries, mama) honey,
        directed to my chest)
    Now, when I leave you now, little mama . . . you will never see me back
        here again[93]

Wheatstraw represents himself in mythic terms that deliberately tweak
Christian sensibilities: he's a Dionysus (or Legba) of the jukes, a promiscuous love god whose dozen bragged-on lovers (l. 7) form a countercom-
munity of disciples to his scandalous not-Jesus. The prelude to his self-
invocation as the devil's son-in-law is his humorous imaging of romantic
disrepair (ll. 1–3); that fictive rattlesnake wrapped around his neck is both
a play on Eve's temptation in the Garden and—for Wheatstraw's black
southern audience—an edgy bit of joke-work signifying on lynching. The
song flows outward from the threatened immobilization and death imaged
in that third line toward the final line's escape, the trickster flying the coop
in the face of painful romantic "special deliveries" imaged as shotgun blasts
to the chest: "Now, when I leave you now, little mama . . . you will never
see me back here again." Baker has argued that the paradigmatic blues-
gesture is self-erasure: I been here and gone.[94] That dynamic registers not
just in the concluding line but also as a repeated oscillation between bold
proclamations and sly indeterminacy, both of which augment Wheatstraw's
mystique. "The other way that I love you, mama . . . honey, now don't
nobody know," for example, titillates even as it cloaks erotic trancing—a
love god's ministrations—in a veil of privacy. Again, in the third stanza,
Wheatstraw invokes his "eleven women" and "one little Indian squaw" only
to flirt coyly with the rumors that pursue him: "I'm liable to be the devil's
son-in-law." Undergirding his braggadocio and deepening the humor is the
implication-within-the-rumor that the devil with whom he claims kinship
by consummated marriage is the worldly white one rather than the Prince
of Darkness. He's got a pointedly diverse array of women clamoring to share
his bed, after all. Who is to say he's *not* sleeping with the devil's daughter?

And of course he was, in a sense. Infrapolitics proceeds by the lofting of such scandalous but disavowable innuendos.

If "Devil's Son-in-Law" represents Wheatstraw's first formal self-annunciation, then "Peetie Wheatstraw Stomp" and "Peetie Wheatstraw Stomp No. 2," both recorded at the same session in 1937, consolidate the lover/trickster/badman persona that had by then become his stock in trade. Both songs are marked by a good-timing, piano-driven buoyancy that contrasts markedly with the slower earlier recording. In the first of those latter recordings, music and lyrics work together to suggest that his Dionysian bad behavior makes everybody in his community feel good:

> Women all ravin' about Peetie Wheatstraw in this land
> Women all ravin' about Peetie Wheatstraw in this land
> He got so many women, they're goin' from hand to hand
>
> Don't tell all the girls what that Peetie Wheatstraw can do
> Woo-hoo-well, that Peetie Wheatstraw can do
> That will cause suspicion now and you know they will try him, too
>
> [spoken] Now play a little bit, boy, let's see how good it sounds
>
> If you wanna see the women an' men clown
> If you wanna see the women 'n men clown
> Just let that Peetie Wheatstraw come into your town
>
> I am Peetie Wheatstraw, the High Sheriff from Hell
> I am Peetie Wheatstraw, the High Sheriff from Hell
> The way I strut my stuff, woo-well now, you can never tell[95]

In James C. Scott's terms, these four verses offer an exemplary image of the bluesman as locus of overt and covert resistance against status domination. Wheatstraw invokes himself in all four verses but defers the "I" until the last verse, as though he has finally come to lay claim to the festive, pleasure-giving redeemer-god who bears his name. He reinforces his mystique by simultaneously thrusting himself forward—a fearless full possessor of public space—and playfully drawing back from full visibility in a way that suggests masculine power in reserve. "Don't tell all the girls what Peetie Wheatstraw can do," he crows, and later, "The way I strut my stuff, woo-well now, you can never tell." Here is public assertion of worth by gesture, dress, speech—he's strutting his stuff and singing about it—along with a brazen appropriation (if not quite desecration) of a key status symbol of the dominant: the white beat-cop's right to swagger through the neighborhood.

Here too is a hidden transcript that deploys gossip and rumor to reframe black collective life—and perhaps a curious white girl or two—as a carnival of on- and offstage delights.

Wheatstraw sounds essentially the same notes in "Peetie Wheatstraw Stomp No. 2," beginning with a bold inscription of the scandalous nickname that rhymes with his stage name and concluding with playful repartee that gives his recording the feel of a neighborhood beer joint:

> Everybody hollering, Here come that Peetie Wheatstraw
> Everybody hollering, Here come that Peetie Wheatstraw
> I'm better known by the Devil's Son-in-Law
>
> Everybody wanna know what that Peetie Wheatstraw do
> Ooo-hoo well, what that Peetie Wheatstraw do
> But every time you hear him, he comin' out with something new
>
> [spoken during piano solo] Show 'em what Peetie Wheatstraw do, boy
>
> He makes some happy, some he make cry
> Whooo, makes some happy, some now he make cry
> Well now he made one old lady go hang herself and die
>
> This is Peetie Wheatstraw, I'm always in [*sic*] the line
> This is Peetie Wheatstraw, then again I'm always on the line
> Save up your nickels and dimes, you can come up and see me some time.
>
> [spoken] Play it a little bit, boy
>
> [spoken] Now good folks, I said, and the girls especially, save your nickels and dimes, you can come up and see me some time.[96]

The trickster is ascendant, and the lover is close behind: here is Spencer's Wheatstraw-as-Legba, instigator and master of the revels, neither wholly good nor wholly bad but instead a force of constructive disorder; an "up-setter," in the vernacular. The "something new" he repeatedly "com[es] out with" is a figure for innovative songwriting and musicianship, but it reso-nates more broadly as a kind of endless self-reinvention that, compelling "everybody[s]" attention, might be heard as a hero's prod to black collective renewal in the face of practices of domination that corrode self-respect and diminish morale. There is harsh laughter indeed in Wheatstraw's claim, distanced by the third-person address, that "he made one old lady hang herself and die"; this is the sort of claim—the fruits of fornication, unrepen-tantly celebrated—that led black Christians to demonize blues performers as "lowdown," but it also shows us the power of the blues, as attitude and ethos, to transform despair-inducing materials—crying and dying—into thigh-slapping release. Profit, too: the "nickels and dimes" that he hopes to earn from his adoring public, especially the women, suggest an accessible love-god willing to trade companionship for cash.

THE POWER

In our own post–civil rights, post–Black Power moment, where the former U.S. president is the product of an interracial marriage and southern police forces are largely integrated, the sort of covert signifying strategies employed by Wheatstraw, Broonzy, and other black male blues performers to tweak the tail of the white devil rarely materialize as such. Plausible deniability is no longer required as a guarantor of personal safety. "When I was coming up on the plantations around here," Willie King, a Mississippi bluesman, told a journalist after the release of his unusually frank 2002 recording, "Terrorized,"

> we were terrorized. We were hung for nothing, whipped for nothing, worked hard for nothing, and we still wound up at the end of the year with no money. But back then the people were so oppressed that they couldn't come out and say it was the bossman who created all these problems. . . . As my granddaddy used to say, "If you don't call no names, you won't get the blame." So instead of calling the bossman's name, the blues singers called the woman's name. But the time has come to be straightforward and come right out and say it. After the Civil Rights movement, they stopped lynching and whipping us, so you can say whatever's on your mind. They might not like it, but they can't hang you for it.[97]

If the South, for all its vaunted changes, remains considerably less than a postracial utopia, then the tentacles of the carceral network remain of pressing concern. Clyde Woods, Angela Y. Davis, Houston A. Baker Jr., and Michelle Alexander have argued for an essential continuity between the ancien régime described by Honeyboy Edwards—where capricious and draconian vagrancy laws allowed white southern lawmen to "get themselves another set" of unrecompensed field hands for the county farm—and the prison-industrial complex of the present day. It might also be argued, in line with John Egerton's southernization-of-America thesis, that black frustration with what is felt to be unfair, violent, and excessive policing driven by a racial differential is more likely to surface these days in Ferguson, Missouri, or in Brooklyn than in the Mississippi Delta—and, when given musical form, is likely to dispense with veiled signification in favor of blunt talk, as in NWA's "Fuck tha Police" (1988).[98] It is tempting in retrospect to take LeRoi Jones's Clay, the soft-spoken but agitated and finally rage-filled young black poet of *Dutchman* (1964), as the guardian of the threshold that distinguishes the signifying-on-the-white-devil blues of yore from black music's later insistence on calling out the white devil by name. "If Bessie Smith had killed some white people," he tells Lula, his white female antagonist who goads him by trivializing blues as "belly rubbing music," "she wouldn't have needed that music. She could have talked very straight and plain about the world. No metaphors."[99] The devil—in this one specific form, as the coded way sublimated aggression conjures with white disciplinary power—is a metaphor whose time has passed, at least in the blues tradition.[100]

Two recent recordings from the contemporary period reveal continuities with that earlier tradition even as they suggest just how much has changed. Chris Thomas King is a younger blues performer from Baton Rouge, Louisiana; his father, Tabby Thomas (1929–2014), was an Excello recording artist during the 1960s and ran a local juke joint for many years in which his son was exposed to the full range of Deep South blues as well as national touring acts. In 2000, King played Delta bluesman Tommy Johnson in the feature film *O Brother, Where Art Thou?* The following year, King released a pioneering album of blues/rap hybrids titled *21st Century Blues . . . from da Hood* (2001). In "Mississippi KKKrossroads," King revisits the most resonant location in blues mythology and encounters not Legba but the white devil of southern (in)justice, a figure of unalloyed evil:

It's like this y'all . . .

Went down to the kkkrossroads but all I found was a tree and a dusty road
I was looking for the devil; I put down my shovel, I started thinking on a
    higher level
He appeared as the county sheriff with his good ole boys hellhounds and
    a bailiff
He was a big porky pig he said you better make it good boy it's gonna be
    your last gig.
He asked for my name with his light in my face I said my alias is
    Jesse James
Some call me the backdoor man, men don't know but women understand

You wanna buck with me I'm from the danger zone
Bad to the bone, well let's get it on

Mississippi God damn, God damn Mississippi . . .
Mississippi God damn, God damn Mississippi . . .

He said fellas like me make for good decorations on his Christmas tree
He keep heads in a trophy case
That's when I started running hellhounds they began to chase me
Into a barn trapped like a rat on Mr. Charlie's farm
So I jumped out the window and I locked the door
I bet them motherfuckers won't howl no mo'
I set it up in flames then I heard them good ole boys scream my name
They wanted me dead but my name ain't Fred 'cause I always pack
     my lead

You wanna buck with me I'm from the danger zone, etc.

They had me on the run still I managed to drop 'em one by one
A new clip in the chamber I was wounded, tired, and filled with anger
Somebody's in danger I'm gonna teach that pig how to treat a stranger
The big showdown me and the devil, no one else around
He had it comin' so I called him out
But you know he started runnin'
But he was just too slow
I popped three in his back and another just below

You wanna buck with me I'm from the danger zone, etc.[101]

King's rap is an epic reassembly, in Keith Cartwright's terms: a restaging of the primal southern scene of discipline—a lone black man on the run; a sheriff, a white posse, and hounds in pursuit—that tells its story by sampling a wide range of black aesthetic investments drawn from blues (Howlin' Wolf, Robert Johnson, John Lee Hooker), soul (Nina Simone, Marvin Gaye), rock (George Thorogood's appropriation of black vernacular), gangsta rap, and gangsta rap's occulted origins in Western braggadocio and gunplay.[102] King's brag exemplifies a central argument of this chapter: the challenge posed by the devil of white discipline is what provokes the singer to declare himself not just a badman but a trickster lover par excellence, an incorrigible "backdoor man." The narrative courts and rejects the hellish dreamscape of black abjection imaged in Sylvester Weaver's "Devil Blues" as the fleeing singer traps and incinerates the hellhounds, picks off the posse members one by one, and soon finds himself alone with the devil. As the "big show-down" transpires, King inverts the contest imaged in Lightnin' Hopkins's

"The Devil Jumped the Black Man," shooting the fleeing devil from behind rather than outrunning him from the front. What "Mississippi KKKrossroads" offers us, finally, is an image of black blues masculinity defining itself, through improvisational dexterity in the face of the carceral network, as *that which refuses to be spatially contained*. The segregated South was the danger zone in which blues masculinity was forged; the slave South was its prehistory. The devil—white, black—presides over and emerges from that pressured southern space.

In "I Got the Power" (1996), New York City blues performer Guy Davis stages a very different but equally resonant encounter with the devil, one that conjures with familiar crossroads poetics to reconstruct the badman/trickster/lover pose. Rather than an emblem of evil whiteness, as in King's rap, the devil evoked by Davis is a conventional Faustian tempter who offers the singer a range of worldly and otherworldly powers. The transaction itself is elided, so that it seems less like a soul-sale than an effortless transmission, a passing-of-the-torch without any downside risk except one: its inability to grant the singer the love of the one woman he craves:

I went to the devil, you know the devil said to me
I'll give you more power than you ever thought could be
I'll give you the power to make gold out of lead
I'll give you the power to raise up from the dead
I got the power
I got the power
But it don't mean nothing, baby, honey if I don't have you.

When you have the power to make you a man amongst men
Why make love to one woman when you can make love to ten
I can go out in the desert, make diamonds out of sand
I can call down the thunder with a wave of my hand
'Cause I got the power, etc.
But it don't mean nothing, not one little thing, baby if I don't have you

I can go to the city, buy up everything I see
Got politicians in my pocket, kings and presidents know about me
I can drink a river of poison, be feeling just fine
I can wrestle with the angels and kick the devil's behind
I got the power, etc.
But it don't mean one little thing, baby, if I ain't got you.[103]

Davis's singer effortlessly assumes the devil's powers and—channeling Stagolee—brags of his ability to kick's the devil's behind. The familiar Deep South revenge-against-whiteness motif lingers behind this plot point, but faintly; it's no more than a whisper of ancient history. (Davis is the son of actor Ossie Davis, a native of rural Georgia whose father, a railroad engineer, was threatened with death by the Ku Klux Klan but laughed it off.)[104] The shadow of Jim Crow is palpable in the architecture of the singer's will-to-power: a hunger for achieved masculinity, the ability to attract and pleasure multiple women, money enough to fulfill every desire (in part by literally *making money* in the form of diamonds), but, above all, and underlying those compensatory fantasies, a seemingly unlimited freedom of action in public space. Davy Crockett and the Western tall-tale tradition, mediated through Bo Diddley ("I walked forty-seven miles of barbed wire, I use a cobra snake for a necktie"), are one source for this material, but of course Diddley himself was a black refugee from segregated Mississippi whose masculinist fantasies—here, a transfiguration of the lynching noose—bespoke his time in the danger zone.

Davis's song is a response to the call leveled by Big Bill Broonzy in "Hell Ain't but a Mile and a Quarter." That earlier song was a cagey, veiled, evocation of the singer's imagined incursion into white-patrolled Deep South space—and a profoundly insubordinate one, ending with his supplanting of the devil as hell's ruler and a marriage to the devil's daughter in which he puts her "up on a shelf," trivializing her as he pretends to ennoble her. The fantasy compensates for the subject's disempowerment, the narrowness and low status of the social "place" to which Jim Crow's hell consigns him. Davis's singer, by contrast, is fully empowered on all fronts. He's the king of infinite space, an unbounded epic hero. That dream achieved, he yearns not for the devil's daughter—she's neither imaged nor desired here—but for the one woman who will delight and complete him. Having taken on the full panoply of devil's powers, he's now prepared *not* to play the devil but simply to become the man he is: wise and self-governed, rather than ungovernable, "crazy," dangerous, unpredictable. He's ready to settle down.

With achieved freedom comes responsibility. But that is a very late development in the blues. For most of its history, blues song has been an arena in which freedom—especially the radical sexual freedom of the footloose or errant lover—has engendered pain and confusion. The figure of the devil mediates that dialogue, too.

4, THE DEVIL'S GONNA GET YOU

Blues Romance and the Paradoxes of Black Freedom

My gal made me a devil, just as cruel as I can be
Now my gal made me a devil, just as cruel as I can be
Lord I let her run around . . . and then she made a
    chump of me

—ROBERT PEEPLES, "Wicked Devil's Blues" (1929)

THERE'S THE DEVIL

In *Blues Legacies and Black Feminism* (1998), a groundbreaking study of women's blues, Angela Y. Davis justifies the music's frank preoccupation with sexual love—desired and desiring bodies and souls—by reading it as a register of the transformed experiential horizons enjoyed by African Americans in the post-Emancipation period. Although the former slaves' economic status was only slightly less dismal than before, she argues, the "status of their personal relationships," which is to say their romantic relationships, was revolutionized:

> For the first time in the history of the African presence in North
> America, masses of black women and men were in a position to make
> autonomous decisions regarding the sexual partnerships into which they
> entered. Sexuality thus was one of the most tangible domains in which
> emancipation was acted upon and through which its meanings were
> expressed. Sovereignty in sexual matters marked an important divide
> between life during slavery and life after emancipation.[1]

To be a slave was to be chattel property, bound by law and by customary practice to the whims of a master and/or slave trader: bound spatially to the plantation, the coffle, the slave pen; bound to submit sexually to the master's (or trader's) advances or to the master's edicts about which other slaves one should breed with. Sexual violence against slave women was, as Saidiya Hartman notes, airbrushed out of juridical existence, and thus implicitly endorsed, "by virtue of the law's calculation of negligible injury" to the black female slave in question.[2] Although white men, especially employers of black female domestics, continued to assert their right of unfettered sexual access after Emancipation—which is why concerned black parents sought to keep their daughters out of domestic service—Davis's central claim is sound. To grow up in the post-Reconstruction South, the freeborn child or grandchild of slaves, was to possess a significantly broadened, if unevenly distributed, freedom of choice over whom one slept with, cohabited with, and per-chance married. Blues song vividly registers this hard-won sovereignty. Precisely because the working-class creators and consumers of the blues were relatively impoverished and had few worldly possessions, the bod-ies that individual sexual subjects *did* possess took on a range of new and exciting meanings in a self-determined sexual economy where one could sell it, trade it, shake it, make somebody go wild about it, take it down the block, give it away. New freedoms in the matter of sexual partner-selection were abetted, as Davis notes, by a second significant transformation, the removal of restrictions on "free individual travel," and this new freedom, too, registers in the blues as a familiar set of restless motifs: I'm going (to New York, Chicago, Louisiana), baby take a walk with me, don't you wanna go, been there and gone. "In both male and female blues," Davis argues, "travel and sexuality are ubiquitous themes, handled both separately and together. But what finally is most striking," she reiterates, "is the way blues registered sexuality as a tangible expression of freedom."[3]

This is all true. But the opposite is also true, at least where sexuality is concerned. What is finally most striking about blues song is the way it regis-ters sexuality as *unfreedom*—or more precisely, as an unstable, antagonistic relationship between two freely choosing sexual subjects, a zero-sum game in which one or the other participants, often as not, ends up in thrall to insatiable desire, murderous jealousy, an aching sense of loss, or ontologi-cal confusion about the maddeningly fickle "devil or angel" who has cast the singer into a hell on earth. "It ain't very many blues that ain't made up about a woman," insisted Delta bluesman James "Son" Thomas, and although some of those blues were cock-of-the-walk brags or adulatory odes to a particular woman's attractions, most were testimonials to men in pain.[4] "What you love best is what can hurt you the most" is how pianist Henry Townsend put it, and his female peers agree.[5] Davis has argued that in "preach[ing] about sexual love," blueswomen such as Ma Rainey and Bes-sie Smith "[gave] voice to the most powerful evidence there was for many black people that slavery no longer existed," but the truth was that blues song often preached about sexual love as a form of slavery.[6] When things were going well, to be sure, sexual slavery could be an impossibly hot and delicious form of submission to carnal knowledge—as in Smith's "You've Got to Give Me Some" (1929), composed by Spencer Williams, where "meat" is playfully invoked as a focus of near-desperate sexual hunger:

Lovin' is the thing I crave,
For your love I'd be your slave,
You gotta gimme some,
Yes, gimme some!
Can't you hear me pleading?
You gotta gimme some!

Said Miss Jones to old butcher Pete,
"I wanna piece o' your good old meat!
You gotta gimme some,
Oh, gimme some!
I crave your round steak,
You gotta gimme some!"
. . . .

Hear me cryin' on my bended knees;
If you wanna put my soul at ease
You gotta gimme some,
Please gimme some!
Can't stand it any longer,
You gotta gimme some[7]

As a bracingly frank discourse of desire proclaiming its "rootedness in an ethos of eros,"[8] blues lyricism and the performers who deployed it incurred the wrath of religious folk who viewed such sex-talk not just as idolatry—the mutable, knelt-to beloved, in Smith's case, substituted for the immortal Cross as a source of soul-solace—but also as a full frontal assault on respectability. Blues is the devil's music, in this respect, because the devil is the avatar of ungovernable sexuality, an evil spirit that incites private heartbreak and public mayhem. The devil is Eve's tempter in the Garden, and she, incarnating him, is man's downfall, the Devil Woman.[9] From the bluesman's perspective, dwelling in shocked disbelief at the visceral reality of sexual abandonment, the devil is the "must have been" that "changed [his] baby's mind" and made her "take up" with some other "so and so." Yet, syncretized with Legba and transmuted into a crossroads

guide, a Deep South spirit of place, the devil is also the phallic impetuous-
ness of that same rambling bluesman, a quality that enrages some women
(and men) and drives other women wild. When Delta bluesman Son House
was visited late in life in his Rochester, New York, home by two young white
blues musicians, Brian Williams and John Mooney, he startled them with
a confession about the devil and his own sexuality. "He would talk about
the devil," Williams reported, "and when he would say that, he would point
down, he would point at his genitals. And he would say 'There's the devil.'
Almost as though to suggest that in his younger days when he—I don't
know that this is the case—but if he was unfaithful to his wife, or having
affairs, or maybe just out womanizing, that that was part of the devil. It
wasn't him doing that. It was the devil that was occupying him. And it was
interesting that whenever he talked about it, he would point to his penis.
And sometimes he would even touch himself there."[10] The devil made
me do it! If the bluesman's penis is the devil—disruptive, chaos-sowing,
a disavowed Tempter preying on the will—then the question of who has
sovereignty in sexual matters on the post-Emancipation landscape is far
more vexed than Davis's formulation suggests.

The devil figure, in truth, has proven to be extraordinarily useful for
blues singers striving to articulate what Hartman terms "the contradictions and antagonisms of freedom" in the sphere of sexual love.[11] If you
and I are both free to travel as we see fit, encounter and woo one another
as self-possessed sexual subjects, and couple to our mutual delight, that is
indeed a fortunate development, one that lifts us above the condition of
our slave-born parents and grandparents. But if, having coupled, one of
us chooses to extend his or her freedom beyond the bed we've been sharing—our freedom to travel, our freedom to encounter, woo, and couple with
other self-possessed sexual subjects—then contradictions and antagonisms
besiege us. The devil figure helps blues people make sense of this train
wreck of frustrated desires, shattered idealizations, and devouring possessive investments. At once behavioral exemplar, scapegoat, and agent of
vengeance, the devil mediates the heartbreak—"the burdened individuality
of freedom," in another of Hartman's resonant phrases—and helps blues
singers enlarge their soul burdens into epic disappointments that can be
shared with the world.

On this point, Hartman's *Scenes of Subjection: Slavery, Terror, and Self-
Making in Nineteenth-Century America* can offer us deeper insight into the
problematics of post-Emancipation black life, not to mention a needed
corrective to the overly sanguine view of sexual sovereignty offered by

Davis. Rather than seeing Emancipation as a watershed moment, Hartman asks us to attend to the way white planter power quickly reconfigured itself "through contractual and extralegal means"—labor contracts, lynching, vagrancy laws, convict leasing, behavioral manuals addressed to black laborers, all later consolidating themselves into a sharecropping regime—and how this of necessity resulted in "the paradox of emancipation," one that involved "the coupling of coercion and contract, liberty and necessity, equality and subjection."[12] Hartman is speaking in Foucauldian terms about the interlinking of socioeconomic life (especially productive relations) and individual psychology: newly "free" black laboring subjects who found their mental horizons unexpectedly pressured by external and internalized coercions:

> Emancipation announced the end of chattel slavery; however, it by no means marked the end of bondage. The free(d) individual was nothing if not burdened, responsible, and obligated. Responsibility entailed accounting for one's actions, dutiful suppliance, contractual obligation, and calculated reciprocity. Fundamentally, to be responsible was to be blameworthy. In this respect, the exercise of free will, quite literally, was inextricable from guilty infractions, criminal misdeeds, punishable transgressions, and an elaborate micropenality of everyday life.[13]

Hartman is speaking about white/black relationships in the post-Emancipation South, an entirely unequal partnership in which whites impose all the burdens, obligations, and responsibilities while blacks are adjudged—by whites but also by their own consciences—to have committed all the infractions, misdeeds, and transgressions. But her words offer a rich and suggestive gloss on the blues lyric tradition when the subject at hand is the dance of freedom and responsibility within male-female relationships and the vagaries of sexual passion that animate the dance.

"To be responsible was to be blameworthy": here, distilled, is the paradox of black freedom that undergirds blues romance and enables an imaginative space within which the devil performs his work. When love relationships fail and the white slavemaster is no longer pulling the strings, who or what is to blame? Blues people, according to Spencer, fall into the "somewhat religious" category—neither thoroughgoing church members (although often socialized in the church as children) nor nonbelievers, they had imbibed black Christianity's familiar stock of devil-lore and the devil remained for many the reflex explanatory mechanism when bad shit, so to speak, went down.[14]

The devil was the go-to icon for black folk struggling with the paradoxes of freedom and unable or disinclined to psychologize themselves or their romantic antagonists. In Hartman's terms, the blues-devil became a way of explaining and pronouncing guilt, punishing misdeeds and transgressions, and inflicting a range of penalties on lovers and competitors. Slave-era law may have declared "negligible injury" when slave women were raped by white men, but the voice of the emancipated blueswoman spoke forcefully against the emotional wounds inflicted by her no-good black man, and the devil played a crucial enunciatory role in that condemnation—as the devil played a key role in her man's condemnation of her. Nothing marks the passage from slavery to freedom more decisively, in fact, than the way the blues-devil surges into view at the intersection of sexual romance and black popular music during the 1920s and 1930s: a discourse at once parallel to and wholly at odds with the God-and-Jesus-centered conversation within black evangelical circles during the same period, and unprecedented within the chaste precincts of antebellum black religious song. Yet as Hartman's gloss suggests, the theme of black subjectivity struggling mightily for freedom against the imprisoning bonds of coercion remained in place.

IF I WAS THE DEVIL

The prelude to the blues-devil's lyric emergence as a mediating figure in failed or problematic black romantic pairings is the role played by white slave owners in controlling the circumstances under which such pairings took shape in the decades preceding Emancipation. White ministers also played a coercive role, one that made the devil's residence part of the conversation. The Christianization of the slave community, according to John Blassingame, "brought ambivalence toward sex to the [slave] quarters" on nineteenth-century plantations, in part because ministers preached ardently "against the continuation of the African tradition of polygamy":

> They called upon the slaves to adopt Christian monogamy and to cleave to one mate throughout their lives. [The slaves also] learned they should avoid "impure thoughts," "lewd and filthy words," that fornication was "a great sin," a disgrace, "a sin against God," leading to "falsehoods, and jealousies, and murders, and loss of health." God would punish adulterers in "everlasting Hell" or, like the people of Sodom and Gomorrah, destroy them. . . . Christian slaves often taught their children . . . that "shame" and premarital sex were the same.[15]

Even as white slave owners routinely forced their black female slaves to violate this creed as they (or their sons) preyed sexually on them, the closing of the transatlantic slave trade gave such men a material incentive to encourage stable, child-generating pairings between their male and female slaves, and they exercised immense—although not always determinative—control over slave marriages. Not only did the masters of most slaves have the final say about whom those slaves married, but the majority of slaveholders, according to Blassingame, "feeling that the children their male slaves had by women belonging to other planters was so much seed spewed on the ground, insisted that they marry [slave] women on their own estates."[16] Yet there were limits to this total control—a margin of romantic self-determination that slaves were sometimes able to exercise in the face of white coercive power. In *'Til Death or Distance Do Us Part: Love and Marriage in African America* (2010), historian Frances Smith Foster notes that "unless they lived on a large plantation, married [slave] couples were most likely not to live together" but instead to work on nearby plantations and spend Saturday evening and Sunday together in one of the two locations—a practice that the slaves termed "abroad marriages." Husbands were more likely than their wives to be the traveling partner in such marriages, in part because of the danger of sexual violation slavewomen risked when traveling alone but also because male slaves were sometimes granted the right to seek work at locations far removed from their home plantation.[17]

If we fast-forward from the antebellum plantation to the Deep South of the 1920s and 1930s, we can discern the afterimage of slavery's social practices and attitudes within the new domestic freedoms enabled by Emancipation. Freed to travel in the immediate aftermath of the war, many ex-slaves took the opportunity to track down long-lost spouses and families and to reconfigure "abroad marriages" under one roof. Marriage remained not merely a priority but the norm, as Herbert Gutman reminds us, for the typical black family between 1880 and 1925, whether middle class or working class, southern or northern.[18] African American religion upheld this ideal—the long tail of antebellum white evangelicalism—as did a black elite preaching economic uplift and a clubwomen's movement preaching respectability. But the particulars of class location made a difference, as sociologist Charles S. Johnson notes in *Growing Up in the Black Belt: Negro Youth in the Rural South* (1941). The "people who create the 'blues' and the secular songs of the demimonde," he explains, are sited in "the underworld," the bottommost of four lower classes—he terms these the "upper-lower class," the "lower-lower class," and the "folk Negro"—that sit in turn below a small middle class and a tiny upper class:

> The "underworld" is a group which does not, perhaps, constitute a class, but which nevertheless is a social category. It is composed of individuals who fall outside the recognized and socially sanctioned class categories, that is, those persons who are free from the demands of society—the "wide" people, the vagabonds, the "worthless" and "undeserving poor" who are satisfied with their status, the "outcasts," the "bad niggers," prostitutes, gamblers, outlaws, renegades, and "free" people. Life in this underworld is hard, but its irresponsible freedom seems to compensate for its disadvantages.[19]

Johnson's repeated use of the word "free" is striking here. It dovetails with Davis's foundational claim that the freedom to travel and the freedom to choose one's sexual partners, ever-present twin themes of the blues, are the ways black folk (especially those lower on the ladder) decisively marked, lived, *knew* their freedom in the post-Emancipation decades. This underworld, the world of the blues, stands furthest from the behavioral and attitudinal protocols of the black church and the uplift-oriented middle class, even as many of its members, as Spencer reminds us, retain a biblical frame of reference that inflects their categories of judgment. The phrase "irresponsible freedom" suggests, among other things, a thoroughgoing promiscuity free from localized subcultural condemnation, but of course there *were* consequences for such behavior, and those consequences—enacted sexual freedoms wreaking psychological havoc and worse—are the very stuff of the blues. They are where the devil enters, in fact. Or at least that is how some blues singers represented the situation, if not always when describing their own behavior.

"I run up on a woman everywhere I'd go," Honeyboy Edwards remembered of his life as a traveling musician. "If you could play guitar and harp, you could have any woman you wanted. . . . Women would come to where you're playing at, even with their husbands with them, and flirt with the musicians. Well, no man likes that. . . . He'll kill you about her. He'd rather be dead than lose her."[20] Spencer has argued that Legba is the emulative model for this sort of rambling, promiscuous bluesman, and although that Dahomean deity's name would not have been known to the black southern masses of the time—or indeed to almost any American, white or black, outside the precincts of academic anthropology and comparative religion—his shadow hovers behind the troublemaking figure at the heart of Bumble Bee Slim's "Busy Devil" (1934):

The devil's so bad . . . he rambles all the time (2x)
That's why so many women . . . keep the devil in their mind

Now here's one thing . . . the devil always do (2x)
He will get in your home . . . and break it up for you

Once I had a woman . . . she was so nice and kind (2x)
But she give me trouble . . . when that man got in her mind

He ain't no stranger . . . but I can't see his face (2x)
All I know . . . I lost a husband's place

That busy devil . . . is a dangerous man (2x)
Wherever my woman was . . . he made her understand[21]

In the preceding chapter I argued that the rambling bluesman's capriciousness, his refusal to be pinned down in space and time—to a plantation, a boss, a woman—was, to a significant degree, an adaptive response to the economic and disciplinary pressures of Jim Crow. Such men, imaged lyrically, turn the phallic insubordination of Legba to infrapolitical purposes; they become uncontainable tricksters, all-night-long "upsetters" of routinized and exploitative dawn-to-dusk southern agricultural life. In his study of African trickster gods, Robert Pelton notes of Esu and Legba that "[both figures] emphasize a pursuit of intercourse so relentless that it shatters every worn-out pattern to enlarge the space of human life. Both, therefore, are troublemakers, disturbers of the peace and disrupters of harmony."[22] When "harmony" and "peace" are merely code words for a southern way of life in which a minority white plantation elite works the levers of power to keep a black majority labor force terrorized, immobilized, disfranchised, and profit-producing, a figure who disturbs, disrupts, and shatters this pattern is surely a good thing. Or is he? "Busy Devil" suggests that African American society pays a price for harboring such underworld characters, swaggering lover-badmen of the Stagolee variety, a notion corroborated by the murderous possessiveness Edwards attributes to jealous husbands. The "busy devil" of the song might as well be Bumble Bee Slim himself, a Georgia-born, Chicago-honed blues performer whose stage name suggests both wide-ranging mobility and phallic proficiency: I'll fly in out of nowhere and sting you, ladies. His lyric complaint, voiced from the perspective of a cuckolded husband, is thus richly ironic, defending the sanctity of home and marriage even as it configures the bluesman-devil as an irresistible focus of attention for the women of the community.

In "If I Was the Devil" (1939), Leroy's Buddy (Bill Gaither) celebrates himself—albeit in fantasy—as a harsher version of Bumble Bee Slim's up-setter, a ladies man from hell for whom sovereignty in sexual matters is a license to do cold-hearted evil:

> If I was the devil . . . then I would have everything going my way (2x)
> The way I would torment these women, I'd keep them weary both night
>   and day
>
> You talk about trouble, I would really be trouble king (2x)
> I'd be a lowdown dirty mistreater, a peace-breaker and most everything
>
> If I saw that you was happy, I would have to do you a dirty deal (2x)
> Get your mind all upset, then ask you mama how do you feel
>
> I would send you to the river, make you jump overboard and drown
> If I'd send you to the river, make you jump overboard and drown
> And I would stand right on the banks and watch your little body go
>   floating down
>
> So I was the devil, it would be a low-down dirty sin (2x)
> You couldn't have no more good times, and there would be trouble
>   until the end[23]

The imagined devil figure here confers on the black male blues singer a trickster's freedom of action, an unlimited field of opportunity ("everything going my way") for the wreaking of romantic havoc—first on the women of the world ("these women") and then, in the last three stanzas, on one particular unfortunate. Yet here, and strikingly, the devilish bluesman has also invested himself with the overweening power of the white slavemaster and his post-Emancipation successors: he's the "trouble king" who rules the roost, calls the shots, makes and breaks the rules, and, most important, uses that power to inflict his will on the (black) women within his purview. He's the Boss. This devil figure's ability to wreak havoc on black intimate rela-tionships, in other words, is haunted by something that brought continuing anguish to the black men who sang and listened to such songs: the power of white men to claim black women sexually—including married black women—and to prevent black men from retaliating or responding with similar incursions across the color line. (In "Busy Devil," white malevolence is similarly signified on by the devil who "will get in your home . . . and break it up for you.") "That's how it was down south," Honeyboy Edwards remembered of his life in Depression-era Mississippi. "If I'm a black man and a white man is going with my wife, I couldn't do nothing about it. And if I look at his wife, he'd want to hang me." [24] But bluesmen could sing songs in which they revenged themselves on the white man, in symbolic terms, by reconfiguring his imperial possession-taking powers as their own. That uneasy dynamic is simmering under the surface of "If I Was the Devil," even as the song's overt malevolence is focused entirely on the black women who are being (re)possessed by the devilish black trickster/lover.

In *After Freedom: A Cultural Study in the Deep South* (1939), centered on the Delta town of Indianola, sociologist Hortense Powdermaker discovered that the "freest," most promiscuous lower-class black men, paradoxically, were least inclined to allow their wives and lovers that same freedom. "The men who 'run around' most with other women," Powdermaker discovered, "are often the ones most quick to punish such lapses on the part of their wives by beating or shooting." [25] This black masculine rage was driven, in part by a dismaying continuity between slavery and Jim Crow: the fact that many white men in Indianola took black women as lovers, in situations ranging from domestic rape to the full consent of the black beloved, while black men, like their enslaved forebears, stood by powerless to intervene or reciprocate. Powdermaker's analysis aptly sums up the paradox explored in this chapter: the thoroughly compromised—indeed, tortured—nature of "sovereignty in sexual matters":

> The Negro takes his wife and mistress from his own race and usually from his own class. In doing so he must contend with rivalry from the men of both races. Against the white rivals he is helpless, but his Negro rivals he can fight and shoot, and he does.
>
> Conflict is inherent in such a situation. The more lax a man is in his own sex life, the more resentful he appears to be of his wife's indiscretions, and the unfaithful wife resents her husband's infidelities. Some colored women do not want to hear of their husband's infidelities, some husbands do not want to hear of their wives'. For the most part, however, these Negroes have not adapted themselves to the situation. The women fight each other and, far more often, the men fight each other and beat their wives, out of sexual antagonism and because they want exclusive possession of some one individual. [26]

Although it dates from a later period, Lightnin' Hopkins's "Devil Is Watching You" (1962) offers a richly suggestive meditation on the theme of black masculine anger generated by Jim Crow's tortured sexual politics and the outsized hunger for possession and control that the situation seems to have bred in some men. Seeking to corral his woman's freedom of action in every direction, the singer conjures up the devil as her ceaselessly watchful antagonist in a way that harkens back to white mastery on the plantation and the slave patrols that upheld it, even as it represents a phantasmic projection of his own jealous fury:

> You better be careful . . . 'bout what you do
> I just wanna mind . . . the devil watching you
> Yes, you better be careful woman . . . 'bout every little thing you do
>
> You may go to make grocery . . . in a grocery store
> But I want tell you the devil gonna watch you . . . everywhere you go
> You better be careful . . . you know the devil is watching you
>
> You can beg, cheat, and borry . . . you can steal a little too
> You may hide it from me . . . but the devil is watching you
> Whoa . . . the devil is watching you
>
> You may take my money . . . go have some fun too
> But you better be careful . . . the devil is watching you.
> He gonna bring it back . . . just like you take it from me.
> . . . .
>
> The devil will get you worried . . . and go home to his wife
> He'll hug her naked and kiss her, see I got . . . I got him goin' twice
> You know there ain't nothing unpossible . . . naw for the devil to do[27]

The "busy devil" of this song is anything but carefree, footloose, and promiscuous — at least until the final verse, when Hopkins sends him home to his marriage bed in a way that suggests, mischievously, that what is being signified on is precisely the situation Powdermaker evokes: a tomcatting white man who has spent most of the song "worrying" the women of Darktown before crossing back over the tracks and returning to his wife. For most of its length, however, this is a song about a black intimate relationship animated by two diametrically opposed freedoms: the singer's "woman," at large in her small-town world — shopping for groceries on his dime, perhaps squirreling away some change and stopping by a local juke to have some "fun" — and the singer, imagining himself through his devil-proxy as a King of Surveillance who ranges unopposed through that same world, furiously determined to mark her every step and punish her slightest transgression.

He's not looking to have fun, he's looking to shut down *her* fun. But of course, as that final verse suggests, the devil may just be able to have it all. The entire song, in Hartman's terms, stages its male-female relationship from the man's perspective as an elaborate micropenality of everyday life. The woman's freedom—and thus the man's—is hopelessly compromised by the man's paranoid need to possess and control.

In a study titled "'The Blues Ain't Nothin' but a Woman Want to Be a Man': Male Control in Early Twentieth Century Blues Music," Matthew B. White analyzed more than 600 blues songs recorded by men during the 1920s and 1930s and discovered that 113 of them "depicted women in a manner which allowed for easy categorization (e.g. woman as gold digger, woman as unfaithful wife/lover, etc.)."[28] Not surprisingly, 38 percent of these "women blues" dealt with infidelity. Although infidelity is sometimes presented as a legitimate male goal—there are "many songs which idolize the promiscuous male, whose fame rests upon the number of women (especially married women) which he can bed"—it is most certainly *not* legitimate when the bluesman confronts it in his own woman. "Songs which dealt with a specific act of infidelity had as their intended audience the particular women involved and were accusatory in tone," White observes. "The bluesman is, in effect, having a conversation (no matter how one-sided) with his lover." But in male-addressed songs on the subject, White argues, "the bluesman presents his life as an example for other men to learn from and in the process [he] universalizes the image of the unfaithful wife/ lover" in a way that "promote[s] a generalized mistrust and suspicion of all women."[29] Left out of this neatly bifurcated scenario are songs in which the male blues singer combines the two modes to warn his male rival, the devilish inciter of his woman's infidelity, to back off. Lonnie Johnson does this in "Sam, You're Just a Rat" (1932):

Sam, you say you my friend, but your ways I just don't like (2x)
Soon as I leave my home you trying to bite me in my back

Now Sam, you not my friend, and my home you better stop hanging
   around (2x)
'Cause I've paid for your coffin, and I mean that you graveyard bound

Sam, if you want a woman, go get one, and let my wife alone (2x)
'Cause if I ever catch you with my wife, you hellbound sure as I'm born

Sam, a real man can live happy, but no-good men like you (2x)
You trying to wreck my family, and some other man's family too

Sam, I thought you was my friend, I thought you just was swell
Sam, I thought you was my friend, I thought you was just too swell
So I'm going to give you a vacation, that's a round-trip ticket to hell[30]

Speaking on behalf of besieged monogamy and bruised male comrade-ship, a friendship shot to hell, Johnson repeatedly names and castigates his Legba-spirited rival in a way that dovetails with uplift ideology—low-class behavior must be condemned—even as, in a fury, he sidesteps Christian self-restraint to enlarge himself into an avenging angel, a devil's minion hurling Sam down the road to perdition. A round-trip ticket to hell, rather than the expected one-way ticket, suggests a badman's outsize powers: the singer's ability not merely to send Sam to the devil but to snatch him back as well. His jealous rage, in other words, transforms the singer himself into a devil of sorts, albeit one insisting on his own righteousness.

In "Wicked Devil's Blues" (1929), singer Robert Peeples again blurs the lines between White's categories of female-addressed and male-addressed songs of infidelity, lashing out at his errant woman in a midsong apostro-phe before resuming his public meditation on his own cuckolding. Like Johnson, Peeples compensates for his humiliation by arrogating to himself the devil's power—or God's power?—of hell-consigning vengeance, but he foregrounds his identification with the devil much more explicitly, worrying it like a string of rosary beads:

So jealous of my baby . . . I hate to see her go
I'm so jealous of my baby . . . I really hate to see her go
But if she's got another fellow . . . Lord I'd rather see her down below

'Cause I got ways like the devil . . . believe I'm the devil's child
Lord I got ways like the devil . . . believe I'm the devil's child
I'm so doggoned evil . . . I haven't got the heart to smile

I'm mean as a devil . . . when I begin to feel blue
I'm mean as a devil . . . when I begin to feel blue
And if I ever catch her flirting, baby I'll make it hot for you

My gal made me a devil . . . just as cruel as I can be
Now my gal made me a devil . . . just as cruel as I can be
Lord I let her run around . . . and then she made a chump of me

Going to play to the devil . . . see why men let my baby alone
Going to play to the devil . . . see why men don't let my baby alone
And if the devil give me the power . . . I'll turn my baby into stone[31]

This song is animated by the "if"s that drive the answering line of the first, third, and fifth stanzas: markers of male anxiety in the face of woman's lived sexual sovereignty that lead, in every case, to threats that seek to reassert control. The bluesman's blues arise from his woman's excessive (sexual) mobility—the fact that she "go[es]," flirts, runs around—and by the willingness of his male competitors to take advantage of the situation. Rather than call *them* devils, however, he embraces the devil-persona himself, making the best of a bad situation by going all the way bad. (Better a devil than a chump, or so the cuckold furiously insists.) The song ends with a final revenge fantasy, an inversion of the Medusa myth. The bluesman imagines himself as an evil Perseus, turning his insatiable gorgon of a woman into stone rather than, as in the myth, severing the gorgon's head and using it to turn others into stone. The devil, grasped in a moment of emotional extremity, is the bluesman's all-purpose talisman, one that fills the void created by failed love.

MUST HAVE BEEN THE DEVIL

The devil of "Busy Devil," "If I Was the Devil," "Devil Is Watching You," and "Wicked Devil's Blues" functions as both a behavioral model—for the bluesman and/or his romantic competitors—and an empowering ally. Hovering behind this region of the devil-blues tradition, I have argued, is the specter of plantation-centered white mastery: the slave owner's claimed right of sexual access to his black female chattel, a prerogative that was extended more broadly among white men during the Jim Crow period, pressuring the "new-found sovereignty in sexual matters" enjoyed but also suffered by black southerners in the long aftermath of slavery. African American women in the post-Reconstruction South often vigorously resisted the sexual overtures of white men, girded by the intertwined strictures of the church and the respectability movement, but sometimes they complied, and not always involuntarily, even as they sought to live out their sexual freedom on the black side of town. African American men, denied comparable access to white women even as they witnessed their own masculine prerogatives eroded by the daily indignities of Jim Crow, reaffirmed their masculinity in a variety of ways, some of which show up in blues songs. This roiling complex of fears, desires, grievances, and possessive investments was a motive force animating many black southern lives, especially those on the lower end of the socioeconomic spectrum. It lies at the heart of the blues tradition, in fact. And the devil—endlessly polyvalent and resourceful—was one of its most useful expressive tools.

Sometimes, to paraphrase Freud, the devil of blues-romance is just the devil: a troublemaker and vengeance-wreaker, not a screen-figure behind which infernal whiteness or the promiscuous, Legba-incarnating "creep" of the black competitor is visible. At its most benign, this devil is merely a familiar and frustrating figure of marital discord, the nonaligned spirit Peetie Wheatstraw summons in "Sweet Home Blues" (1936): "Home is a happy place . . . if you can make it that way / Now if you can't keep a happy home . . . ooo well well, will be the devil each and every day."[32] In "Mr. Devil Blues" (1929), Big Joe Williams blames the devil, through the instrument of an unnamed "woman" he's been dating, for breaking up his marriage: "Now look Mr. Devil, see what you done done / You done wrecked my family . . . caused me to leave a happy home." When black male bluesmen sing of this devil, they are retailing what Spencer has termed the "devil-lore" of the Deep South, a collection of motifs, tales, and attitudes attributed to the devil and broadly sourced in early modern European folks beliefs, beliefs conveyed to the slaves by their white masters and neighbors and reinforced by the Calvinism of the Great Revival in a way that found expression, among other things, in the conversion narratives of Afro-Christianity.[33] Invoking the devil in such ways, bluesmen—many of whom had grown up in the church and knew the Bible well—are revealing the profoundly Christian roots of their art. One important element of devil-lore that percolates through blues song is the perennial theme of woman's alliance with, and subjection to, the devil. Women *are* the devil, bluesmen insist, or they're his evil handmaidens, or his easy prey. They're inconstant and craven temptresses, daughters of Eve who deserve to be cast into hell, where they can dwell with the devil in eternal damnation. They are scapegoats, in a sense, for the mutability of the very desires they incarnate. In "Blues as a Secular Religion" (1970), musicologist Rod Gruver argued that "blues poets made a religion of their blues by distilling behavior into the single point of sex, by creating a sacred realm of charged atmosphere conducive for the appearance of Men and Women, the gods of the blues." He illustrates his claim by contrasting the Christian demonization of women with blues' celebration of woman's erotic power:

> The Christian fear of woman is evident in a medieval couplet by Cardinal Hugues de St. Cher: "Woman pollutes the body, drains the resources, kills the soul, uproots the strength, blinds the eye, and embitters the

voice." The Cardinal's hatred of woman contrasts sharply with Sonny Boy Williamson's exaltation of her and the good she does: "Every time she starts to lovin' she brings eyesight to the blind." Sonny Boy's Woman not only brings eyesight to the blind, but she makes the dumb talk, the deaf to hear and the lame to walk. So in Sonny Boy's blues Woman has become a more than mortal female, she has become a god.[34]

Gruver's claim is incontestable: When bluesmen sing of successful love, especially the affirming thrill of sexual love, or merely the thrill of the chase, they do indeed often celebrate their women as Aphrodite's incarnation, possessor of "that same thing" that "makes a preacher man lay his bible down." But how long does such love last? And what becomes of Woman-as-goddess when it fails? She becomes the devil in a blue (or red) dress, the blues' incarnation of Keats's *belle dame sans merci*: a cruelly disillusioning shape-shifter who, shrugging off all possessive investments, vanishes in the night—or transfers her affections to another suitor, or emotionally abuses her "good man"—and strews emotional wreckage in her wake. "She act like an angel in the daytime," complains Blind Boy Fuller in "Crooked Woman Blues" (1940), "[and] crooked as the devil at night."[35]

Lonnie Johnson, New Orleans–born guitarist, recorded a handful of blues of this sort. A brilliant, innovative instrumentalist, Johnson lived a long and productive life marked by two comprehensive personal disasters, and it is tempting to read his lyric production in light of them. In 1919, when he was on an extended tour of Europe, nine of his ten siblings—five sisters and four brothers—were wiped out by the influenza pandemic that was ravaging New Orleans; only one brother and his parents survived.[36] He moved to St. Louis, began playing on the excursion boats, and, in 1925, he married Mary Smith (1900–1970), a Mississippi-born blues singer who later recorded as "Signifying" Mary Johnson. She bore him one child a year, six children in all—reconstituting his devastated family of origin, in symbolic terms—before the couple dissolved their common-law relationship acrimoniously in 1932. (Some of the acrimony may have been generated by the fact that Johnson carried on an affair with Bessie Smith while touring with her "Midnight Steppers" show in 1929.)[37] "For a time," writes blues historian Francis Davis, "[Johnson and his wife] squabbled on their individual records."[38] Speaking of devil-invoking blues recordings by Johnson and several other performers, scholars Pearson and McCulloch insist that "in most of these songs the devil was not a source of terror but a convenient shared reference, often offered in a humorous context, to explain or characterize a woman's actions."[39] In Johnson's case, the humor is dark, bitter, bruised, as in "She's Making Whoopee in Hell Tonight" (1930):

> Baby, you've been gone all day baby . . . set to make whoopee tonight
> You've been gone all day . . . set to make whoopee tonight
> I'm gonna take my razor and cut your late hours . . . I will be serving
>   you right
>
> The undertaker's been here and gone, I give him your height and size
> Undertaker's been here and gone, I give him your height and size
> You'll be making whoopee with the devil in hell tomorrow night
>
> You made me love you . . . just got me for your slave
> You made me love you . . . just got me for your slave
> And from now on you'll be making whoopee in your lonesome grave
>
> Devil's got ninety thousand women . . . he just needs one more
> Devil's got ninety thousand women . . . he just needs one more
> You just the type of woman for him, mama . . . you booked out and
>   you've got to go
>
> I told you the next time you go out, please carry your black dress along
>
> Told you the next time you go out, please carry your black dress along
> 'Cause the coffin will be your present, and hell will be your brand
>   new home[40]

What Hartman calls the burdens and antagonisms of post-Emancipation black life are present here in modernist full force, beginning with the title, which signifies on a recent pop hit. In "Making Whoopee," from the 1928 Broadway musical *Whoopee!*, vaudevillian Eddie Cantor had mined a familiar comic vein in which the sexual enticements with which women entrap men into marriage quickly fade into disillusionment—on the wife's part, Cantor tells us, since she suspects her neglectful husband of fooling around with an outside woman.[41] Johnson's composition retains the woman-as-temptress theme but reverses sexes to make her the straying partner as well, then personalizes and supercharges the marital discord with a familiar image of blues violence—the razor wielded in anger—raised to gothic excess with the help of an undertaker, a black dress, a coffin, a lonesome grave, and the devil, not to mention the devil's massive legion of fallen women. The entire song is the singer's furious attempt to reassert control in the face of his woman's surfeit of achieved freedom—sexual, spatial, temporal—and the condition of love-slavery into which he feels himself to have been cast. As a third party in this particular dispute, the devil is complexly positioned, both friend and foe to the singer. His infernal domain is the scene in which retributive justice will be carried out—in that sense he's a useful ally—but as an outlandishly promiscuous woman-accumulator, a pimp's pimp, the devil's ethics contrast sharply with the singer's wounded monogamy.

Johnson was immensely productive during the period circumscribed by his ill-fated marriage, recording more than 140 sides between 1926 and 1932. As Barry Lee Pearson has noted, it's unwise with blues musicians to presume a one-to-one relationship between biography and repertoire, no matter how emotionally invested they sound in the first-person narratives they retail.[42] Still, making whoopee with the devil was a theme Johnson returned to. He recorded a second song in a similar vein, "Another Woman Booked Out and Bound to Go" (1930), in the session that produced "She's Making Whoopee in Hell Tonight," and twelve years later he released an almost-verbatim remake titled "The Devil's Woman" (1942). The only significant (and minor) change is that song's final line, where the singer's wedding "present" to his cheating woman is the devil rather than a coffin, as though he, too, has become a pimp, reasserting control by sexually reassigning his errant lover: "'Cause the devil will be your man, and hell will be your brand new home."[43] Then in 1960, at the beginning of his final comeback, Johnson recorded "She-Devil," an original composition that feels like a retrospective pronouncement on his failed marriage:

I almost lost my mind, tryin' to hold onto you
Aaaaaaalmost lost my mind, tryin' to hold onto you
I know you didn't love me, baby, you only wanted the things that
    don't belong to you

I built my whole life around you, said we would never part
Built my whole life around you, said that we'd never part
And I'm left alone to cry, you're off to break somebody else's heart

Yes, you ain't nothin' but a she-devil . . . yes, you wouldn't do right
    if you could
Yes, you ain't nothin' but a she-devil . . . you wouldn't do right if
    you could
That's why I'm gonna let you go, baby, 'cause you don't mean me
    no good[44]

When Pearson and McCulloch mock the romanticism of those who view the blues-devil as a source of hellhound-like terror rather than seeing him as a shared masculine reference point used to make (comic) sense of woman's mercurial behavior, they draw our attention away from the deep, anguished feeling at work in songs of failed romance such as this one. Johnson condenses a lifetime of pain into three verses. His woman, a chaos-sowing evildoer, has *become* a devil rather than merely consorting with the fiend. The song moves from the past tense ("you didn't love me") into the present tense ("I'm left alone to cry") before ending in the future tense ("I'm gonna let you go, baby"). The pain, repossessing him, refuses to remain retrospective.

Masculine bitterness in the face of women's sexual faithlessness is a ground note in the blues tradition. Some male blues singers may have crowed about being footloose and promiscuous "wicked devils," but others preferred to dramatize their lovers' sins, emphasizing their own constancy and consigning their female antagonists to hell. At its most forgiving, such bitterness is merely a deep disappointment, as in "She Belongs to the Devil" (1941) by Washboard Sam, which begins, "She belongs to the devil . . . Lord, I cried a-many day / Yes, that child is so weakened . . . hoo-well, who could change her way?" The woman in question seems to have been the singer's boyhood sweetheart and muse, a schoolyard nymphet who taught him how to "sing the blues" but has now gone bad: "Yeah, she belongs to the devil . . . hoo-well, she have wrecked a-many home."[45] In "Shake Hands and Tell Me Goodbye" (1931), an angrier song, Walter Vinson of the Mississippi Sheiks tells his "sweet baby" to "shake hands and tell your daddy goodbye" after she betrays the vows that he, with great effort, has kept: "I worked all the winter, the winter was tough . . . with another man just struttin' your stuff. . . . / . . . I was good when you were sick and good when you was well / No use to prayin' when you get in hell."[46] Damning souls to hell was the Lord's prerogative, but bluesmen routinely blurred that line. "Treat me good . . . Lord will bless your soul," sang Isaiah Nettles, aka Mississippi Moaner. "If you treat me bad . . . mama to hell you'll surely go."[47] "In many [blues] songs," White notes, "a woman's failure to obey was criticized not only as unnatural, but also contrary to religious prescriptions. Biblical authority was frequently used by bluesmen to justify male dominance."[48] By the same token, the devil was routinely invoked to justify a man's failure to dominate: in familiar parlance, it "must have been the devil" that changed his baby's mind, turned her around, chained her down in hell, or otherwise intervened in the couple's troubled romantic life.

The earliest song in this particular cluster is probably Papa Charlie Jackson's "The Cat's Got the Measles" (1925), one of the first blues recordings issued by a man after the near-total dominance of the market by women blues "queens" in the first half of the 1920s:

Now the cat's got the measles . . . the dog's got the whooping cough (2x)
Doggone a man . . . let a woman be his boss

Now I ain't no devil . . . crawl in a lion's den (doggone my soul, Lord
    Lord) (2x)
But my chief occupation's taking women from their monkey-men
. . . .

Now I think I heard a rumbling . . . deep down in the ground (2x)
Well it must have been the devil . . . chaining my good gal down

Now the men don't like me . . . just because I speak my mind (2x)
But the women cry, "Papa!" . . . just because I take my time

Now the cat's got the measles . . . the dog's got the whooping cough (2x)
Doggone a man . . . let a woman be his boss[49]

Here Jackson, incarnating Legba, plays the wicked devil role: his ability to "take [his] time," make love slowly, lets him to steal other men's women at will. But he also invokes the "real" devil as a subterranean menace who is chaining his "good gal down" for no obvious reason—except, perhaps, for trying to boss him, a point underlined by the repeated refrain. The deep-down-in-the-ground devil figure, the defining feature of this song cluster, is adapted from Revelations 20: "And I saw an angel come down from heaven, having the key of the bottomless pit and a great chain in his hand. And he laid hold on the dragon, that old serpent, which is the Devil, and Satan, and bound him a thousand years, and cast him into the bottomless pit, and shut him up, and set a seal upon him, that he should deceive the nations no more, till the thousand years should be fulfilled: and after that he must be loosed a little season." The thousand stipulated years having passed, hell is now apparently the devil's command center in the world evoked by "The Cat's Got the Measles," the bottomless pit into which he, supplanting the angel of heaven, casts and enchains women who deserve better.

Jackson's comic temperament, honed in minstrel and medicine shows and issuing elsewhere in "hokum" blues, shapes the lyrics in the direction of lighthearted braggadocio rather than pained deep feeling. But that deep feeling soon becomes a part of the tradition; the "good gal" goes bad and deserves her hellish fate. In "Blue Devil Blues" (1928), "Texas" Alexander delivers a roundhouse right, one that quickly narrows from a general observation about women to a fuming indictment of one specific wife:

> I heard a mumbling . . . deep down in the ground (2x)
> It must been the devil turning them women 'round
>
> . . . .
>
> When you see that smoke . . . settling to the ground (2x)
> That's some married woman has gone . . . and she can't be found
>
> Sometime I think . . . my woman too good to die (2x)
> Then again I think she oughta be buried alive
>
> You talk about trouble . . . I had it all my days (2x)
> 'Cause I ain't got but one woman . . . man that trouble my grave[50]

Alexander's substitution of "mumbling" for "rumbling" evokes the devil as a low-down, out-of-sight seducer, laying his rap on the women he has "turn[ed]." The "smoke . . . settling to the ground" paints a scene at once infernal (the devil's corrupting influence has manifested as a married woman flouncing offstage with a theatrical *poof!*, intent on fornication) and psychological (the afterimage of a cuckold's fuming rage). The third stanza, juxtaposing a lover's idealization with a cuckold's revenge fantasy, offers an exemplary instance of the blues' powerful ambivalence in matters of love. "The blues removes us from the polar reality of non-unitary experience," writes Jungian analyst Mark Winborn, "because it doesn't tend to separate experience into polar categories in which one pole cancels out the [o]ther. . . . Often love and hate (or aggression) exist side by side in the blues just as they do in the unconscious. . . . Within the unitary reality of the blues, good and evil, love and hate, staying or leaving coexist side by side without an experience of internal contradiction."[51] Winborn is surely right about love and hate existing side by side here, but he is surely wrong about the absence of internal contradiction. That palpable antinomy, that torn-in-half incommensurability of two opposed and primal orientations, *is* the blues. It's the charged feeling—the embodied equivalent of double consciousness—that arises from a specific sort of romantic double bind and demands expression as this sort of blues song, one that bends relentlessly toward the judgment pronounced in the final stanza. In sociohistorical terms, it's the aftershock of black romantic freedom of choice enabled by Emancipation: the married woman who abandons her freely chosen husband for a lover or lovers who await elsewhere. The devil is a helpful explanatory mechanism in such circumstances: the perennial mischief maker who "must have" been responsible for what went wrong.

John Lee "Sonny Boy" Williamson's recording, "Deep Down in the Ground" (1938), offers yet another variant on the pattern: neither Alexander's bitter cuckold nor Jackson's lighthearted braggart but a juke joint player who has been played:

> You hear that rumbling, you hear that rumbling . . . deep down in the
> ground, oh Lord
> You hear that rumbling . . . deep down in the ground
> Now it must be the devil, you know . . . turning my womens around
>
> Now stack of dollars . . . stack of dollars . . . just as high as I am tall,
> oh Lord
> Stack of dollars . . . just as high as I am tall
> Now if you be my baby . . . mama you can have them all
>
> Well a great big woman . . . great big woman . . . head right full of hair,
> whoa Lord
> She's a great big woman . . . head right full of hair
> I call her tailor-made, but her . . . people they don't allow me there
>
> Now here's my hand, baby . . . now here's my hand . . . if I never see you
> anymore, whoa Lord
> Now here's my hand . . . if I never see you anymore
> Well now I'm going to leave you alone . . . to go with Mr. So-and-So
>
> Now tell me baby . . . now tell me baby . . . where did you stay last night,
> oh Lord
> Now tell me baby . . . where did you stay last night
> Now with your hair all tangled and your clothes . . . ain't fitting you right[52]

The devil is "turning my womens around," Williamson protests: the complaint of a promiscuous lover rather than a faithful husband, and one whose self-confidence has been compromised by the faithlessness of one specific paramour. The "stack of dollars" stanza, a gambler's come-on, traces back at least as far as Sleepy John Estes's and Yank Rachell's "Stack o' Dollars Blues" (1930).[53] The third stanza conveys the gambler's admiration for the statuesque focus of his attentions—her "head right full of hair" evokes not just her sexual attractions but the fact that she has money enough to *buy* that kind of hair—and suggests that she is a high-class woman who has descended into his demimonde from precincts where her "people" consider him an undesirable. The last two stanzas displace this portrait downward into grumbling accommodation: nobody controls *this* juke-joint queen, much as they might like to. She's a promiscuous mess, no question, but he's still got feelings for her as he bids her goodbye.

Born in Indianola, Mississippi, in 1904, harmonica player Bill "Jazz" Gillum recorded "The Devil Blues" (1947), one more example drawn from this lyric grouping, toward the end of his active career as a session musician at Victor's Bluebird label in Chicago. Gillum's life ended unhappily, as blues lives go. He was stabbed to death by a woman in 1966, according to a contemporary,[54] and when white blues guitarist Michael Bloomfield visited him on a suffocatingly hot and humid day in the summer before his death, Gillum struck him as a man dwelling in madness—"the craziest man I'd ever met":

> [Big Joe Williams and I] drove out to the West Side and stopped in front of a tiny frame house—just a shanty, really. When I walked into the place, I thought I'd hit Hell City—as hot as it was outside, it was insufferably worse within. All the windows were shut down tight. Clad in a huge brown overcoat and sweating profusely, Gillum stood beside a wood stove stoking a raging fire.
>
> He was extremely paranoid. He'd written the very successful "Key to the Highway" and had never gotten the publishing money for it, and he was afraid I'd come to steal his other tunes. We didn't stay long enough to change his mind.[55]

Bloomfield's characterization of Gillum's residence as "Hell City" seems apt. He offers us a portrait of an aging bluesman raging against his dispossession by the powers that be, retreating in fury to a torture chamber of his own creation as if to outdevil the (white) devil that threatens him. This tableau was almost twenty years in the future when Gillum recorded "The Devil Blues," but the rage at dispossession—a woman taken from him, not a song—was already there, as was the violence through which blues people sometimes arbitrate such disputes:

> Yes I went to the graveyard . . . and I fell down on my knees (2x)
> And I asked the good Lord . . . to give me back my baby please
>
> And I heard an awful rumbling . . . and it came from under the
>   ground (2x)
> It must have been the devil . . . chaining my sweet woman down

Yes I went to the devil . . . but he said there really ain't no use (2x)
Of you sighing and crying . . . I won't turn your sweet woman loose

Now Mr. Devil, you took my rider, and I think that's a dirty shame
Yes, you have took my rider . . . and I think that's a dirty shame
I'm gone make you ride this razor . . . like a hobo rides a passenger train[56]

What might at first seem a straightforward song about a bereaved man who refuses to accept the death of his "sweet woman" turns out to have unexpected features. Both God and the devil are apostrophized here—a rare pairing in blues songs—and while the "good Lord" remains mute, the devil is quite willing to dialogue. If the singer's woman is "sweet," why has she ended up in the devil's clutches? Gillum's biography offers a suggestive clue. He spent the first nineteen years of his life in and around Indianola—that Delta town in which, as Hortense Powdermaker discovered in the mid-1930s, an African American man hungering for the romantic favors of black women was forced to compete not just with his "Negro rivals" but also with white men whose predation he was helpless to contest. Yet helplessness in the face of white domination may be offset by fantasies of vengeance. The singer's anger at a certain "Mr. Devil" who "took my rider," with its racially loaded honorific "Mr.," bespeaks bitter resentment at a white man's claiming of his black lover or spouse, a "sweet woman" who is lost to him forever. Precisely the same racial complaint is suggested by Sonny Boy Williamson's invocation of "Mr. So-and-So" as his woman's claimant in "Deep Down in the Ground." Such a meaning may be latent rather than primary but acknowledging its presence helps explain the striking intimacy with which Gillum's song addresses the devil figure, first petitioning and then threatening vengeance on him in a way that suggests earthly rivals rather than metaphysical ones. Honeyboy Edwards had insisted that a black man "couldn't do nothing about" a white man who consorted with his wife.[57] But the passions bred by such intolerable strictures and the revenge fantasies they engendered could indeed find issue in blues song.

DEVIL GOT MY WOMAN

The devil's traditional role as an opportunistic and deceitful shape-shifter makes him a supremely useful figure, I am arguing, for blues singers struggling to enunciate what Saidiya Hartman has termed "the contradictions and antagonisms of freedom" in the realm of sexual love. Like a gemstone angled in the light, the devil that bedevils black romance may reveal himself in turn to be the "real" devil in his metaphysical aspect as trouble-sower, avenging punisher, and/or negative ideal; the singer himself, in his role as Legba's oversexed, tricksterlike embodiment; and the singer's black and white romantic rivals, in the same role. What Winborn writes about the blues in general—that it "removes us from the polar reality of non-unitary experience"—is indisputably true where devil-invoking blues are concerned. The devil wears many hats; sometimes he wears more than one hat within a given song.

Skip James's "Devil Got My Woman" (1931) is a good illustration of this last claim. Born in Bentonia, Mississippi, in 1902, the same year as Son House, James was, like House and Charley Patton, a man who straddled the fence where God's music and the devil's music were concerned. His father, a bootlegger-turned-preacher, set the pattern. After James's career as a blues recording artist sputtered out during the Depression, he joined his father in Birmingham, where he led a church choir and worked at a Baptist seminary his father was directing. Both career developments were still to come when, in the late 1920s, James married Oscella Robinson, the sixteen-year-old daughter of a local clergyman—his "first significant relationship with a woman who was not a barrelhouse floozie or prostitute," according to his biographer, Stephen Calt.[58] The marriage was short-lived, dissolving unexpectedly when Robinson became romantically involved with a second man, a Great War veteran and friend of James's who had been traveling with the couple. The precise relationship between "Devil Got My Woman" and this failed marriage is unclear. Although James had been singing the song before he and Robinson married, both the people of Bentonia and James himself later thought of her as the song's "devil woman," according to Calt. Calt quotes James on the song's origins in what seems to be that earlier, premarriage relationship:

> I came in contact with a companion, and she was so contentious, unruly, and hard to get along with, I just compared her with the devil—one of his agencies. Since doin' that, I just turned her over to him, and I just give her to know that I would rather *be* the devil than to be her man, because she was so contentious and I couldn't get along with her in no way. . . . I just decided that I would quit worryin' with her so much. . . .
>
> You can lay down happy at night. You and your companion will be in harmony. Everything goin' well. Satan'll creep in that house overnight. She may get up the next mornin' and you can't get a good word out of her. Why? Because Satan has got the bill of sale over her.[59]

James's sovereignty in sexual matters is undercut on all sides by the devil's maddening interposition between the musician and his female companion—nowhere more so than in that striking final image, drawn from the slavery era, of Satan holding "the bill of sale over her," as though he's a white man who owns her. And yet the devil, for precisely this reason, is extraordinarily useful to James, almost a necessity. He's an all-purpose signifier who rushes in to fill a void that would otherwise be filled by troubling ideas about personal responsibility and individual psychology. James's woman is at once the devil's equal ("compared . . . with"), the devil's instrument ("one of his agencies"), and the devil's possession ("turned . . . over" by James, and owned outright). But the devil is also, for James, a negative aspirational ideal that helps convey his frustration with his contentious, unruly mate: he would "rather *be* the devil than to be her man."

That last sentiment, profane and irreverent, is not one that finds a home in God's music. Blues is the devil's music not just because it makes a space for profane expressions of aggrieved masculinity but also because it juxtaposes those expressions with others that reflect a biblical perspective and sees nothing wrong with that juxtaposition—as in the first two stanzas of "Devil Got My Woman":

> I'd rather be the devil . . . than to be that woman[']s] man
> I'd rather be the devil . . . tuh be that woman[']s] man
>
> Oh nothing but the devil . . . changed my baby's mind
> Oh nothing but the devil . . . changed my baby's mind
>
> I laid down last night . . . laid down last night. . . . I laid down last night,
>   tried to take my rest
> My mind got to rambling . . . like a wild geese from the west . . .
>   from the west
>
> The woman I love . . . woman that I love . . . the woman I love . . .
>   stoled her from my best friend
> But he got lucky . . . stoled her back o-gain
> And he got lucky . . . stoled her back o-gain[60]

The first two stanzas orchestrate romantic triangulation as a kind of Möbius strip logic: If James were to become the devil that his woman's maddening behavior drives him to imagine, he would presumably have the power to reclaim her love from the devil who has destroyed it. The third stanza brilliantly elaborates Davis's claim about the thematic prominence of travel and sexuality in blues song originating in post-Emancipation African American social history. Travel materializes here not as physical freedom but as psychological unfreedom: the restless, obsessional night-thoughts of a frustrated lover, configured as a Canada goose's overflight. Freedom is indeed present—the singer's baby is thinking and acting for herself, rather than as James would have her act—but James, incapable of appreciating that freedom *as* freedom, configures it as the devil's handiwork. Or man's handiwork? Love, suggests the final stanza, is a zero-sum game. A woman's romantic freedom is no freedom at all, since she is merely a counter to be exchanged by men. Your loss is another man's gain.

In 1968, several years after James was rediscovered by three young white blues fans and brought back on line as part of the acoustic blues revival, he recorded a sublime update of "Devil Got My Woman." It concludes with two verses that aren't part of the original:

> You know my baby she don't drink whiskey . . . my baby she don't
> drink no whiskey
> And I know she ain't crazy about wine
> Now it wasn't nothing but the devil . . . he done changed my baby's mind
>
> You know I could be right . . . you know I could be right
> Then again I could be wrong
> But it wasn't nothing but the devil . . . he done got my baby and
> he done gone.[61]

The devil for James—and not only for James—is a comforting fallback when conventional explanations for failed love fall short. Denizens of the jukes, blues singers were intimately familiar with the damages wrought by alcoholism and addiction. In "Whiskey Headed Woman" (1939), James's fellow Mississippian Tommy McClennan had sung of a "whiskey headed woman" who "stay drunk all the time"; "If you don't stop drinkin,'" he warned her, "I b'lieve [you] gonna lose yo' mind."[62] How, then, to explain an abandoning lover whose fickleness can't be blamed on whiskey or wine? The devil fills the space in James's lament that would otherwise be occupied by personal attacks, self-recrimination, or stunned incomprehension. This devil is worldly as well as otherworldly, taking his identity in part from the singer's hell-of-a-fellow "best friend" who "done got lucky" with the singer's woman and "got her back again." James embraces the maddening instability of his "baby's mind" as his own creed in a moment of meditative equipoise:

he "could be right," but then again he "could be wrong." The only thing he knows for sure is that the devil "done got my baby and . . . done gone."

DEALING WITH THE DEVIL

One more song cycle deserves mention in this catalog of male laments about the devil's hand in destroying black love relationships. "Dealing with the Devil" was recorded and copyrighted in 1940 by both Brownie McGhee and John Lee "Sonny Boy" Williamson (the latter as "I Been Dealing with the Devil"); Eddie Burns covered the song in 1953, as did James Cotton in 1995. Grounded in the enduring idea of woman as Satan's instrument, the song reconfigures the bluesman's ill-behaving lover through the use of humorous exaggeration and folk cultural materials:

> Now my baby wasn't even excited about our wedding ring
> When it comes to our marrying, it didn't seem to amount to a thing
> But I've been dealing with the devil
> I been dealing with the devil
> I believe I've been dealing with the devil, my woman don't love me
>   no more
>
> Well now I've got the meanest woman . . . the meanest woman you most
>   ever seen
> She sleeps with a ice pick in her hand, man, and fights all in her dream
> I'd sooner be sleeping with the devil
> I'd sooner be sleeping with the devil
> I'd sooner to be sleeping with the devil, my woman don't love me no more
> . . . .
>
> Now baby you know I ain't goin' down, you know this big road by myself
> Now and if I can't take you, I'm gonna carry somebody else
> Because I been dealing with the devil, etc.[63]

"The protagonists in women's blues," notes Angela Y. Davis, "are seldom wives and almost never mothers"; in Ma Rainey's songs, she adds, "the institution of monogamous marriage often was cavalierly repudiated with the kind of attitude that is usually gendered as male."[64] That boisterous womanly assertiveness registers here, on the receiving end, as masculine dismay: a loyal husband whose wife has fallen out of love with him and become a mean mistreater. Here, as in Skip James's "Devil Got My Woman," the singer's bitter disillusionment manifests through his invocation of multiple devils—not just the woman-become-devil but also the "real" devil as a potential bedmate who, in a comic touch, seems desirable by comparison. In McGhee's version, this devil-woman heaps vindictive abuse on her spouse, again to comic effect:

> Put lotta salt in my gravy, potash in my tea
> I know by that she's trying to poison me
> Been dealing with the devil, etc.

> Got a shotgun in the corner, blackjack on the bed
> Wants to catch me sleeping so she can whoop my head
> I been dealing with the devil, etc.

The singer's disillusionment in the face of love gone bad has collapsed the distinction between his woman and a devil who, in other lyric contexts, might have chained her down, preyed on her, stolen her away. She has *become* the devil in her husband's eyes—or, alternately, has been recruited by the devil as an instrument of evil. Rather than lost to her husband, she's oppressively present to him, a masculinized tormentor who betrays every wifely intimacy—marital vows consecrated by rings, the domestic hearth, the marriage bed. In "Characteristics of Negro Expression" (1931), Zora Neale Hurston celebrated the "black gal"—the dark-skinned woman—as "queen of the Jook," describing her reputation among men in terms that anticipate McGhee's violent abuser:

> Even on the works and in the "Jooks" the black man sings disparagingly of black women. They say that she is evil. That she sleeps with her fists doubled up and ready for action. . . . Wake up a black woman, and before you kin git any sense into her she be done up and lammed you over the head four or five times. When you git her quiet she'll say, "Nigger, know whut I was dreamin when you woke me up?"
> You say, "no honey, what was you dreamin?" She says, "I dreamt you shook yo' rusty fist under my nose and I split yo' head open wid a axe."[65]

The bluesman's fantasized response to this epic romantic fail, as evoked by Williamson, is to head off down the big road, fleeing the devil-woman and the hell she has created for him while hoping for a more congenial helpmeet. McGhee inscribes the devil-woman's romantic freedom as well as his own:

I'll tell you something, I ain't goin' by myself
Now if you don't want me, I'll get me someone else.
Been dealing with the devil, etc.

I'll tell you little girl, I ain't gonna tell you again
If you don't want me, find you another man
I been dealing with the devil, etc.

Travel and sexuality, twin themes of the blues, intertwine under the sign of masculine lament, with the devil high in the mix: the road here is the route through which one *escapes* the devil-woman and replaces her with a more felicitous partner rather than the crossroad-space within which one encounters a trickster devil envisioned as male.

THE DEVIL'S GONNA GET YOU

Although they almost never ventured out to the crossroads, blueswomen, too, had stories to tell about romantic disasters, one in which male devils could be helpful as well as hurtful.[66] Like their male counterparts, if not quite as frequently, female blues singers have found the devil to be a useful ally in articulating the contradictions and antagonisms of freedom in the sphere of sexual love. When bluesmen—and their nonmusical African American brethren—embody the phallic, footloose "wicked devil" archetype as a way of enjoying in their freedom and evading the behavioral constraints of Jim Crow and the black church, women sometimes thrill at the result and sometimes rage at it. Hurston's Janie Starks, in *Their Eyes Were Watching God* (1937), illustrates this foundational ambivalence. Her new lover, a bluesman named Tea Cake, disappears for three days after first making love to her, and his absence transforms her euphoria into despair. "In the cool of the afternoon the fiend from hell specially sent to lovers arrived at Janie's ear. Doubt. All the fears that circumstance could provide and the heart feel, attacked her on every side." On the fourth day he returns driving a battered car, "ready with his grin." "She adored him and hated him at the same time," Hurston tells us. "How could he make her suffer so and then come grinning like that with that darling way he had?"[67] The devil-equivalent "fiend from hell" shows up here, significantly, *not* as a figure for the absent bluesman but as an uninvited phantasm that gives Janie a way of symbolizing what haunts her: Tea Cake's hungered-for but absent presence—which is to say, the existential challenge of her own awakened sexual and romantic hunger grasping at a freely choosing human subject, a highly unstable amalgam indeed.

Blues song registers this challenge from the woman's perspective in several different ways. The most familiar is a condemnatory mode that takes its power from the black preaching tradition, offering an example, as Spencer has argued, of the way many blues singers not only came of age in the church but also continued to draw on its spiritual and rhetorical grounding. Bessie Smith's father, William Smith, was a Baptist minister who died when she was eight years old; her recording of Porter Grainger's "Devil's Gonna Get You" (1928) pronounces on the sexual sins of her man with fundamentalist wrath:

> It's a long, long lane that has no turning
> And it's a fire that always keeps on burning
> Mister devil down below
> Pitchfork in his hand
> And that's where you are going to go
> Do you understand?
>
> [chorus]
> Devil's gonna git you
> Devil's gonna git you
> Oh, the devil's gonna git you
> Man, just as sure as you born
> Devil's gonna git you,
> Devil's gonna git you,
> Oh, the devil's gonna git you,
> The way you're carryin' on
>
> You go away, stay for weeks
> On your doggone spree
> Come back home, get in my bed
> And turn . . . your back on me
> Oh the devil's gonna git you, etc.
>
> Dirty two-timer, dirty two-timer,
> Dirty two-timer, you ain't coming clean
> Oh the devil's gonna git you, etc.
>
> I don't want no two-time stuff
> From my regular man

Don't want nothing that's been used
'Cause it's secondhand

The devil's gonna git you
Oh the devil's gonna git you
Man the devil's gonna git you
Sure as you're born to die[68]

Even as it reveals its distant origins in a tradition of evangelical oratory stretching back to Jonathan Edwards's "Sinners in the Hands of an
Angry God" (1741), Smith's recording anticipates Aretha Franklin's soul
hit "Respect" (1967), anchored as it is in the fury of a woman scorned—
abandoned by her man, cheated on, and then sexually disrespected when
he finally returns home. Blues is the devil's music here because it erases
God from the picture, elevates the female blues singer into a preacherly role
forbidden to women within the church itself and, most significantly, foregrounds sexual disappointment in a coarse and unseemly way, as though
her man's "stuff" is all this woman lives for.[69]

Davis is surely right that blueswomen such as Smith "summoned sacred
responses to their messages about sexuality," but they also turned religion's
ritual forms and enunciative powers—in Smith's case, a repeated invocation of the devil—to the purpose of plain old vengeance-taking, driven
by sexual jealousy. This is the spirit in which Koko Taylor admonishes her
man in "The Devil's Gonna Have a Field Day" (1987), invoking not just the
devil but the undertaker to underline the depth of her wrath, annealing
pain with bitter comedy:

Yes I saw you last night . . . you and your woman too
But I'm just like poison ivy . . . I'll break out all over you
So don't try to use me . . . 'cause I refuse to be your fool
'Cause the devil's gonna have a field day . . . and the undertaker
    will get the news[70]

The devil lends himself handily to this revenge scenario. But he undercuts
it as well. The devil of blues song has always been a syncretic figure, one
imbued with the disruptive energies of Afro-diasporic folk religion, especially masculine sexual energy. And of course the Christian devil himself, as
Andrew Delbanco reminds us, is a transcultural assemblage, a locus of charismatic phallicism: "A great deal of the European lore about Satan in fact
derived from pagan traditions, from figures in Teutonic and Scandinavian
folklore like Wotan and Loki, while the visual image of the devil had im-

mediate sources in such predecessors as the Celtic horned god Cernunnos, the satyrs, and the Greek god Pan."[71] The devil of the black spirituals wasn't just an emblem of absolute evil or a stand-in for the white slaver, it must be remembered; he was a conjure man, a bearer of ancestral (i.e., African, "heathen") black magic whom the evangelicalized slaves had been urged, by white and black male preachers alike, to disown. That conjure man reemerges on the post-Reconstruction landscape as the Legba-incarnating bluesman, a New World Pan. The blues-purveyor, according to Spencer, is "often perceived to be a divine lover, and he often portrays himself . . . as akin to the sexually gluttonous trickster always wearing a prodigiously erect phallus."[72] Bluesmen were never shy about proclaiming their sexual attractions, but in some cases (and perhaps cynically, because magical powers sell records) they attributed them explicitly to voodoo and hoodoo: they were love-gods, not just lovers. In "Snake Doctor Blues" (1932), J. D. "Jelly Jaw" Short (1902–62) from Port Gibson, Mississippi, bragged about flying through the air like a voodoo priest and gazing down at the legions of female admirers that his skill with roots and herbs had gotten him:

> I am a snake doctor man, gang of womens everywhere I go
> I am a snake doctor man, gathers a gang of womens everywhere I go
> And when I get to flying sometime, I can see a gang of women standing
>   out in the door
>
> Lord, I know many of you mens are wondering what the snake doctor
>   man got in his hands (2x)
> He got roots and herbs, steal a woman, man everywhere he lands[73]

The "doggone spree" that Bessie Smith accuses her man of having enjoyed behind her back in "Devil's Gonna Get You" is Short and his "gang of womens" seen from the distaff side through a scrim of Christian judgmentalism from which God has been banished. The devil will wreak revenge—or so Smith hopes—on her promiscuous lover, but he too is of the devil's party. The devil is everywhere and nowhere in the drama of black blues romance. The he-devil is painfully absent or unavailable; the she-devil is relentlessly too-present and torturing; the he-devil is an agent of vengeance, ready to be called on. The devil, he or she, is sexy, maddening, dangerous, liberating, undependable, endlessly mutable: the avatar of black freedom as a lived erotics of intimate relationships.

In *A Bad Woman Feeling Good: Blues and the Women Who Sing Them* (2005), cultural historian Buzzy Jackson argues that Smith's "righteous indignation, the emotion that fueled so much of her best work, usually was inspired by her demand for equity in a relationship."[74] But it was also a way of projecting her sins onto others and disavowing responsibility for her own misbehavior. "Smith's loves and her life," writes Jana Evans Braziel,

> —in more conventional terms, her "love life"—defied the conventions of marital heterosexuality: her sexual and amorous affiliations were many and were often queer. In straight terms, she was philandering, infidelitous, unreliable, unfaithful, and perverse; in queer terms, Smith enjoyed the pleasures, often at a great personal cost, of men, women, teenage girls, buffet flats, gay sex shows, and whatever else enticed her. . . . Smith had a long and close relationship with Ruby Walker, niece of Jack Gee, her second husband; she also had extended, passionate, and open sexual relationships with two girls in her dancing entourage, Lilian and Marie.
>   . . . Smith had a volatile, even violent, relationship with Gee, who often beat her for what he regarded as her sexual transgressions. Once, after finding Smith in bed with Marie, Gee hollered, "Bessie, come out here, you bitch; I'm going to kill you tonight.[75]

"Devil's Gonna Get You," in other words, is as much Gee's lament as Smith's. The righteous indignation Smith vents is an emotion she knows well because her own philandering placed her on the receiving end of her husband's wrath. Gee was simultaneously the bedeviled husband and—as violent avenger of his own wounded pride—the husband-as-devil.

When the devil makes an appearance in black women's blues, an absent (or emotionally absent) male lover is almost always to blame. "Women usually do not joke about loss," insists Daphne Duvall Harrison, "and are more likely to sing about their grief and its results: extreme depression, bad health, hallucinations and nightmares, suicide attempts, or violence. There are basically two causes for the loss of the lover sung about in women's blues—infidelity and death."[76] In "Black Mountain Blues" (1930), Smith's lover's sexual abandonment—he's the "sweetest man in town" but has now "throwed her down" for a "city gal"—leads her to transform herself into a violent, devil-driven outlaw, intent on murdering him:

> I'm bound for Black Mountain . . . me and my razor and my gun
> Lord I'm bound for Black Mountain . . . me and my razor and my gun
> I'm going to shoot him if he stands still . . . and cut him if he run
>
> . . . .

Got the devil in my soul . . . and I'm full of bad booze (2x)
I'm out here for trouble . . . I've got the Black Mountain blues[77]

Bessie reaches for a high D flat on the word "devil," the highest note she sings on the recording. That one word sums up her bluesy, vengeful, heart-sore condition. "Black Mountain Blues" exemplifies the sheer toughness of spirit that Ralph Ellison saw as blues song's creative response to the travails of black life—a characteristic stance for Smith, but one she occasionally departs from in order to evoke more abject subject positions.[78] The devil is a useful ally in those cases as well. In "Dyin' by the Hour" (1927), authored by George Brooks, Smith ventriloquizes the plaint of an abandoned woman far more helpless than she herself seems to have been. The song starts with a funeral dirge, evoking not toughness of spirit but capitulation to heartbreak:

It's an old story, every time it's a doggone man! (2x)
But when that thing is gone you . . . you just drift from hand to hand!

I'd drink up all this acid, if it wouldn't burn me so (2x)
Then telephone the devil, that's the only place I'd go

Once I weighed two hundred, I'm nothing but skin and bone (2x)
I would always laugh, but it's nothing but a moan and a groan[79]

"Dyin' by the Hour" resembles Clara Smith's "Done Sold My Soul to the Devil" (1924): a fallen woman sings of her fall, dramatizing the state of emotional disrepair and joyless promiscuity into which she has descended after losing her man. In Clara's case, the singer spins romantic loss into a brassy spirit of resistance, one that leads her to brag about "drink[ing] carbolic acid" and "[toting] a Gatling gun." Here, Bessie's suffering victim *thinks* about drinking the acid but demurs, fearing the pain. The devil remains a touchstone in both songs: a charismatic figure, implicitly or explicitly male, whose attentions, malign as they are, fill the void left by failed love. The devil gives you somebody to call, someplace to go, or merely somebody to rail against, when the man you care about has abandoned you.

Blues song, in short, offers female recording artists a range of attitudinal orientations, from resigned and abject to wrathfully self-actualized, with which to frame their romantic frustrations with the help of a devil figure. Georgia White doesn't actually name the devil in "Your Hellish Ways" (1936), just configures her "daddy" in behavioral terms that make the association, and her bitter resentment, clear. "You go out in the evening," she sings, "and don't come home until daylight / When you do come home, you wants to fuss and fight / Your hellish ways . . . are killing poor me / You may beat me, daddy, for every woman you see. . . . / I'm just sick and tired of your low down hellish ways."[80] In "Send Me to the 'Lectric Chair" (1927), Smith wrings dark humor out of a murderess's courtroom plea not for leniency but for the death penalty and the sense of emotional completion it will confer. She slit her "good man's throat," she acknowledges, after finding him with a "triflin' Jane," then stood over him laughing "while he wallowed 'round and died":

> Judge, judge, please, mister judge, send me to the 'lectric chair
> Judge, judge, good mister judge, let me go away from here
> I want to take a journey to the devil down below
> I done killed my man, I want to reap just what I sow
> Oh judge, judge, Lordy, Lordy, judge, send me to the 'lectric chair[81]

Here the blueswoman is proclaiming her own hellish ways more loudly than her lover's, insisting on the rightness of her pairing with the devil—but also, paradoxically, submitting herself to the demands of earthly and biblical justice, petitioning the male judge nine times in one verse and accepting her state-sanctioned death without protest. This is something very different from the thoroughgoing insubordination usually manifested by the male badman. In "Rough and Tumble Blues" (1925), by contrast, Ma Rainey evokes a scene of romantic disappointment in which her good-looking man, clothed in the "struttin' suit" she bought him, has been consorting with multiple outside women. "Every little devil got on my man's road," complains Rainey, describing how she pushed through the door of a party to discover "Miss Shorty Toad" and her man "shimmying down to the floor." "I got rough and killed three women," she declares proudly in the final stanza, "'fore the police got the news / 'Cause mama's on the warpath with those rough and tumble blues." The devil in this case isn't *the* devil, merely convenient shorthand for the sexual competitors she dispatches with a swaggering lack of remorse, an attitude echoed many decades later by the black comedian Mo'Nique in a routine immortalized on YouTube as "Skinny Bitches Need to Be Destroyed."[82]

Denise LaSalle's "Hell Sent Me You" (2007), authored by veteran Memphis songwriter Raymond Moore, offers a fitting coda to this discussion. Although it falls just outside the chronological boundaries of this study, it illustrates the blues tradition's continuing reliance on the devil as a mediating figure within the troubled realm of black romance. Deploying a disco beat and the harmonic patterning of a soul-blues dance tune, Moore's witty composition evokes the texture of failed modern love as a see-saw battle between sacred and secular consciousness within the soul of a generous woman who is bitterly disappointed by her man's flagrant disrespect:

> We got a problem . . . you can't keep your pants on
> If you can't get a woman in bed . . . you just look at them in lust
> I know I'm a good woman. . . . I try to supply your every need
> And still you've got the nerve boy . . . to go out and cheat on me
> I've been looking for a good man . . . someone honest and true
> I prayed to heaven . . . ohhhhhhhhh, but hell sent me you
>
> Oh you kiss other women . . . right in front of my face
> And you say if I don't like it . . . I can just turn and walk away
> Boy, you're just a devil . . . with an angel's charm
> I thought you were from heaven . . . but hell is where you're from
> I was looking for a good man, someone honest and true
> I prayed to heaven . . . oh, hell sent me you
>
> I been hurt so many times . . . I really had my doubts
> But once you put that thing on me . . . it was much too late to back out
> You showed up at the right time . . . oh you really rang my bell
> I thought it was a sign from heaven . . . but it had to be straight from hell
> You took away my freedom . . . and all the things I used to do
> I prayed to heaven . . . oh, hell sent me you[83]

LaSalle, the inheritor of a blues queen lineage established by Ma Rainey, Bessie Smith, and Dinah Washington, reactivated her career in the mid-1980s by purveying sex-charged, double-entendre-heavy songs such as "Pay before You Pump" and "Lick It before You Stick It," and her live performances feature notably raunchy language. In the late 1990s, after her husband James Wolfe, a DJ and radio executive, announced that he had been called to the ministry, she temporarily retreated from her blues queen role to record several gospel albums, including *God's Got My Back* (1999). "I believe that God has a plan for me," she said in an interview, "and all of this is preparing me for something else."[84] "Hell Sent Me You" shrewdly synthesizes both sides of her persona, potty-mouthed love queen and righteous true believer, in a way that aligns the search for sexual ecstasy with the quest to know God. By framing her romantic journey in religious terms, as an answered prayer for intimate companionship, LaSalle inflects the morally suspect juke-joint mating game in the direction of holiness. But by simultaneously acknowledging the way sensual satisfactions ("you really rang my bell") blinded her to her lover's character flaws, flaws that ultimately revealed the devil in the angel and the hell behind the heaven, she redeploys the language of religion in ways that blues people understand.

When you hitch your happiness to the transient delights offered by a human lover rather than the eternal joys offered by God in heaven, you're sometimes going to get stung. You're going to get conjured by a devil with an angel's charm, which is to say played by a playa who made you feel good for a while. Theologian Anthony B. Pinn has argued that because the blues "lack the certainty of a teleological arrangement of history," those who embrace the music tend to hedge their spiritual bets. "Whereas the boundaries between [good and evil] forces and their effectiveness in human life are clear and based on the Christian faith for those singing the spirituals," he insists, "for those motivated by the blues there is a more utilitarian approach—one that allows for flirtation with both angelic and demonic forces depending on which might offer the most effective assistance."[85] Even as it draws on the language of evangelical Christianity, in other words, blues song articulates experiential complexities that rigid moral schemes can't or won't account for. As Kalamu ya Salaam puts it in his exploration of the blues aesthetic, "Life is not about good vs. evil, but about good and evil eaten off the same plate."[86] Like so many other devil-invoking blues, "Hell Sent Me You" deploys church-bred judgmentalism in the service of worldly vengeance, using religious vocabulary to express furious outrage at the failure of human love. The right to choose freely in love always entails the possibility of hooking up with a lover who, like LaSalle's, takes away your freedom even as he lives out his own. Love hurts, or can. The blues knows all about this paradox. The devil helps blues people articulate it.

5 , SELLING IT AT THE CROSSROADS

The Lives and Legacies of Robert Johnson

> You have an overwhelming mythology here. The whole
> selling-his-soul-to-the-devil thing seems pervasive and
> sticks with people.
>
> —LARRY COHN, producer, Roots n' Blues series,
>   Columbia Records

THE DEVIL'S BUSINESS

To the extent that the devil remains an active force in the twenty-first-century blues world, he does so primarily through a series of investments made in the figure of Robert Johnson (1911–38) and the Mississippi Delta crossroads tableau within which Johnson is imagined to have sold his soul in exchange for unearthly talents on the guitar. The range and number of these investments—emotional, capital, intellectual, juridical, legislative—is staggering. They include not just Johnson's platinum-selling *The Complete Recordings* (1990) and the limited edition *Complete Original Masters—Centennial Recordings* (2011, at a price of $345), along with homage albums to Johnson, numberless remakes of "Cross Road Blues," and Eric Clapton's triennial Crossroads Guitar Festival, but also a handful of documentaries, a feature film (*Crossroads*, 1986) that helped incite the ensuing mania, several dozen novels and short stories (including Ace Atkins's *Crossroad Blues*, 2000), a growing shelf of children's books, a Mississippi flood of academic and biographical studies, two authenticated, copyrighted photos as well as two others whose provenance and authenticity remain questionable, a U.S. postage stamp bearing Johnson's likeness from which the dangling (and cancer-causing) cigarette had been airbrushed, a paternity case prosecuted in the Mississippi courts that established Claud Johnson as Robert's legitimate heir and instantly transformed him into a royalty-receiving millionaire, a state-sanctioned road sign topped with a trigon of stylized blue guitars marking "the" crossroads in Clarksdale, Mississippi (the devil is mentioned several times in the resolution adopted by the town's Board of

Mayor and Commissioners), and, last but not least, a deluge of "crossroads" knickknacks proffered by the Clarksdale Tourism Commission in the years that followed the sign's erection, including foam beer sleeves and the sort of moist towelettes used to clean barbecue sauce from sticky fingers.

I will have more to say later about Walter Hill's *Crossroads* and about Clarksdale's civic branding of a particular urban intersection; both events help consolidate the contemporary legend of Robert Johnson as a restless, devil-haunted Delta phantom, a "James Dean of the blues." The prelude to that discussion is a frank acknowledgment of how completely Johnson's legend has come to dominate the conversation about the devil and the blues, so that the devil's many and various roles in the blues tradition have been obscured. "Was His Greatness Due to Satan?" asked *USA Today* in 1990 as *The Complete Recordings* provoked an unexpected sensation. "Speak of Robert Johnson and you speak of the Devil—the two have become so entangled."[1] To some extent this reduction of the blues-devil to the status of Johnson's muse-antagonist is the result of broader cultural dynamics. Even as Johnson has loomed large in a post-1960 blues world dominated by English blues-rockers and nostalgic white boomers, the specific emotional investments that African Americans have made in that devil figure over the long twentieth century have faded. Although the occasional black preacher warning against the devil's music can still be found in rural Mississippi, the phrase no longer holds much meaning for the mass of African Americans. The role played by Clara Smith, Sippie Wallace, and the classic blueswomen of an earlier era in conjuring up the devil as a troubling or empowering intimate is all but unknown to contemporary white blues fans; the condemnation that such women risked from their congregations for daring to participate in the world of secular black entertainment has faded from memory, too, in a postmillennial moment dominated by Oprah and Beyoncé, both of whom have fused spirituality, sexuality, and commerce in profitable and empowering ways. With the notable exception of Chris Thomas King's "Mississippi KKKrossroads," the blues lyric tradition has relinquished whatever interest it once had in using the devil and his hellish purview to signify on white southern violence, even as rap music, invigorated in the late 1980s by the Nation of Islam's black nationalist ideology, found in the devil a useful symbol for white malfeasance. In the matter of relationships between men and women, the devil—as instigator of discord and instrument of vengeance—surfaces only occasionally in the black soul-blues tradition and the globalized, multiracial blues mainstream.

"Sold It to the Devil," "Hell Ain't but a Mile and a Quarter," and "She's Making Whoopee in Hell Tonight" were then; this is now. Mention, as a researcher, that you are working on a book about the devil and the blues, and everybody knows at least one thing about the subject, or thinks they do. "Educated, secular Americans who would not speak of the Devil in any other context," notes media studies scholar Eric Rothenbuhler, "'know' that that is how Robert Johnson learned to play guitar." Rothenbuhler's claim bespeaks the extent to which the figure of Johnson-as-Deep-South-Faust has achieved hegemony, even in certain scholarly precincts and despite significant critical interventions. A 2003 article published in the *Journal of Adolescent and Adult Literacy* argued that "blues music—specifically the life of 1930s blues guitarist Robert Johnson—can be used to teach the Faust theme of selling one's soul to the devil for personal gain while developing students' literacy skills for the modern world," adding that the soul-selling theme was "a common motif expressed in many lyrics coming out of the Mississippi Delta region in the United States during the 1920s and 1930s." The latter claim is entirely spurious: there isn't a single Delta blues recording from that period, by Robert Johnson or anyone else, in which selling one's soul to the devil is directly imaged. Pedagogy has been piggybacked on mythology. But as two of the most vigorous scholarly debunkers, Barry Lee Pearson and Bill McCulloch, have noted, "The simple reality is that the Johnson legend—the whole selling-his-soul-at-the-crossroads business—cannot be eradicated at this late date; it belongs to the people now, and the fact that people embrace it as a part of American music history is as important as the question of whether it is true."[2]

From a scholar's perspective, "Robert Johnson" is haunted ground: a heavily freighted discursive construction whose twenty-nine extant recordings and accumulating biographical traces, including a sizeable number of interviews with fellow musicians and lovers, have been variously alchemized by successive generations of romantics, revisionists, and postrevisionists. In this chapter I intend neither to dismiss nor to embrace the devil-lore that suffuses contemporary academic and popular understandings of Johnson but rather to frame the talented young musician in relation to that lore in a way that complicates our picture of what he was about. The question "Did Robert Johnson *really* sell his soul to the devil at the crossroads?" isn't just unanswerable but, from a scholar's perspective, uninteresting—although the aesthetic and material investments it generates, including *Crossroads* and Clarksdale's guitar-topped monument, are fascinating indeed. A much more interesting question is, "Did Robert Johnson ever tell anybody that he had sold his soul to the devil at the crossroads?" and, if the answer is yes, "Was he sincere or seeking deliberately to mislead?" The primal scene out of which answers to those questions begin to emerge is, I will argue, Johnson's apprenticeship in Beauregard, Mississippi, with guitarist Ike Zimmerman between 1930 and 1932. An attentive reading of the testimony offered by Zimmerman's daughter and grandson can help us understand the way the elder musician's guidance helped shape Johnson's subsequent social performances, both in and out of the recording studio, including those that spoke to the younger musician's relationship with "the whole selling-his-soul-at-the-crossroads business."

Playing for the Haints
Ike's Protégé and Crossroads Folklore

'Twere profanation of our joys
To tell the laity our love.
—JOHN DONNE, "A Valediction: Forbidding Mourning" (1633)

SELL SELF TO THE DEVIL

To the extent that it is sourced in his recorded output, the devil legend that has attached itself to Johnson is grounded almost entirely in three songs, spread out across a pair of recording sessions in November 1936 and June 1937: "Cross Road Blues," "Hell Hound on My Trail," and "Me and the Devil Blues." (A fourth song, "Preachin' Blues (Up Jumped the Devil)," makes no reference to the devil apart from the title.) I discussed "Me and the Devil Blues" earlier in this study, reading it as an irreverent and essentially comic provocation, a manifestation of Johnson's cocky, hipsterish "young modern" sensibility. Although "Cross Road Blues," as blues researcher Gayle Dean Wardlow has noted, makes no mention of either the devil or a crossroads pact in which a soul is mortgaged in exchange for musical prowess, both popular and scholarly interpretations quickly veer from the lyric particulars of the song into a body of folklore sourced, to varying degrees, in Europe, Africa, and the American South. Within such an interpretive framework, "Cross Road Blues" is then understood to signify on the ritual elaborated in the folklore, and "Hell Hound on My Trail" is read as a companion piece: a cry of panic as the devil, in canine form, threatens to claim the soul that he has earlier purchased.

This last point deserves to be clarified: as suggestive and surcharged with terror as they are often imagined to be, neither "Cross Road Blues" nor "Hell Hound on My Trail" offers anything like a full-frontal rendering of the devil-at-the-crossroads tableau that waxes so large in the folklore. This becomes apparent when we encounter a song that *does* vividly render that tableau: "Crossroads," a 1957 recording by Cousin Leroy, a Georgia-born blues singer:

Well I walked down . . . by the crossroads
There to learn how . . . play my guitar
Well a man walked up. . . . "Son, let me tune it"
That was the devil . . . that was the devil
Oh Lord now
Oh well now
Sho nuff now
Oh Lordy now

Well my mama . . . told my pappy
Just before . . . I was born
I got a boychile . . . yes, he's comin'
Gonna be a rolling stone
Gonna be a rolling stone
Oh well now
Sho nuff now
Alrighty now

[Play the guitar!]

Oh well, oh well my baby
Walked up to my door
Will you tell me . . . where did you learn?
Well I walked down . . . by the crossroad
That's where I got my lesson
That's where I got my lesson
Oh Lord now
Sho nuff now
Alrighty now[3]

Leroy Rozier (1925–2008), born the same year as B. B. King and audibly influenced by Muddy Waters, was a minor figure in the blues—as much of a mystery as Robert Johnson—until an article in *Living Blues* (2012) filled in a few details.[4] He spent most of his life in south-central Georgia, below Macon, although his sixteen-odd recordings were all made in New York City. "Crossroads," which was released in 1960, three years after the recording date, is notable for several reasons. First, it's a touchstone for what Robert Johnson could have done but didn't do, twenty years earlier in "Cross Road Blues": speak directly about a crossroads transaction with the devil, rather than saying nothing about the devil or the (presumed) transaction. Second, the timing of the song's release, one year before a previously unreleased alternate take of Johnson's then-obscure song was included on *King of the Delta Blues Singers* (1961), makes clear that Rozier was drawing directly on the folk tradition for his imagery, not capitalizing on a roots-music trend. This distinguishes him from the many blues and rock artists, beginning with Cream in 1968, who have covered Johnson's composition and, in the long aftermath of Hill's *Crossroads* and *The Complete Recordings*, fed the blues audience's hunger for gothic themes.

What folklore, precisely, was Rozier drawing on? Several core elements of the crossroads pact show up in his song. A musician in search of instrumental mastery goes to a crossroads; a devil figure approaches, asks for the musician's guitar, and tunes it; and the result is a "lesson," a transactional exchange that presumably confers on the musician some new prowess, or mystique, or both. What Rozier's song pointedly does *not* say is that the musician sold his soul to the devil in a way that will incur an unpleasant settling of accounts later on—although the second stanza arguably implies that the devil-encounter helped bring forth the musician's rootless, peripatetic rolling-stone side prophesied by the musician's mother. The soul-sale element, as it happens, isn't an intrinsic or necessary component of devil-at-the-crossroads folklore, at least prior to 1970, although it is a fairly common motif. Some of the confusion on this point has to do with the way two different folklore streams, one from Europe (featuring the biblical devil, Satan) and one from Africa (featuring a pair of related crossroads trickster deities, Esu and Legba), seem to have fused on American soil, coalescing into a folktale that was well known in African American communities below the Mason-Dixon line. A Christian/Manichean worldview that understands the devil as the wholly evil antagonist who claims wayward souls doesn't smoothly align with and subsume an African worldview that understands Esu and Legba as figures of constructive disorder who are also, when properly petitioned, teachers and guides.[5] But where the subject of crossroads pacts is concerned, additional confusion has entered the picture thanks to a familiar problematic: the demonization of the blues by God-fearing black parents and ministers. Blues is the devil's music to such people *not* because any formal exchange with the devil has taken place at a crossroads but because a young man who traffics in such profane, unsanctified, low-class stuff has, de facto, "sold himself to the devil"—a metaphorical accusation that packs ontological weight.

This was the spirit in which Jimmy Rogers (1924–97), Muddy Waters's best-known guitarist and a contemporary of Cousin Leroy, found himself condemned. Born in the Mississippi Delta town of Ruleville, Rogers was raised by his grandmother in nearby Vance, where he hung out with Snooky Pryor and John Lee Hooker. By his midteens he'd dropped out of school—his grandmother, who cleaned railroad cars on the Illinois Central, took him along to St. Louis and elsewhere—and he was "just scufflin' around, dealin' with musicians. . . . I'd walk across the bridge from St. Louis to East St. Louis where the clubs were," he told a journalist. "Cost a nickel. My grandmother gave up the switch by then. I was getting to be a pretty good sized boy. She'd always say, 'I better leave him alone but he done sold hisself to the devil.'"[6] "Sold" in this context implies nothing like the sort of talent-accruing crossroads encounter evoked by Rozier. "Sold hisself to the devil" simply means "He's gone to the devil": a moral condemnation leveled at a wayward young musician who would rather juke all night than work or attend school. Rev. Booker Miller (1910–68), a contemporary of Johnson's from Greenwood, Mississippi, expanded on this theme in an interview with Wardlow. "Them old folks did believe the devil would get you for playin' the blues and livin' like that"—meaning, according to Wardlow, engaging in the sins of adultery, fornication, gambling, lying, and drinking. The idea of "selling your soul to the devil," Miller insisted, traced back to "those old slavery times."[7] In "Hell Is a Name for All Sinners" (1931), Lonnie Johnson addresses himself, with cheerful resignation, to an imagined congregation of murderers, thieves, gamblers, crooks, and whiskey drinkers, acknowledging the collective fate that lies in store—one that has nothing to do with crossroads: "So come on you sinners, let's join in an' sing this song. / Come on, let's join in an' sing this song. / We sold our self to the devil, now hell is our everlastin' home."

There is a colloquial Christian meaning of "sold himself to the devil," in other words, that carries general behavioral overtones, and a much more specific evocation of a crossroads encounter with the devil. Both show up with some frequency in the blues tradition and in African American culture more broadly. But they aren't the same thing—although blues aficionados and scholars alike often conflate them, and although they may sometimes have flowed together in the minds of those in prewar black southern communities who were inclined to slander blues musicians. No crossroads pact is required of the young bluesman in order to find himself disparaged for having "sold his soul" to play "the devil's music." Yet the ritual did exist, and its presence in the social field—as brag, insinuation, or condemnation—clearly increased the legend-generating capacity of blues musicians as a group.

The Robert Johnson legend, according to Pearson and McCulloch, first crystalizes through just such an insinuation—a doubled insinuation, more precisely, in which blues historian Pete Welding quotes Son House in his 1966 *Downbeat* interview with the Delta bluesman and then superadds a layer of mystique. At issue was young Robert's seemingly miraculous transformation, in roughly half a year, from a mediocre guitarist into a legitimate phenom who showed up at a juke where House was playing and stunned the older musician with his prowess:

> "Me and Willie [Brown] was playing out near a little place they call Banks, Miss.," House said, "and he come in that Saturday night with the guitar. . . . So he wiggled on through and got where we was." I said, "Well, boy, what are you doing with that thing?" He said, "Aw, get up and let me have your chair and I'll show you what I can do with it." I said, "Oh, nothing— that's all a lot of racket." He laughed and said, "Well, let me try." So I said, "Well, okay." We gets up, you know—laughs at him. So he sets down and he starts playing, and when he got through, all our mouths was open . . . yeah, what happened was a big surprise—how he did it that fast. . . .
>
> Johnson was at this time about 21 or 22, House said. The older blues man recalled that when Johnson came to the dance near Banks, his guitar style was fully shaped, revealing the same mastery as is evident on his recordings a few years later. House suggested in all seriousness that Johnson, in his months away from home, had "sold his soul to the devil in exchange for learning to play like that."[8]

House, we should note, doesn't say that Johnson *himself* claimed to have sold his soul to the devil. Nor does House say anything about a crossroads location. Still, the transactional element of House's insinuation—that young Robert must have traded his soul "in exchange for learning to play like that"—strongly suggests that House is referencing a crossroads pact. Sociologist William F. Danaher has suggested that such legendry on the part of Johnson's blues-playing peers might be understood as an occupational myth: a story floated by a subculture that helps its members retain self-respect and unity in the face of an extraordinary individual. "By crediting Johnson's talents to supernatural powers and placing Johnson in another category from themselves, musicians who did not display his virtuosity, even after years of playing, legitimated their continued participation in the subculture and maintained in-group solidarity."[9] This explanation helps us see House's invocation of the devil as a response to status anxiety produced by the sudden shifting of the Delta blues pecking order: a young wannabe reappears to vanquish his former masters, wiping the patronizing smiles off their faces. It *must* have been the devil, since a more mundane explanation—Johnson had greater natural talent, or practiced harder—could only cast aspersions on House's and Brown's own artistry. Pete Welding, in any case, chose to emphasize the gothic atmospherics lurking within House's characterization by concluding his article with a comment from Johnson's traveling companion, Johnny Shines, that Johnson's death by poisoning at the hands of a no-good woman had (or so he'd heard) "something to do with the black arts." "The story," Welding pronounced, "certainly details an appropriate end for a man who all through his adult years felt the hounds of hell baying loudly and relentless on his trail. In the end, he just couldn't outrun them any longer."[10]

Welding's sort of overheated romanticism, along with earlier effusions by Rudi Blesh (1946) and Samuel Charters (1959), is viewed with disdain by many contemporary commentators. "I can be as fascinated by occult musings as the next guy," writes Elijah Wald, "but it is long past time for music journalists to get over the cliché of always linking Robert Johnson and the Devil. . . . I propose a moratorium on sentences like 'Persistent themes in his blues were religious despair and pursuit by demons.'"[11] Pearson and McCulloch go so far as to accuse Welding of inaugurating a "counterfeit story line" by conjuring up Johnson as a twentieth-century Faust, and they indict a long list of legend-augmenting coconspirators, Eurocentric and Afrocentric alike, including Robert Palmer (1981), Peter Guralnick (1982), and Julio Finn (1986).[12] "The debunking of Johnson's involvement with the supernatural," as musicologist David Brackett observes, "has entered a boom period in the new millennium."[13] (Or at least that's true for scholarship. Journalists, fans, and the people overseeing blues tourism in Mississippi show little interest in jettisoning the phrase "legend has it.") One line of revisionist counterattack insists that Robert Johnson's legend is grounded in a case of mistaken identity: the general public's confusion of the author of "Me and the Devil Blues" and "Cross Road Blues" with another, older Delta bluesman, Tommy Johnson (1896–1956), who did indeed speak forthrightly about having sold his soul to the devil at the crossroads. The elder Johnson's account, which epitomizes the folkloric paradigm, was conveyed to ethnomusicologist David Evans in the late 1960s by his younger brother LeDell, a bluesman-turned-preacher:

> He [Tommy] could sit down and just think up a song, which is blues, and make 'em hisself without anybody learning him. . . . He could make a song in ten minutes. Now if Tom was living, he'd tell you. He said the reason he knowed so much, said he sold hisself to the devil. I asked him

how. He said, "If you want to learn how to play anything you want to play and learn how to make songs yourself, you take your guitar and you go to where a road crosses that way, where a crossroad is. Get there, be sure to get there just a little 'fore twelve o'clock that night so you'll know you'll be there. You have your guitar and be playing a piece sitting there by yourself. You have to go by yourself and be sitting there playing a piece. A big black man will walk up there and take your guitar, and he'll tune it. And then he'll play a piece and hand it back to you. That's the way I learned how to play anything I want." And he could.[14]

This is one of the only extant accounts of a crossroads pact that specifically mentions blues music. Its veracity is confirmed by Wardlow, who was told the same story by both LeDell Johnson and Ishmon Bracey, a musical associate of Tommy's, during his own Mississippi fieldwork in the 1960s. Bracey, according to Wardlow, "downplayed [Tommy's] claim, saying he had played the blues 'as good as Tommy' and he never sold his soul for musical talent."[15] Evans, an early skeptic, argued in *Tommy Johnson* (1971) that Tommy's story "was almost certainly a device to bolster his fame and reputation and augment his trickster image."[16] Where Evans views Tommy's narrative as calculated self-legending, a "device" designed to increase his cultural capital as a blues performer, Bracey takes Tommy's claim more personally, as a brag that implicitly downgrades his own creative gifts and thus needs to be rebutted. Both Evans and Bracey dovetail on a key point: *any* claim about selling one's soul to the devil at the crossroads in exchange for a superior skill set, whether it is made by a blues performer himself or by his relatives, peers, or critics, should be viewed as an attempt to claim power within a specific social context. This is the deep logic that links Tommy Johnson's crossroads narrative, as retold by his brother and Bracey, with Son House's comment about Robert Johnson.

Associating oneself with the devil was, at least potentially, a source of useable power for a blues performer, a form of subcultural one-upmanship that could also translate into profitable mystique on the streets and in the jukes. Associating another blues musician with the devil could serve a similar function—asserting one's "natural" priority in the matter of musical talent (no special deals needed)—but it could also be a way of seconding the devil's-music slander leveled by Christian judgmentalism. This last impulse was clearly at work in both LeDell Johnson and Bracey. The context within which LeDell offered up his brother's story of crossroads soul-selling was his own rebirth in Christ, a religious conversion that led him to swear off the blues, put down his guitar, and leave behind what he termed "a devil's life." Bracey, too, had renounced the blues to become a preacher and a performer of religious music by the time Wardlow interviewed him. Neither convert was inclined to see Tommy Johnson, an incurable alcoholic, as anything other than an object-lesson in the wages of sinfulness. As for Son House: he was a conscience-stricken bluesman haunted by his own inability to toe the Christian line, but he was also Robert Johnson's elder and competitor on the guitar.[17] We will never know precisely why he leveled the soul-sale insinuation at Johnson, long after the younger man's death, but he had something to gain on both fronts, spiritual and professional, by leveling it.

Over the past fifty years, and despite the sort of scholarly parsing I've offered here, the association of Robert Johnson and the blues with a devil-pact at a Mississippi Delta crossroads has come to seem natural and inevitable, as though the man and the music were of a piece with the folklore. And of course they are—but only if one is speaking of the white folklore that has emerged during that period, a time in which white romanticism about such things has come to dominate the popular imagination. The African American folklore of an earlier era, a large and unruly body of material in which Cousin Leroy's recording and Tommy Johnson's account were both sourced, tells a more complex story. The best guides to that material are a pair of white investigators, Newbell Niles Puckett (1897–1967) and Harry Middleton Hyatt (1896–1978). Puckett, a native Mississippian, published an expanded version of his Yale dissertation as *Folk Beliefs of the Southern Negro* (1926); Hyatt, an Episcopal clergyman who grew up on the Illinois side of the Mississippi River across from Hannibal, Missouri, did extensive fieldwork among African Americans in the southeastern United States between 1936 and 1940, eventually publishing a compendium titled *Hoodoo—Conjuration—Witchcraft—Rootwork* (1970).[18] Puckett offers one representative version of the crossroads pact in a section titled "The Faust Legend"; Hyatt offers more than thirty-five under the heading "Sell Self to the Devil." Although Puckett's tale and a handful of Hyatt's are about improving one's guitar skills with the help of the devil or a "big black man," many of Hyatt's tales involve other instruments—banjo, fiddle, accordion, piano—and a fair number concern nonmusical pursuits through which impoverished, oppressed African Americans can gain a hand up, such as improving one's gambling skills, evading the police, and escaping from jail. None of the accounts come from Mississippi, although that may simply be because Hyatt didn't visit there. None of the informants—not a single one—mentions blues. Nor does the phrase "the devil's music" show up in these accounts, although the devil's connection *with* music, his conferring of instrumental prowess in nonsanctified forms of music more specifically, is a notable theme. Several of Hyatt's tales feature subjects who curse God and swear fealty to the devil. Although midnight at the crossroads is a characteristic time and place for devil-encounters, the hour called "morning"—dawn or near-dawn—is even more common, and graveyards are an important secondary location. Multiple visits, generally seven or nine, are almost always required in order to complete the transaction.

The tales diverge wildly on what might be called the Faust question: does "sell[ing] self to the devil" in exchange for musical talent mean that one is, in fact, irreversibly damned to hell? Puckett's informant, an unnamed "New Orleans conjuror," says yes. "You will be able to play any piece you desire on the guitar and you can do anything you want to do in this world, but you have sold your eternal soul to the devil and are his in the world to come."[19] Several of Hyatt's tale-tellers suggest a similar fate, including one from Ocean City, Maryland, whose narrative shares some features with Tommy Johnson's:

> If you want to know how to play a banjo or guitar or do magic tricks, you have to *sell yourself to the devil.* You have to go to the cemetery nine mornings and get some of the dirt and bring it back with you and put it in a little bottle, then go to some fork of the road and each morning sit there and try to play that guitar. Don't care what you see come there, don't get 'fraid and run away. Just stay there for nine mornings and on the ninth morning there will come some rider riding at lightning speed in the form of the devil. You stay there then still playing your guitar and when he has passed you can play any tune you want to play or do any magic trick you want to do because you have sold yourself to the devil.[20]

In the great majority of these tales, however, the transaction with the devil is interpreted in a way that undercuts any Faustian idea of eternal damnation. None of the narrators makes even a token attempt to convey the horrors that are routinely alleged to have haunted Robert Johnson; most of the tales, in fact, treat the devil figure as a conferrer of talents who fades from the picture after gifting the petitioner, as in the following from the South Carolina piedmont:

> If yo' wanta be a professional gambler, why yo' git chew a deck of cards an' go in de cemetery aftah hours in de night, jes' aftah twelve o'clock, an' go to de first man in de cemetery an' straddle de grave. When yo' straddle

de grave, somebody will come dere an' play a game or two with you, until you see a light comin' 'cross de cemetery an' dat'll be de ole devil. If yo' kin stan' de temptation till he git dere wit dat light, den he'll play wit chew, an' when he git through plain' wit chew, why yo' be a 'fessional gambler.[21]

In three of Hyatt's tales where the devil does return after a stipulated pe-riod of time to stake his claim, the pact-maker is able to trick him quite eas-ily by giving him a piece of shoe leather—a "sole" rather than the promised soul. Several other informants describe easily reversible crossroads pacts in which one can simply throw down a guitar and walk away from the devil to "break the tie" or, alternately, "go right back to the same crossroads and make a vow to reform." ("That's all you have to do is make the vow there[?]" asks Hyatt of his Florida informant, incredulous. "Nothing else[?]")[22]

Who *is* this devil of the crossroads—a fear-inducing soul-snatcher one moment, an empowering teacher the next? Over the decades, a scholarly consensus has emerged that traces his bifurcated character in African Amer-ican folklore to his creole origins in both Europe and Africa. Or at least a scholarly consensus *should* have emerged, especially where Puckett's and Hyatt's crossroads tales are concerned. What has happened instead is that the African cultural origins of the African American crossroads story and the devil figure at its center have come to be overemphasized, at least among blues scholars, perhaps to compensate for a corresponding overemphasis of the Faust theme by a general public hungry for horror stories about poi-soned bluesmen barking like dogs. This process began innocently enough with Zora Neale Hurston; "The devil," she wrote in *Mules and Men* (1935) of the figure she'd encountered in the folktales of Florida blues people, "is not the terror that he is in European folk-lore."[23] In *Myth of the Negro Past* (1941), anthropologist Melville Herskovits reiterated Hurston's insight—"So different is this tricksterlike creature from Satan as generally conceived, in-deed, that he is almost a different being"—and he attributed that difference to the survival, in the African American folk mind and by way of slavery's transatlantic cargoes, of Legba, the trickster deity from Dahomean-Yoruba mythology who "rules the crossroads."[24] Europe's devil, the Satan of the Bible, has of course long been associated with crossroads: they were the place where black magic transpired, witches lingered, and the bodies of condemned criminals were left to rot. The tradition of a devil-compact is widespread in European history and can be traced back beyond the Bible into the Zoroastrianism of ancient Persia.[25] But the dialectic of European and African cultural origins that underlies crossroads folklore has, in the years since Hurston and Herskovits, been elaborated into an Afrocentric idea, one that understates the European contribution to the crossroads devil in order to configure the bluesman as a particular kind of culture hero. Brought to North America in the early nineteenth century by slaves imported from the Caribbean, argues Samuel Floyd in *The Power of Black Music* (1995),

> this new incarnation of Esu as the Devil took hold as he emerged at the crossroads sometime in the late nineteenth century to deliver superior creative skills to black songsters, and exerted a powerful influence on the development of the blues. . . . This African-American legend [that is, Puckett's folktale] seems to me remarkably consonant with, and a logical extension of, the Yoruba myth—an embroidered and African-Americanized revision of it. . . . In the first thirty years of the twentieth century, African cultural memory was vivid. This myth engaged the imagination of Robert Johnson, Tommy Johnson, Peetie Wheatstraw, and other bluesmen who would, in turn, perpetuate it in their life-styles and their music. Robert Johnson became obsessed with and fatalistic about "the forces against him," eloquently expressing this obsession and fatalism in "Hell-Hound on My Trail," "Crossroads [sic] Blues," and "Me and the Devil Blues."[26]

Floyd's basic premise about the persistence of African religious and cultural forms in New World settings is valid in the broadest sense, but his rhetoric can't hide a yawning evidentiary gap. Postulating Esu's "emergence" on Deep South terrain isn't the same thing as offering an interpretive framework that can actually account for the complexities of Robert Johnson's life and art, including the subcultural world of Mississippi bluesmen within which he sought distinction. With his evocation of an "obsessed" and "fatalistic" Johnson, Floyd offers us an Afrocentric version of the Eurocentric Johnson famously evoked by Greil Marcus (1975): "He walked his road like a failed, orphaned Puritan . . . framing his tales with old echoes of sin and damnation. There were demons in his songs—blues that walked like a man, the devil, or the two in league with each other—and Johnson was often on good terms with them." Both Johnsons are figures of romance, not least because Floyd and Marcus, like many others, stake so much of their portraiture on three songs chosen from a much larger repertoire. But there is a truer Robert Johnson to be found.

He is not, as the revisionists would have us believe, a young man so focused on professional success, so set on "escaping the Delta" by crafting saleable pop songs, that he was essentially unconcerned with God and the devil. Nor, as Ted Gioia has argued in a recent study (in line with researcher Robert "Mack" McCormick's stated position), can Johnson's career and repertoire be explained as a guilt-driven embrace of the devil's-music slur leveled at him by black townspeople furious that his young wife Virginia Travis had died in childbirth while he was out on the road playing the blues.[27] The Robert Johnson I seek to evoke is something else: a sly hipster, determined to stay out of the cotton fields and harvest pleasure from Delta womanhood with the help of his prodigious talents; a young man who looked askance at the supernatural, thanks to his mentor, but knew how to turn devil-talk to his own purposes. He is Ike's protégé.

'CROSS THE ROAD

The legend of Robert Johnson at the crossroads depends on missing time—a phrase, coincidentally, that waxes large in the contemporary folklore of alien abductions—and a disappearing act.

Johnson disappeared from the Robinsonville area of the Mississippi Delta late in 1930. His wife had died that April; during roughly the same period, Son House and Willie Brown began playing local dances that drew the inexperienced young musician like a moth to a flame. Johnson would pick up a guitar when the older men went on break and, as House later recalled, "go bamming with it" until the crowd complained.[28] House and Brown considered him a pest. So Johnson left town. When he returned, after an absence of "six or seven months" in House's estimation, he had suddenly—miraculously—been reborn as a prodigy, somebody who must have "sold his soul to the devil" in order to gain such talents, as House famously insisted to Welding three decades later. The power of the legend, to the extent that House's story anchors it, depends as much on the brevity of the interlude as on the increase in instrumental proficiency. No mere human could have made that sort of great leap forward in so short a time, it is presumed, without divine, or demonic, intercession.

Scholars have known at least since Robert Palmer's *Deep Blues* (1981) that Johnson was gone from Robinsonville for somewhat longer than House realized—at least a year and, by some recent estimates, as long as three years.[29] (I explore this issue in detail in part 3 of this chapter.) It has long been known that Johnson retreated to the Hazlehurst area, his birthplace, roughly thirty miles south of Jackson, and that he studied guitar with an older Alabama-born bluesman named Ike whose last name has been variously misspelled Zinneman, Zinnerman, Zinman, and Zinemon. Ike, according to Stephen C. LaVere's liner notes for *The Complete Recordings* (1990), "had always told his wife that he had learned to play guitar in a graveyard at midnight while sitting atop tombstones," a fact that led Gioia (2008) to characterize the older man as "devilish."[30] Virtually nothing else was known of Ike and his relationship with Johnson until cultural historian Bruce Conforth published an article in *Living Blues* (2008) based on extensive interviews with Isaiah "Ike" Zimmerman's unnamed daughter and grandson.[31]

According to those two, Robert Johnson—whom they called R. L.—lived for "a long time" with Zimmerman's family, right in the family house; Conforth recently specified seven months as the term of Johnson's residency.[32] Although Conforth withholds the family's precise location to maintain their privacy, another researcher has identified the town as Beauregard, Mississippi, five miles south of Martinsville (where Johnson met Callie Craft, who would become his second wife, during that period) and ten miles south of Hazlehurst.[33] The Ike Zimmerman evoked by his daughter and grandson was a "strong" and "good" man, a family man with a well-paying job working for the highway department, but also a "womanizer" who "played guitar to chase women." He played guitar behind his head, his daughter remembered, and "did all of that."[34]

Ike had one other character trait, an eccentricity of sorts that he imparted to his protégé: he not only practiced in the local graveyard at midnight, but he teased his family, in a way designed to both frighten and amuse them, about the evil spirits with whom he held court there. "Daddy," insisted his daughter, laughing at the recollection, ". . . would always scare people and say he'd go pickin' the guitar and the *haints* would come out, at the graveyard":

> He said (he'd go to the cemetery) 'cause he could play better 'cause it was still . . . real quiet. Real quiet. But he'd come back and tell them he played for the, he said the *haints*. He said I been up there playing for the *haints*. They'd make a big laugh out of it. They sure would. . . . And I think when he was carryin' Robert up there it was so Robert could really concentrate on his guitar. . . . He (Ike) was determined not to let him [Robert] fail.[35]

"It was always at twelve o'clock," added Ike's grandson, and Ms. Zimmerman concurred: "They would leave and go to that cemetery. It's . . . got them old tombstones. . . . He'd sit back there with him (Robert Johnson). He wasn't at no crossroads. . . . There wasn't no crossroads. They went '*cross the road* (laughs). 'Cause you gotta go across (the) road and go to that cemetery. They went over there and sat on the tombstones. Exactly. And that's where they was. Sitting there playing. . . . When everybody was asleep. I think because it was quiet and nobody around to walk and interfere. He [Ike] wasn't never scared, but he wasn't meeting the devil neither (laughs)."[36]

Both Ike and his descendants exhibit a playful irreverence toward conventional pieties — not just Christian piety, which would have looked disapprovingly on midnight visits to graveyards, but also the world of black folk religion or hoodoo as well. According to sociologist Katrina Hazzard-Donald, haints, along with witches and so-called demon spirits, were part of a regional Afro-diasporic belief system that spread across the South in the aftermath of the Civil War.[37] Whites had always denigrated such things as "superstition," but by the 1930s, according to sociologist Hortense Powdermaker, younger Mississippi blacks themselves, especially in the Delta, were rejecting *both* hoodoo and Christianity (especially hellfire-and-brimstone threats) as antiquated, out of touch. "The same forces operate against both," argued Powdermaker — which is to say, the pressures of an accelerating modern world — "and the same people tend to discard them."[38] "I don't believe in those lies," Delta bluesman Johnny Shines (1915–92) told an interviewer the year before he died. "I never did believe in it. There's a whole lot of stuff I used to hear when I was a kid. I was glad when I got big enough to get the heck out of the house so I wouldn't have to hear any more of that stuff. . . . I mean, my daddy was well educated but he believed that stuff."[39] To the extent that devil-lore about selling one's soul at the crossroads is sourced in both Christian demonology and the residue of African spirituality, it is precisely the sort of thing that Robert Johnson, his young modern sensibility activated by Ike's irreverence, would have viewed with considerable ironic distance. This is why Julio Finn's claim about Robert Johnson — that in all likelihood during his "wanderings in the bayous" he had sought out or met a "Hoodoo Doctor" who had "initiated him into the cult" so that he could "invoke Legba . . . master of the crossroads" — is so unpersuasive.[40] Johnson, following in Ike's footsteps, would have been far more likely to mock than take an audience with such a conjure man (or woman). As the testimony of Zimmerman's family makes clear, what Robert got from Ike was a mentor who offered close personal instruction over an extended period of time; a model for guitar-playing as a mode of seduction; and an attitude toward the supernatural that might be termed instrumental skepticism: using spirit-talk (haint-talk, devil-talk) as a form of ironic banter that sometimes scares or mystifies noninitiates, sometimes jokes with them, but in all cases maintains a protective shield around the deeply serious and purposeful activity of blues musicianship.

The word "protégé" means "protected." Robert, only four years younger than his master teacher, was Ike's protégé in every sense. Ike was determined not to let him fail. "He came for my daddy to teach," remembered Ike's daughter, "and my daddy taught him. He lived there with my daddy. . . . he stayed a long time (because) he was staying to learn how to play the guitar. . . . It seemed to me like he just took him for his family 'cause . . . he was always, protected . . . and he just fitted in."[41] Johnson was engaging in a range of other activities during his extended sojourn with Ike: romancing and marrying Callie Craft, ten years his senior; sleeping with and impregnating a teenaged preacher's daughter named Virgie Mae Smith; and performing at local jukes, both solo and with Ike. But it was the bond forged during those late night training sessions in the graveyard "'cross the road," I suggest, that profoundly shaped not just Johnson's guitar style but also his approach to life and art. Ike and Robert formed, in effect, a subculture of two nested within Mississippi's extensive blues subculture—a clique, to use the term invoked by sociologist Erving Goffman to describe "a small number of persons who join together for informal amusements."[42] Cliques are sustained in part by the way they generate, protect, and in some cases exaggerate the importance of secrets that help distinguish their members from nonmembers, both their professional peers (i.e., in Goffman's terms, persons of one's own "rank") and the general public. The secret shared by Ike and his protégé was that there *was* no secret. There wasn't a crossroads pact of the sort evoked by the folktales that both men were surely familiar with. Nor were there the dark dealings with the devil, or "haints," imagined by Christians, black and white, who had always consigned bluesmen to the devil's party regardless. There was only masculine fellowship, the shared endeavor of transmitting acquired knowledge from master to apprentice and the hard, patient work it took, in the quiet of a graveyard, to do that. But why dissipate the mystery, if others insisted on summoning it up? Why not work with it—playfully, directly, obliquely, whatever it took to keep others off balance, gain the advantage, and keep the clique's secret?

The attitude I'm evoking here in the bond between Zimmerman and Johnson is merely one instance of a more general predisposition that sociologist Howard S. Becker discovered in his research among Chicago-area professional jazz and dance musicians in the late 1940s. Such musicians, he found, were powerfully invested in the project of differentiating themselves from the "squares," as they termed their audiences, and they continually performed their own hipness for each other in a way that even some within the subculture found oppressive. "I'm glad I'm getting out of the business," one young musician told Becker. "I'm getting sick of being around musicians. There's so much ritual and ceremony junk. They have to talk a special language, dress different, and wear a different kind of glasses. And it just doesn't mean a damn thing except 'we're different.'"[43]

That attitude—we're different, they're square; we get it, they don't; we know how serious we are about our midnight training sessions, they think it's all a bunch of devilish hoodoo—is the attitude that Ike Zimmerman transmitted to Robert Johnson. When the lessons were finished, Johnson, now married to Callie Craft, left his mentor behind and moved back to the Clarksdale area. But the attitude remained alive, internalized and projected as one brilliant young musician's aggressive cultivation of mystique, at least with those whom he considered below him in rank (or equal in rank but deserving of being kept out of the clique), which was almost everybody: friends, fellow musicians, female lovers, the general public. Ike's signature phrase after returning home from the nearby graveyard, "I been up there playing for the *haints*," became, in Johnson's hands, an inclination to flirt with crossroads devil-lore—for a joke, for real, anything to keep the squares guessing. Pearson and McCulloch have insisted that "no one who spent time with [Johnson] in the years following the loss [of his first wife, Virginia] could recall him saying or doing anything to promote the idea that he was in an ongoing partnership with the devil," but this isn't true.[44] Evidence exists that he told at least four people—a friend, a fellow blues player, a girlfriend, and a random passerby—that he had sold his soul to the devil, and two out of four were quite sure he was putting them on.

The friend was Willie Coffee, an aging Mississippi sharecropper who had been Johnson's boyhood pal and who remained in touch with him through the years. Interviewed by LaVere on the front porch of his shack in the late 1990s, Coffee reminisced about how Robert, back then, had been "gone awhile with that guitar" before returning a much better player:

WC: How he got up that way so quick, I don't know. But he say he sold his self to—soul, to the devil. . . .

SL: When Robert told you that he had sold his soul to the devil, did you . . . think he was being serious?

WC: No, I never did think he was serious, because he'd always, when he'd come in here with us, he always come in, you know, with a lot of jive and . . . you know, joking, cracking a lot of jokes like that. I never did believe in it.[45]

Coffee's recollections evoke Johnson as a self-conscious crafter of the legend that would ultimately be attached to him, playfully undercutting his own sincerity in a way that created masculine fellowship even while allowing an air of uncertainty, of unsettling possibility, to remain in play. Later in the interview, Coffee added that Johnson "had a record out, about he's standing at the cross roads, trying to flag a ride, and everybody kept on passin' him by, nobody didn't stop." Unlike many who have bought into the legend, Coffee seems disinclined to confuse the song's vividly evocative lyrics with his memories of Johnson's tongue-in-cheek "confession" about selling his soul to the devil. Most notable, however, is the striking correlation between Johnson's joking and Ike's, as reported by friends and family. Each man, reentering the world of his intimates, aggressively makes light of his (imagined) rendezvous with the Dark Side, engaging a familiar folkloric theme while preserving the sanctity of his actual musical labors in the woodshed.

Honeyboy Edwards, a musical peer of Johnson's, reports a similar encounter and draws the same conclusion as Coffee. Here it is important to note, as many scholars have, that Honeyboy's responses to interviewers have been inconsistent through the years. Speaking with folklorist Alan Lomax in Mississippi in 1942, for example, Edwards responds compliantly to a series of leading questions but says nothing about a crossroads soul-sale:

AL: You think Robert Johnson went the wrong way?
HE: Yes.
AL: You think he did, huh?
HE: Yes, I don't believe he was saved.
AL: So you think blues and all this is the Devil's business?
HE: Well, I believe the blues is.
AL: You're just the Devil's child right now, aren't you?
HE: I'm the Devil's child right now.[46]

In *Delta Blues* (2008), Gioia mischaracterizes Edwards's contribution to this exchange, claiming that Edwards "[offers] his opinion that Johnson [was] . . . caught up in the 'Devil's business.'"[47] But the phrase is Lomax's, not Edwards's, and the issue both men are speaking to isn't crossroads pacts but the broader Christian indictment of blues as the devil's music rather than the sort of music "saved" church members sing and enjoy, an indictment that Edwards readily capitulates to here, perhaps out of a desire not to contradict his white interlocutor. Still, Gioia's larger claim, that Johnson may have helped propagate his own legend long before white blues writers came along, is correct, supported by another interview with Edwards conducted by British music journalist Paul Trynka in 1994. The Johnson evoked by Edwards is consistent with the jokester evoked by Coffee and the Ike Zimmerman remembered by Ike's family. As Edwards put it,

> Before he left [Robinsonville] they [Son House and Willie Brown] wouldn't let him play with them. He went off, I guess off to the Crossroads. He told me he went to the crossroads. Matter of fact he spoke that he went to the crossroads, and I didn't know exactly what he mean, and what he'd done. . . . He probably did (say that to frighten people) he said he went down to the crossroad and went down on his knees and met a man, but I never met a man! Robert was a big bullshitter man. Robert went under Lonnie Johnson, he went under two or three different names.[48]

Johnson's story impressed Edwards enough at the time that he shared it with his cousin Willie Mae Powell, who was dating Johnson. "He told Honey 'bout it . . . that he sold hisself at a fork in the road. Twelve o'clock one—at night. Honeyboy says it's the truth. He told him so. He did."[49] But there's a difference between Johnson truly having *said* that he sold himself to the devil and truly having *meant* it. If Powell isn't attuned to the distinction, then Edwards clearly is. His summary judgment—"Robert was a big bullshitter"—crystalizes the way Johnson kept alive his mentor Ike's irreverent spirit by winking at the very mystique that he was aggressively cultivating. (It makes perfect sense, in such a context, that Robert would adopt Lonnie Johnson's name as an alias, since the older musician had recently recorded several devil-blues songs, including "She's Making Whoopee in Hell Tonight," 1930, and "Hell's a Name for All Sinners," 1931.)

A skeptic might argue that Edwards's statement appears to mingle memories—or apparent memories—of Robert's boast with a line from "Cross Road Blues": "I went to the crossroad . . . got down on my knees." Is it possible, as Patricia R. Schroeder suggests, that Edwards simply fabricated Johnson's claim about soul-selling, telling Trynka, as he told Alan Lomax, what he presumed the white man wanted to hear, especially at a mid-1990s moment when Johnson's *Complete Recordings* and crossroads legend were hot currency in the blues world?[50] "I didn't invoke the crossroads story," Trynka recently asserted in his own defense. "We were just talking about Johnson as a guitarist, it was [Edwards] who mentioned the crossroads story first."[51] But then what about Johnny Shines, who traveled and performed with Johnson over a period of several years—far more extensively than Edwards—and who has always vigorously denied ever having heard Johnson speak of selling his soul at the crossroads? "No, he never told me that lie, no,'" Shines told an interviewer. "If he would have, I'd have called him a liar right to his face, because I know it's a lie."[52] Robert Junior Lockwood, too, disputed the soul-selling legend in a way that suggests Johnson never made such a claim in his presence. "All that bullshit about him selling hisself to the devil, that's bullshit."[53] But if Shines and Lockwood are telling the truth, is it possible that Coffee and Edwards are also telling the truth?

Goffman's writings about cliques can help us reconcile these conflicting accounts. "Cliques," according to Goffman, ". . . often function to protect the individual not from persons of other ranks but from persons of his own rank. Thus, while all the members of one's clique may be of the same status level, it may be crucial that not all persons of one's status level be allowed into the clique."[54] Johnson's aggressive joking or "bullshitting" about soul-selling with Coffee and Edwards reflects, I am arguing, his felt sense that the two men are either below him in rank (Coffee, who submitted to a sharecropper's life) or equal in rank but not deserving of being included in the clique (Edwards, a peer/competitor). Johnson's refusal to tell either Shines or Lockwood that "lie" about the devil and the crossroads, by contrast, suggests that he perceived both men as equals and thus deserving of being allowed into the clique—which is to say, allowed into the tightly knit circle of two that Johnson had forged with Ike and carried forward into the world as his secret talisman, a psychological disposition to hold himself above and apart from the squares. Shines was his traveling and performing partner for several years: his longest lasting partnership apart from the one with Ike. Lockwood, whose mother, Estella Coleman, had a long-term relationship with Johnson, became Johnson's student-apprentice. Johnson saw Shines, in other words, as a kind of aftermarket Ike, a serious musician with whom he could simply *be*, rather than joking, fronting, and jostling for status. He saw Lockwood, similarly, as his protégé—a "junior" Robert Johnson with whom he now enjoyed the sort of master-student relationship that Ike had forged with him. Lockwood, like Shines, became a member of the clique.

There is no reason, in other words, to presume that Johnson "bullshitted" everybody in precisely the same way, or, conversely, to argue that the testimony offered by Shines and Lockwood undercuts all claims that Johnson engaged in aggressive self-legending. There are at least two other informants, in any case, who corroborate the accounts offered by Coffee and

Edwards. One is the redoubtable "Queen Elizabeth," a former girlfriend of Johnson's who spars on camera with John Hammond Jr. in the documentary *The Search for Robert Johnson* (1992):

> QE: He say I went to the crossroads and learned. Got in the . . . [inaudible] of the cross. And I started to play. And I done heard. I axed 'em. If I want to know a thing, I axed 'em. Well that's where you have to play! You sold your soul to the devil.
>
> JH: You think a lot of folks who play the blues . . .
>
> QE: That's right!
>
> JH: . . . have sold their soul to the devil?
>
> QE: Yeah! Yeah. He done sold his soul to the devil. He sold his body there.
>
> JH: All blues singers have sold their souls in order to be able—
>
> QE: Yeah!
>
> JH: —to play?
>
> QE: You singin' the blues, ain't you? Huh? Do you sing?
>
> JH: I sing. But I didn't sell my soul.
>
> QE: Don't you sing?
>
> JH: Yeah I sing.
>
> QE: Well. Ain't you done sold your soul?
>
> JH: No, not at all.[55]

Queen Elizabeth's testimony illustrates the way some black southerners could conflate two different claims about selling one's soul to the devil: a crossroads pact made by a specific individual, on the one hand, and a more general charge against blues musicians grounded in the devil's-music slander, on the other. Pearson and McCulloch argue that her testimony is "tainted by the fervor of her negative feelings about blues, blues singers, and Johnson," and that may be true.[56] By the same token, she is speaking, like Coffee and Edwards, as a firsthand witness to Johnson's soul-selling claim. Her repeated insistence on her own agency vis-à-vis that claim—"I axed 'em. If I want to know a thing, I axed 'em"—suggests that she is speaking from her memory of a specific conversation rather than simply inventing the conversation out of whole cloth.

Finally, there is the curious tale told by blues researcher Michael Leonard, as reported by Jim O'Neal in *Living Blues* (1990). Leonard, he said,

> met a man named Walter Hearns a couple of years ago who claimed to have known Robert Johnson and who said that Johnson told him he had made a deal with the devil at a graveyard in Crenshaw, Mississippi.

Leonard was canvassing for 78s when he met Hearns at the intersection of Greenwood and Saxon Streets. After a short discussion about Memphis Minnie and Son Joe, Hearns asked Leonard if he had heard of Robert Johnson. He then told Leonard about the night Robert Johnson had spent in the graveyard. In the morning, when he emerged from the graveyard, Hearns and some other children followed him down the street as he sang lines from Preaching Blues. When Leonard returned to visit Hearns and get this story on tape, Hearns was dead.[57]

The Leonard-Hearns encounter took place in Memphis (Greenwood Street and Saxon Avenue cross there); Crenshaw, due east of Helena, Arkansas, is a town on the eastern edge of the Delta, equidistant from Robinsonville and Clarksdale.[58] As Hyatt's compendium makes clear, the folklore of soul-sales is sited almost as frequently in graveyards as at crossroads, but of course Johnson, Ike's protégé, had his own reasons for viewing graveyards as impromptu woodsheds, perfect for uninterrupted practice sessions. Hearns's tale rings true. It is easy to imagine Johnson, on emerging at daylight, masking his serious (and noninfernal) intent by invoking the sort of superstition that most of the people he encountered would have been quite willing to believe about a blues musician who passed the night in a graveyard. He was following in his mentor's footsteps. Talking a lot of trash about playing for the haints.

HELLHOUNDS AND BITCHES:
IMAGINING ROBERT JOHNSON

What is cast off, laughed off, disowned, always returns. We should not assume that Robert Johnson's relationship to the counterdivine remained stable over time—however much he sought to differentiate himself from the squares by invoking that old-fashioned devil shit and seeing if they bought it.

The devil that haunted him, to the extent that a devil *did* haunt him, was an extension of the lived realities of post-Emancipation black life. What characterized him—and everybody who knew him agrees on this—is the relentlessness with which he lived out the freedoms that were available to him. He was highly mobile, highly promiscuous, willfully alcoholic. He had many aliases and was known by a different name in every town: Robert Dodds, Robert Dusty, Robert Spencer, R. L. Spencer, R. L., Robert Lonnie Johnson, Robert Sax, Robert Saxton, Robert Moore, Robert James, Robert

Barstow. He refused to be tied down to one woman or one cotton field, and he contrasted himself with Willie Coffee on the latter point. "Robert, he was my main friend," Coffee wistfully told an interviewer:

> He always told me, said, "Now you gonna take and plow these old long-eared mules until you die, rather than give up and follow me. If you follow me, you won't know nothing about them mules no more. Won't care anything about 'em." But I never did follow him no way. I just didn't have the nerve . . . to travel like him. He traveled all over the state, I reckon.[59]

Like the majority of his blues-playing peers, only more so, Johnson refused to be corralled, attitudinally or behaviorally, by the immobilizing protocols of Jim Crow or the "rock" of Christianity. He sang "me and the devil" and "hello Satan," but he also cried "to the Lord above for mercy"—even as, when drunk, he cursed God in a way, according to Memphis Slim, that could empty a bar of its customers. His personality was capacious; it enabled a multitude of stances. (There is no particular reason to doubt the deathbed conversion related by his mother to Alan Lomax, much disputed as it has been by scholars; it, too, was a part of the palette of choices that constituted his lived freedom.) He could make his guitar signify on human speech—"repeat and say words with him like no one else in the world could," according to Johnny Shines, who added that "this sound affected most women in a way that I could never understand."[60] Johnson configured himself, lyrically, as a ladies' man, a player, not a faithful husband—except for one song, "Honeymoon Blues," where he insists that he will return to his beloved Betty Mae someday "with the marriage license in my hand" and will "take you for a honeymoon / in some long, long distant land." Johnson was a trickster, a "bullshitter," and his songs are a congeries of different voices, full of playful spoken asides—but he's deeply serious, too. His characteristic trickster's mode is to flit between seriousness and play. His repertoire, considered in isolation, isn't his biography. But the songs he chooses to write and sing, the way he sings them, and the way he references himself ("poor Bob," "Mister Johnson"), his associates (Willie Brown), and his female lovers (Willie Mae, Beatrice) offer significant—although not, in isolation from the testimony of friends, determinative—evidence for who he was. The "hellhound" on his trail, to the extent that there was one, was the overhanging threat of white violence that any traveling black musician would confront in the Mississippi Delta and the Jim Crow South as a whole, *and* it was the woman, many women, whom his faithless love had infuriated, along with their jealous boyfriends and husbands.[61] Willie

Coffee remembered a woman named Lucille who "chased him one day on the road" after discovering that he'd been "shanking" another woman:

> He was goin' out to his mama's. I don't know where he had been, but
> he come in. And he'd been kind of shanking' around with a, you know.
> Somehow or another they got into it. She chased him right 'cross the ditch
> from one side across the ditch to the other side, and back and forth. He'd
> jump the ditch. She go around to the bridge and come back. Go up, he'd
> jump back, 'cross on that side, until somebody from Conway's come along
> in that old T-Model, lowered the top off just about, and picked him up and
> carried him on out to his mama's. She swore she gonna kill him. She had a
> icepick at Robert, and trying to carve him.[62]

"[He was] asking for trouble all the way down the line," Keith Richards famously pronounced. "All his deals with the hellhounds and the bitches—one of them will get you."[63] But of course there were no deals, just the life he'd lived. The devil, for Robert Johnson, was his own disavowed fear, something that hovered outside the safety of the clique he'd formed with Ike and carried with him into the world—a fear fostered by the way he lived his freedom on a landscape of post-Emancipation unfreedom. The devil was that fear, that multiplicity of fears. Fear of abandonment, fear of violent death, fear of the cessation of unlimited mobility. Fear that his life of restless movement, reckless promiscuity, chronic alcoholism, overt flouting of religious faith, easy busking money, and the dazzling musicianship that bound it all together was as likely, someday, to lead to disaster as to liberation.

But the devil was also just a bunch of old folks' foolishness, and he knew that, too.

CROSS ROAD AND HELLHOUND

What, then, of the songs themselves? If we grant their composer and performer the full measure of his human complexity, including an attitude toward the counterdivine—the devil and crossroads mythology—that trended heavily ironic, what do "Cross Road Blues" and "Hell Hound on My Trail" add to our understanding of Robert Johnson?

We might begin by acknowledging that revisionist scholarship has significantly altered the prevailing view of Johnson, demanding that we hear those recordings not as the confessions of a tortured soul in the process of breaking down but as the calculated choices of a youthful recording artist hoping to please a record company and find an approving audience. If we imagine, as part of our romantic view of Johnson, that he was devil-haunted, then how do we explain the fact that he held off recording "Cross Road Blues" until the third day of his first recording session, after he'd recorded first and second takes of eleven other songs? "He was well aware of the current blues market," Wald explains, "and naturally started with his most commercial material."[64] This included his first hit, "Terraplane Blues," a cleverly modern signifying blues in which a man complains about his female lover's lack of sexual response by comparing it with the malfunctioning parts of a late-model Hudson automobile. Putting out hit records and getting laid were more pressing concerns to Johnson, goes this line of argument, than arbitrating soul-sale issues with the devil. The much vaunted "urgency" of "Cross Road Blues" in regards to spiritual matters is somewhat less compelling when we're forced to acknowledge how many other songs, most of them about seducing and losing women, took precedence on Johnson's studio set list.

If we are confused about this point, then that confusion, insist the revisionists, is a direct result of how Johnson was first presented to us as a recording artist. "Us," in this case, refers not to Johnson's contemporaneous black audience but to a much later cohort of white baby boomers in their youthful incarnation as the folk revival audience, eager to encounter a raw, untutored, tormented black artist from the deepest recesses of the Jim Crow South. Exhibit A, suggest Pearson and McCulloch, is an LP titled *King of the Delta Blues Singers* (1961), the first significant reissue of Johnson's work:

> The album began with "Cross Road Blues" and ended with "Hellhound on My Trail." The fourteen cuts in between included "If I Had Possession Over Judgment Day," "Preaching Blues," and "Me and the Devil Blues." The titles conjured images of religion and the supernatural and supported the perception of Johnson as an artist who was troubled by psychological demons. The song selection, particularly the first and final cuts, also supplied fodder for the Faustian story line that would soon be linked to Johnson.[65]

Producer Frank Driggs helped embed that story line in white imaginations, Pearson and McCulloch argue, through liner notes that underscored the gothic theme. "He seemed constantly trapped," Driggs wrote of Johnson. "He was tormented by phantoms and weird, threatening monsters. . . . Symbolic beasts seemed to give him a great deal of trouble."[66] Just as important is Driggs's decision not to begin the album with the first take of

"Cross Road Blues"—the version issued in 1937—but instead to substitute the previously unreleased second take: a slower, slightly shorter version that ends, one verse earlier than the first take, with what has struck some listeners as an ominous invocation of a hell-bound man's fate:

> You can run, you can run . . . tell my friend-boy Willie Brown
> You can runnnnn . . . tell my friend-boy Willie Brown
> Lord, that I'm standin' at the crossroad, babe. . . . I believe I'm
>   sinkin' down[67]

The first take has a slightly different version of those lines as its fourth verse, but the fifth and final verse brings the theme back to the search for female companionship in a way that might well have helped the song catch the sympathetic ear of a juke-house woman. It is addressed to such a "mama" and "baby," in fact:

> And I went to the crossroad, mama. . . . I looked east and west
> I went to the crossroad, baby. . . . I looked east and west
> Lord, I didn't have no sweet woman . . . ooh-well, babe, in my distress[68]

In his influential biographical study, *Searching for Robert Johnson* (1982), Peter Guralnick speaks of the song's "immediate evocation . . . of the devil's bargain," but the devil's bargain, as I noted earlier, is pointedly *not* represented in the song, at least when compared with Cousin Leroy's "Crossroads" and Tommy Johnson's folkloric account.[69] The devil is not mentioned at all, nor is any teaching-encounter involving a guitar. Nor is anything said, in so many words, about the sale (or claiming) of Johnson's soul. All the song offers us is the crossroads location itself—symbolically freighted, admittedly, given the folkloric tradition—and an apparent surfeit of loneliness, helplessness, and fear, along with several conflicting time stamps and a prayer to the Lord for salvation. Is Johnson lyrically revisiting the scene of an earlier devil-pact on the day the bill has come due? For those like Palmer and Guralnick who find the Johnson legend compelling, the song's cues are ample evidence for that, especially when fit into a tapestry that includes conventional (i.e., devil-haunted) readings of "Hell Hound on My Trail" and "Me and the Devil Blues." For Pearson and McCulloch, Wardlow, and other skeptics, those same cues merely enable an unjustified projection of gothic legendry onto a skilled, self-aware artist who deserves better.

The romantics, in other words, imagine that Johnson was "truly" devil-haunted; the revisionists insist that Johnson had no interest in such silliness. A fresh interpretation of "Cross Road Blues" becomes possible, however, if we contextualize the song as the product of Ike Zimmerman's protégé, a young man who was willing to engage in devil-talk if it served his purposes. From this perspective, both versions of "Cross Road Blues" become calculated seduction pitches in which Johnson, pushing his voice hard and with complete control—now breaking at the top of his range, now growling down low—is playfully signifying on crossroads folklore in a way that heightens his own emergent mystique as a hell-bound man. Whether one accepts this interpretation depends in part on the particular emotion one imagines that one hears in Johnson's voice. Debra DeSalvo hears a man "crushed by existential dread"; David Evans hears a man who has "fallen into a state of utter spiritual despair."[70] I hear nothing of the sort. I hear a man who is using abjection rather than surrendering to it, skillfully milking sympathy from an imputed female listener, a "sweet woman" he addresses seven times in five verses (as "babe," "baby," and "mama") and hopes to bed. Lonely bad boys—poor boys, far from home—are sexy:

> I went to the crossroad . . . fell down on my knees
> I went to the crossroad . . . fell down on my knees
> Asked the Lord above "Have mercy, now . . . save poor Bob if you please"
>
> Eeeee, standin' at the crossroad . . . tried to flag a ride
> Eeee heee heee . . . I tried to flag a ride
> Didn't nobody seem to know me, babe . . . everybody pass me by
>
> Standin' at the crossroad, baby . . . risin' sun goin' down
> Standin' at the crossroad, baby . . . heee hee-ee, risin' sun goin' down
> I believe to my soul, now . . . po' Bob is sankin' down
>
> You can run, you can run . . . tell my friend Willie Brown
> You can run, you can run . . . tell my friend Willie Brown
> 'at I got the crossroad blues this mornin,' Lord . . . babe, I'm sinkin' down
>
> And I went to the crossroad, mama . . . I looked east and west
> I went to the crossroad, baby . . . I looked east and west
> Lord, I didn't have no sweet woman . . . ooh-well, babe, in my distress

If Johnson, as Memphis Slim claimed, was known to curse God when drunk and scare juke-joint customers when he did so, why does he beg the Lord for mercy and salvation in this song?[71] Has he suddenly come to regret his earlier heresies? Or perhaps the attitude of repentance expressed in the song doesn't reflect Johnson's own attitude. Pearson has warned against the dangers of "constructing biography from repertoire"—which is to say, assuming that "the sentiments and exploits expressed in Johnson's lyrics" are autobiographical and meant to be taken literally.[72] By the same token, when Johnson references himself twice as "poor Bob," he is asking his listeners to do just that. One way of reconciling these conflicting perspectives is to hear the entire composition as a constructed dramatic monologue: Johnson bullshitting about the haints—and, in this case, the Lord. Gesturing obliquely but legibly at crossroads folklore that his audience would have imbibed from their parents without necessarily subscribing to themselves, configuring himself as abandoned and abjected, "sinking down" twice into a presumptive hell, he is asking his imputed female listener to feel a shiver of fear on his behalf. More than that: he's creating a lyric space within which she might envision herself as his angel of mercy, rescuing him from the fate to which the Lord, unresponsive, seems willing to consign him.

Johnson's invocation of Willie Brown makes more sense if we remember that Brown, like House, was Johnson's patronizing elder, somebody the ambitious young guitar-slinger would have had good reason to chide for underestimating him. Anything but a sincere cry for help, the fourth verse of "Cross Road Blues" is, as I read it, Johnson's playful way of calling out the older guitarist, a respected member of the Delta's blues subculture. "Hey old man," he seems to say, "you and Son House were wondering how I learned to pick my box so much better than you? It musta been the devil. And now I'm paying the price. Ain't that sad." Johnson never told Johnny Shines "those lies" about selling his soul, but he's signifying on them in his indirect apostrophe to Brown, a form of rough in-group humor. "Friend" is meant facetiously. Although equal in rank, Brown clearly isn't a member of the clique.

The Robert Johnson I am evoking here isn't the familiar devil-haunted avatar of existential dread or spiritual despair, in other words, but a calculating young ironist who aims to seduce lots of women and enjoys laughing at those who mistake his "sincerity"—especially in metaphysical matters—for the real thing. Some readers will find this portrait impossible to accept. They will reflexively find themselves siding with Evans and his claim that "by the time of his final [recording] session Johnson appears to believe that he is in the clutches of Satan and has been abandoned by God."[73] What *is* Johnson if not sincere, impassioned, and agonized, the epitome of a Delta truthteller? Surely his artistry isn't just a con game? Here it may be useful to remind ourselves of what actually transpired on Friday, November 27, 1936, in the recording studio set up in San Antonio's Gunter Hotel. Four days earlier, on Monday, Johnson had recorded two takes each of eight different songs, including "Sweet Home Chicago," "Ramblin' on My Mind," and "Terraplane Blues." On Thursday, Johnson returned to the studio but cut only one additional side. There's scant record of what Johnson did during his two days off, or during his evenings, although producer Don Law claimed to have bailed him out of jail on a vagrancy charge and also reported a telephone conversation in which Johnson, "lonesome," asked to borrow a small sum in order to pay the prostitute he'd brought up to his room. In any case, the Robert Johnson who hit the studio on Friday was, to judge from his first recording of the day, ebullient. The song he opened with, "They're Red Hot" (1937), is generally considered by blues scholars to be a one-off novelty — "so unlike his other recordings," as Wald puts it, "that it might almost be by a different person."[74] The song, as Gioia aptly notes, evokes the pitch of a street vendor, "look[ing] backward to the world of medicine shows and itinerant merchants," and it showcases the "versatility of Johnson's vocalizing," so that "it almost sounds as if the singer is creating several separate personas on this one song, each with a distinctive timbre, evoking a dialogue between them."[75] This is Johnson as arch-trickster, sexually signifying with a vengeance. The song is a pimp's come-on, a brag about the red-hot lover whose matchless wares he's offering to all comers:

> Hot tamales and they're red hot . . . yes, she got 'em for sale
> Hot tamales and they're red hot . . . yes, she got 'em for sale
> I got a girl, say she long and tall. . . . She sleeps in the kitchen with her
>   feets in the hall
> Hot tamales and they're red hot . . . yes, she got 'em for sale, I mean
> Yes, she got 'em for sale[76]

On and on Johnson sails, nine verses in exactly three minutes: a lyrically inventive and thoroughly dazzling vocal performance drenched in sexual innuendo. In formal terms, "They're Red Hot" is a slightly extended sixteen-bar blues: precisely the same harmonic structure as "Whitewash Station Blues" (1928) by the Memphis Jug Band, and a form, as Wald has noted, much more typical of East Coast ragtime guitarists than Mississippi players. "This is the most lighthearted interlude in all of Johnson's oeuvre," Gioia concludes, "opening up a different perspective on this supposedly devil-haunted soul. Yet at the close of the San Antonio sessions," he continues, "the darker, more apocalyptic side of Johnson's work emerges. . . . Johnson himself . . . seems to intend that these songs should be heard as revelations of his own private demons."[77]

"Private demons"? "Different person"? Gioia and Wald are both in error here, and for the same reason: they find it impossible to accept "They're Red Hot" as a representative, even exemplary, work within Johnson's recorded canon. Far from a one-off novelty, "They're Red Hot" is a skeleton key to Johnson's entire aesthetic. In its rapid-fire timbral and perspectival shifts, all of which undercut sincerity for the sake of humor, energy, and virtuoso display, it sums up and radically extends an original approach to vocal stylization that is clearly in evidence in the eight songs he'd recorded earlier in the week. More than that: if Johnson in his personal life was, as Honeyboy Edwards claimed and Willie Coffey seconded, a "bullshitter," someone who could tell a tall tale with a straight face and laugh to himself as he was doing so, then "They're Red Hot" reveals *that* Robert Johnson in full flower. And it was *that* Robert Johnson who—after following up this exercise in double-entendre hokum with "Dead Shrimp Blues," a double-entendre complaint about a mistreating woman—moved on to "Cross Road Blues": one more pitch for companionship animated by a sexual hunger that casts its calculating eye across its audience and says what it needs to in order to close the deal.

We are making a foundational error, in other words, if we conjure up a devil-haunted Johnson who has been "abandoned by God" and make him our interpretive norm, even as we marginalize the seemingly "different person" who tossed off "They're Red Hot." Yet this is precisely the mistake that Wald and Gioia reiterate in their discussions of three more songs, "From Four Until Late," "Hell Hound on My Trail," and "Little Queen of Spades," that Johnson records in sequence during his final pair of sessions on June 20–21, 1937.

"From Four Until Late" does indeed showcase a softer side of Robert Johnson: not the seductive trickster but the abandoned and tenderly pained (rather than vengeful) lover. He croons rather than cries. Metaphysical and religious concerns are absent. Most strikingly, his lover's lament ends with the possibility of comic redemption—comic in the Shakespearian sense of forgiving his woman her sins and reestablishing community:

> When I leave this town . . . I'm 'on' bid you fare . . . farewell
> And when I leave this town . . . I'm gon' bid you fare . . . farewell
> And when I return again . . . you'll have a great long story to tell[78]

This was the final song that Johnson recorded on June 20. When he returned to the studio on the following afternoon, he began with "Hell Hound on My Trail." "Whatever its strengths," Wald writes, nothing in "From Four Until Late" hinted at the tortured poetry Johnson would unleash in "Hell Hound on My Trail." . . . Johnson made a complete about-face into his darkest, most anguished performance on record. . . . It is his poetic masterpiece, a nightmare of hellhounds and magic powders, illuminated by lightning bolts of sharp, natural imagery. . . . It is the cry of an ancient mariner, cursed by his fates and doomed to range eternally through the world without hope of port or savior.[79]

Although Wald spends much of *Escaping the Delta* upending conventional understandings of Johnson, he drops the revisionist pose here for an unrepentant romanticism more typical of Marcus, Palmer, Guralnick, and Banks, a gothic miasma energized by the words "tortured," "nightmare," "anguished," "cursed," and "doomed." We have seen this before. We see it again in the way Gioia contrasts "Hell Hound" with "Little Queen of Spades":

> Haunting and haunted, it steps on perilous ground where popular songs rarely go, trespassing on the rightful domain of the confessional or counselor's couch. . . . "Hellhound" was the first song he recorded on his final day in the studio on that Sunday in Dallas. The next song he records, "Little Queen of Spades," returns to the casual, carefree delivery we associate with Johnson the traveling musician. It is hard to believe that the same person is singing these two songs, so different is the tone and timbre.[80]

But of course the same person *is* singing these two songs, along with the mellow and forgiving "From Four Until Late." And the "casual, carefree delivery" that Gioia attributes to "Little Queen of Spades" by way of contrasting it with the "haunting and haunted" "Hell Hound" is, as I'll discuss in a moment, something that shows up briefly in "Hell Hound" as well—in the sly, knowing, lover's come-on delivered as a spoken aside in the second verse.

"Hell Hound on My Trail," like "Cross Road Blues," is the work of Ike's protégé: the crafty self-projection of a young man seeking love and shaping his own mystique for the purposes of seduction, like a spider spinning a web. It opens, to be sure, with a verse that seems entirely sincere and that many have found chilling:

> I got to keep movin' . . . I've got to keep movin'
> blues fallin' down like hail . . . blues fallin' down like hail
> Ummmmm mmm mm
> blues fallin' down like hail . . . blues fallin' down like hail
> And the day keeps on worryin' me . . . it's a hellhound on my trail
> hellhound on my trail . . . hellhound on my trail

Johnson's voice begins notably high and seemingly strained—he's at the very top of his nonfalsetto register—but then, in the middle of each two-line sequence, he suddenly drops his voice an octave, creating a downward melodic slope that emphasizes the directionality of the blues that is "fallin' down like hail" and the location of the dim infernal region into which the hellhound is presumably tracking him. Johnson's invocation of that hellhound takes its power from a deep reservoir of black Christian imagery sourced in the slavery period. One of the slave narratives collected by the WPA in the 1930s, for example, describes the hellhounds that pursued the narrator just before his conversion to Christ: "I heard it thunder again three times and then I looked and I was at the gates of hell. I saw old Satan and his hell-hounds. He set them after me."[81] But the use to which Johnson puts this spectacle of abjection is the opposite of a conversion narrative. It is deliberate sacrilege, in fact:

> If today was Christmas Eve. . . . If today was Christmas Eve . . .
> and tomorrow was Christmas Day
> If today was Christmas Eve . . . and tomorrow was Christmas Day
> [spoken] Aw, wouldn't we have a time, baby?
> All I would need my little sweet rider just . . . to pass the time away,
> uh huh . . .
> to pass the time away

That spoken aside gives away Johnson's game—a game that Ike would have appreciated. It makes clear that the entire performance to that point has been an exercise in cultivating a beleaguered pose for the sake of attracting feminine attentions. How bad is this bad boy? Neither cowering in fear of the hellhound nor meditating on the proposition that Christ died for his sins, he views Christmas Eve and Christmas Day as the ideal time to . . . well, spend two whole days in bed fucking his little sweet rider. Gioia is right when he notes that "churchgoers of the day—a group that accounted for the vast majority of Mississippi's residents, circa 1937—would have been very familiar with the image of hellhounds hunting the souls of desperate sinners," but he misses the degree to which Johnson designs the second verse so as to violate the sensibilities of those same church people in the most flagrant possible way.[82] This is the same Robert Johnson who will, later that afternoon, record "Me and the Devil Blues," with its casual and (to Christian believers) shocking apostrophe, "Hello, Satan, I believe it's time to go" and its spoken aside, "Baby, I don't care *where* you bury my body when I'm dead and gone," the latter a rejection of every Christian's deathbed wish to be buried in the church graveyard. All of these sacrileges show Johnson simultaneously seducing his imagined (female) audience with bravado and mocking anybody square enough to take his devil-and-hellhounds talk at face value. He's hip, they're not. And that difference is important to him.

In the third stanza of "Hell Hound on My Trail," Johnson offers the striking suggestion that the hellhound and the lover are one and the same: an angry woman who has hoodooed him, driving him to distraction as he makes his way through the world:

> You sprinkled hot foot powder, mmm around my door
> all around my door
> You sprinkled hot foot powder . . .
> all around your daddy's door, hmm hmm hmm-mm-mm
> It keep me with ramblin' mind, rider . . .
> every old place I go . . . every old place I go

Hot foot powder was, as Katrina Hazzard-Donald has noted, a commodified modern adjunct to an African American hoodoo practice known as track gathering that traces back to West and Central Africa. Older African Americans, especially in the South, believed that the human soul rested in the palms of the hands and the soles of the feet; "hoodoo adherents believed that a conjure fix, or spell, could be put on someone . . . by either gathering the dirt tracks where you had left your footprints or by dusting or pouring a mixture onto the footprint."[83] By 1935, according to Hazzard-Donald, conjure's older practitioners, the herbalist root-workers whom Hurston called "swampers," "were giving way to a more specialized practice, limited and heavily commercial," especially in the urban North.[84] Hot foot powder, often manufactured and "marketeered" by non-African merchants, was the epitome of such commercialism. Johnson's invocation of that commercial product here, in other words, marks him as modern rather than old-fashioned. But of course *all* hoodoo practices were old-fashioned from Johnson's relentlessly skeptical young modern perspective. There is no reason to think that he takes hot foot powder any more seriously than he takes crossroads folklore or hellhounds. All are versions of the haints that Ike jokingly told his family he had been communing with when he returned home from the graveyard. Only someone not in on the joke, or too credulous by far, would believe such superstitious nonsense. Or a prospective lover, of course—someone who might be moved by Johnson's (apparent) loneliness, thrilled by the audacity of his God-forsaken persona, and intrigued by his repeated turns from the metaphysical to the carnal. The fourth and final stanza has its eye on such a lover, lingering in the corner of an imagined juke and waiting to supplant the "little sweet woman" who isn't there:

> I can tell the wind is risin' . . . the leaves tremblin' on the tree
> tremblin' on the tree
> I can tell the wind is risin' . . . leaves tremblin' on the tree,
> hmm hmm hmm mmm
> All I need's my little sweet woman . . . and to keep my company,
>   hey hey hey hey . . . my company[85]

Between 1931 and his death in 1938, in the words of blues historian Andrew James Kellett, Robert Johnson "cut a sexual swath through the Deep South."[86] Johnny Shines claimed that "[women], to Robert, were like hotel or motel rooms; even if he used them repeatedly, he left them where he found them. . . . Heaven help him, he was not discriminating."[87] None of us can say for sure what was going through Johnson's head, and heart, when he recorded "Hell Hound"; for all we know, he might have been overtaken by memories of Lucille, the jealous girlfriend who chased him with a knife one day out on the road because he'd been "shanking" another woman. But we can, if we're willing to, hear a somewhat different Robert Johnson than scholars and fans have previously offered us.

Doing so depends on our willingness to adjust our received ideas about Johnson so that we acknowledge the way his extended apprenticeship with Ike Zimmerman critically shaped not just on his guitar playing but also his skepticism toward the spirit-world, his self-conception as a ladies' man, and his willingness to deploy the former in the service of the latter. Johnson did indeed invoke the devil-haunted folklore of crossroads soul-sales, both in his life and in his lyrics, but he did so with far more irony than his romanticizers have understood, and with much more boldness and discernment—distinguishing, for example, between Johnny Shines and Honeyboy Edwards in the matter of devil-talk—than his revisionist scholars have acknowledged. This chapter's argument rests on a pair of statements made by two of Johnson's musical associates: Ike's "I been playing for the *haints*" and Honeyboy's "Robert was a big bullshitter." The latter statement proceeds from the former. The bullshitter described by Honeyboy is a brilliantly subversive young artist who is retelling, in his own fashion, the ghost-story-as-joke told by his mentor. "Cross Road Blues" was that sort of spooky tale, as were "Hell Hound on My Trail" and "Me and the Devil Blues." The spoken asides that interrupt the latter two songs are Johnson's version of winks and nods—the bullshitter showing his hand, daring us to laugh at his outrageousness, if we get the joke. In "Malted Milk" (1937), recorded midway between "Hell Hound on My Trail" and "Me and the Devil" in Johnson's final studio session, he describes his booze-induced dizziness in "hainted" language that Ike himself might have used: "My doorknob keeps on turnin' . . . it must be spooks around my bed / My doorknob keeps on turnin' . . . must be spooks around my bed / I have a warm, old feelin' . . . and the hair risin' on my head."[88] Boo! Most of us recognize a ghost story for what it is, delighting in the skill with which it manipulates our fears and engages our sense of humor. Robert Johnson has had the curious distinction of being a brilliant ironist whose ghost stories have been embraced by the multitudes as testimonials of torment rather than jokes about haints. "The simple reality," as Pearson and McCulloch note with justified exasperation, "is that the Johnson legend—the whole selling-his-soul-at-the-crossroads business—cannot be eradicated at this late date; it belongs to the people now, and the fact that people embrace it as a part of American music history is as important as the question of whether it is true."

That legend, as I noted at the beginning of this chapter, has in our own time come to dominate not just public understandings of Johnson but also the long and variegated history of the devil in the blues tradition. Two of the most significant signposts along that road, a Hollywood film and civic monument, are the focus of what follows.

I Got a Big White Fella from Memphis
Made a Deal with Me

Black Men, White Boys, and the Anxieties of
Blues Postmodernity in Walter Hill's Crossroads

Ain't too many left that play the real *deep* blues. There's John Lee
Hooker, Lightnin' Hopkins—he have the Texas sound, and Texas
blues is very, very good blues—and let's see, who else? Ain't too many
more left. They got all these white kids now. Some of them can play
good blues. They play so much, run a ring around you playin' guitar.
But they cannot vocal like the black man.

—MUDDY WATERS (1981)

THE PROBLEM OF SUCCESSION

Blues fans of a certain age may remember *Crossroads* (1986), a Hollywood
feature film about a Mississippi blues pilgrimage that stars Ralph Macchio
as Eugene "Lightning Boy" Martone, a sulky but determined Long Island
guitarist, and Joe Seneca as Willie Brown, an irritable old harmonica player
and former sidekick to Robert Johnson. The film has had a troubled critical
reception, to put it mildly. (My chief intent here is to make a case for its
importance as a prophetic register of the way blues culture has developed in
our time, even while acknowledging its aesthetic weaknesses.) Released at a
cultural moment marked by widespread public anxiety about the generative
connection between Satanic worship and heavy metal music, the film struck
many as an anachronistic piece of romantic fluff: a southern-fried interracial
buddy flick, *Karate Kid* (in which Macchio had starred two years earlier)
crossed with a wily, bluesed-up Uncle Remus telling tales of bad old Mississippi. The titular crossroads, drawn from the blues' hoariest mythology,
was evoked in the film's sepia-toned opening sequence. Johnson, suited, a
guitar slung over his shoulder, strides into the intersection of two parched
gravel highways as the tracking shot rises and hovers above him; there's a
blasted leafless tree up ahead, stubbled cotton fields stretching away on all
sides. Cut to a side shot of Johnson, gazing anxiously over his shoulder as
though cringing inwardly at thoughts of the devil who has already—we're
led to imagine—purchased his soul here on some prior occasion. Or is about

to purchase it? Willie, we learn in another sepia flashback, took the same shortcut to fame and fortune and found neither—which is why, haunted by nightmares and with Macchio in tow, he is so keen to escape from his high-security rest home in New York City (he murdered a fellow musician many years ago in a dispute over pay) and head on back down to the crossroads, hoping to steal his soul back.

The film is rich in gothic implication early on, but by the time Macchio and Seneca reach the conclusion of their one-week road trip, the devil of the crossroads has been bodied forth, without sepia distancing, as Scratch, played with dapper elegance and a wicked grin by Robert Judd, an African American stage actor. Waving off Willie's objections, Eugene, callow as ever, snorts, "I don't believe in any of this shit anyway," as he accepts Scratch's challenge of cutting heads with Jack Butler, a heavy-metal shredder played by real-life heavy-metal shredder Steve Vai. Eugene, seemingly overmatched, wins the battle in an unexpected reversal, saving Willie's soul into the bargain. As the film ends, the two men—old and young, black and white—stroll off into a bright new day, one that slowly fades to sepia, casting them into the past even as they chatter happily about Chicago, the blues, and the future that awaits them.

Shot on location in the Delta in the spring and summer of 1985, *Crossroads* was released the following year and did poorly at the box office; the prevailing tone of contemporary reviews was derision. "The Karate Kid comes to know his mojo in the calamitous '*Crossroads,*'" sneered a reviewer in the *Washington Post*. "[The film is] a misbegotten mishmash with Ralph Macchio as a Julliard guitarist who exorcises a bedeviled old Delta blues man. . . . Macchio has got all the soul of a Spaghettio." The *Toronto Star* mocked the "laughably mythic concept" at the heart of the film—the idea of making a crossroads pact with the devil in exchange for musical prowess—as "half-baked mysticism passed off . . . as authentic blues folklore." Ry Cooder, a roots music standard-bearer and the film's musical director, "[surely] has the background to know what this movie will do to true blues lovers. First, it will intrigue them. Then they will laugh. Then anger and confusion will set in, leading to raw, unbridled fury."[89]

Scholars Barry Lee Pearson and Bill McCulloch, authors of a revisionist study of Robert Johnson, dismiss *Crossroads* as "formulaic fluff," but the academic response in general has been more prosecutorial, indicting the film for racial bad faith. The two most significant studies, by Lorna Fitzsimmons and Patricia Schroeder, both agree with the critique tendered by George Lipsitz, author of *The Possessive Investment in Whiteness* (1998).

Crossroads "plays in the dark," in Toni Morrison's terms. Rather than offering a realistic, culturally informed, and sociohistorically grounded vision of the world from which Robert Johnson, Willie Brown, and their deep blues emerged, the film distorts its black cultural materials in an egregious way, giving full flower to white blues romanticism. That romanticism shows up not just in the film's gothic hyperinvestment in the crossroads devil-pact, so that the callow white boy is given the power to rescue his black elder from the black devil's clutches, but even more pointedly in the figure of Martone himself, driven by a familiar profit-taking fantasy of the blues. To Fitzsimmons, Martone is a blackface minstrel without the makeup, a craven appropriator of black culture whose repeated demand that Willie teach him the never-recorded "thirtieth song" by Robert Johnson so that he can record it and become a big-time bluesman epitomizes the parasitic relationship that white America inflicts on its national Other. "Martone's unambivalent attraction to the plenary potential of commercializing African American music," Fitzsimmons writes, "is symptomatic of white hegemony. . . . It is as the object of the white youth's imperialist gaze that Brown's body is first depicted, sitting in a wheelchair gazing at himself in the mirror." To Schroeder, the central action of the film, an abbreviated road trip that takes the young white man and the elderly black man deep into the blues' southern homeland, is where our moral and aesthetic disapproval should be sourced. Where the film seeks to convince us, through the mouthpiece of Joe Seneca, that what Martone lacks is "mileage," which is to say the experiential background possessed by Robert Johnson, Willie Brown, and other bluesmen worthy of the name, Schroeder sees the film's narrative attempts to confer that "mileage" on Martone as hopelessly inadequate. "Eugene's adolescent attempts to live the life of an early twentieth-century bluesman," she writes, "fall ludicrously short of what those blues musicians endured."[90]

No scene has proved more controversial than the film's extended final sequence, a burlesqued, cartoonish guitar battle in which Martone goes head to head with Butler. Butler, Judd's "big white fella from Memphis" who has "made a deal" for his unearthly talents, grimaces and prances across an indoor stage in a fictive hell as an audience of black congregants, imprisoned souls presided over by Judd's chuckling deviltry, gaze on, willing to bestow their approval on whichever gunslinger ravishes them most compellingly. Both Martone's and Willie Brown's souls lie in the balance. Brown has bequeathed a mojo bag on Martone before the headcutting begins, but its power seems to have been nullified. Then, just as Martone appears to have been vanquished by Butler's technical wizardry, Eugene reaches deep into his own arsenal and pulls out . . . classical music? In a sequence memorialized on YouTube as "Eugene's Trick Bag," Martone, the renegade Julliard student who has given up his studies to chase after the blues, tosses off a percussive, heavily amped-up mashup of Paganini's Fifth Caprice. Butler, try as he might, can't replicate Martone's performance. He throws down his guitar and slinks offstage, defeated. Judd's devil, crestfallen, tears up the contract for Willie Brown's soul.

What sort of blues story is this? Schroeder refers to the film's "puzzling abandonment of blues music in the climactic guitar contest." Fitzsimmons insists that Butler's "inability to reciprocate" in Martone's "disidentification with blackness" is the deciding factor that leads Legba/Scratch—which is to say, Judd's character—"to tear up Brown's pact." As I will argue, both Schroeder and Fitzsimmons are mistaken about Martone's apparent disidentification with blackness, but for the moment I should note that academic and journalistic disapproval are matched by the dismay of the scriptwriter, John Fusco, and the cocomposer of the guitar music, Arlen Roth, both of whom were interviewed about their participation in the film. The headcutting scene originally penned by Fusco in his award-winning NYU film school script was, the author insisted, nothing like the scene that director Walter Hill ultimately decided to shoot and use. In Fusco's draft, Martone's antagonist was an older *black* guitarist, a former nemesis of Willie Brown's, not a young white metalhead, and the entire guitar contest took place outdoors, in a rail yard, before a raucous black audience enjoying a fish fry. The process of transforming the script into the film, in other words, led not just to a heightening of the sinister "devil's theater" element, but to a radical reconfiguring of racial meanings conveyed by the blues battle. More critically, from this perspective, the original script included a second young guitarist—a young black guitarist that Fusco described as a "really hot" Gary Clark Jr. figure—who cuts heads with the older black guitarist, and loses to him, just before Martone gets his turn. "There was no Steve Vai character," Fusco reiterated. "It was the old black guy. So I didn't have white boy against white boy. Not in the original."[91]

As it turns out, the young black blues guitarist made it not just into the revised script but onto the set and onto the cutting-room floor. He was played by Shuggie Otis: the biracial son of white rhythm-and-blues bandleader Johnny Otis and a guitar phenom in his own right. According to Roth, four or five days were spent on the Hollywood soundstage filming Otis doing battle not with the older black guitarist, since that character had been revised out of existence, but with Vai's Jack Butler. "The idea is that when you first come into that wild room where they're gonna have the final thing," Roth insisted, "you see Shuggie losing to Vai, and walking out, dejected. . . . He tries a little bit, and he can't make it, and then he leaves." That is the scene that was filmed. And then, according to Roth, director Hill left the scene on the cutting room floor. "Walter said, You can't have a white guy beating a black guy. You just can't have that in a film. It's not politically correct, or whatever the words were at the time. And it was just something that they felt . . . they couldn't put across, that they would be severely criticized for that."[92]

Walter Hill's solution, the film's solution, to the dilemma posed by Shuggie Otis, the young African American bluesman in a mid-1980s vision of the blues, was to airbrush him out of the picture rather than showing him being beaten by a young white bluesman—a young white bluesman who was in fact not a bluesman at all but a heavy-metal shredder committing sacrilege on the music. We know what the filmmakers ended up with after this erasure: a pair of white boys, each of whom is the protégé of an older black southern male figure, duking it out for the right to claim, in symbolic terms, "I am the future of the blues."

We would do well, I think, to attend, and closely, to this last symbolic formation: black men, "their" white boys, and the future of the blues.

Far from a piece of formulaic fluff, I view Crossroads as one of the most significant blues texts of its time, precisely because it resonates powerfully, on a symbolic level, with the transformations that were actually occurring in the mainstream American blues world of the early and mid-1980s. Framed in that fashion, it becomes legible as an anxiety formation: a fantasy about the problem of succession as it materializes within an increasingly white "legitimate" blues scene constituted by aficionados and fans, blues societies and organizations, magazines (especially Living Blues), festivals and club gigs, but above all by awards ceremonies, including the W. C. Handy Awards and the Grammys.[93] What happens to the blues when white blues performers begin to win the big awards? What happens to the blues when the African American elders die off and the white inheritors are all that's left? Is there such a thing as a "fit" white successor to a black blues elder, and, if so, how will he be produced? How will we recognize him?[94]

In the headcutting scene staged at the end of Crossroads, an essence that might be called white bluesness is split between two young men. The good stuff—the "mileage," the mojo bag, the supportive interracial partnership—is conferred on one young man. The bad stuff—the overtheatricality of heavy metal, the narcissistic self-regard, the technical wizardry—is conferred on the other young man. White bluesness sanctifies itself by abjecting, throwing away, what it hopes it is not: the dead-souled heavy-metal shredder in black leather pants who diddles all over the twelve-bar changes. What remains behind, triumphant, is the real thing, which is to say the white boy who can really play the blues and deserves to take over when the old black guy is gone—his old black guy, the master who teaches him the trade and hands him the torch.

Or at least that's how the fantasy world of *Crossroads* would have it. And the fantasy hopes, desperately, that we fail to notice that Shuggie Otis and his symbolic equivalents have been left out of the picture. Because if we notice the presence of the young black bluesman in the contemporary moment *outside* the film's frame, the fantasy of succession falls apart. As it happens, one particular young black bluesman's presence most definitely was being noticed at the time, especially in the pages of *Living Blues*, the self-described "journal of the black American blues tradition," along with the disruptive presence of his most famous white guitar-playing peer.

Crossroads is heavily invested in precisely this fantasy, these questions, because the American blues scene was undergoing a significant transformation between 1983 and 1986 when the film was being brought into being. Four names take you to the heart of that transformation: Muddy Waters, Albert King, Stevie Ray Vaughan, and Robert Cray.

YOU KNOW HE'S GOT A BLACK DADDY

On April 30, 1983, when John Fusco was dreaming up the screenplay for *Crossroads* as a student at NYU's Tisch School of the Arts, Muddy Waters died. "No single event has ever focused so much worldwide attention on the blues," argued *Living Blues* editor Jim O'Neal. Next to B. B. King and John Lee Hooker, Waters was the preeminent Mississippi-born master of the postwar blues scene. "His music," Robert Palmer had recently noted in *Deep Blues* (1981), "was widely imitated by a generation of young white musicians. His blues sounded simple, but it was so deeply rooted in the traditions of the Mississippi Delta that other singers and guitarists found it almost impossible to imitate it convincingly." Several days after Waters's death, accompanied by a front-page obituary in the *New York Times*, a thousand friends, fans, and musicians, including James Cotton, Willie Dixon, and Johnny Winter, a white Texas guitarist who had produced and played on several albums that helped revive Waters's career in the mid-1970s, paid their respects at a funeral service on Chicago's South Side. "It's impossible to think of never hearing that voice again," said John Hammond Jr., a then-forty-year-old white blues guitarist whose own primary model, Robert Johnson, was one of Waters's significant influences. "It's so hard to believe he's really gone."[95]

That November, at the fourth annual W. C. Handy Blues Awards in Memphis, Waters was posthumously awarded Blues Single of the Year (first place) and Classics of Blues Recording (first and fifth place). The awards, as usual, were selected by "an international voting panel of several hundred blues authorities, critics, producers, musicians, promoters and representatives of the recording and radio industries." Every single winner, in every category except Classics of Blues Literature, was African American. In fact, every single nominee in every category, ten nominees per category, was African American—with one small but notable exception: Stevie Ray Vaughan, a Texas-born, twenty-nine-year-old soon-to-be megastar of the blues guitar, whose debut album, *Texas Flood*, was tied for tenth in the Contemporary Blues Album category. All this would change, to the distress of many, over the following three years.

A few weeks after the Handy Awards, in December 1983, Vaughan joined Albert King, another Mississippi blues guitar legend, on a Hamilton, Ontario, soundstage for a ninety-minute performance—a performance that was, in hindsight, a ritual moment in which a black blues elder anointed his young white successor. King was preternaturally well-qualified for the task. An African American blues performer with impeccable chitlin' circuit and Memphis soul/funk credentials, King also had a long history as a crossover artist, happy to court white blues fans and musicians; he'd been a mainstay at Bill Graham's Fillmore Auditorium in the late 1960s, recorded an Elvis tribute album (*Albert King Does the King's Things*, 1970), and jammed onstage with the *Doors*. King and Vaughan had first crossed paths in 1973 at Antone's, a blues club in Austin; as King told a journalist in April 1985— the same moment that *Crossroads* began filming in Mississippi—"I gave him some of his first lessons," and King's influence on Vaughan's style was evident.[96] As the Ontario session got under way, King took a moment to preach. "Boy," he said, "there's lotsa guitar players out here." "That's the truth," Vaughan agreed. "They just play," King continued. "They play fast, they don't concentrate on no soul. But you got 'em both." On September 15, 1984, at the Delta Blues Festival in Greenwood, Mississippi, after Vaughan and his band had impressed the largely African American crowd, King took the stage at midnight for his headliner's set and took public credit for his protégé. "He's white," King joked with the audience, "but you *know* he's got a black daddy."[97]

We have become familiar, these many years later, with such ritual moments: the elder black bluesman pronouncing on the bona fides of the white blues boy—onstage, in interviews, in carefully calibrated recording projects. Passing the torch, sanctifying him, confirming his fitness as a successor. Buddy Guy has claimed Jonny Lang and Quinn Sullivan as his protégés in this way; Muddy Waters himself made an album called *Fathers and Sons* in 1969 in which he partnered with, and implicitly sanctified, his white successor-designees, Paul Butterfield and Mike Bloomfield. The exchanges between Vaughan, King, and their blues-consuming public were certainly not the first such moments, but they were watersheds nonetheless, for two reasons that bear directly on the headcutting scene in *Crossroads*.[98]

First, King's comments highlight a problematic in the black-and-white succession drama, which is the idea that white blues guitarism trends toward the fast and the soulless. White blues guys have technique, to be sure—or at least they have speed—but do they have soul? That's the million-dollar question, one that bespeaks white anxiety in the face of a presumed African American inclination to judge, and condemn, white cultural appropriation. Black people invented soul: that claim was a commonplace within Black Aesthetic circles in the 1960s.[99] Blues is, or should be, soulful music. But do white bluesmen have soul? King's anointment of Stevie Ray accomplishes its task by insisting not just that the kid has soul but also that he combines speed *and* soul—which is to say that no matter how fast he plays, he isn't just diddling. He isn't just Steve Vai, or Jack Butler. And here my interview with Arlen Roth dislodged another surprising revelation: when *Crossroads* was in preproduction, *Vaughan was initially considered for the part of Jack Butler*. Ry Cooder, the musical director, flatly rejected him. According to Roth, Ry said, "Aw well, Stevie Ray, you're talking about watered down blues. . . . That's like second-generation watered down blah blah blah." We might adapt Thorsten Veblen's *Theory of the Leisure Class* and argue that the search for reputability in white blues circles proceeds by invidious comparisons of precisely the sort that Cooder engages in here: watered-down, second-generation, no soul, not real blues. The legitimate white bluesman knows himself as legitimate only to the extent that he is able to distinguish himself from those whom he is able to frame as white blues poseurs—assuming, of course, that he doesn't have a blues-playing black elder to vouch for him. The aesthetics of blues performance are a key marker: Eugene Martone proves himself legitimate, within the headcutting scene that finally took shape on the set of *Crossroads*, by distinguishing himself from a competitor who is saddled not just with soulless machine-gun technique but a fey affect and a burlesque style that veer cartoonishly away from anything resembling established blues practice for signifying deep and earnestly conveyed emotion. Martone doesn't explicitly have to distinguish himself from Butler, of course, he just has to beat him, because Butler's musical and gestural vocabulary, along with his tight black leather pants, tiger-striped singlet, and headbanger hair, already delegitimizes him in the eyes of a significant portion of the film's audience, from snobbish blues aficionados hipped to the film by *Living Blues* (which highlighted the participation of Frank Frost, a noted Mississippi juke joint harmonica player) through rock-blues fans recently brought into the fold by Vaughan's explosive ascendance.[100]

Although the argument I am elaborating focuses primarily on cultural politics within the early-to-mid-1980s blues scene, it's worth pausing for a moment to note how the choice of Vai as devil-sponsored villain, Scratch's "big white fella from Memphis," allows *Crossroads* to signify on one of the period's most explosive social issues: the moral hysteria or "Satanic panic" swirling through American culture during the film's production cycle. Much of that hysteria concerned the (imagined) ritual abuse of children by Satanic cults, but the culture warriors who drove the panic also had a particular subset of rock music firmly in their sights. The rise of the Christian Right, marked by the founding of the Moral Majority (1979) and the Family Research Council (1981), coincided with the sudden eruption of heavy metal onto the pop music scene, a music animated by technically dazzling male guitar heroes, especially Eddie Van Halen and Yngwie Malmsteen, along with audible and visible investments in Satanic imagery, including Van Halen's "Runnin' with the Devil" (1978) and Mötley Crüe's *Shout at the Devil* (1983), which featured a pentagram on its cover. The year 1985 was the watershed. As *Crossroads* moved into full production with Vai and Macchio battling on a Hollywood soundstage, Tipper Gore helped found the Parents' Music Resource Center and sponsored Senate hearings at which Joe Stuessy, then a music professor at UT San Antonio and author of "The Heavy Metal User's Manual," indicted the music for promoting Satanism and other sins.[101] In May of that year, the sensationalist television newsmagazine *20/20* aired a documentary titled *The Devil Worshippers* that found the problem lurking in

> the neighborhood record store under the category of "Heavy Metal music." The Satanic message is clear, both in the album covers and in the lyrics, which are reaching impressionable young minds. And the musical

message comes across loud and clear, at concerts and now through rock videos. The symbolism is all there: the Satanic pentagram; the upside-down cross; the blank eyes of the beast; the rebellion against Christianity; and, again and again, the obsession with death.

In 1985, Vai was just bursting onto the heavy metal scene as a member of a new supergroup led by Van Halen's former lead singer, David Lee Roth. Only a year earlier he would have been familiar primarily to the reader-ship of *Guitar Player* for his July 1984 transcription of Eddie Van Halen's dazzling instrumental set piece "Eruption" (1978), a performance which helped establish the fusion of blues-rock guitar and classical violin under the sign of virtuosic hammer-on technique as heavy metal's signature sound. The casting of Vai as a decadent metal-head shredder, in any case, a "big white fella" wholly beholden to Robert Judd's leeringly devilish Scratch, should strike us now as a witty literalizing of the indictment leveled by Gore, Stuessy, "The Devil Worshippers," and the rest of the Christian Right. The devil owns him! But that fact alone can't grant Butler blues legitimacy.

In 1985, not surprisingly, when Walter Hill and his producers selected Vai for the role, a role that was originally to have been played and acted by Cooder himself, Cooder was furious. "Yep," Roth remembered him saying dismissively of Vai, "[he doesn't] know nothing about blues, nothing at all." And then Cooder "just walked out . . . in an angry way, walked out of the trailer." Vai turns out to be the perfect choice for the part precisely *because* the character he plays knows "nothing about blues," at least as an idiomatic performance style consistent with long-standing African American tradi-tion. Jack Butler just knows how to shred all over the twelve-bar changes in a way that convinces us—we anxious white blues audience—that we definitely do not want the blues to go in *that* direction once the old black guys have died off and the white boys have taken over. But if Butler beats Martone, that's where the blues are going. Because you've got two old black guys, Willie Brown and Scratch, and each of them has a white boy in this particular cockfight. The soul of the blues, the *soulfulness* of the blues, is at stake. Which is why we, and the film, end up rooting for Martone, no matter how callow he might first have seemed.

Even as *Crossroads* was being dreamed up, reshaped, and wrestled onto the screen, even as Muddy Waters was being laid to rest in Chicago, Stevie Ray Vaughan, sanctified by Albert King and sneered at by Ry Cooder, was exploding onto the American blues scene as the next great guitar hero. *Texas Flood*, Vaughan's debut, was released in June 1983—the Canadian concert with King took place at the end of the tour—and what becomes clear from early concert and album reviews is that Vaughan was being framed in the mainstream press as neither a traditionalist nor a futurist, neither a soul-man nor a psychedelic speedster, but as an unprecedented combination of all those things: a latter-day Johnny Winter, in some sense, but deeper in the pocket and with more Hendrix in the mix. "What we have here," wrote one reviewer, "is a remarkable blues talent with his feet planted firmly in the soil of tradition and his head in some uncharted progressive galaxy." "He is about as close to a blues-rocking purist as can be found these days," wrote another, "[but he] owes a great deal to the futuristic vision the late great guitarist"—meaning Jimi Hendrix—"introduced to basic blues." What *Crossroads* offers us in the figures of Eugene Martone and Jack Butler are exaggerations of these two tendencies, the traditionalist and the futurist, that Vaughan was in the process of fusing, to powerful effect, on hundreds of stages across North America. But the release of *Crossroads* was still two years in the future when something remarkable happened—something that helps account for the uncanny power generated by the film's racial and generational dynamics.[102]

In November 1984, a year after being nominated for Grammys in the Rock Instrumental Performance and Traditional Blues category, Stevie Ray Vaughan became the first white performer in the five-year history of the W. C. Handy Awards to win an award. He triumphed in not one but two major categories, Instrumentalist of the Year—where he beat out veteran guitarists Albert Collins, Buddy Guy, and Gatemouth Brown—and Entertainer of the Year. (He also came in #2 for Contemporary Male Blues Artist of the Year.) His triumph was made possible by a change in the voting rules, one that expanded the voting base to include anyone who subscribed to *Living Blues*. This democratizing gesture had the unintended and alarming consequence of allowing white-blues-loving barbarians through the door, literally as well as figuratively. In his report on that year's Handy Awards ceremony in *Living Blues*, David Kerrigan decried "the obnoxious calls of 'Stevie Ray! Stevie Ray!' which came from too many drunk fans. Many of Vaughan's fans seem hell-bent on disgracing themselves in public, as they did at the Delta Blues Festival by calling for him in the midst of applause for Bo Diddley."[103] Other white blues artists were borne aloft by the barbarian hordes as well, most notably Johnny Winter (#2, Contemporary Blues Album) and John Hammond Jr. (#2, Traditional Blues Album).

In 1985, as the filming of *Crossroads* was ginning up down in the Mississippi Delta, Vaughan repeated his Handy Award triumph as Instrumentalist of the year, reaffirming his public image as the white blues guitar-slinger to whom the torch had been passed. His spiritual father, Albert King, was honored at the Handys that year as well, but in a way that consigned him to the past rather than the present: *Born under a Bad Sign*, King's 1967 album, was inducted into the Blues Foundation Hall of Fame in the "Classics of Blues Recordings" category.

If Vaughan was, as *Living Blues* noted in its report on the 1985 awards ceremony, "still the only white musician to ever be voted a Handy," then by 1986 things had reached what felt to many, including editor O'Neal and his longtime contributors and subscribers, like a full-blown crisis, with ill-informed recent subscribers—Stevie Ray's blues-rock crowd—overturning the old order. Vaughan, as it happens, won no awards in 1986, but The Fabulous Thunderbirds, also out of Austin, were voted Blues Band of the Year, and Johnny Winter, in the biggest shock, was elected to the Blues Hall of Fame. "When a rock guitarist [Winter] is selected to a Blues Hall of Fame," wrote Ron Weinstock in a special two-page *Living Blues* forum, "while commonly acknowledged major figures in blues history are by-passed, then something is seriously wrong with these awards. . . . Hey, do us a favor," he sneered, calling out the magazine's newest readers, "if you want to vote for Johnny Winter or Clapton as a blues guitarist, do it in *Guitar Player* or some similar magazine." "Look at the results of the 1986 Hall of Fame voting," agreed Bob Donnelly. "How can you explain Johnny Winter and Mike Bloomfield getting more votes than Clarence 'Gatemouth' Brown? Are there not more deserving bluesmen than Johnny Winter? It's ridiculous."[104]

The mainstream American blues world, in other words, suddenly found itself at a tipping point in the mid-1980s, as though the bill for *Fathers and Sons* had finally come due, fifteen years down the line. The black Mississippi-born elders—Muddy Waters, Albert King—were passing from the scene, and passing the torch. Their white allies and apprentices were mourning them, declaring them irreplaceable, but also moving into position as their anointed successors, and, for the first time in the person of Vaughan, Winter, and the T-Birds, winning the big awards. Guitar was the medium through which many of the younger white players, including Winter and John Hammond Jr., worked this miracle. But the miracle, I'm suggesting, was accompanied by an anxiety—a sense that white prevailing over black, in the blues world of all places, was a terribly vexed proposition. And yet the blues would have to find a way of surviving, and the white boys would have to be a part of whatever future would guarantee that survival.

Crossroads, taking shape during the three-year window between 1983 and 1986, resonates powerfully with, and helps us see more clearly, the broader cultural, or subcultural, anxieties at work. What the film renders invisible, in this respect, is just as important as what it makes exceedingly visible, which is white male blues guitarism gone wild. If we schematize the long final sequence, which begins with Brown and Martone revisiting the crossroads and ends with Martone's triumph over Jack Butler, as the saga of two black blues fathers in conflict, each represented in performance by his designated white blues son, then what the film leaves out is the possibility of a *black* blues son taking part in the succession struggle—which is to say, it erases Shuggie Otis, whose scenes were edited out of the final cut. And here it is important to remember that the character played by Otis had a real-life equivalent: Robert Cray. *Crossroads* makes no space whatever, in its fantasy of succession, for somebody like Cray: a young black blues artist capable of inheriting the tradition and taking the blues to a new place. Yet that is precisely the role that Cray was playing on the mainstream blues scene as *Crossroads* was being filmed down in the Mississippi Delta.

Cray was, in the minds of some (but not all) of the *Living Blues* faithful, the great black hope: the Pacific Northwest's answer to Texas shuffles, one step behind Vaughan in accolades and popularity, but gaining fast. In 1984, in fact, *Living Blues* had led its Handy Awards report by noting that "Robert Cray became the first artist to win four Handy Awards in one year when the voting results were announced." Unlike the great majority of African American artists celebrated in the pages of *Living Blues*, most of whom had cut their teeth before rural and urban black audiences, Cray's core constituency was white and rock-oriented; his quartet was half-black, half-white. "Handys now apparently go to the highest bidder," complained subscriber A. V. Sykes after the 1986 awards, "and in 1985 and 1986 this was Robert Cray. The awards have lost credibility. There is no way Cray could be that good when (1) grassroots, long-time blues fans don't even know him, and (1) he is not really an authentic bluesman." But the stars were aligning on his behalf; Cray was, for better or worse, the best chance white blues aficionados of African American blues had of outflanking the onslaught of white bluesmen—especially where singing and songwriting were concerned, areas in which African American blues artists traditionally excelled.

In 1985, even as Vaughan won his second straight Handy award in the Instrumentalist category, Cray won a Handy for best Contemporary Blues Male Artist and released his second album, *False Accusations*. (A back-cover ad in *Living Blues* that year in described Cray as "America's best blues modernist.") He also took part in a stunningly successful group project, *Showdown!*, which paired him with two older black Texas guitarists, Johnny Copeland and Albert Collins. *Showdown!* won a Grammy in 1986 for Best Traditional Blues Recording and a Handy for Contemporary Blues Album, a year that also saw Cray take home his third consecutive Handy for Contemporary Male Blues Artist plus awards for Blues Single, Blues Song, Blues Vocalist, and Blues Entertainer.

Showdown!, as it happened, set Cray up for the explosive success of *Strong Persuader*, the 1987 solo album that won a Grammy for Best Contemporary Blues Recording and vaulted Cray onto the pop charts. *Showdown!* did for Cray in 1985–86 what Albert King did for Vaughan in 1983: it placed him in dialogue with his black blues-playing elders—literally, since the album was leavened by studio repartee—and it welcomed him into the brotherhood. Copeland and Collins anointed Cray as their protégé, gave him a chance to prove himself their equal, and made space for him as their eventual successor. "It was real nice to see him," said Cray of Collins in a 1986 cover story in *Living Blues*, referring to the *Showdown!* recording session, "and have him treat me like his son."[105] As the cover photo for *Showdown!* makes clear, the premise of the album—a young black gunslinger does battle with a couple of wily older axe-men—is actually closer to John Fusco's original vision of the *Crossroads* headcutting sequence than the Martone-and-Butler fantasia that dominated the film. In this respect, the final version of *Crossroads* is both an anxious evasion of the Cray-figure in contemporary blues culture and a strategic consolidation of white male blues power. *Crossroads* kills off the heavy-metal monster, so to speak, in order to create a sanctified white blues guitar-guy who might just be able to carry the future of the blues on his shoulders, but it also erases (or merely ignores) the young black bluesmen of the mid-1980s moment—not just Shuggie Otis and Robert Cray, but Sugar Blue, Kenny Neal, Billy Branch and the Sons of Blues—who were working just as hard as their white peers, if not harder, to honor the tradition and carry the blues forward.

ACQUIRING MILEAGE, REALING THE BLUES

The phrase "blues postmodernity," the subtitle of this particular investigation, is a way of evoking the anxieties, the sense of groundlessness, circulating through the mainstream American blues scene in the mid-1980s. There are almost as many definitions of the word "postmodern" as there are definitions of the blues; here, I'm drawing on Jean-François Lyotard's idea that the postmodern condition is characterized by "incredulity toward metanarratives," a loss of belief in the big cultural stories that anchor our social and imaginative lives. If the face of the blues, real blues, in the national imagination, is an older southern-born African American man, preferably from Mississippi, and if the history of the blues is most powerfully evoked by the story of Muddy Waters taking his deep country blues north from Mississippi to Chicago as part of the Great Black Migration and adding electricity when he gets there, what does it mean for the blues story when Muddy dies—and Stevie Ray takes over? One response to postmodernity is a what-me-worry attitude, a willingness to mix and match various cultural elements, an embrace of paradox and uncertainty. The slogan "No black, no white, just the blues" embodies this sort of stance, clearing aesthetic space for white blues performance even as it configures the blues scene as an antiracist utopia enabled by the collapse of Jim Crow. The other characteristic response to postmodernity is fundamentalism, which is to say, a retreat to reductive explanations, a return to origins and origin-figures, a purging as illegitimate of whatever cultural elements are unwanted or inconvenient. In the blues world, we are all familiar with fundamentalist gestures. The irritable assertion, "Blues is *black* music," is one such gesture. Both slogans represent a retreat from the complexities of history into the reassurance of myth.[106]

Crossroads is a key text for the period because it illustrates both responses to the postmodern condition of the blues. On the one hand, the entire mechanism of the film's black-and-white buddy plot, including Willie's handing over of the mojo bag before Eugene's trial by fire in the headcutting sequence, is designed to achieve a leveled postmodern playing field in which blacks and whites are suffering together, and triumphing together, under the sign of the blues. The most resonant scene in this regard is the moment when Martone, having been abandoned by his new lover, picks up the guitar after both men have downed shots of whiskey and plays "feelingfully" for the first time. The camera focuses on Willie's face as Eugene plays on, and the blues Eugene plays are suddenly Willie's blues: the story of his life, the pretext for his spoken reverie. "Lots of towns," Willie murmurs. "Lots of songs. Lots of women. Good times. Bad times. The only thing I want people to say is, 'He could really play. He was good.'" Yet as hard as *Crossroads* works on behalf of its worthy-white-successor plot to bring Martone and Brown into a spiritual alignment that transcends race, it works even harder to recuperate and consolidate the black-blues origin story, sourcing the real blues back in the 1930s and deep down in the Delta, and anchoring the story in the sepia-colored figure of Robert Johnson: not just his fictive crossroads encounter with Legba (which is never shown on screen) but also Willie's own crossroads encounter, which is dramatized quite vividly, and Willie's spiritual proximity to Johnson. "Now that's where Robert made his deal," Willie instructs Eugene, speaking of the crossroads, "and after he told me about it, that's where I made mine."

Given the popular and scholarly fascination with Johnson that has prevailed in the nearly quarter century since his platinum-selling *Complete Recordings* (1990) was released, abetted by documentaries, tribute albums, and at least one full-scale academic conference, it may be hard for some to remember that R. J. hasn't always loomed this large in the popular imagination.[107] Johnson had, of course, been a passion shared by British blues-rock royalty ever since the release of *King of the Delta Blues Singers* (1961) on LP—a source of inspiration and occasionally of repertoire ("Love in Vain," "Crossroads," "Rambling on My Mind") for The Rolling Stones, Cream, and Eric Clapton in particular. But although the live version of Cream's "Crossroads" enjoyed a long afterlife in classic rock rotation, one indelible rock cover is not the same thing as a high profile for the blues artist being covered. The truth is, even Clapton had turned away from Johnson by the mid-1970s; none of his solo or live albums between 1976 and 1986 features so much as a single composition by Johnson. *Crossroads* helped launch Johnson's name back into widespread circulation, consolidating the crossroads-pact idea, fusing it with a vivid and haunting (if brief) screen image of the legendary bluesman, and firmly situating both the "real blues" and its surrealist origin myth in the Mississippi Delta.

The film benefited in this regard from extraordinarily fortuitous timing: on February 13, 1986, shortly after the Rock and Roll Hall of Fame had included Johnson as an "early influence" in its very first group of inductees and only one month before the film's theatrical release, *Rolling Stone* magazine published the first known photograph of Johnson, posed in a pinstriped suit with a guitar clasped to his chest, grinning. He was *real*, suddenly. The ur-ancestor figure for rock as well as blues was now a poster boy, literally. The material reality of the photo should have undercut the spooky surrealist element of the film. Instead, the reverse seems to have happened. The general public, and a certain kind of pilgrimage-hungry blues aficionado in particular, took *Crossroads* to heart—abetted, as Tom Graves has noted, by the film's "near-continuous rotation on cable television in the years after its initial release, [which] put it in the living rooms and minds of millions of viewers worldwide." Not long after Patty Johnson and former *Living*

Blues editor Jim O'Neal opened their Stackhouse Delta Record Mart in Clarksdale, Mississippi, in 1987, they found themselves confronted by blues tourists in search of "the" crossroads. "We [got] to the point," Johnson told an interviewer, "where . . . we were saying 'Ask us about a lot of things, but please just don't ask us where the crossroads are, because there's a zillion of them. Do you want to know where the ones were that were used in that particular movie? That's called a location, in a movie, on a set.'"[108]

Here again the story is more complicated than one might think. For it was O'Neal, a decidedly unromantic scholar of the blues, who provided the producers of *Crossroads* with the blues ephemera—old issues of *Living Blues*, Sheldon Harris's *Blues Who's Who*, Peter Guralnick's article "Searching for Robert Johnson"—that show up in an early montage scene filmed in Martone's dorm room at Julliard, an aspirational bluesman-cave in which he first conjures up the fantasy of tracking down Johnson's unrecorded thirtieth song. And it was Guralnick's biographical essay and Robert Palmer's equally influential book *Deep Blues*, it turns out, both of them published in 1981–82, that helped John Fusco shape his original screenplay for *Crossroads*. The aspiring young writer burrowed deeply into both works when he was a film student at NYU. "I remember it was a goldmine," he said of Palmer's book, and he added, "That's where Legba came from." One of the unremarked curiosities of *Crossroads* is the fact that Robert Judd's devil figure is never, for all his gothic trappings and palpable malevolence, actually referred to as the devil but is instead, at least when Willie Brown speaks of him, given the moniker of what might loosely be called his African ancestor, the Dahomean spirit of the crossroads. The name "Legba" is not one that Johnson, Brown, or any other black Deltan of his time would have used in talking about a crossroads pact. Nor does Legba, by that name, show up in the multiplicity of crossroads-tales collected by folklorist Harry Middleton Hyatt. Brown's invocation of Legba in the film is anachronistic—a nod to comparative religion, academic anthropology, and the Afrocentric idea as distilled by the *New York Times* pop music critic, and thus a notably postmodern touch.[109]

Both Guralnick and Palmer, in other words, helped give intellectual heft to the crossroads theme that had long hovered over Johnson's story, creating a scholarly consensus of sorts that Fusco drew on for the architecture of his plot. Although the sign-on-the-dotted-line literalism of *Crossroads* isn't something that Guralnick and Palmer can be blamed for, neither is it fair for the *Toronto Star* to accuse the film of "half-baked mysticism [masquerading] as authentic blues folklore." The truth lies somewhere in between. And to the degree that *Crossroads* seeks to represent Johnson's blues musicianship as the epitome of brilliance and premodern authenticity, Fusco is again working within the interpretive frame offered by Guralnick. "Robert Johnson's music remains the touchstone," Guralnick wrote, "against which the achievement of the blues is measured."[110] Fusco dramatizes this claim in a memorable exchange between Martone and Brown. "Listen," says Martone excitedly when Brown acknowledges that he's Johnson's former sideman, "I know I'm not Robert Johnson, I . . ." "No, you ain't!" interrupts Brown. "You ain't even the beginning of a pimple on the late great Robert Johnson's ass! You might have a little bit of lightning in you, but you're missing everything else."

The narrative arc of *Crossroads* is designed to supply enough of that "everything else" so that Martone emerges from the mists of youthful arrogance and a deficit of salient experience—with women, with southern racism, with cutthroat competitors—in a way that lets him take his earned place as Brown's sideman and successor. Willie is his irascible guide to the blues underworld, the conductor who helps him accumulate mileage, and here the casting director chose actors with impeccable credentials. Joe Seneca came to the part fresh from a yearlong stint as Cutler, a blues and jazz trombonist, in the original Yale Rep and Broadway productions of August Wilson's play *Ma Rainey's Black Bottom*. Robert Judd played opposite Seneca in both productions—he was Cutler's bandmate Toledo, a pianist—which created a sort of minireunion on the *Crossroads* set. Written in the early 1980s but set in the 1920s, *Ma Rainey's Black Bottom*, like *Crossroads*, dramatizes a struggle for succession within the blues world: Levee, a young black trumpeter in Rainey's band, can't stand her "old jug-band shit" and is looking to cash in on his own peppier compositions. The figure of Ma Rainey, brought vividly to life by Wilson, may help us recognize that *Crossroads* achieves its purposes not just by erasing younger black male aspirants to the blues throne, but by leaving blueswomen—young and old, white and black—entirely out of the picture. Koko Taylor, a Memphis native and inheritor of Rainey's crown, did very well at the 1985 Handy Awards, winning Contemporary Female Blues Artist of the Year for the sixth straight time, along with Blues Entertainer and Blues Vocalist of the Year. *Crossroads* could not be less interested in making Taylor and her female peers a part of the contemporary blues story.

Ma's example, and Taylor's, might lead us to notice something else that no previous commentator seems to have remarked on: the fact that neither of the white boys in *Crossroads* ever sings. The future of the blues, as the film envisions it, is all about the guitar. It's a guy thing, a white-guys-taking-over-from-black-guys thing, and an instrumental thing. Joe Seneca rasps his way through one memorable vocal performance in a black juke, but Ralph Macchio doesn't so much as hum a note, and Steve Vai is entirely mute. What are the blues if not a form of song—a descending vocal strain, a lyric utterance? If *Crossroads* is heavily invested in crafting a vision of what the blues have been and where they're going, this silence at the heart of the film conveys a powerful ambivalence in mid-1980s America about whether the white boys, skilled and soulful as they may be, can fully claim the tradition they would presume to inherit. That ambivalence was voiced with singular candor, as it happens, by Muddy Waters. "They got all these white kids now," he told Robert Palmer in an interview from *Deep Blues* reprinted in *Guitar Player* in 1983. "Some of them can play *good* blues. They play so much, run a ring around you playin' guitar. But they cannot vocal like the black man." [111]

POSTMODERN MISSISSIPPI AND EUGENE'S CREOLE TRICK BAG

I want to return now to a pair of critiques leveled at *Crossroads* by Patricia Schroeder and Lorna Fitzsimmons, respectively. Schroeder, as I noted, indicts the film for presuming to grant Eugene Martone all the experiential "mileage" he needs in order to become a bluesman during a few days in the Delta, even while failing to represent "the lifelong hardships of Depression-era Mississippi that shaped Robert Johnson and the historical Willie Brown." Fitzsimmons faults Martone, and the film, for turning away from the blues at the Paganini-powered climax of the headcutting scene, finding in his winning gambit against Jack Butler a "disidentification with blackness" that critically undercuts the quest-for-the-blues theme. On the first point, Schroeder is entirely right to draw our attention to the film's representational shortcomings in the matter of African American social history. The handful of sepia-tinged flashback scenes we get are restricted to the Dallas recording studio where Johnson records "Cross Road Blues" and the Mississippi crossroads where he and Willie make their deals. To the extent that evil is imaged in these old-time southern scenes, it has a black face—not just Robert Judd as Legba/Scratch but his sneering assistant played by Joe Morton—and that is indeed a betrayal of social realism, which is to say the experiential grounds of the Delta blues, a world in which the evils of Jim Crow, including lynching, most assuredly had a white face. (It should be noted, in the film's defense, that the devil encountered at the crossroads is often described in African American folklore as a "big black man.")[112]

By the same token, Schroeder pushes a good point too far when she characterizes the film's plot as "Eugene's adolescent attempts to live the life of an early twentieth-century bluesman [that] fall ludicrously short of what those blues musicians endured." *Crossroads* is animated, in fact, by a productive tension between the remembered but essentially unrepresented premodern Mississippi Delta that generated Johnson's and Brown's blues and the postintegration landscape into which Brown and Martone make their quest. Brown is the pivot through which this tension is effected. Early in the film he serves as the film's fundamentalist oracle, a consolidator of black blues wisdom in the face of postmodern flux. "There ain't but one school, straight down in the Delta," he tells Martone after Martone tells him about Julliard. "That's where it all started." When the two men first set foot on Highway 61 in the Delta after being dropped off by an old pickup truck filled with clucking chickens, Brown chides Martone for complaining. "I understand why *you* ain't happy. This is the real thing. This ain't no book!" But the real thing that they encounter as their trip proceeds is not the violent, segregated Mississippi of Johnson's or Brown's youth—and is therefore incapable of confronting Martone with the stringent demands that Mississippi made on those men—but rather a contemporary social landscape significantly reshaped by the civil rights struggles of the intervening decades. There are no water fountains marked "white" and "colored." None of the Mississippians they meet, white or black, seem particularly scandalized by the interracial duo—or the teenaged white girl (Jamie Gertz) who accompanies black man and white boy for part of the trip. When that trio runs afoul of the law, the swaggering, big-bellied Mississippi sheriff is black, not white, as are his deputies, although the law still has "vagrants" in its sights and is happy to consign all three travelers to that category.[113]

Postmodern Mississippi, as evoked in *Crossroads*, is an uncanny mixture of old and new. The residue of segregation does finally manifest as a small town's rigidly bifurcated night life—a black juke on one side of main street, a redneck bar on the other—and the flagrant but relatively benign racism of a white hotel owner who tells Martone to take his "mud duck" of a friend and scram. "I didn't know that kind of thing still went on," Martone mutters incredulously after the owner departs. "Well now you're startin' to learn some deep blues," Willie replies. Neither episode presumes to burden Martone with the life of an early twentieth-century bluesman, since such experience is necessarily inaccessible to him in the narrative present. The film's purpose is instead to recapitulate certain touchstones of that Jim Crowed life on a believable contemporary landscape in a way that underscores the film's two key ideological claims about the blues, which is that the music's meanings, including its racial meanings, must be lived, earned, and that hands-on mentoring makes a difference.

The most stunning moment in *Crossroads*, arguably, comes shortly after Willie and Eugene have arrived in the Delta. Willie, unimpressed by Eugene's attempt to replicate the chug-a-chug of a passing train on the bass strings of his guitar, says, "You ain't never gonna get that lost song if you can't make the train talk. The way you playin' it's gonna take you ten years!" "Well maybe I'll just have to do what you did, Willie," Eugene snorts. "I'll go down to the crossroads and strike up a deal with the devil and that'll take care of the whole thing." Willie slaps him across the face and barks, "Don't you ever say that again," then turns and walks away. Echoing Jim's prideful chastising of Huck as "trash" in *Adventures of Huckleberry Finn*, the scene underscores the change wrought on Mississippi's social landscape— slapping a young white man would have been a lynching offense in Willie's youth—even as it demands that Eugene deepen his sense of blues ethics and aesthetics in a distinctly old-school way. Black Delta father figures could be rough on their sons. Howlin' Wolf, according to his biographers, "physically intimidated" the younger black musicians who played in his band, and "used his fists to keep order." "If they playin' wrong," Roscoe Gordon insisted, speaking of Wolf's Memphis recording sessions and West Memphis gigs, "he would beat 'em up or punch 'em." Willie's correction emanates from, and hints at, such a bygone world. Eugene can't possibly live the life of an early twentieth-century bluesman during a brief sojourn in the contemporary Delta, but he can be made to attend to one who has lived that life, forging the outlines of an authentic partnership.[114]

For all its gothic investment in Legba, the crossroads, and the ritual of soul-selling, *Crossroads* ultimately endorses the mentor model of blues education. It is Willie's boy, after all, not Scratch's boy, who prevails in the headcutting session. Foreshortened as Eugene's apprenticeship may be, the film nevertheless insists that there is no shortcut to blues mastery. Neither book-learning nor the devil will get you very far. Experience is needed, as is hands-on guidance, both of which are facilitated by a pilgrimage to the music's spiritual homeland. And here we arrive at what has, in many eyes, proved to be the film's ultimate scandal: Eugene's apparent turn away from the blues at the climax of his contest with Jack Butler. Schroeder and Fitzsimmons see Eugene's recourse to Paganini's Fifth Caprice as a sign of the film's ideological confusion and aesthetic failure, a Eurocentric retreat from the skillful marshaling of blues energies. My counterargument rides on three points and begins with an observation: the mano a mano battle between white boys is actually, for a significant portion of its length, an asymmetrical contest in which Eugene and Willie, on guitar and harmonica, are holding down the "traditional" side of the equation against Butler's blues-metal futurism. While each black elder has "his" boy, in other words, only one of the two black elders actually stands shoulder to shoulder with a musician he has mentored. Jack Butler stands alone—isolated, the film ultimately suggests, in his narcissistic, technique-driven vision of white blues futurity, one ungrounded in any conception of Deep South community. Here, in any case, are three quickly sketched reasons why Eugene's Trick Bag is not a disidentification with blackness but a decisive embrace of the blues tradition.

First, playing Paganini's Fifth Caprice on the steel strings on an amped-up Fender Telecaster is not at all the same thing as playing that composition on the nylon strings of a classical guitar, especially when a range of rock-blues hammer-ons, pull-offs, and glissandos are tossed in. Eugene's fastidious Julliard professor, Dr. Santis, would have been scandalized at the sonic reconfiguration and ritual redeployment of classical repertoire effected by his renegade student. Eugene's Trick Bag is, in fact, an inspired act of creolization. Edouard Glissant, speaking of Faulkner's fiction in a way that implicitly indicts the mandarin distaste of the likes of Dr. Santis, evokes creolization as a "conjunction that opens up torrents of unpredictable results . . . the unpredictability that terrifies those who refuse the very idea, if not the temptation, to mix, flow together, and share." Eugene doesn't abandon the blues; he fuses the African-sourced, New World tradition of electric blues guitarism with the European tradition of classical virtuosity in a way that expresses what Keith Cartwright would call "gumbo consciousness." Linguist Michael Montgomery describes creole societies as "cauldrons of crisscrossing and competing cultures, nationalities, and influences"; Eugene's fusion-move reminds us that America has always been a cauldron of this sort.[115]

Second, in pulling nonblues music into a blues orbit, Eugene is behaving much as Robert Johnson did. As Elijah Wald reminds us, Johnson and his Delta blues cohort, along with their counterparts in Texas and the Piedmont southeast, maintained their freedom from stoop-labor by serving as human jukeboxes, priding themselves on being able to pull a wide range of songs out of their trick bags at a moment's notice. Johnny Shines remembered Johnson performing everything from hillbilly tunes to Hollywood cowboy songs and Bing Crosby numbers. "He did anything that he heard over the radio," Shines insisted. "Popular songs, ballads, blues, anything. It didn't make him no difference what it was. If he liked it, he did it." He could play in the style of half a dozen other well-known blues guitarists, and the country singer Jimmie Rodgers was a particular favorite, according to Shines. "Me and Robert used to play a hell of a lot of [Jimmie's] tunes, man. Ragtime, pop tunes, waltz numbers, polkas—shoot, [Robert] was a polka hound, man." By surprising and delighting his audience with a well-chosen piece of repertoire from outside the formal confines of the blues, Eugene is proving that he has, in fact, grown appreciably in the direction of Brown's former partner.[116]

Third, and perhaps most important, by reaching deep into himself at a crucial moment in the guitar contest and finding a way of wringing victory from the jaws of defeat, Eugene is fulfilling a crucial function of the blues, one evoked by Albert Murray. "The legacy left by the enslaved ancestors of blues-oriented U.S. Negroes," Murray writes, "includes a disposition to confront the most unpromising circumstances and make the most of what little there is to go on, regardless of the odds. . . . The improvisation that is the ancestral imperative of blues procedure is completely consistent with . . . [that] of the . . . fugitive slave, and the picaresque hero, the survival of each of which depended largely on an ability to operate on dynamics equivalent to those of the vamp, the riff, and most certainly the break, which jazz musicians regard as the Moment of Truth, or that disjuncture that should bring out your personal best." In other words, the bluesiest thing Eugene does in *Crossroads* is reach back into his Julliard School past and, in a moment of improvisational genius, pull out and repurpose an old song, creolizing it with such virtuosic panache that it proves unanswerable, saving Willie's life and his own in the process. In doing so, he signifies on the creole mix that defines heavy-metal guitar—the blend of blues-rock tonality and lightning-fast arpeggios drawn from classical violin—and bluesies it up, adding his own spin to an idiom that was supposed to have been Butler's sweet spot, not his own. Signifying and personalizing: these are core blues values, even if the sound that bodies them forth isn't what anybody would call blues. This is why Willie hugs him onstage as the screen fades to black. The white blues inheritor has done his own thing in a daring and inspired way, rather than merely parroting back an established, black-owned idiom.[117]

Crossroads is a flawed, often clichéd work of art. But it is, despite its shortcomings, much more than a piece of formulaic fluff. It resonates powerfully with a mid-1980s moment when an increasingly mainstreamed American blues scene was struggling to navigate a racial crisis that was also an ethical and aesthetic crisis. The crossroads, in this sense, wasn't about devil-sponsored black magic but about aging black blues masters and the younger men who would succeed them. As the face of the blues trended increasingly white, who owed what to whom? What were the music's core values, and what sort of transmission process would ensure that they remained vital? Jack Butler loses the battle, *Crossroads* suggests, because he gained his prowess the easy way—selling his soul, selling out—rather than through focused practice time in the woodshed, improvisational dexterity, and the guiding, chastening hand of a self-respecting older man. Those seem like useful and important lessons; the film deserves credit for endorsing them. Yet we should attend as well to what *Crossroads* excludes from the frame in its determination to dramatize one young white man's emergence as a worthy inheritor of the blues crown: it banishes the black sons. It precludes any potential successor-relationship they might create with Willie Brown and other black blues fathers. Leaving Shuggie Otis on the cutting room floor, the film averts its eyes from Robert Cray, Sugar Blue, and Billy Branch and the Sons of Blues. It is far too invested in educating Eugene Martone and purging itself of Jack Butler's rocked-out blues-metal to pay the slightest attention to either white player's black peers. That is the great failure of *Crossroads*—its signal evasion, along with the fact that blues guitar entirely supplants blues singing in the brave new blues future, and the fact that female blues artists have no role at all. But those silences are also why the film has much to teach us, if we're willing to listen.

III   Local and Private Legislation
Branding the Crossroads in Clarksdale, Mississippi

There's not enough money to buy the branding we own.
—BILL SERATT, president, Mississippi Delta Tourism Association

CROSSROADS SOUVENIRS

One of the more surprising developments in American popular music is the way a rich, variegated, and long-standing relationship between the devil and the blues tradition has been crystalized, in our own day, into one iconic sculptural installation on a tiny patch of ground in Clarksdale, Mississippi. Few contemporary blues tourists are unfamiliar with "the crossroads": a MapQuestable and Google Image–searchable intersection of Highways 61 and 49—actually, DeSoto Avenue and North State Street—where an interlocking trio of large blue electric guitars topped with a pair of state highway signs sits on a small triangular traffic island. "A can't-miss-it roadside structure," performance scholar Paige McGinley calls it, "a kitsch classic of American vernacular architecture."[118] This is where "legend has it" that Robert Johnson sold his soul to the devil. All but the most skeptical blues tourist knows that much, and has a selfie or on-location YouTube performance video, guitar in hand, to prove it.[119]

By the same token, it is all but impossible to find a tourist, visiting journalist, or scholar, who can answer the most basic questions about the monument: who commissioned, designed, and built it, what year it was installed, whether those two highways actually crossed at that location during Johnson's lifetime, even how many guitars the monument actually sports. (Like others, McGinley mistakenly claims that the "Graceland-style marker" has "two guitars.")[120] Many Clarksdalians know, or know of, their townsman Vic Barbieri, the retired shop teacher who dreamed up and constructed the monument, but his name recognition ends at the city limits.[121] May 11, 1999, the date his assemblage was erected, has fallen out of public memory. (A recent issue of *Living Blues* devoted to Mississippi blues tourism sites placed the monument's installation as some time "in the past 20 years.")[122] In her 2009 study of Clarksdale's hip-hop scene, anthropologist Ali Colleen Neff voiced a justified skepticism when she dismissed the crossroads monument

Road crew in Clarksdale, Mississippi, reassembles Vic Barbieri's crossroads monument. The three-guitar headpiece was taken down for a cleaning in 2012, thirteen years after first being installed. © Jesse Wright.

as "a landscaped shiny landmark recently constructed by the Chamber of Commerce for the sake of tourists' photo albums," but she was wrong about the Clarksdale/Coahoma Chamber of Commerce: that office played no role in the monument's creation, although it has avidly capitalized on the monument's attractions in the years that followed.[123] Neff, in the manner of other skeptics, insists that "the 61/49 crossroads has shifted half a dozen times since Robert Johnson's heyday," as though that "fact" self-evidently delegitimizes the monument, but here, too, as I intend to show, facts on the ground are considerably more complex than received widsom.[124] The truth is that Clarksdale's new crossroads, the intersection of two rerouted, freshly paved state highways, was in place and fully functioning by the summer of 1935—in plenty of time for Robert Johnson to have floated into view, paused, and dreamed up "Cross Road Blues" before recording the song more than a year later. The truth is also that "the crossroads" did not exist, as such, during the 1930–32 window when Johnson made his great leap forward as a guitarist. At the beginning of that period it was the nondescript T-junction of two city streets, DeSoto and Sycamore, that had no connection to the state highway system; two years later it was an unseemly jumble of mule-graded roadbed and disputed routing: the epicenter of a big fight between the city of Clarksdale and Mississippi state highway authorities. Who sells his soul in a construction zone? Robert Johnson most certainly did not. Yet there was, for all that, a legitimate reason based in long-standing civic tradition for Clarksdale to formally commemorate the intersection in 1999, even though Johnson played no part in that tradition.

If neither popular mythology nor scholarly skepticism about Clarksdale's crossroads accords with historical truth, one reason for this is the heavy investment that Clarksdale's civic and cultural elites have made in branding the monument and its location in the international blues-touristic imaginary—a branding that depends on historical erasure. One important participant in the monument's creation, Clarksdale's mayor, Bill Luckett, dropped the usual modifier "legend has it" when Headline News anchor Robin Meade asked him what he wanted the world to know about Clarksdale and the blues: "It's the epicenter. It's ground zero for blues music. It's the birthplace of John Lee Hooker, Ike Turner. Sam Cooke. All the blues greats have played there. Muddy Waters lived right outside of town. Anybody who was anybody in the blues music came through there. Robert Johnson sold his soul to the devil to play blues guitar at our crossroads, our intersections of 49 and 61 Highways."[125] Although Barbieri's name is never mentioned in such commentaries, both his iconic design and the legend it commemorates are omnipresent in the web pages, print brochures, and souvenirs offered by Clarksdale's tourist- and investment-focused organizations—a cultural clamor that seems to corroborate Mayor Luckett's bold claim. One reason for the clamor, as it happens, is Luckett's broad reach as both politician and entrepreneur. Clarksdale Revitalization Inc., a 501c3 nonprofit advocacy group Luckett helped found in 2008, features Barbieri's sculpture framed by a brilliant blue sky on its homepage and offers tourists "Chasin' the Ghost of the Crossroads," a four-page brochure that blues tourism scholar Stephen A. King describes as offering "an image of the crossroads sign located in a deserted countryside, a cotton field in full bloom. Underneath the sign is an African American (presumably Robert Johnson) holding an acoustic guitar and looking into the distance, apparently waiting for Satan to materialize. These mythic representations of the crossroads dislocate the sign in time and space, turning the sign's commercialized surroundings into a far more enjoyable tourist fantasy."[126]

"Keepin' It Real!" is the motto of Clarksdale Revitalization Inc., but the organization's intention is, as King suggests, precisely the opposite: to craft a surreal dreamscape divorced from history in order to incite touristic hunger and stimulate business investment. The homepage of Clarksdale City Hall features Mayor Luckett at his desk beneath yet another photo of the crossroads sign; further down the page, a paragraph headlined "Clarksdale History" informs visitors that "Clarksdale is the 'Birthplace of the Blues' and is the location of the legendary Crossroads where Blues pioneer Robert Johnson purportedly sold his soul to the devil."[127] The word "purportedly" here suggests that the mayor adjusts his pitch in the matter of the legend's veracity, depending on the audience. The prevailing local style of legend-purveying, in any case, ranges from earnest to tongue-in-cheek; the cumulative effect is to cement Clarksdale's claim on both Johnson *and* the devil, for fun and profit. The city/county tourist map offered by the Chamber of Commerce, for example, features Barbieri's sculpture on its cover and an unattributed quote from Johnson's "Cross Road Blues" ("I went down to the Crossroad, I tried to flag a ride"), plus an ad for City Hall—again, featuring the guitar-draped sign—headlined "Bring Your Business to the Crossroads . . . Let's Make a Deal."[128]

A tourist who visits the Chamber to pick up a map can harvest a cornucopia of free crossroads souvenirs, including foam beer sleeves, squeezable gray toy guitars, and moist towelettes, all of which feature stylized versions of Barbieri's guitars-and-road-signs design. But the market leader in Clarksdale's crossroads merchandise operation is the Delta Blues Museum:

the chief civic instrument, one would have assumed, for soberly assessing Robert Johnson as a historical and cultural actor. Not so. The museum happily dispenses with scholarly accuracy, blurring the line between history and myth to arrive at a kind of tantalizing truthiness that shores up the ideological basis for Clarksdale's claim on Johnson-at-the-crossroads and, more pointedly, helps the museum sell stuff. The DBM homepage features a pair of aged, overlapping road signs for Routes 61 and 49 and a "quote" from Son House that is actually an airbrushed assemblage of fragments from Pete Welding's 1966 interview: "When Robert Johnson got through playing, all our mouths was open. He sold his soul to the devil to get to play like that."[129] A visitor who clicks through tabs and links marked "educational programs," "explore and learn," and "follow Robert Johnson" ends up on a pop-up page headlined "Follow Robert Johnson Down to the Crossroads." Several more clicks and one arrives at the third stage of Johnson's "journey," a sepia-colored popup with "If You Want To Make a Contract with the Devil" on the left—it offers a vivid conjure man's tale related by Puckett—and, on the right, "Clarksdale, Mississippi 1936: The Legend of the Crossroads" bracketed by a photograph of Barbieri's looming sculpture.[130] The legend-biography, as the museum iterates it, is animated by Johnson's grief at losing his young wife and baby in childbirth:

> This was the end of farming for a bereaved Robert Johnson, who, legend has it, took the dark path to the Crossroads and the Blues. The Crossroads legend is as old as Legba and, to many, the legend explained Robert's astounding leaps in musicianship. Perhaps, Robert simply drowned his sorrow in music, studying intensely with Ike Zimmerman in Copiah County during his short marriage to and immediate desertion of Callie Craft. Nonetheless, his fabled musical rambling throughout the Delta and points beyond now began in earnest.

The fact that the Delta Blues Museum spells Zimmerman's name correctly—indeed, the fact that his possible role in Johnson's musical education is mentioned at all—suggests scholarly due diligence on the museum's part. But curatorial theatrics quickly trump scholarship. Hovering in the mists below Johnson's legend-biography is artwork featuring a parchment scroll headlined "Contract" in gothic typeface and a tarot card of a bare-chested, horned, cloven-hoofed devil labeled "The Devil." The museum's narrative offers no evidence that Clarksdale's crossroads—the present-day location of the sign that illustrates the legend—is where Johnson's dark path and fabled rambling took him. Why Clarksdale, and why 1936? By 1932, according to Son House's biographer, Johnson's guitar playing had reached "critical mass," and by 1933 or 1934 he was publicly manifesting his brilliance, in Helena and beyond.[131] By 1936 his soul-selling phase is long past, factitious as that phase is. Perhaps what is being gestured at without actually being named is "Cross Road Blues," which Johnson recorded at his first studio session in November of that year—although the song, as Gayle Dean Wardlow and others have noted, doesn't mention the devil, or soul-selling, or musical skill. Nor does it mention Clarksdale, or Highways 61 and 49.

The distinction between truth and truthiness—which is to say, legendry peppered with factoids—becomes moot the moment one enters the Delta Blues Museum's online gift shop.[132] "Get Your Crossroads Souvenirs!" barks the headline, beneath which are images of Crossroads Hwy Signs (Single $19, Pair $35), several different black Crossroads Tees ($20), and a Crossroads Poster ($15), all of which are traversed by a diagonal banner, "Welcome to the Crossroads!" An explanatory greeting beckons just below:

> Highways 61 and 49 meet in Clarksdale, MS—the legendary "crossroads" where Robert Johnson (and other blues musicians) were said to have sold their soul to the devil to play the blues so well. Now you can own special souvenirs of this magical "land where the blues were born" with a tee, poster, and replicas of the famous highway signs.
>
> Your purchases support our work at the Delta Blues Museum. Thanks!
>
> Order your Crossroads Souvenirs today!

Other blues musicians? At *Clarksdale's* crossroads? There isn't a shred of legendry, much less historical evidence, to justify such a claim. Drilling down into the gift shop's subdirectories, one can find a Limited Edition Crossroads Hoodie to promote the Deeper Roots Campaign ("Hoodie is black with colorful graphic of bluesman at the Crossroads of Highways 61 and 49 in Clarksdale"), a Crossroads Pin (a stylized one-guitar version of Barbieri's sign), and Crossroads Coffee ("Pays tribute to the legendary site of guitar mastery, and delivers a satisfyingly soulful taste as only a gourmet coffee can").

From one perspective, all of this legend-proffering and profiteering is merely harmless chicanery: a small Deep South city, long laboring under a depressed postplantation economy, seeking to take advantage of its legitimate inheritance as the intersection-point of two famous blues highways and the birthplace of blues stars (Muddy, Hooker, Ike) by working a little three-card monte in the matter of Robert Johnson. Some local entrepre-

Abe's Bar-B-Q, a Clarksdale eatery located adjacent to the "legendary" crossroads, is one of several local businesses that plays up the town's supposed connection with Robert Johnson's devil-haunted mythology. Courtesy of Jimmy Thomas.

neurs, such as Pat Davis, owner of Abe's Bar-B-Q, a Clarksdale culinary landmark adjacent to The Crossroads, are clearly enjoying the ride. "In 1924," Davis told a reporter from National Public Radio, "my father opened up a barbecue restaurant. Robert Johnson used to sit around where those sycamore trees were, playing his blues guitar, drinking a Bud and eating one of our barbecues. And we think that's where Robert Johnson made a deal with the devil to play good blues music."[133] Although the Budweiser reference is pure malarkey—Mississippi didn't repeal Prohibition until 1966—the construction history of the crossroads site and the relocation of Abe's from Fourth Street to its current location in 1937 offer some factual basis, surprisingly, for Davis's tongue-in-cheek claim about Johnson eating and playing blues on location. *That* much, at least, could actually have happened.

From another perspective, that of competing regional interests in the world of contemporary Mississippi blues tourism, Clarksdale's stunningly successful escapade in civic branding—not just *a* crossroads but *the* crossroads, home to Johnson and the devil—is an infuriating power grab based on a lie of monumental proportions. "You know damn good and well that

Highway 61 and 49 are not the crossroads," insisted Bill Seratt, a Greenville-based member of the Mississippi Blues Commission in a 2008 interview. "Clarksdale laid claim to being the crossroads thirty years ago so, therefore, a lot of not very deep blues enthusiasts really think they're at the crossroads. But we all know they're not." [134] "Is the so-called official crossroads there?" laughed Pat LeBlanc, host of the *Southern Crossroads* blues radio show and creator of the Crossroads Blues Festival in Greenwood. "Look at where Robert Johnson was before he made these records. How much time was he in Clarksdale before he sold his so-called soul? I would think you'd probably be better off looking around Robinsonville and these other parts, even outside the Delta." [135] King notes that four Delta counties (Coahoma, Bolivar, Sunflower, and Copiah) currently lay claim to possessing the "definitive" crossroads site. But when the four locales—Clarksdale, Rosedale, Dockery Farms, and Hazlehurst—are considered as a group, it becomes apparent that Clarksdale has achieved overwhelming market dominance. "Clarksdale has always been one step [ahead] of the game when it comes to marketing blues to tourists," LeBlanc adds, and the creation and installation of the guitar-laden crossroads marker in 1999 was clearly the watershed moment: a brilliant marketing idea that reinvigorated Clarksdale's civic identity and gave the legend a photogenic home.

"People go to Mississippi," wrote blues historian Francis Davis in 1995, "to look at things that aren't there anymore." [136] But they also go to Clarksdale, these days, to gaze as pilgrims at a specific piece of sculpture located on a specific patch of ground over which the city of Clarksdale and the state of Mississippi have come into serious conflict not once but twice: first in the early 1930s and again in the late 1990s. In both cases, what was at stake was the routing of, and legal jurisdiction over, intersecting state highways. In the latter case, the devil's connection with Robert Johnson was promoted by Clarksdale's political leadership as a way of breaking a jurisdictional impasse. Neither conflict is a part of Clarksdale's current civic narrative, much less the "legend of the crossroads." Yet an honest accounting of both conflicts has a great deal to teach us about the way the temptations of crossroads mythology obscure important but fugitive histories—histories that can profoundly enrich our understanding of Clarksdale as a struggling community and Robert Johnson as a cultural actor and focus of touristic fascination. In their own uncanny way, it turns out, Clarksdale's civic and cultural elites have followed in Johnson's footsteps—singing "Me and the Devil Blues" with a wink and a nod and allowing the gullible public to buy in.

Those who believe in the legend of Robert Johnson making a crossroads pact with the devil, and those skeptics who deride the legend, all tend to presume that such legendry is exempt from, or immune to, the workings of logic: the former because, as fans, they yearn to see Johnson as a mythic figure in touch with supernatural forces, the latter because they know that this is how fans think. But the fans and skeptics are both mistaken. The moment one takes the legend seriously—even if only as a strictly conditional exercise—and asks, "Okay, then: when *did* Robert Johnson sell his soul to the devil in order to play guitar like that?," it becomes clear that the legend is subject to real, if somewhat fuzzy, temporal constraints. Since the legend insists both that Johnson's extraordinary prowess was conferred by the devil in very short order and that Johnson's amazed peers bore witness to the results (if not the transaction itself), the legend demands, through its own internal logic, that we take Johnson's Great Leap Forward as incontrovertible evidence not just *that* the soul-selling took place, but *of when* it took place. Just because legends ask us to suspend the usual rules of evidence doesn't mean that they are exempt from all rules. In Johnson's case, there is a date on the calendar prior to which those who knew him agreed he just wasn't a very good guitarist. And there is a date by which he is suddenly impressing people with his dazzling new skills. From that point on, Johnson was on a roll—rambling widely, whoring indiscriminately, and remembered as a preternatural talent by Johnny Shines, Honeyboy Edwards, and other guitar partners and peers. As hard as this may be for the legend-embracers to accept, there is a temporal window—a specific period of calendar time—within which the soul-sale at the crossroads, if one believes that sort of thing, must have happened. The magical broomstick simply won't fly beyond those bookending dates. The questions then become *What are those dates? When is the window?* Either you take the legend seriously or you don't. If you take it seriously—and the civic and cultural leaders of Clarksdale clearly want us to—then you are required to answer, or at least entertain, those questions.

Begin, once again, with the twice-told testimony of Son House. Although he was Johnson's elder and later his competitor on the juke-house circuit and is therefore not necessarily to be trusted as an objective observer, he is the only contemporary of Johnson's whose direct personal witness offers us a before-and-after portrait of the young musician. In interviews with Julius Lester (1965) and Pete Welding (1966), House tells essentially the same story.[137] The offstage prelude to that story is two events: the death of Virginia Travis, Robert's young bride, on April 19, 1930, which led Johnson to move back in with his parents on the Abbay and Leatherman Plantation in Robinsonville, Mississippi, some fifty miles north of Clarksdale; and House's recording sessions with Willie Brown in Grafton, Wisconsin, on May 28 of that same year—the latter date offering a key front-end time stamp for the legend-besotted. Any crossroads pact cannot possibly occur before this date. But of course the lead witness hasn't even weighed in yet. By the middle of June, after a two-week stay in Lula, Mississippi, House was making music with Brown and Charley Patton in the Robinsonville area, playing "those old plantation balls" on Saturday nights. Johnson, nineteen, caught wind of the residency and began dogging the two men from gig to gig. "He was just a little boy then," House told Lester, insisting to both interviewers that Johnson's habit of picking up a guitar when he and Brown were on break and "blamming" on it revealed such a lack of skill that juke-house customers would demand that he silence the young pretender. Johnson, according to Palmer, was "often an object of ridicule when House, Patton, and Brown were drunk and feeling mean." At some point, either because the younger musician was tired of being ridiculed or tired of farming for his father or broken-hearted and restless in the aftermath of his wife's death, or some combination of all those reasons, Johnson abandoned Robinsonville for points south. He soon ended up in Hazlehurst, his downstate birthplace, before traveling another ten miles south to Beauregard, where he settled in with Ike Zimmerman and his family and began his studies in earnest.[138]

When did Johnson actually leave Robinsonville? The date matters not just because it would stand, if available, as the front-end doorstop on the soul-selling legend but because some who purvey crossroads legendry—such as Bill Lester, longtime resident/docent of Dockery Farms—suggest that the demonic transfer was accomplished shortly after that moment, during Johnson's long swoop south to Hazlehurst.[139] Scholars, it turns out, are at some variance about Johnson's departure date. Palmer and LaVere, a romantic and an archskeptic, respectively, in the matter of Johnson's learning process, both use the slippery phrase "before too long" to describe how many Saturday nights passed before Johnson, tired of suffering insults from House and Brown, decided to take off.[140] An August 1930 departure, perhaps? Pearson and McCulloch, for their part, date Johnson's southward flight from Robinsonville as "late 1930 or early 1931."[141] Komara, former head librarian of the Blues Archive at the University of Mississippi and author of a monograph on Johnson's musical development, offers "late 1930" and specifies that "Paramount released its [Son] House 78s from October 1930 through the next 12 months; this time coincided with Robert Johnson's study in Hazlehurst."[142] If the math remains slightly fuzzy, the outlines of a scholarly consensus are clear. October 1930, give or take a month, is a reasonable estimate of Johnson's Robinsonville departure date. At that point, the game clock governing the crossroads legend springs to life. If you believe in the legend, you can't argue for a date much earlier than this and expect anybody to take you seriously. The very ground of your legend is a before-and-after scenario that requires House's time-sensitive testimony about Johnson's lack of talent and a suitable period of hazing before the frustrated young musician leaves town, resolving to break bad.

Now that the clock is ticking, how much time passes before our young guitar hero flashes back into view, transfigured? House told Lester that Johnson had "stayed [away] . . . about six months," and Welding described House (without directly quoting him) as having said that Johnson returned home "six or seven months later."[143] Taking House at his word and using October as our front-end anchor date, we can place Johnson's return to the Robinsonville area at some point in April or May 1931. At that point, according to House's twice-told tale, Johnson showed up one night with a guitar in hand at a juke house in Banks, near Robinsonville, where House and Brown were working, and asked to play. "I winked my eye at Willie," House told Lester. "So he sat down there and finally got started. And man! He was so good! When he finished, all our mouths were standing open. I said, 'Well, ain't that fast! He's gone now!'"[144]

The devil's intercession goes unmentioned in Lester's 1965 interview, but a year later, in a "quote" that Welding was never able to substantiate with a tape recording and that many scholars view with skepticism, the blues journalist makes the familiar claim: "House suggested in all seriousness that Johnson, in his months away from home, had 'sold his soul to the devil in exchange for learning to play like that.'"[145] The brevity of the interregnum, as I argued earlier, helps establish the legend: what else *but* a deal with the devil could explain so rapid a progression in so short a time? House says nothing about a crossroads location, it should be noted, here or in any other published interview, and it is entirely possible that his statement, if one assumes its veracity, was a somewhat more generalized accusation of the sort that religious black southerners were inclined to level at any young person who manifested an interest in, much less a surpassing talent for, nonsanctified music. Virtually every scholar who has investigated the issue, in any case, disputes House's time assessment, insisting that Johnson was absent from Robinsonville for significantly more than six months. (For reasons that will become clear, the Delta Blues Museum and others who promote Clarksdale's connections with the Johnson legend have the most to lose by endorsing House's abbreviated chronology, although they clearly don't realize this.) The earliest that any scholar places Johnson's return to Robinsonville is "during or just after [cotton] harvest time when the local farmers had money to spend" (Komara), which translates to October 1931.[146] House's biographer, Daniel Beaumont, argues that "Johnson's guitar playing attained 'critical mass'"—the requisite for his ability to astonish House and Brown—"in late 1931 or 1932."[147] Conforth, who is completing a full-length biography of Johnson, recently insisted that Johnson moved back to the Delta "in early 1932," running into House and Brown in Banks not long after that.[148] Both Graves and LaVere argue for an even later return, in 1933, when Johnson and Craft relocated from Hazlehurst to the New Africa settlement south of Clarksdale; LaVere, the distant outlier, places that move and Johnson's subsequent encounter with House and Brown in "late 1933."[149]

This two-year spread in the dates offered by serious scholars for Johnson's triumphant return to Robinsonville's jukes—some point between October 1931 and October 1933—is alarming to those who seek certitude in such things, and it helps explain why Johnson's legend has flourished. Legends thrive on uncertainty. Bodies that can't be decisively placed in space and time have a habit of sprouting wings and swooping through the air, at least in certain overheated imaginations. The spread narrows somewhat if we're willing to grant even the slightest weight to House's time sense: if his claim about Johnson's six-month absence bespeaks a memory playing tricks on an aging bluesman, it seems even more unlikely that Johnson was gone for three full years without House noticing. Also implicitly disputing that elongated time frame, Komara argues that Johnson moved to Helena, Arkansas, "in late 1932 or 1933."[150]

Where does this little thought-experiment, an attempt to place firm chronological bookends on Johnson's legend-has-it encounter with the devil, actually take us? On the front end, October 1930 remains a good, solid anchor for the soul-sale window. Johnson could theoretically have decamped from Robinsonville as early as July, having gotten his fill of House and Brown a few weeks after they arrived in town after the late May recording session. But that early date is unlikely, and earlier than that is impossible. As for when the window shuts: with a two-and-a-half-year divergence in the extant accounts, stretching from House in the spring of 1931 to LaVere in the fall of 1933, a conscientious scholar is forced to make hard choices. If October 1933 is the latest possible moment that Johnson could have traveled more than 200 miles north from Hazlehurst, stopped off at the crossroads, summoned the devil, signed the contract, flexed his fingers, paid his devastating visit to the Banks juke, and still had time to cross the bridge to Helena, then even those who fervently embrace the legend would have to admit: that's a challenging itinerary. For all the reasons I have suggested, it makes sense to close the soul-selling window somewhat earlier—agreeing not with House (April 1931) or even Komara (October 1931), but siding with Conforth and settling, for the sake of argument, on April 1932.

October 1930 to April 1932: the best current estimate of the only period of time within which Johnson, were he so inclined, could actually have bargained away his soul. If you are one of those who sincerely believes that Johnson made a deal with the devil at the crossroads in order to become the dazzling guitarist he became—rather than, for example, studying with Ike Zimmerman, as I argued earlier and virtually all scholars believe—then you must take your stand on that patch of temporal real estate. Of course some true believers will insist, over all reasonable objections, on granting Johnson the widest possible window of entrepreneurial action, and they will demand the "hard" bookends: July 1930 to October 1933. And that's perfectly fine, too. At least where Clarksdale's crossroads is concerned, it makes absolutely no difference whether you opt for the shorter window or the longer window. Clarksdale's crossroads, the intersection of Highways 61 and 49 on the spot where the world-famous monument currently sits, did not exist *as* a crossroads at any point in time within either window, although it was slouching toward completion by the fall of 1934 and open for business a year after that. You can't sell your soul to the devil at the crossroads if the crossroads—"our crossroads," as Mayor Luckett told Robin Meade—literally isn't there.

This claim, one inimical to the blues touristic agenda of Clarksdale's civic and cultural elites, requires evidence. Before reviewing that evidence, I should note that a somewhat different version of this claim, one that offers an important counterstatement to Luckett's triumphalism, has been made by skeptical commentators in the years following the monument's installation. That cohort, which includes a cultural anthropologist, a local Clarks-

The so-called old crossroads, where Highway 49 and Highway 61 intersected in the early 1930s before being rerouted to their present location Photograph by the author.

dale historian, a specialist in African American literature, and a founding member of the Mississippi Blues Commission, argues for the importance of what it calls the "old crossroads": not the DeSoto/Sycamore intersection at what was then, in the 1930s, on the outskirts of town, but the intersection of East Tallahatchie Street and Fourth Street (now Martin Luther King Boulevard) at the center of the so-called New World entertainment district.[151] In Robert Johnson's day, this was the bustling heart of blues-loving black Clarksdale. More important for those who stake Clarksdale's identity as "the crossroads" on its linking of two storied blues highways, East Tallahatchie and Fourth Street were, in fact, Highways 49 and 61—or at least they were the Clarksdale terminus for those two highways, in all their meandering packed-gravel glory, until the "new" Highways 49 and 61, intersecting at the current (i.e., "legendary") crossroads, were surveyed, designed, dug, graded, paved, and opened to the world in the summer of 1935. At that point, East Tallahatchie and Fourth Street began the slow descent into becoming what they are now: "old Highway 49" and "old Highway 61," which is how they are labeled on the current tourist map if you follow both streets past the city limits into the Coahoma countryside.[152]

In the fall of 1930, when Robert Johnson headed south out of Robinsonville with Hazlehurst as his destination, he would almost certainly have taken old Highway 61 south to Clarksdale. His other option would have been

to travel east to Hernando on Route 3—much of it is coded "unimproved" on the best available highway map from the period—and then swing south on Highway 51 through the hill country borderlands of Senatobia, Batesville, and Grenada.[153] Clarksdale, the heart of Delta cotton country in harvest time, is where the action was, and it's impossible to imagine Johnson, blues-hungry as he was, bypassing the city for a slower, less exciting route. Which means that he would have rolled, or walked, into town by way of Fourth Street and, as he came even with the train station looming behind the Bornman Lumber Yard to his right, run smack into East Tallahatchie: the "old crossroads." That is where Highways 61 and 49 crossed in the fall of 1930. It is an entirely reasonable conjecture to place Robert Johnson—young, agitated, ambitious—on that spot at that particular moment in time. Some will find this an exciting proposition. Is *that*, then, where Johnson made a deal with the devil—if you believe in that sort of thing?

Cultural anthropologist Neff makes precisely that claim. She writes as an advocate for Clarksdale's younger African American musicians, both rappers and blues players, a dispossessed blues community that, she argues, has not only gained little or no benefit from the "legendary" crossroads marker and the blues boom it has abetted, but has watched its elders' history be erased from the civic narrative. "These routes," she writes of old Highway 61 and 49, quietly mark the crossroads of American music. The famed Blues Highways were filled with traveling, working, creating, and living blues people, and their sounds and styles continue to resonate far beyond this patch of loamy soil. World-famous folklore claims that Delta bluesman Robert Johnson sealed his fate at this very location, selling his soul to the devil for a set of guitar licks in the 1920s.

. . . Today, the historic roads are outstripped by channels of fast grey pavement that claim the Blues Highways' names—61 and 49—while bypassing the neighborhoods that built their legacy.[154]

Neff is right about the cultural importance of the old Blues Highways, although there is good reason to think that the "fast grey pavement" that unrolled across the Delta during the 1930s and the much higher speeds those new highways enabled were a creative stimulant to the blues musicians who encountered them. (When Robert Johnson sang "Mr. Highwayman, please don't block the road" in "Terraplane Blues," 1936, he was thinking of a late-model Hudson with a terminal velocity of eighty miles per hour, a speed that would have been inconceivable on the dusty gravel of old Highway 61, where thirty miles per hour was the limit, but a thrilling possibility on the just-installed, paved, straight-as-an-arrow thoroughfare that replaced it.) But Neff is mistaken about the dating of that "world-famous folklore"—no extant version of the Johnson legend specifies the 1920s—and she shares with Clarksdale's blues boosters a problematic insistence on broadening the crossroads-concept in a way that serves her ideological purposes rather than remaining anchored in established material facts.

What made the East Tallahatchie/Fourth Street intersection the "crossroads of American music" in 1930 was its location at what was, in effect, Clarksdale's Times Square. That is precisely the same thing that makes it an extremely unlikely venue for Johnson's private consult with the devil. The Yazoo and Mississippi Valley railroad line runs adjacent and parallel to East Tallahatchie, only thirty feet from the old crossroads, bisecting Fourth Street and arcing ninety degrees to the right through an urban switching yard before joining up with the Illinois Central tracks in front of what was, in Johnson's day, the new and bustling Clarksdale Passenger Depot. Robert Birdsong, a noted local historian, argues that Clarksdale had a reputation among African American musicians for having "the toughest crowd to please" between New Orleans and Chicago because the New World district, with the old crossroads as its symbolic and geographic center, was an unusually compact transit hub, showcasing talent from all directions.

"Whether coming by rail or coming by road," he observed, "for a hundred years of outmigration from the 1860s to the 1960s, that outmigration came through Clarksdale."[155] One block from the old crossroads, Issaquena Street, although subsisting in a state of near-abandonment and disrepair today, was a thriving entertainment zone as late as the 1970s, remembered with equal fondness by the black and white Clarksdalians I interviewed.

Why would Robert Johnson have traveled from the far reaches of rural Coahoma County into the raucous, clanging midst of metropolitan Clarksdale in order to transact intimate business with the devil? The nearby jukes and cafés would have been rocking long past midnight, driven by street and sidewalk traffic. The urban soundscape would have made it difficult for Johnson to hear his own hands on the strings, much less the devil's suave entreaties. "The city's concrete and noise," writes Spencer, speaking of Chicago and the urban North in words that find unexpected traction here,

> helped diminish the rural residue of southern religious cosmology [in the blues lyric tradition] because it, respectively, covered up nature and muted its sounds, nature being the key conduit with the spirit world. A city or urban blues singer was unable to go to the crossroads at midnight to learn his or her virtuosity from "the devil," for the city had innumerable crossroads, all of which were busy with the traffic of industrial trucks that did their carrying at night.[156]

The old crossroads has a legitimate claim on our attentions as a symbol of Clarksdale's long, illustrious, now vanished and somewhat obscured history as a bustling urban center of black southern blues life. Robert Johnson almost surely passed through that intersection more than a few times—turning southeast on East Tallahatchie in the fall of 1930, perhaps, and heading toward Tutwiler, Greenwood, and points south. That likely occurrence in itself deserves commemoration. There is no more reason, however, for the legend-hungry to call East Tallahatchie and Fourth Street *the* crossroads, Johnson's rendezvous point with the devil, than to call the current spot the same thing—except, of course, for the fact that the former location actually existed *as* a crossroads, the intersection of two state highways, during Johnson's (fictive) soul-selling season.

ROAD FIGHT

The story of Clarksdale's crossroads in the 1930s—the new crossroads—is best summarized as a tale of two maps.

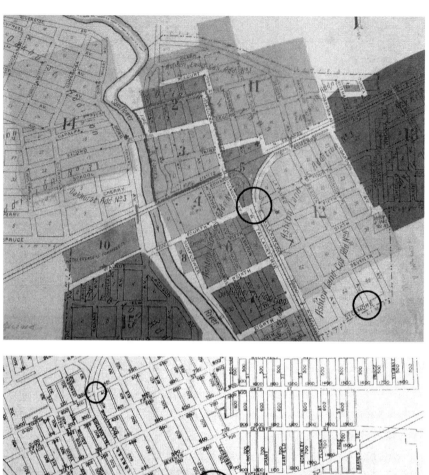

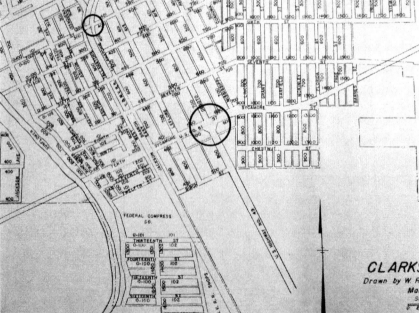

Sanborn Fire Insurance maps of Clarksdale from 1918 (top) and 1938 (bottom), showing the circled locations of the old crossroads (upper left) and future/new crossroads (lower right). Photographs by the author.

A researcher who consults a 1938 Sanborn Fire Insurance Map for Clarksdale can easily find the present-day crossroads location.[157] U.S. Highway 49 rises in a long diagonal line to meet U.S. Highway 61 at the southeastern edge of the city. The two highways junction at right angles in a distinctive trapezoidal shape that, although not visible on the Sanborn map, are spelled out in the final revision of the original blueprints for the intersection. Sixty-one years later, Vic Barbieri's monument was erected on the more easterly of those two triangles, where it currently stands. Highway 61 is also identified on the 1938 map by the pair of local streets it becomes as it passes through the city: Sycamore in the vicinity of the intersection, Tenth Street to the west of the railroad tracks. Highway 49 has no other name south of the crossroads, but north of the intersection it becomes DeSoto Avenue.

A researcher who consults a 1929 edition of the map finds nothing, at least at first, because nothing is there.[158] No highways, no trapezoid, no crossroads. Sycamore is there: flush against the city's southerly limits at its midpoint, it runs slightly more than a quarter of a mile in either direction, dead-ending in Florida Street on the east and Sunflower Avenue, next to the river, on the west. DeSoto, in turn, dead-ends in Sycamore at its southernmost extent. It doesn't extend south beyond Sycamore because Highway 49—new Highway 49—has not yet been built. There is nothing to distinguish the junction of DeSoto and Sycamore from half a dozen such junctions on the outermost ring of the Clarksdale city grid. There is no reason whatsoever to imagine that Robert Johnson, or any other blues musician on the prowl for a crossroads, would have chosen *that* spot, of all places.

What happened between 1929 and 1938? How was such an unprepossessing location transformed into "our crossroads," the future site of so much fabricated legend?

Both the transformation itself and the troubles that accompanied it were sourced, ultimately, in the actions of one man: Horace Stansel, a civil engineer and Mississippi state legislator who was appointed in 1928 by then-governor Theodore Bilbo to head a special committee charged with studying and proposing improvements to the state's notably lagging highway system. Public pressure for road improvements had been building for some time; worried not just about being left behind but routed around, Clarksdale's elites were a party to those complaints. "Gravel road states," wrote the editor of the *Clarksdale Daily Register* in 1928, "are unable to compete with the hard-surface road states for desirable motor travel and the superhighway system will establish routes that will be difficult to change."[159] The five-member Stansel Highway Commission traveled the state in 1929, discovering, among other things, that only 26 of the roughly 200 miles of U.S. 51, the principal highway between Jackson and the Tennessee line, were paved.[160] The result, in 1930, was the Stansel Highway Bill, an act which wrested power from the state's counties, including the power of eminent domain, and transferred it to a streamlined state highway department overseen by three (rather than eight) commissioners. According to the new statute, "The State Highway Commission [was] hereby given complete control and supervision, with full power and authority to locate, relocate, widen, alter, change, straighten, construct, or reconstruct any and all roads on the State Highway system."[161] In late November 1930, eager to move ahead, the white citizens of Clarksdale voted 362 to 14 in favor of a $200,000 bond issue, matched by federal aid, to build hard-surfaced highways in Coahoma County. The state highway commission was the conduit for that aid as well as the final arbiter of routing. According to the *Daily Register*, M. J. (Marshall) Bouldin, an important cotton planter and president of the Coahoma County Board of Supervisors, would be traveling to the state capital to meet with the commission and advocate on Clarksdale's behalf. "The route for the hard surfacing road program," cautioned the paper, "has not been definitely decided. It is being selected by highway commissioner engineers, who haven't yet announced even a probable route."[162]

The new route for Highway 49, as it turned out, was easily settled on and without controversy: an arrow-straight thirteen-mile stretch or "air line" from Tutwiler to Clarksdale, parallel to and several hundred yards east of old 49, that would bisect Sycamore Street and become DeSoto Avenue as it entered town. By late February 1931, advertisements seeking construction bids were put out in the *Daily Register*; by late March, the contract had been awarded and work had begun, starting from the Tutwiler end and working north. "Several hundred laborers were put at work as well as 66 mule teams and drivers, all recruited from the ranks of Coahoma county's unemployed."[163] The original plan was to complete grading and construction of the gravel roadbed by September so that it could settle over the winter before being paved the following spring, but that schedule proved slightly too optimistic. The "Road Map of Mississippi" published in *Mississippi Highways* in October 1932 ("correct to June 1, 1932"), still shows the somewhat meandering, gravel-coded outlines of old Highways 49 and 61.[164] But paving was under way by June, after Commissioner Abe Linker had visited Clarksdale in May and finalized plans for the concrete surface. Although no evidence exists for precisely when new Highway 49 was completed, a reasonable guess would be the late fall of 1932.[165]

One new highway, however, does not a crossroads make. Clarksdale's other new highway was soon bedeviled by division within the community and a struggle to wrest control from state authorities. The chief demand of Clarksdale's white elites was that new Highway 61 run through downtown for at least some portion of its length, much as its predecessor currently did; a secondary topic, vigorously debated by businessmen and planters alike, was whether it should run through the west or east side of the city. The state highway commission, charged with overseeing the routing and construction of fifty miles' worth of road stretching from the Tunica County line down to the Bolivar County line, had their own set of pragmatic concerns. By the beginning of June 1931, state engineers had already surveyed the western route, a dead-straight "air-line" from Cutrer Mansion north through Lula, but engineer Paul Claxton was back, the *Daily Register* reported, to survey a more easterly route that would follow the gas pipeline of the Mississippi Power and Light Company through Coahoma County. The new crossroads is mentioned for the first time in this story:

> A suggested route for the connection of Highway 61 with Clarksdale is at Sycamore street, which is the end of Highway 49, now under hard-surface construction. From Sycamore street the highway would follow DeSoto avenue North to Fourth street, then up Fourth to Mullens' store.[166]

As a follow-up story made clear, this suggested route, with its pair of awkward ninety-degree doglegs, was an attempt by Clarksdalians to shape the dialogue in a way that steered the highway through the eastern portion of downtown rather than missing Clarksdale completely, as a route strictly aligned with the pipeline would do.[167] Rumors swirled for the next several months. In early August, local point man Bouldin shared an impatient letter from Linker, the Oxford-based highway commissioner in charge of the project, and urged "opposing factions in this fight [to] leave the selection of the route to the good judgment of the Highway Commission, supported by the neutral findings of their engineers."[168] One week later, on 12 August, the *Daily Register* reported on the results of a large public meeting called by Bouldin with headlines that perfectly expressed Clarksdale's taut civic mood: "Resolution to Leave Road Up to Engineers—Proviso Is That They Must Select Route through This City." The "mass meeting of Coahoma county citizens," 200 in all, took place at the offices of the Clarksdale and Coahoma County Chamber of Commerce. The compromise resolution indicated by the headline, driven by a collective sense of urgency, was introduced by the Young Businessmen's Club of Clarksdale and passed with only two dissenting votes, bringing "several weeks of controversy between two factions" to a close.[169]

The simmering multiparty dispute faded from view as the summer of 1931 drifted toward fall, only to erupt into open warfare in November when the state highway commission issued its final decision about the routing of new Highway 61. "Club Re-opens Road Fight" read the banner headline in the *Daily Register*. "Leaders Renew Battle to Get Right Routing." The outrage, according to a resolution adopted by the Clarksdale Rotary Club, was that the commissioners had dared to choose a route that ran "on the East side of the railroad . . . through tenth and Sycamore streets of the city of Clarksdale," hugging the city limits rather than doglegging down through town. They had chosen precisely the route, with precisely the crossroads that Mayor Luckett and the city's twenty-first-century leaders now celebrate as "our crossroads." But in the fall of 1931, as Robert Johnson continued his studies with Ike Zimmerman down in Beauregard, that route was an insult to the town's leading white men, a nightmare come true. "Our committee was 'washed out' and we all received a 'cold' deal from the powers that be," fumed Dr. E. LeRoy Wilkins, a Rotarian who had met with Linker and a second commissioner. "It seems to me," he continued, "that if we want to get a hard surfaced road through Clarksdale, other than along Tenth street and Sycamore avenues we will have to fight for a West Side route which would automatically bring the highway along one of our principal streets."[170] In an editorial published the following day, the *Daily Register* applauded the Rotary statement as a "new turn in the civic tide," invoking the $200,000 bond issue and condemning the state's action as taxation without representation. "To satisfy their own friends, to meet their own purposes," summarized the editors, "state commissioners decide arbitrarily in favor of Sycamore and Tenth Street route against wishes and pleasure of a majority."[171] Clarksdale's Young Businessmen's Club immediately allied themselves with the Rotarians, and a special committee consisting of representatives from both groups traveled to Jackson to meet with the commissioners in a last-ditch attempt to save Clarksdale from the abyss of disadvantageous routing. There, reported the *Daily Register*, "they ran counter to an unchangeable NO." There was something devilish about all this, suggested the newspaper—"something sinister in the flat refusal that came from the lips of commissioners."[172]

When all else failed, one final option remained available to Clarksdale's white elites: demanding that the state highway commission return the

$200,000 raised by the bond issue, which would stop the new highway dead in its tracks. But as the special joint committee discovered, this option was "legally impossible."[173]

Three months of steady winter rain descended on Clarksdale at that point, and new Highway 61, along with the future site of "our crossroads," languished like an infected wound. Then the skies suddenly brightened in late February 1932 and the dispute suddenly resolved itself. Commissioner Linker drove over from Oxford to meet informally with the Coahoma County Board of Supervisors, offering a detailed report on "all activities of the federal, state and county authorities" related to the planned highway, along with an itemized account of all expenditures so far. "His talk," noted the *Daily Register*, "was concise and to the point and gave the interested persons present a very clear and intelligent idea of all that has been done. . . . Mr. Linker was heartily endorsed by the members of the board, planters from different sections and by representatives of the Tax-payers League. . . . Following the talk by Mr. Linker the meeting resolved itself into a round table discussion and the highway commissioner graciously and intelligently answered all questions to the satisfaction of all present."[174] The die was cast. The city and state had settled on the future location of Clarksdale's new crossroads.

If Robert Johnson had visited that intersection at precisely that moment, of course, he would have found nothing that looked like the crossing point of two blues highways. He would, instead, have found more or less the same thing that existed on that spot between November 1931 and June 1932: the unfinished junction of a relatively unimportant city street (albeit one with a suddenly promising future) and the muddy (or dusty) butt end of "new" Highway 49—freshly dug and graded, settling over the winter, awaiting the paving that would finally begin in June, and closed to traffic. Such an unprepossessing construction zone offers little traction for the sort of romance that many latter-day blues fans, imaginations enlivened by Clarksdale's coordinated marketing plan, have attached to the site. An attentive reader may notice, too, that the April 1932 date established earlier as the reasonable bookend for Johnson's soul-selling window—assuming one believes in such things—has come and gone with one of the two highways not yet paved and the other not even contracted to the highest bidder. Even a hardcore aficionado holding out for the widest possible soul-selling window would have been frustrated by the measured, incremental process of bringing those new highways into being. Due in part to the long annual break necessitated by winter rains and in part to the complexity of the project, which included a handful of smaller bridges and one large, expensive bridge over the Sunflower River, Highway 61 was not fully operational as a throughway, with automobile traffic flowing both directions across the Highway 49 intersection, until July 1935, almost five years after the $200,000 bond issue was first floated.[175] By that point, of course, Johnson's bravura performance for Son House at the juke joint in Banks was long behind him, along with the period of intensive apprenticeship to Ike that had helped him accrue his dazzling skills. He'd been out on the road, crisscrossing the South, for a couple of years.

A funny thing happened to Clarksdale's new crossroads after it opened for business. Clarksdalians, having fiercely opposed the routing that created it, quickly embraced it as though it had been their idea to begin with. The transformation becomes visible with a new listing in the city's 1936 telephone directory: "Cross Roads Service Station Milton Hughes mgr cor DeSoto junction hwys 61 & 49."[176] The following year, a Lebanese immigrant named Abraham ("Abe") Davis relocated his pit barbeque restaurant, the Bungalow Inn, from Fourth Street and Florida—only seven-tenths of a mile from the old crossroads—to a location directly adjacent to the new crossroads.[177] The city's center of gravity, trembling a little, had suddenly shifted. Nothing illustrates this shift more clearly than the plaque installed in 1938 by the Coahoma chapter of the Daughters of the American Revolution on the traffic median where, sixty-one years later, the City Beautification Commission would install a second memorial with a radically different valence. Extending an implicit invitation to the larger world, the plaque offered Clarksdale's best face to travelers passing through, or pausing for refreshment, while in transit on those fast new highways:

Clarksdale

County seat of Coahoma County was founded in 1869 by John Clark, for whom the town was named. Situated in one of the most fertile regions of the world, it has grown into one of the leading cities of the Yazoo Mississippi Delta. It has a just pride in its library, its schools, and its churches, and is an important market for long staple cotton.

That was Clarksdale's brand in 1938, the year Robert Johnson died: books, schools, God, and cotton. The devil was nowhere to be found—certainly not at *that* crossroads. All that would change in the decades that followed.

Bronze plaque erected in 1938 at the site of the new crossroads in Clarksdale, celebrating the town's achievements: library, schools, churches, cotton. Photograph by the author.

THE 10,000TH PERSON CALLING ABOUT ROBERT JOHNSON

One enduring mystery of Clarksdale's crossroads is how that particular location managed to accumulate the word "the," signifying its exclusive claim on the Johnson legend. Were the words "legend has it," which are ritually attached to the spot in our own day, simply the opportunistic invention of a local huckster—one determined to corner the market and leave other aspirant crossroads locations out in the cold? Or is there a more innocuous explanation for why and how the legend became attached to the location?

The outlines of an answer become apparent the moment one realizes just how quickly that new 49/61 intersection became known as "the crossroads" to the citizens of Clarksdale—not in connection with Johnson, but simply as an important civic center. In 1973, a local entertainment weekly called *Here's Clarksdale* took a walk down memory lane. Back in 1940, the magazine reminded its readers, "The city limits . . . could roughly be defined as Cheyenne in West Clarksdale, Cutrer Hill, Fairland, Coahoma Ave. and Highway 61. Cross-Roads and 4th Street were burgeoning, but there were few homes and businesses beyond these limits."[178] Not *the* crossroads, but still: in the space of four years, the intersection point of two new highways had blossomed into a vibrant neighborhood named for the intersection. Assisting that transformation was Cotton Boll Court, a multiunit motor court just off the southeast corner. Listed in the 1941 *Clarksdale City Register*, it was the brainchild of S. H. Kyle, owner of the Roundaway Plantation four-teen miles south of the city. Postcards from the period locate it at "Hiways 61 and 49" and boast of "Innerspring Mattresses—Tile Bath—Shower over tub—Insulated—Gas Heat—Garages—Telephones." Remembered by several elderly Clarksdalians as an important fixture at the crossroads, it eventually burned down, almost taking Abe's Bar-B-Q (the renamed Bungalow Inn) with it, leaving the U-shaped set of crumbling concrete foundations that remain a visible blight on the current intersection.[179]

A twenty-first-century visitor to that intersection, finding Crossroads Furniture and several other similarly titled businesses nearby and knowing nothing of local history, might assume that their owners were seeking to capitalize on the presence of the crossroads monument. The truth is that the location's crossroads brand—indeed, the name "the crossroads"—considerably predates both the monument's installation and Johnson's association with the location. "It was always known locally as the crossroads," insisted James Butler, the former director of public works who supervised the monument's installation in 1999. "Everything in the area was named Crossroads, because that's just what the community had called the intersection: the crossroads."[180] Anchored by the twenty-four-hour service station (remembered by Abe's son Pat Davis as a place that had "thrown away the front door key"), the intersection quickly accumulated a series of businesses in the 1940s and 1950s that adopted the crossroads motif and were still remembered vividly half a century later. The 1964 telephone directory lists not just Cross Roads Serv. St & Wrecker Serv, but Crossroad Laundry & Cleaners, Crossroad Shell Service Station, and Crossroads Branch Bank of Clarksdale, all located within a hundred yards of where the monument now stands.[181] "As long ago as I can remember," concurred Hunter H. Twiford III, Clarksdale's former city attorney, "which would be probably mid-50s, late 50s would be. . . . Everything in that area was called the crossroads."[182] Octogenarian Nell Smith, a Clarksdale native and doyenne of the City Beautification Commission, remembered a social life back in the 1950s that featured late-night excursions to the crossroads:

> Even when I was married, we used to go to—that's where we'd go to that crossroads café, the restaurant back there, after the Planter's Ball. The crossroads were always just . . . important to us. . . . We'd go there after the big dance or something, some of the couples would want to go get some coffee and some scrambled eggs. You know, it was kind of late, and we'd go there. There was the service station, and in the back part of it you had

a different entrance. They would stay open late after the dances and we'd have breakfast and coffee, and talk about what a good time we had.[183]

Even Vic Barbieri, the monument's creator, had vivid childhood memories of the crossroads dating back to 1948 or 1949, when his father purchased a duplex just off the intersection. He ticked off a list of businesses in the immediate vicinity named Crossroads, including the service station, the cleaners, a drugstore, a pawnshop, and a truck stop. "Before this blues thing came along it was always the crossroads," he summarized.[184]

Clarksdale's blues thing—which is to say, white touristic interest in the blues and formal public acknowledgement of the music by white elites— took a long time to arrive. Mayor Luckett may brag now about Clarksdale's being "the epicenter . . . ground zero for blues music," but his predecessors, both locally and statewide, ran in the opposite direction for many years, according to William Ferris, Mississippi's best-known blues folklorist. "The reality is that blues was an embarrassment for Mississippi until fairly recently," Ferris insisted. "I spent much of my life trying to make happen what is now happening. But we could not get support from any tourism budgets for the work we did with *Living Blues*."[185] Still, Ferris noted, Clarksdale ultimately become an important player in the blues tourism market because of a "series of high-powered long-term commitments," including the founding of the Delta Blues Museum by Sid Graves (1979), the arrival of Rooster Blues Records in Clarksdale (1986), the expansion of the Delta Blues Museum (1999), and the sudden visibility of actor Morgan Freeman as Luckett's business partner in the Ground Zero Blues Club (2001). The first two developments, which considerably predate the apotheosis of Clarksdale's crossroads, are the ground on which the city's later blues touristic success was built, and they were movements from below—labors of love organized by scholarly aficionados rather than administrative or profit-focused initiatives organized from above. The relocation of Rooster Blues from Chicago to Clarksdale, in particular, signaled the arrival of Jim O'Neal, a founding editor of *Living Blues*, and paved the way for the emergence of what might be called crossroads tourism. In 1988, O'Neal and his partner Patty Johnson opened the Stackhouse Delta Record Mart in downtown Clarksdale and staged the first Sunflower River Blues Festival on the street in front of their emporium. Much to their surprise, they quickly found themselves fielding requests from a small but steady stream of out-of-state visitors for directions to "the crossroads." You know, came the invariable addendum, the place where Robert Johnson made his deal with the devil.

Reflecting later on this late-1980s moment, O'Neal and Johnson attributed much of that early touristic interest to the film *Crossroads* (1986)—"a charming little movie," Johnson said, "[that] had nothing really to do with Robert Johnson."[186] Nor, of course, did it mention Clarksdale's crossroads; the soul-sale scenes featuring Robert Johnson, Willie Brown, and various devil figures were filmed forty-five miles south, in Beulah. But the film's Mississippi locations and evocative dramatizations apparently awoke a hunger for adventure in a scattering of pilgrims around the globe, and Clarksdale, an easy drive down from Memphis, was a frequent first stop. O'Neal traces the beginning of blues touristic interest in Clarksdale's crossroads, however, to one specific moment earlier in the decade—a textual moment that, ironically, helped inspire John Fusco to write his *Crossroads* screenplay as a film student at NYU. "A lot of that goes back to Robert Palmer," O'Neal insisted, "his chapter in *Deep Blues* (1981). . . . That's exactly where it all started." The passage in question argues that "in a region as perfectly flat as the Delta," a crossroads, *any* crossroads, is "one of the few features of the landscape that really stands out," and is therefore something that finds its way into the names of local businesses:

> Driving south toward Clarksdale in 1979, I noticed at the junction where Highway 49 crosses Highway 61, running off west toward Lula and Helena and east toward Sledge and the central hills, a combination gas station/ restaurant called the Crossroader. When I got to Clarksdale, I bought gas at the Crossroads Service Station, Highway 61 and DeSoto Street. Curious, I looked in a local telephone directory and found a Crossroad Laundry and Cleaners, Crossroad Sporting Goods, Crossroads Branch Bank of Clarksdale, and Cross Roads Wrecking Service. The familiarity and ubiquity of the crossroads in Delta iconography lends an added immediacy to Johnson's tale of terror.[187]

Johnson's "tale of terror" is of course "Cross Road Blues." Palmer doesn't explicitly claim that Clarksdale's crossroads is the crossroads referenced by Johnson, nor does he seem to know that Clarksdale's crossroads is the second place where Highways 61 and 49 intersect—that is, that DeSoto becomes 49 as it crosses 61. The crossroads-themed businesses he finds in the phone book testify, as Clarksdale's residents have asserted, to the continuing vitality of the neighborhood. But Palmer's insinuation asks us to connect the dots. "Familiarity," "ubiquity," and "immediacy" somehow align themselves with "terror," and thus with Johnson's (imagined) transaction with the devil. "He didn't come out and say it," O'Neal said of Palmer. "He kinda, just . . . hinted, you know."[188]

Was this, then, the original source of Clarksdale's claim on Johnson: a music journalist's tendentious travelogue, misread by others in a way that enabled the legend? Or perhaps those early blues pilgrims to Clarksdale, fanning out across the town's crumbling, postplantation landscape and armed with the question *Can you tell me where the crossroads is?* encountered locals, white and black, who, never having met a blues tourist and knowing nothing about Robert Johnson, took the question literally and said, "Head out DeSoto Avenue until you hit Highway 61." Eventually, as the tourists kept coming, the locals figured out what was going on and accommodated themselves to the legend—or so we might surmise.

The 1990 release of Johnson's *Complete Recordings*, which went platinum and won a Grammy Award, was a watershed moment in the history of crossroads fandom, triggering what Jeff Todd Titon has called the "new blues tourism" and further stoking Clarksdale's through-traffic in the years that followed.[189] Although two elements of that new blues tourism, historic markers and Chamber of Commerce literature, were not yet present in Clarksdale, two others were: tour maps and "a growing group of presenters and musicians who interpret the music for outsiders." For O'Neal and Johnson, both the legend and the pilgrims it brought through the door of their record store were a source of great amusement and occasional frustration. Neither host made a case for Clarksdale's crossroads—they were thoroughgoing skeptics with regard to any such devil-talk—but they were quite willing, at least at first, to offer the credulous, especially those with cars, a range of scenic options across the state. "Sometimes a film crew would be looking for a location," O'Neal recently remembered,

> that looked like a crossroads. Whether it was one, or "the" one or not, just something to use as background for another little documentary news item about the Delta. There were always tourists that came in and wanted to know where it ["the" crossroads] was, you know. I would give them the list of places and say, "It's probably none of 'em, it probably doesn't exist," but that's not what they wanted to hear. The funniest one I wish there had been a camera on. It was like something from a Cheech and Chong movie. They'd been out and around. They were both covered with dust and one of 'em looked at the other and said, "I'm telling you, man, there *ain't* no crossroads!" [And the other one] was talking about, "We're gonna keep looking." They were just beat. Worn out and covered with dust.[190]

As curator of the Delta Blues Museum during the mid-1990s and a tourist guide during those years, blues guitarist John Ruskey frequently confronted the same scenario, especially with overseas pilgrims. "There was such a mystique around the crossroads that the legend grew larger than the reality. In a lot of peoples' minds there was a physical place that had to exist somewhere in the Delta." Rather than taking people to the 61/49 intersection, Ruskey, a seasoned river guide, offered them a wilderness encounter:

> When people would press me for it, I had a special place. It was just a really kind of powerful-feeling crossroads out on a hump of land on a high rise of ground inside a giant old loop of the Mississippi River, just north of downtown Clarksdale. Four hundred years ago the Mississippi did flow right alongside downtown Clarksdale, and it created this wetland and a giant loop, and Stovall Road is actually on one side of that loop. And where Muddy Waters used to play as a kid, they call it the Little Sunflower River. Some people say his grandmother gave him that name, "Muddy," because he used to like to go down into this wetland and play, and he'd come home covered in dirt. In the middle of that [loop] is this really rich soil that is on the King and Anderson plantation. And there were two farm turn-roads that crossed each other out in the middle of that big open area. It just had a good feel to it, a powerful feel. And at nighttime the stars are really there. And that's where I would bring people to, when someone would press me and they just had to see the crossroads. I'd say, "Yeah, yeah, I know where the crossroads are." [*Mimics a Japanese accent*] "Ah, ah, Johnny-san, Johnny-san, you take me there?"
>
> And so I brought a few people out there. Some Japanese people . . . a young Japanese guy, and I think a French guy. Most Americans are a little more jaded and not so enthralled by the whole mystique of it. Lots of foreigners.[191]

Facilitated in those premonument years by freelance guides in Clarksdale and elsewhere in the Delta, such crossroads encounters sometimes precipitated strong emotional responses. "I brought a young guitar player out there one time," remembered Ruskey, "who was very serious about his music and was humbled and felt the need to get down on his knees and literally kiss the dust. When I brought him back to town, he didn't say anything until we got back to town, and I didn't press him, but he said that he heard voices when he had his head down on the ground." A similar vignette involving the actor Lou Diamond Phillips was recounted by both Johnson and Pat LeBlanc; the crossroads in question was located not in the vicinity of Clarksdale, but forty miles south, adjacent to Dockery Farms—a more "likely" soul-sale site in the eyes of many aficionados, as even the skeptical Johnson was willing to concede. "That's one of those places that we used to send people to," she said, "because there's train line there, it's just south of Highway 8, which runs right past Dockery, where the old Highway 8 was. . . . Could somebody have gotten on a train there? You know, 'I went down to the crossroads.' That's a possibility."[192]

The intersection of old Highway 8 and Dockery Road, located half a mile south of the current front entrance to Dockery Farms and just past an abandoned graveyard, remains pristine and evocative to this day: a dusty crossing-point of two graveled dirt roads in the middle of the fields, with the southern-bound leg swerving suddenly after it crosses the old highway, snaking left behind some shrubbery in a way that feels ominous. Phillips, a Filipino American actor of part-Cherokee ancestry, made a Mississippi pilgrimage in the early 1990s, perhaps stimulated by his friendship with John Fusco, writer and producer of *Young Guns* (1988), in which he had appeared a few years earlier. "I took Lou Diamond Phillips out there [to the Dockery crossroads] with his little blues band," said LeBlanc, the Mississippi-born host of "Southern Crossroads," a syndicated weekly blues radio show, "and they actually got down in the dirt and rubbed the dirt on their person, you know. Took some of the dirt with 'em. It was very emotional."[193] Johnson told the same story without naming Phillips. "There is an actor who happens to be part native American, and *he* came to the store. . . . We said, 'Okay, you have several options if you want to go to some local crossroads, some places where there's a crossing point.' And he was actually seen being photographed—he got down on his knees and threw the dirt on his body and rubbed it around. It was a very personal moment for him."[194]

Perhaps the most powerful testimony about the emotions unleashed by crossroads tourism was offered by Sandy Bynum, head of communications and advertising for the Mississippi Development Authority's Division of Tourism. During the 1990s, as executive director for the Convention and Visitors Bureau in Greenwood, sixty miles south of Clarksdale, Bynum offered tourists a mimeographed map of local blues sites before sending them on their way. But one particular day she took pity on a young Irish pilgrim, a hitchhiker:

A young man, he was college age. He was on a trek to experience the blues and come to Mississippi. And he came in the door of my office. . . . And he said, "I'm really trying to find the crossroads." . . . I handed him the map, and I said, "I've just been talking to a good friend of mine, Pat LeBlanc. Pat and I found this—we had this map, this original map." And so we got it out and I said . . . "Let's go find—this is where Highway 49 and 61 actually crossed back in the days of people still driving old jalopies and wagons." And so we got in the city van, and we drove way out into the county, following this original map. And I'm telling you: a hot dusty Delta day. It had to be a hundred and one degrees that day.[195]

According to LeBlanc, the map was based on a series of old aerial photographs that he had discovered at the LeFlore County Courthouse, showing how the location of the Three Forks store where Robert Johnson was alleged to have been poisoned by a jealous husband had slowly shifted over the years. Bynum drove her visitor "way out in the country somewhere":

> We followed this old, old map. And we walked out into the middle of
> this cotton field. And I was thinking, "I'm getting really dirty." We were
> talking about the crossroads and the legend of Robert Johnson selling his
> soul to the devil. And we were holding the map, and we looked, and you
> could see that the tree line is missing this way, and the tree line is missing
> this way. Here we are on this adventure, really, together, trying to find the
> spot. This should be where the crossroads actually was located back in that
> time. And whether we were in the right place or the wrong place, I learned
> a valuable lesson that day. It's the telling of the story. It's the emotion in
> a place. Because he stood there and cried. And his tears dropped from
> his eyes to the ground, and they would hit the dirt—poof!—and make
> that teardrop spot pop, just like a petal would do in the water. And he
> looked at me and he said, "I can die happy now, because I've stood at
> the crossroads."[196]

As the testimony offered by O'Neal, Johnson, Ruskey, LeBlanc, and Bynum makes clear, crossroads tourism in Mississippi between the late 1980s and mid-1990s provided both pilgrims and their guides with vivid tableaux and powerful, sometimes transformative experiences. But the deluge of eager visitors could also be wearing on their hosts. By 1997, O'Neal's answering machine greeted prospective pilgrims with "If you're the 10,000th person calling about Robert Johnson and how to find the crossroads, proceed to the intersection of Routes 49 and 61 and wait for further instructions."[197] Although Clarksdale, and the Stackhouse Delta Record Mart in particular, often became the launching point for such adventures, none of the guides interviewed for this study—except O'Neal with his tongue in cheek—directed pilgrims toward that city's as-yet unmarked 49/61 cross-roads, nor did they see any particular reason to do so.

And yet, as the 1990s proceeded and economic troubles shadowed the city, pressure for precisely that intervention began building from various directions, laying the groundwork for Clarksdale's eventual triumph in the crossroads franchise. Back in 1990 the Mississippi Legislature had passed the Mississippi Gaming Control Act, allowing waterfront casino gambling in any county whose voters approved, and by 1993 the citizens of Coahoma County, watching with astonishment and envy as casino revenues flooded into dirt-poor Tunica County next door, had voted "yes" as well. The Lady Luck Casino soon sprang up in Lula, just across the river from Helena, Arkansas; the Coahoma County Tourism Commission was created the same year in the hope of extracting further revenue from out-of-state gamers.[198] Yet Clarksdale, for the most part, saw little immediate benefit from the county's new tax revenues, the fruit of a long-running feud. According to former city attorney Twiford, the county cut the city out of virtually all the gaming revenue and showed little interest in supporting blues tourism. "I'll never vote to give any [funding] to the Delta Blues Museum," Twiford reported one of the county supervisors as having said. "I want to support the Agricultural Museum at Friar's Point."[199] The city's local blues scene, which had remained surprisingly vital into the early 1990s, declined precipitously in the course of the decade as the casinos, several of them with blues-themed lounges, drew heavily on what little disposable income Clarksdale's African American patrons possessed. "People weren't coming out to hear the music," insisted Ruskey. "I think the opening of the casinos siphoned out a lot of the blues audience and the money that people used to spend just to go in and pay a couple of bucks for admission and a couple of bucks for a beer and a bucket of ice. Money is so tight that they couldn't do both things."[200] Shirley Fair, an African American entrepreneur who has managed to survive for many decades on the corner of Issaquena Street and Martin Luther King Boulevard, was curter: "The casino dried up a community that was already hurting."[201]

Even as Clarksdale's African American blues people were experiencing these wrenching changes, white elites, impressed by touristic interest in Robert Johnson, were looking for a way to capitalize on the city's historic importance as a birthplace and rendezvous point for blues legends such as John Lee Hooker, Muddy Waters, Ike Turner, and Sam Cooke. Bessie Smith, her body broken in a high-speed car wreck on (new) Highway 61, had been brought in 1938 to the tiny local African American hospital in town, which was now the seedy Riverside Hotel, a key stop on the blues pilgrim's itinerary. Surely such a rich cultural history could be turned to civic advantage. And then, of course, there was all that talk about the crossroads. In 1993 or 1994, according to Patty Johnson, a reporter for the *Clarksdale Press-Register* named Rebecca Hood-Adams "started the whole ball rolling" in the matter of Clarksdale's claim on the Robert Johnson legend with an article in which she claimed—or so Johnson recalled with dismay—that, "Well, it's a *known fact* that the intersection of Highway 61 and 49 *is* the location of the crossroads." Johnson insisted that "those of us who were real blues aficionados in the city were really scratching our heads and going, 'Oh, come on! Please stop this!'"[202] Whether Hood-Adams, a longtime Clarksdale resident, was drawing on local memory of the crossroads business district or consolidating shards of misbegotten legendry that had accumulated since Palmer's *Deep Blues*, or blending both things together with a civic booster's hunger to get the city *moving* in some urgently needed way remains unclear. But her claim about the crossroads was being echoed elsewhere. Speaking of Clarksdale's evolving self-image, local historian Robert Birdsong cited the importance of *Great Drives* (1996), a short-lived documentary series narrated by The Band's Arkansas-born drummer, Levon Helm, one episode of which took viewers on a weeklong road trip down Highway 61.[203] "Once you get farther south of Memphis," Helm drawled,

> it's hard to miss the big new signs calling you toward Tunica, Mississippi, the Las Vegas of the South. Looking like camels in a snowstorm, the casinos jump out of the Delta landscape. . . . When you pull into Clarksdale, Mississippi, you can feel the blues. [*Panorama of broken-down houses.*] Well, here we are at the crossroads. This is where Highway 61 crosses Highway 49. You have to make a decision here of which way to go. They say the great bluesman Robert Johnson made a big decision here one time; this is where he made the deal with the devil. Sold his soul in order to become as great a guitar player as he was. You may not find the devil they say Robert Johnson did, but you'll still find the blues on the streets of Clarksdale, Mississippi.[204]

At a certain point, the identity of "they" in the phrase "they say" suddenly became irrelevant and the legend of Johnson at Clarksdale's crossroads took on enough ontological solidity to become self-sustaining. Helm's twangy, on-site invocation of the legend marks that moment: a white southern musician's pilgrimage to, and certification of, the mythic ground zero of the Mississippi blues.

As it happens, Helm's pilgrimage precisely tracked the journey that blues tourists were being encouraged to make by a targeted ad campaign sponsored by the Mississippi Division of Tourism, a branch of the Mississippi Development Authority. Titled "Every Crossroads Has a Story," the ad first appeared on the back cover of the November/December 1996 and January/February 1997 issues of *Living Blues* magazine. Featuring a small oval photo in which a younger white guitarist faces an older black guitarist, the two men sitting in angled chairs on the porch of an old store with a "BBQ/Grocery" sign dangling overhead, the ad's text evokes Johnson's soul-sale and the 61/49 intersection from the younger white man's perspective, although it doesn't mention Clarksdale by name:

> A real bluesman can talk to you with his music. Now, I've tried to pick out those soulful notes on my guitar, but could never duplicate that feeling you get when Howlin' Wolf lets you know he is 300 pounds of joy.
>
> With that feeling in mind, I went to Mississippi and got turned on to Robert Johnson.
>
> The real stuff.
>
> Supposedly he went down to a crossroads and sold his soul to the Devil to play like that.
>
> So I drove down Highway 61 to Highway 49 where most folks say the deal was struck. I didn't want to sell my soul, or anything. I just wanted to pay my respects.
>
> I don't know if the Devil got the soul of Robert Johnson that night. But this intersection has still heard its share of music. B. B. King, Muddy Waters and Charlie [*sic*] Patton all had something to say and crossed these roads many times.
>
> *For more information on the museums, memorials and festivals celebrating the blues in Mississippi or to find out about all the other unique attractions in the state, call 1–800-WARMEST for your free Travel Planner.*[205]

Framed with the tag line "Mississippi: The South's Warmest Welcome," the ad masterfully evokes touristic desire by framing the crossroads pilgrimage as a white musician's journey toward everything his playing lacks: blackness, southernness, feeling, "the real stuff." The ad seamlessly incorporates an oft-quoted fragment from Son House's 1966 interview with Pete Welding ("sold his soul to the devil to play like that") into a claim that House never made (House never mentioned a crossroads), softening that claim with the language of legendry: "supposedly" and "most folks say." Finally, in a rhetorical gesture that Clarksdale's elites later incorporated into their city's brand positioning, the ad coyly shifts from the devil-at-the-crossroads claim to the intersection-of-two-legendary-blues-highways claim, so that the mythic idea of a crossroads soul-sale blurs into the fact-based idea of hard-working blues musicians crisscrossing the state back in the day. The ad gestures symbolically, in other words, at a transracial brotherhood of traveling blues people—one that the prospective (white) tourist can bring into being by calling the toll-free number and making his own bluesy trek down to the crossroads.

By 1998, the state-sponsored ad campaign and earlier imaginative investments had worked their magic on Clarksdale's behalf, drawing not just tourists but visiting journalists to the city's still unmarked but now "legendary" highway intersection. "I'm on a ride to the heartland of the blues," Gary Warner told readers of the *Toronto Star* in May of that year, offering a double dose of confected hoodoo. "Tomorrow, Highway 61, the Main Street of Delta Blues, where Sam Cooke was born, Bessie Smith died and Robert Johnson sold his soul to the devil at 'the crossroads' . . . In Clarksdale, 61 and 49 meet. This is the 'crossroads' where Robert Johnson sold his soul to the devil in exchange for a lightning hand on the guitar. Or so the story goes."[206] In August 1998, David Standish offered his iteration of the same tall tale to readers of the *Vancouver Sun*:

> The most notorious spot [in Clarksdale] is the intersection of Highways 61 and 49. Other places in the delta make the claim, but this is generally accepted as the crossroads where Robert Johnson is said to have made his unholy deal with the devil. One dark midnight, the legend goes, he sold his soul here in exchange for playing guitar and singing the blues like a tormented angel. It's the one in his "Crossroads" [*sic*], arguably the quintessential delta blues of the '30s, updated with a vengeance by Cream into one of the most powerful rock songs of all time.
>
> Today the intersection, for a non-blues fan, is unremarkable or worse. It's not a spooky rural meeting place of gravel tracks, but rather a face-off of a Fuel Mart, a Church's Chicken, the Delta Donut Shop and Abe's Barbecue. Still, for me at least, it was kind of a thrill to see after all these years of listening to the song.[207]

Here at last, like botanists in pursuit of a rare jungle orchid, we are confronted with the Thing Itself: major-market journalism, standing on what it imagines to be holy ground, blithely propagating the legend of Clarksdale's crossroads in all its fact-free glory. Since Standish can't even spell Johnson's song correctly—it's "Cross Road Blues"—perhaps it's unsurprising that he, like every other journalist who has written this particular story, fails to exert the slightest investigatory zeal in the matter of the legend's origins and veracity.

Still, Standish gets one thing right: by 1998, Clarksdale's crossroads was an undistinguished commercial hub—a disappointment indeed to romantic imaginations. The small bronze plaque placed on one of the medians back in 1938 was still there, tarnished with age, whispering of the library, schools, churches, and cotton. But nobody was paying attention to tarnished bronze, least of all blues tourists on pilgrimages and journalists on southern junkets. That civic brand was dead, or dying. "Our crossroads" was about to be born.

HONKY-TONK MAN

In September 1998, the Rock and Roll Hall of Fame in Cleveland, Ohio, sponsored a conference-and-concert extravaganza titled "Hellhound on My Trail: Robert Johnson and the Blues." The range of invited journalists, academics, and musicians—including Johnson's three surviving peers, David "Honeyboy" Edwards, Robert Jr. Lockwood, and Henry Townsend—put the capstone on a decade in which Johnson had risen from the grave to become not just the bestselling prewar blues artist of all time but a certified American icon, a folk hero on the order of Davy Crockett or Buffalo Bill, with gothic chiaroscuro added.

Later that fall, the members of Clarksdale's City Beautification Commission gathered for their monthly meeting and, as in past years, entertained suggestions for the coming year's annual project. "The core group was senior citizens," according to James Butler, then director of public works, "and they were just a great group of folks that tried to do good things for the city."[208] Present, among others, were Bill Luckett, an attorney/entrepreneur and the city's future mayor; Newton Dodson, a former mayor; Nell Smith, a formidable advocate for her passions; and Vic Barbieri, a retired shop teacher in Clarksdale's public schools who, with his students' help, had designed and built a handful of other projects for City Beautification over the years, including the sign for the Tennessee Williams Park. On this day, Barbieri and Smith recalled, Luckett made an urgent plea: "We need a guitar or something like that out at the crossroads. . . . People go out there and there's nothing there. We need to do something about the blues." Luckett remembered mentioning Levon Helm and the *Great Drives* video as a part of his pitch.[209] Barbieri had heard this sort of talk before; nothing ever came of it. But this time, perhaps because of cresting journalistic and touristic attention to Clarksdale's (imagined) connection with the Robert Johnson legend, a consensus rapidly formed. Not all members of the committee were familiar with the legend; Smith didn't even know who Johnson was. But everybody knew the crossroads—the tourists had been asking for it—and Luckett's passion was contagious. Someone, of course, would have to do the work.

"I listened to all the input on it," said Barbieri, recalling the moment in his sprightly twang, "and then when they got through I had my say-so. I said, 'Well, I'm gonna build it, and I'm gonna build it like I want it, or I won't build it at all.' So that clinched it right there."[210] Given the go-ahead by his fellow committee members, Barbieri assigned himself a target date of the following spring and returned to his shop to dream up an appropriate design.

When Vic Barbieri enters this narrative, the long and winding story of Clarksdale's crossroads suddenly becomes richer, deeper, and more surprising than it already was. The summary judgment offered by anthropologist Ali Colleen Neff after conducting extensive research in Clarksdale—that the three-guitar monument was "a landscaped shiny landmark . . . constructed by the Chamber of Commerce"—isn't just factually incorrect but ethically problematic, since it fails to acknowledge the way the city's civic identity was profoundly inflected by the creative artistry of one individual—a native, an elder, and a musician, a self-described "honky-tonk man."

Born in Clarksdale in 1933, raised in nearby Lyon, Barbieri was three years old when Robert Johnson recorded "Cross Road Blues" and five years old when the bluesman died. Brought up in an Italian American family, raised a Catholic, Barbieri would seem to have had little in common with Johnson—except the Delta itself, and the fact that he played guitar. All the members of Barbieri's extended family were farmers, and not particularly wealthy ones; after a stint in the Army during the Korean War, Barbieri spent twenty years in the television business, visiting "many a [black] tenant's home" to install antennas and do on-the-spot repairs. "I use to enjoy being around them," he said, his wistful language conveying the remembered social distance experienced by segregation's white witness, "and a lot of times there would always be one at the old country store had a guitar or harmonica. And I would sit there and drink a Coke and smoke cigarettes with them, stuff like that. And, you know, that kind of touched me in a way, because I felt like that's all they really had. They didn't have any money. They didn't have any property or anything. They just worked. They worked. I had a feeling for it. I could understand where the blues comes from, see."

Blues, he insisted more than once, was not his music. "I was always into country," he said. "I just like country music." Barbieri had grown up listening along with his father to WJJD's *Suppertime Frolic* radio broadcast out of Chicago, and by 1947, as a Clarksdale teenager, he had hooked up with a young lap steel guitar player and was playing on-air at local station WROX, imitating his heroes Eddy Arnold and Hank Williams on a show engineered by Sid Graves, future founder of the Delta Blues Museum. "We would play on Saturdays," he remembered, evoking his regular strolls through Clarksdale's black entertainment district,

> and then go down to the city auditorium and play at the Barn Dance at
> night, and then we would walk home down Issaquena, where all the Jewish
> stores were, and all the action was, with two guitars and a Sears Roebuck
> amplifier. And we would sneak back in the alleys and watch those blues.
> Of course they'd run us out. They'd be at you, "You white boys get out
> of here! Get out! Get out of here!" You see, back then the old-timers had
> enough respect. We were juveniles. We were kids. They knew they would
> get in trouble with the law. But it fascinated us, because of those old beat-
> up guitars they had, and drums, and the way they played.

In designing a marker for Clarksdale's crossroads, Barbieri was drawing on a lifetime of memories as an auditor, spectator, and performer in the Delta's rich musical stew, including a long-running gig as a pedal steel guitarist in a western swing band. "Bob Wills," he said, speaking of his current repertoire on the two-necked instrument. "Ray Price. Willie Nelson. We play honky-tonk tear-jerking music on the outside neck, and on the inside neck we play jazz." An untutored artist, his visual aesthetics were molded by a lifelong fascination with commercial logos, particularly the work of Raymond Loewy, the French-born industrial designer. The garage where he built the crossroads monument contains three or four vintage Studebakers from the 1950s and early 1960s: Loewy's celebrated automotive design. "I'm a student of his," Barbieri proclaimed, invoking the designer's best-known logos: Exxon, Shell, Xerox, Greyhound, International Harvester. "I wanted something that when you see it, you don't have to study it or read it. Just the silhouette alone represents what it stands for."

Barbieri worked out his ideas by constructing a 1/12th scale model out of Styrofoam and wood. "This is the Delta," he said, "so it would be three sides. It would come out of Cleveland, it would come out of Memphis, it would come out of Greenwood. And the highways meet. So I decided to put three guitars." In order to avoid copyright infringement suits from

Vic Barbieri, Clarksdale shop teacher and designer, holding his original scale model of the crossroads installation. Photograph by the author.

the major guitar makers, he borrowed design elements from six different instruments, creating a generic one-pickup F-hole model with a tailpiece: not the acoustic guitar Robert Johnson played, but an electric guitar of somewhat later vintage. "I couldn't copy anybody's," he insisted. "You just can't. I can't copy the Gibson Les Paul or the Fender." He placed right-angled Highway 49 and 61 signs at the top "to sort of keep that part of it alive," adding a triangle down below—again, the delta idea—on which he wrote, "The CROSSROADS."

When Barbieri brought his scale model to Luckett's law office, he re-membered, Luckett exclaimed, "My God, what have you got there?" The two men drove across town for an excited meeting with then-mayor Richard Webster; Barbieri got the commission, and informal supply lines were ar-ranged. His unpaid services would be his gift to the city.

Over the next few months, as Barbieri worked through the design details and began cutting out, painting, and assembling his heavy metal installa-tion, both Butler and Luckett regularly visited his shop, occasionally helping out. "One day he took out the cutting torch and started cutting," Barbieri remembered of the attorney. "He [did] a lot of work in a thousand-dollar suit and five-hundred-dollar shoes out there in that mud." The color of the guitars was a key issue. "I picked blue because I thought of blues," Barbieri said. "It's a General Motors medium poly blue that was used from about 1980 through about 1985 on all GM products." Barbieri deflected one kibitzer's suggestion that he make the guitars red, white, and blue by invoking his four years of military service. "I had some suggestions on some other colors," he said irritably. "Purple was one of 'em"—the preference of several young black Clarksdalians who thought that the flat blue he'd selected wasn't lively enough. He put his own initials, V. B., in the headstock of each guitar. When it was time to add the 49/61 element up top, he visited the local Mississippi Department of Transportation office and found skeptical officials unwilling to hand over road signs; Butler vouched for his project and they relented.

By early March, amid growing excitement within the City Beautification Commission and the concentric circles of Clarksdale's white elite—including Pat Davis of Abe's Bar-B-Q, who was "all over it," according to Twiford—Barbieri's crossroads installation was almost ready to go.[211] Barbieri was on the verge of achieving for Clarksdale what nobody had even thought to attempt: the creation of an iconic sign that would indelibly rebrand the city in the public imagination. "[The guitars] are something just like Las Vegas and Hollywood," Barbieri insisted. "Think about those two cities. See, that's what I had in mind. Hollywood was a simple wood sign. And in Las Vegas: 'Welcome to Las Vegas.' When you see that, you don't have to read, you don't have to look. The silhouette, that tells you one thing. That's why I designed it that way." The public was already being drawn to the crossroads—Robert Johnson's legendary crossroads!—by unquenchable touristic hunger. The sign would seal the deal. All that remained now was to install it.

There was one possible complication. The intended location of the sign was one of the two small grassy triangular medians at the intersection of two state highways: the crossroads created by the State Highway Department back in the mid-1930s. It was a state right-of-way, not county or city property. Which meant permission would have to be obtained. That job fell to Butler in his position as Clarksdale's director of public works. In early March, Butler drove forty miles east to the District 2 office of the Mississippi Department of Transportation in Batesville. There he met with James

Dickerson III, the District 2 engineer. "I need to get a permit to put up a sign," he told Dickerson. "We're doing a project for City Beautification, a big crossroads thing at 49 and 61."[212]

"You can't do it," Dickerson replied.

"Now wait a minute, Jim."

"You can't do that on a state highway right-of-way without a permit, and we can't issue a permit because what you're talking about violates our specification for sight flares at that intersection."

A "sight flare," Dickerson later explained, is a term of art: an obstruction-free visual field that ensures the safety of drivers approaching an intersection from all sides. Barbieri's monument would be a huge, illegal blockage. A dangerous distraction, liable to cause accidents.

Shocked, Butler challenged Dickerson. What about several other intersections in Clarksdale and up in Oxford where locals had placed signs? Did those folks have permits? Dickerson didn't know.

"Well then," Butler said, "we'll just have to go and put the damn thing up."

"Do that and we'll take it right down."

Now Butler was scared. Holy cow, he thought. I've killed this thing just by asking! "Jim, look. Look. There's gotta be some way we can do this."

"Well, sure. You can go down to Jackson and tell the governor, just designate that the official state crossroads. It'll be a historical marker."

"Really?"

"Sure. Pass a legislative act and get it signed."

"Hah!" Butler exclaimed. "That's exactly what we'll do."

DEVIL'S ADVOCATE

For the second time in sixty years, the city of Clarksdale had come into conflict with the Mississippi Department of Transportation over the fate of the 49/61 interchange. "Crossroads Sign Runs into State Roadblock," read the front-page headline in the *Press-Register*.[213] Last time around, the city had been forced to submit. This time Clarksdale had a secret weapon: city attorney H. Hunter Twiford III, the devil's advocate.

Like Barbieri, Twiford is a man unknown to the general public but of pivotal importance to Clarksdale's contemporary civic identity. Like Barbieri, he grew up in and around Clarksdale—his father farmed in Alligator, twelve miles south of town—and, like Barbieri, he was a musician and youthful habitué of WROX, someone who fraternized with Delta blues people in a way that helped shape his subsequent orientation toward Clarksdale's emergent identity as a blues capital. "I'm a child of the '60s," he said,

> and a frustrated musician. You know, playing guitar in my little rock 'n' roll band and then hanging out with and listening to some of the blues guys. Although we didn't play much Delta blues. What we did was play the English version of the blues. I'd go down to Hezekiah Patton's place in Winstonville as a teenager and listen to some great music—Bo Diddley, Bobby Blue Bland, Ike Turner. I was only 14 or 15 at the time; Mr. Patton let me sit with him behind the bar. Frank Frost and the Nighthawks were locals who would play at our parties and dances pretty frequently, and we'd hang out with them some, and I'd sit in.[214]

The Harlem Inn, a key stop on Mississippi's chitlin' circuit, was built by an African American farmer, Hezekiah Patton Sr., and opened in 1939 as a roadhouse by the side of new Highway 61 in Winstonville, twenty-five miles south of Clarksdale.[215] Twiford, half a generation younger than Barbieri, was able as a teenager in the 1960s to enter black social spaces that Barbieri was chased away from in the 1940s—a measure of the easing of social relations in late civil rights–era Mississippi, or perhaps merely a measure of the relative laxity of segregation's policing in a country juke compared with downtown Issaquena Street. "Forty years later," Twiford said, "I got really interested in the blues from an historical perspective, and I realized the tourism potential of the blues and the potential impact on Clarksdale while talking to Sid Graves," the Delta Blues Museum's founder.[216]

Eager to see Clarksdale solidify its position in Mississippi's emergent blues-touristic universe, deeply frustrated by the reluctance of the Coahoma County Tourism Commission to support the city's initiatives in that direction, Twiford was in no mood to see Barbieri's monument derailed by the state on a legal technicality. So he did something unprecedented in the 400-year annals of America's organized civic life.

He invoked the devil's name. Not as men of God do, to convey righteous wrath and implacable opposition, but in a way that suggested . . . approval.

More specifically, he drafted both a resolution and legislation—the former for consideration by Clarksdale's mayor and commissioners, the latter for forwarding to the Mississippi Legislature—and in both government documents he proclaimed the legend of Robert Johnson selling his soul to the devil at Clarksdale's crossroads in a way that made clear that *here*, and nowhere else, was where Clarksdale was going to take its stand.[217] This was

Clarksdale's civic brand: a Delta blues stronghold that had been sanctified, *on that very spot*, by the devil's miraculous intercession in the life of the world's most celebrated Delta bluesman. The resolution rang forth like a battle cry, summoning all to behold:

WHEREAS, Clarksdale is commonly recognized by musicians, historians and scholars as the "Birthplace of the Blues," and has a long and rich cultural history relative thereto;

WHEREAS, the Board of Mayor and Commissioners of the City of Clarksdale has taken great strides in preserving Clarksdale's rich Blues Heritage and tradition, and promoting the same as a major tourism attraction; and

WHEREAS, the intersection of Highways 61 and 49 in the City of Clarksdale is commonly recognized by blues musicians, historians, scholars and publishers as the "Crossroads" referred to in the Robert Johnson legend, in which Robert Johnson reportedly sold his soul to the Devil in return for becoming a master of the Blues and one of the pre-eminent Bluesmen of the genre;

WHEREAS, authors, including Gayle Dean Wardlow, Dr. Edward Karmar and Jim O'Neal, have confirmed the probable location of the "Crossroads" as the intersection of Highway 49 and 61 within the City of Clarksdale; and

WHEREAS, the intersection of Highways 61 and 49 is a prominent tourist attraction which draws significant numbers of tourists and Blues aficionados to the site, and should be marked as the "Crossroads" of the Robert Johnson legend, and its potential as a historical and tourism site fully developed; and

WHEREAS, the Board of Mayor and Commissioners of the City of Clarksdale encourages adoption of local and private legislation by the Mississippi Legislature so authorizing and designating, and promoting the signage thereof.

NOW, THEREFORE, BE IT RESOLVED . . .[218]

Civic leaders routinely invoke God's name, despite the Constitution's uneasiness about such things. But the devil? And the deliberate identification of an incorporated American city *with* the devil? One seeks in vain for a precedent, finding nothing—except, perhaps, for the negative ideal offered by Puritan New England during the paroxysm of paranoia culminating in the Salem witch trials. "The New Englanders are a people of God," wrote

Cotton Mather in *The Wonders of the Invisible World* (1692), his official report, "settled in . . . the devil's territories." Here was Clarksdale, 400 years later, flipping the script: a people proudly of the devil's territory, landlocked in God's Bible Belt and yearning for blues touristic certification.

In his zeal to see Clarksdale so certified, attorney Twiford was apparently not averse to massaging the factual basis of his representations: stretching the truth slightly, in the service of a higher good. Here he may well have been inspired by the local blues (and entrepreneurial) tradition, where improvisational dexterity is the accepted way of triumphing over bad facts. It is also entirely possible that he was merely repeating what other civic boosters had told him. His claim that Gayle Dean Wardlow, Dr. Edward Karmar [*sic*], and Jim O'Neal had "confirmed the probable location of the 'Crossroads' as the intersection of Highway 49 and 61 within the City of Clarksdale," in any case, was at odds with the written record. A quick review of their writings reveals that all three blues scholars are skeptical about Clarksdale's purchase on the Johnson myth and about crossroads legendry more generally:

> WARDLOW: "A careful inspection of the lyrics to 'Cross Road Blues' and the other 28 songs Johnson recorded does not reveal any verse that remotely says 'I went to the crossroads and I sold my soul to the devil.' It is not there."[219]
>
> KOMARA: "The legend today most associated with Robert Johnson tells of him selling his soul to the devil at a Delta crossroads for improved guitar skills. . . . Believing the crossroads myth hampers an understanding of Johnson's music."[220]
>
> O'NEAL: "Clarksdalians identify the crossroads as the intersection of Highways 61 and 49. Whether this crossroads is really connected with Robert Johnson mythology is highly dubious."[221]

As Sandy Bynum said when defending her practice of saying "legend has it" to blues tourists in Greenville, "We're pretty good storytellers in Mississippi."[222] Clarksdale's mayor and commissioners were persuaded by the story told by the city attorney, which was entirely in line with prevailing—although not universal—public sentiment. (Several dissenters on city beautification preferred Tennessee Williams as a civic icon, and an occasional Christian, black or white, had expressed displeasure at the proposed monument.)[223] At a meeting on March 15, 1999, Twiford's resolution was unanimously adopted.

The next course of action was introducing the proposed legislation onto the floor of the state legislature. Here the combined efforts of Clarksdale's white elites would not suffice. An interracial alliance would be required: specifically, the services of state Representative Leonard Henderson, a proud and cantankerous African American educator, born and bred in Clarksdale, who had beaten civil rights icon Aaron Henry two years earlier in a close and disputed election. Twiford's firm had represented Henderson in the state Supreme Court appeal that confirmed Henderson's right to the seat. Henderson, when interviewed, balanced skepticism about Clarksdale's elites with an acknowledgment of the need to act with the city's economic interests in mind. "With the new phase of farming," he said, recapitulating local history, "with cotton pickers and various herbicides and stuff to get rid of grass, you don't need cotton choppers. The main objective became, 'What can we do to revitalize Clarksdale?' You know, 'We gotta get something.' And the alleged majority, business people, said, 'We can make this a chic blues town.' And that was what started that."[224]

Having no particular emotional investment in Robert Johnson or the blues, Henderson did, however, have something in common with the architect of the crossroads monument: he and Barbieri worked across the street from each other in Clarksdale's all-black public schools—Henderson as the principal of Riverton Elementary School, Barbieri as the shop teacher at Clarksdale High. "Vic and I worked together," he said.

> I knew Vic. And that's why I went on and did whatever I could to get it [the bill] through. See, Vic used to teach welding in the City of Clarksdale Public Schools and the Vocational Center. He's one of them old Army veterans, and I was in the Army during Vietnam. We never had anything to do but argue and disagree with each other, and tell racial jokes. We used to joke, but it was between the two of us. That's one of the reasons I didn't have any objection to trying to get the statue or sign erected.

In the long chain of contingencies required to effect the official commemoration of Clarksdale's crossroads, Henderson's invocation of "racial jokes" as something that created trust and fellowship between black and white veterans of the U.S. military—the elementary school principal and his shop-teacher buddy—is surely the most unlikely. Yet here is one of the key lessons of the entire episode: buried beneath the airbrushed self-representations of contemporary Clarksdale's blues-touristic PR machine is a much edgier and, in its own way, more redemptive story: more human, more compelling, and far truer to the town's complicated history and intersecting lives.

Henderson, in any case, was supremely attentive to the irony of his position. Happy to help out an old friend and willing to be of service to Twiford, Luckett, and the city government, he was unwilling to make a fool out of himself on the floor of the Legislature. So he vetted the proposed legislation, now titled House Bill 1745, with a considered eye. "Being a legislator at that time," he explained, "whenever your people come to you with a request, if it's not offensive and it can't be proven wrong, then you submit it and try to get it passed." As so-called local and private legislation, it would apply only to the location in question; it had no statewide ramifications—except, of course, for the fact that in conferring the state government's imprimatur on one specific crossroads, the bill would torpedo the touristic value of every other crossroads in the state. As for the idea of creating a state-certified monument commemorating a legend of debatable provenance, rather than a time-specific historical event, Henderson remained agnostic. When pressed on the subject, he offered a taut, casuistic summary of his reasoning on behalf of the legend described in the bill. "People cannot prove that it's not factual. It's not that it's factual. It can't be proven that it's *not* factual."

Satisfied on all counts, Henderson brought Twiford's bill to the Legislature. The devil's name was removed by the legislative drafting staff, along with much of Twiford's flowery language. The city attorney expressed no regrets. "I suspect it was more important to my bosses—the Mayor and Commissioners—that the 61/49 intersection be officially named as the 'Crossroads' of Robert Johnson legend/fame before someone else beat us to it than the specific wording of the legislation." The final bill was short and to the point:

> An act to authorize the governing authorities of the City of Clarksdale to designate the intersection of U.S. Highway 61 and U.S. Highway 49 in the City of Clarksdale as the "Crossroads" in recognition of the legend of blues musician Robert Johnson; and for related purposes.
>
> Be it enacted by the legislature of the State of Mississippi:
> SECTION 1. (1) The governing authorities of the City of Clarksdale are authorized to designate the intersection of U.S. Highway 61 and U.S. Highway 49 in the City of Clarksdale as the "Crossroads" in recognition of the legend of blues musician Robert Johnson and the long and rich

"I wanted to put a mark on this town." The creator stands beneath his creation in the summer of 2013. Photograph by the author.

cultural history crediting that location and the City of Clarksdale as the birthplace of the blues.

(2) The governing authorities of the City of Clarksdale, with the co-operation and approval of the Mississippi Department of Transportation, may place appropriate signs or plaques on or along the highway intersection described in subsection (1) of this section.

SECTION 2. This act shall take effect and be in force from and after its passage.[225]

H.B. 1745 sailed through the legislature. Henderson attributed this, with earned pride, to the mystique he had gained by beating Henry, a multiterm incumbent and one of the most powerful black legislators in the House. "When I beat him and won the legislative seat, nobody questioned anything that I submitted. That's why I had to read it to make sure it wouldn't be a big joke." On April 14, Governor Kirk Fordice signed H.B. 1745 into law, along with a second and much longer bill, also authored by Twiford and sponsored by Henderson, which created a board of trustees and a source of tax revenue for the Delta Blues Museum, paving the way for Clarksdale's emergence as the market leader in twenty-first-century blues tourism.[226]

On May 11, 1999, with the Mississippi Department of Transportation now out of the picture, James Butler and his road crew bolted Vic Barbieri's three-guitar installation into place, down at the crossroads. "The thing is heavy," Butler joked. "We did the concrete the day before. It's a big pipe that goes way down in the ground with a lot of concrete. And you talk about the guitars, they're 385 pounds apiece. But it didn't really take that long to stack the stuff on top of the pipe." Barbieri didn't charge the city anything, Butler noted—"Not a penny for his labor"—nor did he copyright his design. "No," Barbieri explained,

> I wanted to do something for Clarksdale, as bad as it needs it. It needs
> something positive. I'm not one of these guys that every time something
> is done I've got my hand stuck out making my banking. I'm not a rich per-
> son. I'm not broke either. But it gave me satisfaction every time I drive by
> I see people taking pictures. I think it belongs to everybody in Clarksdale.

"I wanted to put a mark on this town," he added proudly. "I wanted this town to be known for something, whether folks like the blues or not. And I tell them I'm not in the blues. But I wanted something that the town would be known for all over the world, and it is."

CONCLUSION

Everybody . . . got a little devil . . . in their soul . . . oh yeah.

—TOMMIE YOUNG, "Everybody's Got a Little Devil in
Their Soul" (1972)

FROM BLACK TO WHITE

The seventy-five-year span that separates Clara Smith's "Done Sold My
Soul to the Devil" (1924) from Clarksdale's erection of a monument at a
peculiarly vexed crossroads location offers an occasion for reflecting on the
birth and flowering of a devil-blues tradition, as well as on the apotheosis
of a somewhat narrowed idea of what that tradition is about. For the first
thirty or forty years, the tradition was shaped primarily by the tastes of a
black record-buying public, one rebelling against the strictures of black
southern evangelicalism and abetted, early on, by a broader Lost Generation
cohort of "misbehaving" urban whites. With the reissue of Robert Johnson's
seminal recordings on *King of the Delta Blues Singers* (1961) and then, just
as significantly, the release of Cream's *Wheels of Fire* (1968) featuring Eric
Clapton's live rock-blues recasting of "Cross Road Blues" as "Crossroads,"
the tradition began to reorient itself toward a white blues public: its taste
for romance (Johnson as a tortured loner), its hunger for Southern Gothic,
its limited understanding of the devil's-music dispute within black southern culture, and its profound ignorance of the broad array of purposes to
which African American blues people had deployed the devil figure in their
songs. It is hard to overstate the importance of Clapton to this process. Although he has personally scoffed at the devil-at-the-crossroads conception
of Johnson's achievement, the continuing popularity of "Crossroads" as a
rock-blues standard—endlessly replayed on classic rock radio and covered
by countless rock and blues performers—along with Clapton's awed testimonials in his autobiography and documentary interviews, his periodic
recorded homages to Johnson, and his triennial Crossroads Guitar Festival,
have combined to foster in aging baby boomers and their children a sense
of Johnson as ne plus ultra: the incomparable Delta blues genius, always

already framed in his empowering-yet-troubled crossroads haunt.[1] In this respect, Clarksdale's opportunistic claiming of Johnson's legend represents not just the opening gambit of that Delta town's drive to become the market leader in Mississippi's nascent blues tourism industry but also the final stage of a much longer canonizing-and-narrowing process.

Although the year 2000 is the effective end point for this study, it is worth briefly sketching three developments from the decade and a half since then, each of which has inflected the devil-blues tradition in a different way. These are, in turn (1) the continued capitalization and racial problematics of Clarksdale's crossroads, (2) an unexpected second flowering of devil-blues recordings by a contemporary cohort of white and black performers, and (3) the stubborn remnants of the devil's-music dispute in contemporary Mississippi.

A BITTERSWEET THING

On July 6, 1999, two months after James Butler and his road crew erected Vic Barbieri's three-guitar monument in Clarksdale, President Bill Clinton swept into town with his entourage, including the secretaries of transportation, labor, and agriculture. It was his first visit to Mississippi as president: one stop on a six-state antipoverty tour termed the "New Markets Initiative." Although Butler, Barbieri, and the good white members of City Beautification weren't the focus of his attentions, the eagerness of Clarksdale's white elites to rebrand the city as a blues-touristic hub, a "crossroads of the blues," makes more sense when considered in light of the region's epic fail in the matter of its African American population. In the 1990 census, 58.5 percent of black families in Coahoma County lived below the poverty line and black unemployment was 21.9 percent.[2] During the five and a half hours he spent in town, Clinton made a point of visiting Issaquena Street, once the heart of Clarksdale's thriving black entertainment district and now a blighted, boarded-up wasteland where, as one account noted, "the long-shuttered Roxy Theater looked like a prop for 'The Last Picture Show.'"[3] His host there was florist Shirley Fair, longtime proprietor of Ooo So Pretty Flowers on the corner of Issaquena and Martin Luther King Boulevard (formerly Fourth Street), one block from the old crossroads. "Nothing has gotten any better," Fair told visiting journalists, speaking about the town's woes in the aftermath of the riverboat casino boom of the previous half decade that had helped spur growth in nearby Tunica County. "There's nothing here to grasp on to. The railroad is closed, the factories have gone.

The good folks move on and the gangbangers take over the streets and that makes it harder for businesses to survive."[4]

Yet only three months after Clinton's visit and less than six months after Barbieri's monument had been launched as what Hunter Twiford called "the recognizable icon for Clarksdale," *New York Times* pop music critic Neil Strauss wrote of a Delta city on the upswing in a piece titled "A Home of the Blues, Singing a New Tune."[5] "Something strange has happened in Clarksdale in the last year or two. As if awakening from amnesia, many whites here have suddenly become aware of the town's blues heritage . . . [One] result may be to take Clarksdale into the next century as one of the South's most irresistible cultural meccas." The crossroads monument was not mentioned, but the relocated and revamped Delta Blues Museum was, along with two newly christened city streets, Blues Alley and John Lee Hooker Lane. Local developer Bubba O'Keefe was hopeful. "We've got gold in the stream that needs mining," he proclaimed, noting, as a way of establishing his and the region's credentials, that the late Mississippi Fred McDowell—a celebrated slide guitarist—"used to pump gas for my father."[6]

If it isn't quite accurate to call the story of Clarksdale since 1999 a tale of two cities—one black and poor, the other white, well-capitalized, and profit-hungry—then there is considerable truth in the generalization nonetheless. One engine of Clarksdale's postcrossroads renaissance, to be fair, has been the much-vaunted partnership between two native Mississippians, black actor Morgan Freeman and white lawyer and entrepreneur Bill Luckett, a pairing that resulted in the opening of an upscale restaurant (Madidi) and a tourist-friendly juke joint (Ground Zero) in 2001. "The media blitz that started when Morgan Freeman came here," insisted Butler, "hit us like wildfire."[7] But there is an unmistakable disconnect between the harsh realities of black Delta life out of which the region's distinctive blues culture has emerged and, in contrast, the often surreal romance that white blues entrepreneurs and civic boosters seem determined to make of Clarksdale's blues inheritance, both real and imagined. The figure of the devil at the crossroads lies at the heart of that romance.

As a parade of journalists passed through Clarksdale in the first few years of the new millennium, reaffirming the legend connecting Robert Johnson, the devil, and the crossroads monument, a range of Clarksdalians, including Luckett and Freeman, the Delta Blues Museum, and the town and county tourism offices, fully invested in the charade. By 2007, Butler and his fellow "Shackmeisters"—a quintet of entrepreneurs who had cobbled together an unlikely motel complex out of refurbished sharecroppers' shacks on the grounds of an old cotton plantation—were invoking crossroads folklore, fancifully, to describe the birth moment of their Shack-Up Inn:

> [The Shackmeisters] wound up at midnight, on the same night, at the same crossroads. There the deal was made. As lightning flashed in the delta skies and thunder rolled across the moonlit cotton fields, the five shackmeisters, cypress prophets all, forged a bond stronger than old oak and new rope. Their mission, to bring the blues home to the cradle and rock the tourists in the process. Like hellhounds on their trail, the shacks have overtaken the Shackmeisters, to the benefit [of] millions of blues lovers from around the world.[8]

The phrase "millions of blues lovers from around the world" is no mere flight of hyperbole but an apt description of the global reach of this particular blues mythology and the blues-touristic attractions of contemporary Mississippi more generally. According to Bill Seratt, executive director of the Vicksburg Convention and Visitors Bureau, "people who come to the Delta specifically for the blues product, especially the domestic travelers, [are] a very small percentage. A greater percentage [is[the international traffic. The international traffic is in the Delta because of the music."[9]

Surely the most ambitious and audacious attempt to capitalize on Clarksdale's self-certification as the blues-devil's home took place in 2008 and was the brainchild of two Canadians: Les Barber, a real estate developer from Toronto, and Earl Klatzel, a Calgary-based artist and visual designer with a website full of blues-themed artworks featuring vivid in situ portraits of Delta bluesmen like David "Honeyboy" Edwards, James "Son" Thomas, and, of course, Robert Johnson.[10] Financed by the Crossroads Group LLC, the Crossroads Hotel and Entertainment Complex, as described in promotional materials at the time, was a "theme-roomed boutique Hotel, Wellness Spa, and Blues Entertainment Venue at Highways 61 & 49," where "according to legend Robert Johnson sold his soul to the devil at the crossroads . . . for the ability to play the best Blues guitar in the world." The more than 150 rooms and amphitheater, spread out across five lots surrounding Barbieri's monument, would be accompanied by a Robert Johnson Crossroads Blues Legend Park. There, wealthy donors and supportive aficionados—"Blues Friends"—would have the chance to purchase bricks on which their names had been engraved, laying a foundation for the park "in honor of the Bluesmen and Blueswomen who paved the way for Blues, Rock & Roll, Gospel, Soul, and Jazz." Other offerings at the complex Klatzel had designed, according to Barber, would include guided tours of the Mississippi Blues Trail, a Crossroads Music School, blues and rock fantasy camps, a cooking school, gospel music on Sunday mornings—at the devil's crossroads!—and mentoring programs in the local schools. "A main target audience," reported the *Clarksdale Press-Register*, "will be European and other international blues fans."[11]

Barber's timing was bad. Bedeviled, one might say. On September 29, 2008, less than two weeks after the *Press-Register* previewed the complex, the Dow Jones Industrial Average dropped 777 points, the largest one-day loss in its history. It had already dropped 449 points on the day the story was published and another 445 points three days later. The Crossroads Group, chuckled Klatzel when interviewed later about the fiasco, "just started folding. I mean they just folded up like nothing."[12] Klatzel's designs for the never-completed complex themselves became a part of local blues lore, subsumed under Barber's vaulting ambition and guilty by association with other reality-challenged schemes. "There was a Canadian developer," blues guide John Ruskey remembered,

> who wanted to build a monstrosity of a hotel right over the crossroads. . . .
> He was literally going to build a castle with the roads running through
> the middle of his hotel . . . so you could literally rent a room and sleep
> in a room located at the crossroads. There was another guy, a Los Angeles
> developer, who wanted to make these holograms of Robert Johnson in a
> giant fountain that would be located out in front of the Blues Museum.
> You know, there'd be the sign, streams of water going in the air, and you'd
> see the face of Robert Johnson in the fountain.[13]

Reflecting on the experience and on his own approach to the blues as a visual artist, Klatzel was both candid and unapologetic. "When I get into something," he said,

> I get into it full blast. . . . I don't make up nothin', I use the real people
> from other photographs of that same era, and put 'em back on the streets.
> I just wanna recreate everything back to what our grandparents saw
> for real. All in color. And as close as possible to the real story. I'd never
> designed a park, but I [knew] everything about Robert Johnson and the
> myths and the reality. . . . I *know* that was just a myth. I like it, because
> it makes it interesting. What that myth does through the blues is what
> draws all these young generation in. They say, "Man, this guy made a
> deal with the devil to play, I wanna hear him!" And that's what drew *me*
> in. And now, as an older person, that is way behind [me]. I'm into the

music and the amazing music that was made through sorrow, through their lifestyles.[14]

"Clarksdale," Klatzel said bluntly, "was just the myth part of the story. Had really nothing to do with Robert Johnson, but look how many people went there over the years. Even Robert Plant went there and grabbed a cup of dirt."

Despite his fervent insistence on the photorealist, documentary fidelity of his blues-based artwork, Klatzel also acknowledged his aesthetic roots in surrealism, "fantasy art," something that his education at the Alberta College of Art never wholly erased. When asked if the devil ever showed up in his paintings, he replied, "The closest I've got to that is 'Hellhounds on My Trail.' That's one powerful painting. I put hellhounds up in the clouds." The three hellhounds in question, looming out of the skies over a pair of shotgun shacks at the edge of a cotton field, look like three very angry German Shepherds—teeth bared, jaws snapping—and their muzzles are echoed, in the foreground, by the gap-toothed open mouth of a black bluesman modeled loosely on Son House, guitar in hand. "Real" is the last word that such art brings to mind. Klatzel is a gifted portraitist, but his landscapes, to one who actually knows those landscapes, are lushly romantic and fanciful in the extreme. Not surprisingly, he has never visited the Mississippi Delta. He has only been to the United States once, in fact. "The only place I been into the States is I took my wife when we first met—I took her to California. I said, 'Everybody's gotta see Disneyland.' So I took her down to Anaheim. We drove down, then drove up through the redwoods. It was a nice holiday."

While it may be tempting to see the Crossroads Hotel and Entertainment Complex and similar investments in devil-blues mythology as harmless fun and games, a field of play for blues-entranced white imaginations, these investments, to the extent that they endorse the City Beautification Commission's original decision about where to place the crossroads monument, have had a cumulatively negative effect on Clarksdale's black residents—at least according to Shirley Fair, the feisty and unconquerable doyenne of Issaquena Street. Fair has a long track record as one of Clarksdale's best-known black entrepreneurs; a passionate blues fan herself, she balances pride of cultural ownership with a disinclination to romanticize the music—an attitude grounded in vivid early memories of her elders' dislike for the blues and its loud, liquor-swilling, sometimes violent clientele. "When I was growing up, when I was in college, I would hear older people saying,

'Don't let your child go to them cafés or those juke joints, because that ain't nothing but the devil. It is nothing good that is coming up out of there.'"[15] When she and her late husband, Leonard, first moved to Clarksdale in the late 1970s, they briefly owned a café-cum-juke joint themselves, one with a juke box and DJs rather than live musicians. "Fair's Hole in the Wall," she chuckled ruefully: "The Hole in the Wall was a hole in the wall! Everything went on. We had a DJ come in and spin records. Folks would pull the mic from the DJ and they would start singing. And you would have a certain group that would [work] the fields hard and come up in there, and they would buy beer. We didn't have a liquor license, but you could bring your liquor in, as long as you had it enclosed. So they would bring their liquor in and buy the beer. And we sold like sausages and pickles and pig's feet and hot eggs and stuff like that. But it was so dangerous, my mother used to be so afraid for me to be going out, to helping at the place."

The Fairs relocated their restaurant to one of the highways outside Clarksdale, remaining there from 1979 to 1987, then purchased the building on Issaquena Street and moved back to the New World district. Fair first heard of Robert Johnson shortly after *Crossroads* was released, when her husband told her that his cousin, a blues singer from Greenwood named Lloyd Johnson, claimed to be related to the "famous blues legend." "I said, 'Well I don't know nothing about the blues,'" she remembered, "and he say, 'Well everybody gonna know about it cause they made a movie about it.'"

Fair's love for the blues developed during her decades on Issaquena Street, surrounded by the remnants of a once-thriving juke joint scene. Looking out the door of her flower shop, she gestured with a proprietary pride at the Boom Boom Room across the street—too dangerous for the tourists, she insisted—and, down MLK Boulevard in the other direction, Red's Lounge. When asked what she thought of the city's decision to erect a monument to Robert Johnson out at the crossroads, her lukewarm response highlighted the racially problematic nature of the decision, especially the struggle of an economically marginal but historically important quadrant of black Clarksdale, one scarred by the violence of disadvantaged young black men, to share in whatever wealth the city's blues-touristic boom was creating:

> I guess everybody in the community that was African American was just
> so glad [at first] to have a symbol representing the blues to be put up
> there on the highway, never really thinking about where they puttin' it
> at, was just so glad to see something coming up in Clarksdale that could

draw attention, that could draw tourists. It was like a bittersweet thing: it was something that was honoring the blues, and that you didn't have to pay anything to get it put up. But you know it was a part of your heritage. So it was good in that sense. But then when you get older and you realize that [the monument] should be somewhere else, too.

The problem, in Fair's eyes, was that the monument in its present location encouraged a kind of cultural misdirection grounded in historical amnesia, titillating blues tourists with stories about the devil rather than framing Johnson as a working musician who plied his trade in the New World. The monument up on the highway, she complained,

takes him out of a community, and it puts him somewhere else. You begin to learn a little about his life, his autobiography, but you don't understand well, if he was supposed to have played the blues in this area, why did they move him so far? . . .By just seeing the guitars, most tourists just take a picture there and don't want to wander off up in the neighborhoods, especially now that the neighborhoods are not what they used to be. You got some tourists that's not gonna never come down into the neighborhood, but it needs to be something that feed[s] back from those guitars, to come back down into the neighborhood where the blues was actually played. . . .It should be more than one [monument], or something showing that the blues really formulated from down in the New World district.

Fair gestured more than once, angrily, at what she called "the other side of town": the portion of Clarksdale's old downtown, including the Delta Blues Museum, Ground Zero, and the Cathead Delta Blues and Folk Art emporium, which serves as the backdrop to the city's two big annual blues festivals. In her eyes, the crossroads monument was working in concert with the downtown blues renaissance to entice tourist dollars, and cultural attention, away from the blues-drenched neighborhood that most deserved it. "*This* is the historical district," she insisted. "That's not the historical district up there. That's a good tourist attraction, which is great. But I have to do something in my lifetime to put a mark here. Now, what I'm gonna do, how I'm gonna do it. I haven't discovered it yet. But it will be known before I leave this earth."

Vic Barbieri, through his gift of an iconic monument, has made his mark on Clarksdale and the blues-touristic imagination; Shirley Fair may yet do so. Memories of Issaquena Street—in its celebrated heyday, in its long period of decline—are something the white and black Clarksdalians share.

They also share a notable lack of interest in the devil-at-the-crossroads mythology that so many of their enterprising white townspeople, along with blues musicians and fans around the world, find compelling.

SOMEBODY LET THE DEVIL OUT

One of the most significant developments in the long arc of the devil-blues tradition is the resurgence in popularity of the devil theme among contemporary recording artists. I am referring here not to the dozens of cover versions of "Crossroads" that are currently for sale on iTunes and Amazon—those were surely to be expected—but to new and inventive compositions by a broad spectrum of blues performers, white and black. This resurgence became apparent when, in an act of scholarly due diligence after completing this manuscript, I used the iTunes and Amazon search engines to see if any devil-blues songs had been released since I first compiled a list in 2008. To my surprise, I found fourteen new recordings. I updated my list, then sorted it by decade.[16] The results were as follows:

       1924–29: 27
       1930–39: 54
       1940–49: 11
       1950–59: 5
       1960–69: 7
       1970–79: 5
       1980–89: 6
       1990–99: 10
    2000–2009: 27
       2010–15: 10

Pearson and McCulloch note in their book on Robert Johnson that "devil references in blues were common in the late thirties and early forties," terming the phenomenon "a minicraze of devil songs."[17] As this decade-by-decade breakdown makes clear, the minicraze was in fact a two-decade phenomenon, lasting from the mid-1920s through the mid-1940s. Then, as a matter of creative output, the tradition tails off, coasts along—until it catches fire all over again in the year 2000 and burns strongly for next the decade and half: a second minicraze of devil songs.

Why, after such an extended fallow period, should the devil once again be captivating the imaginations of blues songwriters at the dawn of the second millennium? Three possible explanations come to mind; each gets at an element of the story, and all three may well be interacting dynamically to produce the renaissance in question, a renaissance I'll example here through selected lyric excerpts:

1. The long decade between the release of *Crossroads* (1986) and the "Hellhound on My Trail" conference at the Rock and Roll Hall of Fame (1998) saw an explosion of interest in Johnson and his devil-haunted mythology, an interest heightened by the release of his platinum-selling *Complete Recordings* (1990) and the publication of the only two known photographs of him (1986, 1990). Covering Johnson's songs was one way American blues culture responded to his resurgent popularity and the market attention that such covers attracted. A more creative response, including Jerry McCain's "My Deal at the Crossroads" (2000), Billy Jones's "At da' Crossroads" (2005), Watermelon Slim's "Devil's Cadillac" (2006), and Anthony Gomes's "The Blues Ain't the Blues No More" (2015) took longer to arrive.

> I went down to the crossroad, I made a deal with the devil for the
>   woman's love
> Yes, I went down to the crossroad, people, and I made a deal with the
>   devil for the woman love
> My mama said, "Son, why did you sell your soul to the devil, when you
>   know there's a good Lord up above?"
>
> . . . I saw nine thousand nine hundred and ninety-nine black cat bones,
>   all stacked up in one pile
> Whoa I saw some nine thousand nine hundred and ninety-nine black
>   bones, all stacked up in a pile
> And then a black fog rolled, and I could see myself way back when I was
>   a baby child (Somethin' wrong!)
>
> Mama said, "You're gonna burn in hell, son, and that fire down there
>   is mighty hot"
> Oh she said, "You gonna burn in hell, and that fire down there is
>   mighty hot
> You see, you sold your soul to the devil, and a little loving is all you got"
>
> Stay away from the crossroad . . . stay away from the crossroad
> Stay away from the crossroad . . . stay away from the crossroad
> Stay away from the crossroad, I don't care what else you do
> —Jerry McCain, "My Deal at the Crossroads" (2000)

I was riding shotgun in the devil's Cadillac
I was riding shotgun in the devil's Cadillac
We was headin' for the crossroads, with a monkey on my back

We was doin' ninety, rollin' on down the road
We was doin' ninety miles an hour, rolling on down the road
We was headin' for the crossroads just as hard as we could go

[bridge]
That Cadillac was so quiet, like the inside of a hearse
The air conditioning was so cold, like a tomb or maybe worse
We stopped, he said, "We're here," I looked out at deserted farmers' fields
I didn't say a word, but I knew that I'd made a deal
—Watermelon Slim, "The Devil's Cadillac" (2006)

2. The run-up to January 1, 2000, including the so-called Y2K apocalypse predicted by many, created considerable premillennial anxiety. But it was the Al Qaeda–sponsored attack on the Twin Towers of the World Trade Center on September 11, 2001, that helped precipitate a clash-of-civilizations *mentalité* in political and intellectual elites, Christian evangelicals, and the American public at-large.[18] In that context, the words "devil" and "evil" took on a new urgency. President George W. Bush referred to Iran, Iraq, and North Korea as the "axis of evil" in his State of the Union Address in January 2002; Venezuelan president Hugo Chávez spoke to the United Nations General Assembly in September 2006, one day after Bush addressed the same body, and lambasted "the gentleman to whom I refer as the devil" for his attempt to create a "world dictatorship."[19] Radical Islam and the terrorists it had spawned were envisioned as agents of the devil, particularly in evangelical imaginations: "As a religious system," suggested one of many such websites, "Islam . . . is entirely of Satanic origin."[20] With so much fear, vituperation, and political polarization circulating through America's public discourse, blues musicians found in the figure of the devil a powerful way to critique post-9/11 life, most notably in Popa Chubby's "Somebody Let the Devil Out" (2002), Cephas and Wiggins's "Stack and the Devil" (2002), and Shemekia Copeland's "Sounds Like the Devil" (2009).

Early one morning I was lying in my bed
The alarm came off, I just shook my head
I said, "Damn I'm late"
Went downstairs and my wife came in

"You wouldn't believe what them bastards just did
They took the whole thing down"
I started shaking I could hardly believe it
When I heard the man on my TV
Somebody let the devil out
Somebody let the devil out
Somebody let the devil out
Take a long shoe to kick him back down to hell.
—Popa Chubby, "Somebody Let the Devil Out" (2002)

Love is tumbling, dreams are crumbling
We are looking for a place to hide
People are hurting, politicians certain
They got God on their side
And they're saying that he's talking to 'em personally
But it sounds like the devil to me!

Hard as I'm slaving, there ain't no saving
I'm never gonna see a dime

I ain't got health care, Lord it ain't fair
I can't even afford to die
They said they treat us all just like family

But it sounds like the devil . . . sounds like the devil. . .
Sounds like the devil to me!
But it sounds like the devil . . . sounds like the devil
Sound like the devil to me!
—Shemekia Copeland, "Sounds Like the Devil" (2009)

3. Although the recent "minicraze" in devil-themed blues recordings is
evenly divided, on the songwriter/performer end, between black and white
artists, the contemporary mainstream audience for the blues is, as many
have remarked, almost entirely white. The preoccupations and concerns
of an African American audience that helped spur several earlier generations of black songwriters to speak of the devil in specific ways have been
supplanted, in our own time, by the preoccupations and concerns of a
very different audience. A desire to reject the strictures of black southern
evangelicalism in a devil-dance of bad behavior has been replaced, in recordings by Walter Trout ("I Thought I Heard the Devil," 1999, covered by

John Mayall in 2002), Jason Ricci ("Done with the Devil," 2009), Jim Suhler ("The Devil in Me," 2009), and Johnny Sansone ("The Lord Is Waiting, the Devil Is Too," 2011), by anxieties about addiction and a hunger for recovery: the long aftermath, perhaps, of a mass white drug culture birthed in the marijuana-mushrooms-and-LSD haze of the 1960s, fueled by cocaine in the 1970s and 1980s, abetted by ecstasy in the rave-ups of the millennials, and underpinned by a dark romance with heroin among rock and blues musicians, including Clapton and Keith Richards. Aging baby boomers anchor the contemporary blues audience; the devil theme offers that cohort a chance to meditate on and reassess their youthful excesses, even as the pleasure-centered Legendary Rhythm and Blues Cruises and similar events tempt them to overindulge. The perennial theme of male-female relationships, meanwhile, remains a place where performers such as Buddy Guy ("The Devil's Daughter," 2013), John Lee Hooker Jr. ("She Wasn't Nothin' but a Devil," 2004), Janiva Magness ("The Devil Is an Angel," 2010), and Tommy Castro ("The Devil You Know," 2014) see the devil's hand at work whenever lies, deception, and betrayal take place between lovers, breaking hearts and destabilizing minds.

> I thought I saw the devil . . . he was standing at the bar
> He was sipping on some whiskey . . . he was smoking a cigar
> He said, "I know some ladies and I brought them just for you
> They're more than willing to do what you wanna do"
> And I said, "I don't think that would be so smart . . . I know
>   you want to tear my world apart
> You want to tear it all apart"
>
> I saw the devil . . . he was walking next to me
> He said, "I'm here to help you . . . to be all that you can be
> I'll take away your pain and help you make it through the night
> Put your trust in me, I'll make everything all right"
> And I said, "I don't think that would be so smart . . . I know
>   you want to tear my world apart
> You want to tear it all apart"
> —Walter Trout, "I Thought I Heard the Devil" (1999)

> It wants to tell you lies
> It wants to advertise
> It won't compromise
> It comes in disguise

It will hypnotize
It can paralyze
You won't vocalize
Feelings of demise

You'll be ostracized
It laughs and does not cry
You'll never exorcise
It sees out your eyes

Three knocks at the door
This ain't no folklore
It's a dirty force
You cannot divorce

Done with the devil, but
Devil ain't done with you
Done with the devil, but
Devil ain't done with you
—Jason Ricci and New Blood, "Done with the Devil" (2009)

She wadn't nothin but a devil . . . tried to play this game on me
I thought she wanted my honey . . . but she was after my money
I knew all the time . . . but damn, she was fine

I knew there was something up her sleeve . . . 'cause she slipped and called
    me Steve
I thought that was kind of funny . . . 'cause my mother named me Johnny
I just need to be very careful . . . when I'm fooling with the devil

So I called 911 . . . and she began to run
Ain't no fun . . . when the rabbit's got the gun
She tried to be so slick . . . with her bag of dirty tricks.
—John Lee Hooker Jr., "She Wasn't Nothin' but a Devil" (2004)

I DON'T PREFER NO BLUES

In *The Holy Profane* (2004), a study of religion in black popular music, musicologist Teresa Reed argues that "before the 1950s, the lines between God and the Devil were so dogmatically (if not clearly) drawn that religious consumers were never expected to patronize secular music. By the 1950s, however, the tide had clearly changed."[21] That change did not occur without struggle; the 1950s ushered in the rock-and-roll revolution and the sacred/secular fusion known as soul music, both of which were met, at least initially, by strong resistance from black (and white) religious circles, including the familiar devil's-music charge that had been leveled at the blues in earlier decades. But the passage of time and the weakening of church power over a secularizing American culture during the 1950s and 1960s did indeed effect a broad, if unevenly distributed, attitudinal transformation.[22] If one were searching for a symbolic moment at which the devil's-music dispute suddenly seemed to fade as a pressing concern within African American communities, one could do worse than "Everybody's Got a Little Devil in Their Soul," a 1972 release by Tommie Young. Young, the gospel-singing daughter of a Dallas minister, was twenty-three and unheralded when producer Bobby Patterson saw her in a local nightclub and produced her debut album for his Soul Power label.[23] Young's song, more than a decade removed from the cultural turmoil of the 1950s, seems to confirm an attitudinal shift, staging what might be called the dedemonization of the devil and embracing of the devil's presence in modern black lives. She mentions religious and community leaders (preacher, teacher) and "innocent" children. The tone is broadly comic: accepting of human weakness rather than pronouncing judgment and banishing evildoers:

> I wanna tell you . . . said everybody . . . got a little devil . . .
>   in their soul . . . yeah
> Said everybody . . . got a little devil . . . in their soul . . . aww yeah
> Said everybody . . . got a little devil . . . everybody . . . ain't quite on
>   the level
> Everybody . . . got a little devil . . . in their soul
>
> Said the preacher . . . got a little devil . . . so I've been told . . . aw yeah
> Well you know the teacher . . . she's got a little devil . . . she can't
>   control . . . oh no
> Said everybody . . . got a little devil, etc.
>
> [chorus]
> Devil in their soul . . . devil in their soul . . . devil in their soul . . .
>   devil in their soul (3x)
>
> I said little sister . . . she's got a little devil . . . on her mind . . .
>   oh yes she has

And you know little brother . . . he's in a little trouble (got a little devil) . . .
  all the time . . . oh yeah
It may not show . . . on the outside . . . but everybody's . . . got a little
  devil . . . they're trying to hide
Everybody . . . got a little devil . . . in their soul[24]

Thanks in part to the call-and-response dialogue between Young and her background singers, the word "devil" is repeated more than forty times in the three-minute-and-forty-second track—a record, surely, for such a cheerful piece of pop music. In formal terms, the song is a sixteen-bar gospel blues, precisely the same form Ray Charles mined in his controversial 1954 hit, "I Got a Woman." The simple fact that the song exists, that it was recorded by a daughter of the church and achieved modest notice in the trade press without apparently causing widespread moral panic or incurring wrathful condemnation from Christian evangelicals, says something about how much had changed over the decades.

Yet how much *had*, in fact, changed? Within three years, Young had renounced her modest career as a soul singer and returned to her church home, altering the spelling of her first name to Tommye in a classic act of self-redefinition. During the three decades that followed, she released a handful of gospel albums with titles like *Believe* (2000) and *Created to Worship* (2008): a prodigal daughter of a sort not unfamiliar to fans of the blues, one who turned decisively toward the Lord after her brief and spectacular flirtation with something like worldly acceptance of the devil's role in human affairs.

Young's example, framed by Reed's pronouncement, might remind us that the shifting valence of the devil figure in the blues is part of a larger cultural conversation, one that encompasses a broad spectrum of black (and black-derived) popular music. In the eyes of black evangelical Christianity, "popular" has long been a synonym for "worldly": music designed for dancing, conducive to dissipation, and intended to provoke sexual idolatry, rather than music consecrated to the service of the Lord and the project of social uplift. The boundary distinguishing black sacred music from black secular music may have shifted and weakened over the years, but it hasn't disappeared. It is being continually renegotiated—in moments, for example, where contemporary black religionists embrace the lives and legacies of famous blues musicians they might in earlier days have condemned. When a memorial marker for Robert Johnson was placed in the Mt. Zion Missionary Baptist Church in Morgan City, Mississippi, in April 1991, Rev. James

Ratliff elegantly finessed the issue of Johnson's crossroads deal—in part, it might be argued, because Sony executives, looking to burnish their image after recently making so much money on Johnson's *Complete Recordings* (1990), had given generously to Ratliff's church. "God works in mysterious ways," the preacher insisted. "Legend says this man sold his soul to the Devil. I don't know about that. All I can say is, when he died, the members of this church had love in their hearts and gave him a resting place, and God wrote that down. Now, I don't know what Robert Johnson told the Lord. *You* don't know what Robert Johnson told the Lord. We *all* have come short of the glory of God."[25]

When musicologist Therese Smith conducted research at the Clear Creek Missionary Baptist Church just outside Oxford, Mississippi, in the mid-1980s, she concluded that "it is generally among the younger members of the church that the distinction between 'good music' and 'devil's music' is most often perceived to be blurred."[26] Even at that late moment in the devil's-music dispute, however, the distinction remained important to many older church members and to their ministers and church musicians:

> Especially in rural Mississippi . . . , the two sub-cultures of Delta blues . . . and fundamentalist Christianity have remained relatively intact and opposed. It is an opposition that is critical to the identity of the Clear Creek M.B.C. membership. Preachers still warn about the evils of the sinner's life: moonshine, women, and "devil's music." And the Delta blues tradition is still strong. By and large audiences for the two traditions are different; not many church folk who go to church on Sunday morning attend a blues session on Friday or Saturday night, and such behavior would be strongly condemned in church. . . . The church choir director and pianist, Herbert Bonner, maintains that there are certain chord progressions specific to "devil's music," which arouse the wrong feelings in listeners and performers alike.[27]

Not all contemporary black southern ministers and church musicians condemn the blues and the feelings it evokes; some enjoy it and a few even perform it. But anecdotal evidence suggests that those who enjoy and perform it are fully aware of the stigma it still carries in church communities—the long tail of an enduring disagreement, even when the term "devil's music" isn't uttered. Interviewed by Alan Young for a book on black gospel singers and the gospel life, Rev. J. W. Shaw, pastoring at the St. John Missionary Baptist Church near Brownsville, Tennessee, grew up "sing[ing] in the cottonfields," and he and his family sang "blues most of the time," he said, "because we knew more about the blues than we did about gospel music."

> I realized that as a pastor I can't go out publicly promoting blues. I don't get in my pulpit and say, "Hey, y'all, listen to the blues next week." But I don't have any problem saying to the people in my church, "I'm a blues lover." I love the blues. . . . If we didn't feel we would be so highly criticized by the public, you would see us in a lot of the clubs, listening to blues. People like B. B. King when he comes to town. But because I'm a pastor . . . they're rather narrow-minded . . . so we stay away for those reasons.[28]

In 2008, Broke & Hungry Records, a small southern label, released *The World Must Never Know*, the debut recording by a seventy-eight-year-old performer and deacon from a "very traditional" church in the Mississippi Delta who, to avoid being condemned by his parishioners, refused to use his real name, choosing instead the pseudonym "The Mississippi Marvel." Interviewed by Clarksdale-based blues promoter Roger Stolle several years after the album came out, the Marvel insisted that he played nothing but "hard blues" outside the church and "church songs" inside; he was unapologetic about his blues playing and cheerfully resigned to his double life. "Sometimes," he laughed, "you ain't supposed to let your right hand know what your left hand is doing. I love blues. But playing the blues . . . It ain't that there's that much wrong with it because you're in the church, it's just the position of the people up in the church—the deacon or something. See, as far as they're concerned, if they want [a deacon] to play in the church, he better not bring his blues down there."[29]

More recently, the blues world has celebrated the late-life emergence of Leo "Bud" Welch (1932–) a guitarist and singer who played the blues until the mid-1970s, then set that music aside to play gospel in the Sabougla Baptist Church near his home in Bruce, Mississippi. Host of a twice-a-week TV show, *The Black Gospel Express*, Welch released a debut album, *Sabougla Voices* (2014), consisting entirely of religious material done in a rough, primitive, electric-guitar-and-drums style familiar to fans of north Mississippi hill country blues. It caused a sensation among those fans and others—in part because Welch's live shows included plenty of the loud, raw blues material he'd performed in days gone by—and consternation in his pastor, who was unsure what to make of his octogenarian parishioner's sudden emergence as a contemporary blues star, an act in hot demand on the club and festival circuit. "I don't prefer no blues," the pastor reportedly said. To which Welch supposedly replied, "I know you don't, 'cause you don't know anything about 'em."[30] Welch's second album, *I Don't Prefer No Blues* (2015), consists entirely of blues: a mocking rejoinder, it would seem, to his minister's disapproval. Like many black southern blues performers before him, skilled at the protocols of synchronous duplicity and determined to taste the fullness of life, Welch rejects the binary thinking through which the black church seeks to parse the world and its music into sacred and secular, God's purview and the devil's. "Leo," according to the promotional material on his new website, "does not believe that Blues is the devil's music but a way of expressing the highs and lows of one's life through song."[31]

Thus, at least in Mississippi, does the struggle continue.

Acknowledgments

During the seven years that it took to research and write *Beyond the Crossroads*, I received a great deal of help from many different people and a handful of organizations. It gives me great pleasure to thank them here. Needless to say, I take full responsibility for this book's failings, whatever they may be, and absolve all who gave so generously of their time, care, and wisdom.

Much of the research was completed during a yearlong sabbatical in 2008–9, for which I thank not just the University of Mississippi, but my two academic homes there, the Department of English and the Center for the Study of Southern Culture (CSSC), and their respective (and warmly supportive) heads, Ivo Kamps and Ted Ownby. The College of Liberal Arts provided additional help with a summer research grant in 2012; a second sabbatical in the fall of 2015 gave me the chance to finish up.

I am uniquely privileged, as a blues scholar, to work on a campus where the Blues Archive, a part of the Department of Archives and Special Collections at the J. D. Williams Library, is a three-minute walk from my office. Greg Johnson, the blues archivist, has assisted me every step of the way, as have others on the archive staff. Humanities librarian Alex Watson not only fielded my occasional requests but demanded updates on the project every time we crossed paths at Uptown Coffee—an invaluable prod. I'm also grateful for the help I received from Debra McIntosh, college archivist at the J. B. Cain Archives of Mississippi Methodism at the Millsaps-Wilson Library of Millsaps College in Jackson, and from librarians Phillip Carter and Joanne Blue at the Carnegie Public Library in Clarksdale. Special thanks to Todd Harvey at the Library of Congress, who tracked down and sent me a scan of Alan Lomax's early interview with David Honeyboy Edwards.

I was fortunate to have the chance to share work-in-progress with my friends, peers, and students in various forums, including the Modern Language Association meetings in 2009 and 2013 and the Southern Studies Brown Bag series at the CSSC in 2009; Mary Hartwell Howorth was nice enough to make space for the latter presentation. I'm indebted to my dear friend, mentor, and inspiration Bill Ferris and his associates at the Center for the Study of the American South at UNC Chapel Hill for inviting me to their campus to give the James A. Hutchins lecture, "The Devil and the Blues," in 2011. Thanks to Greg Hansen and the folks at the Delta Symposium at Arkansas State University in Jonesboro for giving me a chance to work out my ideas about *Crossroads* as keynote speaker in 2014. My former student Rolonda Brown, now the dean of academics at Coahoma Community College in Clarksdale, invited me to her campus so that I could share my research on that town's civic history and the crossroads monument with community college faculty from across the state of Mississippi at the Lamplighter's Conference that same year.

Janelle Collins and Marcus Tribbett, editorial stewards of *Arkansas Review*, have my eternal gratitude for publishing an earlier version of chapter 1 as a pair of articles, "Ain't No Burnin' Hell: Southern Religion and the Devil's Music" (41, no. 2 [August 2010]: 83–98) and "Heaven and Hell Parties: Ministers, Bluesmen, and Black Youth in the Mississippi Delta, 1920–1942" (41, no. 3 [Winter/December 2010]: 186–203), giving me early confirmation that I was on the right track. A portion of chapter 5 also appeared in *Arkansas Review* as "'I Got a Big White Fella from Memphis Made a Deal with Me': Black Men, White Boys, and the Anxieties of Blues Postmodernity in Walter Hill's *Crossroads*" (46, no. 2 [Summer/August 2015]: 85–104). Chapter 2 first appeared in somewhat shorter form in *Popular Music and Society* as "Sold It to the Blues-Devil: The Great Migration, Lost Generations, and the Perils of the Urban Dance Hall" (36, no. 5 [December 2013]: 615–36). Thanks to both publications for permission to reprint.

Three senior scholars made particularly important contributions to this project, two of them more as critics than allies. Although my own interpretations diverge from theirs, I remain grateful for their stern and thorough interventions. David Evans, whose important scholarship on Robert Johnson, the devil, and guitars shows up in my bibliography, read an early version of this project as a referee for the University Press of Mississippi; he offered a long and stringent report, one that not only rescued me from a dozen factual errors but forced me to rethink certain key points in my argument and substantiate my claims with additional research. Tony Thomas, aka "Blackbanjotony," a fearsomely erudite independent scholar, generously agreed to read chapter 1, told me in no uncertain terms that the African-origins section was lamentable, and e-mailed me eight articles that began the process of remedying my ignorance. As for Charles Wilson, my former supervisor at the Center for the Study of Southern Culture, he has long provided a model of interdisciplinary scholarship marked by keen judgment and stylistic grace. Charles contributed to this project at every point: in our periodic and intellectually stimulating rendezvous for "libations" at City Grocery, as an early reader of several chapters, and, not least, as series editor for UNC Press. He never once pressured me to give him this project but was right there for me, as he had always been, when I finally decided to do that. Thanks, bossman!

In Jim O'Neal, Scott Barretta, Mark Camarigg, Brett Bonner, and Greg Johnson, I was lucky enough to have my own little blues mafia, three of them past or present editors of *Living Blues*, that I could call on via e-mail whenever I needed help chasing down a lead or ascertaining a point of fact. Thanks to all, especially Jim, who first hipped me to Cousin Leroy, spoke to me at length about blues tourism in Clarksdale, and contributed significant scholarship of his own to my bibliography.

I interviewed many people in Clarksdale and elsewhere in Mississippi in an effort to disentangle history from myth. Robert Birdsong, local historian, provided particularly important help, including the date when the three-guitar monument was erected. I will always treasure the long interview that Vic Barbieri, the monument's unsung creator, gave me at his home in Lyon and, later, on location at "the crossroads." Shirley Fair, Leonard Henderson, and Maie Smith gifted me with a range of African American perspectives on Clarksdale and the blues. Hearty thanks to Johnny Billington, James Butler, Sandy Bynum, Cathy Clark, James "Jimmy" Dickerson, Patty Johnson, Earl Klatzel, Pat LeBlanc, Bill Lester, Shelley Ritter, Preston Rumbaugh, John Ruskey, Bill Seratt, Nell Smith, Hunter Twiford, Mike Ware, and Jesse Wright. Thanks to my research assistant, Josh-Wade Ferguson, who transcribed many of these interviews and chased down some important research leads. Thanks as well to T. Dewayne Moore, UM doctoral candidate in history, for his fantastic sleuthing in the matter of early newspaper reports on Clarksdale's crossroads.

My colleague Jay Watson and my friends Patti Schroeder and Tim Ryan each read and offered useful feedback on portions of this manuscript. A number of other scholars, writers, and musicians offered me a helping hand during my journey and have my sincere thanks: Adetayo Alabi, Chris Albertson, Ed Berger, Thomas Brothers, Keith Cartwright, Steve Cheseborough, Bruce Conforth, William Danaher, James Dickerson, John Fusco, John Giggie, Ted Gioia, Wayne Goins, Thomas Hale, "Mississippi" Max Haymes, Jeff Konkel, Peter Muir, Charles Shaar Murray, Ali Colleen Neff, Erik Nielson, Barry Lee Pearson, Betsy Phillips, Arlen Roth, Eric Rothenbuhler, Mohammad Bashir Salau, Jon Smith, Paul Trynka, Anne Twitty, Elijah Wald, Gayle Dean Wardlow, Harry West, Alan White, and Ethel Young-Scurlock.

Lastly, but certainly not least, I'd like to thank my wife, Sherrie, and my son, Shaun. They were at my side every step of the way as I chased the demon that has become this book, listening to my complaints and sharing in my delight. They have my enduring love and gratitude for that.

Appendix Devil-Blues Recordings and Selected Sermons,
             1924–2015

When I discovered at the beginning of this project that no comprehensive inventory of devil-blues recordings existed, I began to compile one. My criterion for inclusion was simple: I wanted original blues recordings (not covers or remakes of those recordings, with a couple of significant exceptions) whose lyrics invoked the devil and/or hell. Often, but not always, the titles of these recordings also mentioned the devil or hell. Using every available search engine (including Google, Amazon, iTunes, the U.S Copyrights Office, and the University of Mississippi library with its Blues Archive, along with Harry's Blues Lyrics Online and Michael Taft's concordance/anthology of prewar blues lyrics), I came up with a working song list, then solicited suggestions about what was missing from several friends with a deep knowledge of the recorded archive. Because crossroads mythology has had such a lasting influence on the devil-blues theme, I included both the original and somewhat different alternate take of Robert Johnson's "Cross Road Blues," even though it doesn't meet my stated criterion. I've also included ten recorded sermons; although they don't belong to the archive in question, they are part of the larger cultural conversation that led black southern Christians to demonize the blues. As such, they can help us make sense of the potent imprecation, "devil's music," that has shadowed the blues since the beginning. I've included several devil-invoking jazz and gospel recordings for the same reason: they illustrate the way in which evangelical disapproval of "fast" urban nightlife was being thematized and sometimes satirized in the realm of popular culture, offering broader context for the devil's music dispute.

The following list of devil-blues recordings deserves to be called comprehensive, but it is surely not the final word. I trust that discographers and scholars will supplement it, if they're able to. I am confident that nothing truly essential has been left out—nothing that would fundamentally destabilize the conclusions I have drawn about the lineaments and thematics of the devil-blues tradition.

This appendix does not include every recording referenced in this study, since some of those recordings—Bert Williams's "O Death, Where is Thy Sting," for example, or Little Brother Montgomery's "The First Time I Met You," or Robert Johnson's "From Four Until Late"—weren't blues, or didn't invoke the devil, or both.

YEAR	TITLE	PERFORMER	LABEL / CATALOG NUMBER	RUNNING TIME
1924	"Done Sold My Soul to the Devil"	Clara Smith	Co 14041-D	2:59
1924	"Mad Mama's Blues"	Josie Miles	Ed 51477	3:57
1924	"Thunderstorm Blues"	Maggie Jones	Co 14050-D	3:01
1925	"The Cat's Got the Measles"	Papa Charlie Jackson	Pm 12259	3:03
1925	"Devil Dance Blues"	Sippie Wallace	OK 8206	3:06
1925	"Rough and Tumble Blues"	Ma Rainey	Pm 12311	2:53
1926	"Devil and My Brown Blues"	Bo Weavil Jackson (Sam Butler)	Vo 10 (unissued)	2:57
1927	"Are You Bound for Heaven or Hell?" (sermon)	Rev. J. M. Gates	OK 8552	3:03
1927	"Black Diamond Express to Hell, Part 1" (sermon)	Rev. A. W. Nix	Vo 1098	2:54
1927	"Black Diamond Express to Hell, Part 2" (sermon)	Rev. A. W. Nix	Vo 1098	3:04
1927	"Can't Be Trusted Blues"	Sylvester Weaver	OK 8504	3:09
1927	"Devil Blues"	Sylvester Weaver	OK 8534	3:04
1927	"Devil in a Flying Machine" (sermon)	Rev. J. M. Gates	OK 8515	3:09
1927	"Devil in the Lion's Den"	Sam Collins	Ge 6181	2:44
1927	"Dyin' by the Hour"	Bessie Smith	Co 14273-D	2:57
1927	"Hell Is in God's Jail House" (sermon)	Rev. J. M. Gates	OK 8547	3:01
1927	"Hellish Rag"	Ma Rainey	Pm 12612	3:05
1927	"Hell Bound Express Train" (sermon)	Rev. J. M. Gates	OK 8532	2:59
1927	"Send Me to the 'Lectric Chair"	Bessie Smith and Her Blue Boys	Co 14209-D	3:23
1928	"Blue Devil Blues"	"Texas" Alexander	OK 8640	3:24
1928	"Coal Oil Blues"	Memphis Jug Band	Vi 21278	3:31
1928	"Devil's Gonna Get You"	Bessie Smith	Co 14354-D	3:12
1928	"Devilish Blues"	Stovepipe Johnson	Vo 1203	3:07

YEAR	TITLE	PERFORMER	LABEL / CATALOG NUMBER	RUNNING TIME
1928	"Low-Down Rounder Blues"	Peg Leg Howell	Co 14320-D	2:53
1928	"Death Sting Me Blues"	Sara Martin	QRS R7042	2:47
1928	"Piney Woods Money Mama"	Blind Lemon Jefferson	Pm 12650	3:00
1928	"Whitewash Station Blues"	Memphis Jug Band	Vi V38504	2:46
1929	"Blue Spirit Blues"	Bessie Smith	Co 14527-D	2:55
1929	"Devil in the Woodpile"	Noah Lewis	Vi V38581	2:56
1929	"Is There Harm in Singing the Blues?" (sermon)	Rev. Emmett Dickinson	Pm 12925	3:08
1929	"Sermon on 'Tight Like That'" (sermon)	Rev. Emmett Dickinson	Pm 12925	3:33
1929	"Wicked Devil's Blues"	Robert Peeples	Pm 12995	3:12
1929	"Mr. Devil Blues"	Joe Williams	Vo 1457	3:09
1930	"Another Woman Booked Out and Bound to Go"	Lonnie Johnson	OK 1886	3:14
1930	"Black Mountain Blues"	Bessie Smith	Co 14554-D	3:00
1930	"The Devil and God Meet at Church" (sermon)	Rev. Emmett Dickinson	Pm 13124	2:53
1930	"I'm Feelin' Devilish"	Fess Williams	ViV38131-B	3:18
1930	"Devil Sent the Rain Blues"	Charley Patton	Pm 13040	3:05
1930	"I've Seen the Devil" (sermon)	Rev. F. W. McGee	Vi V38583	3:36
1930	"Moan, You Moaners"	Bessie Smith	Co 14538-D	3:11
1930	"My Black Mama, Part 1"	Son House	Pm 13042	3:07
1930	"She's Making Whoopee in Hell Tonight"	Lonnie Johnson	OK 8768	3:11
1931	"Devil Got My Woman"	Skip James	Pm 13088	3:02
1931	"Devil's Son-In-Law"	Peetie Wheatstraw	BB B5451	3:26
1931	"Fool's Blues"	J. T. "Funny Paper" Smith	Vo 1674	2:52
1931	"Hell Is a Name for All Sinners"	Lonnie Johnson	Co 14667-D	2:56

YEAR	TITLE	PERFORMER	LABEL / CATALOG NUMBER	RUNNING TIME
1931	"Satan Your Kingdom Must Come Down"	Blind Joe Taggart	Pm 13081	3:04
1931	"Seven Sisters Blues, Part 2"	Funny Papa Smith	Vo 1641	2:57
1931	"Shake Hands and Tell Me Goodbye"	Mississippi Sheiks	OK 8951	2:56
1932	"He Calls That Religion"	Mississippi Sheiks	Pm 13142	3:30
1932	"Sam, You're Just a Rat"	Lonnie Johnson	OK 8937	3:22
1932	"Whoopee Blues"	King Solomon Hill	Pm 13116	3:09
1933	"Devil's Island Gin Blues"	Roosevelt Sykes	BB B5342	3:04
1934	"Busy Devil"	Bumble Bee Slim (Amos Easton)	Vo 02713	3:16
1934	"Evil Devil Woman Blues"	Kansas Joe (Joe McCoy)	De 7822	3:13
1934	"I Am the Devil"	Mississippi Sheiks	BB B5516	3:11
1934	"Someday I'll Be in the Clay"	The Mississippi Mudder (Joe McCoy)	De 7008	3:18
1934	"Love My Stuff"	Charley Patton	Vo 02782	2:58
1934	"Worried Devil Blues"	Tampa Red	BB B5744	3:28
1935	"The Evil Devil Blues"	Johnny Temple	Vo 02987	3:13
1935	"Gonna Dig a Hole—Put the Devil In"	Leadbelly	ARC unissued	1:37
1935	"Mississippi Moan"	The Mississippi Moaner (Isaiah Nettles)	Vo 03166	2:31
1935	"My Babe My Babe"	Joe Wilber McCoy (aka "Bill" Wilber)	Ch 50053	2:45
1935	"There's Going to Be the Devil to Pay"	Fats Waller	Vi BS-88994	2:29
1936	"Coon Can Shorty"	Peetie Wheatstraw	De 7159	2:56
1936	"Sweet Home Blues"	Peetie Wheatstraw	Vo 03396	2:48
1936	"Your Hellish Ways"	Georgia White	De 7254	2:33
1937	"Cross Road Blues"	Robert Johnson	Vo 03519	2:38
1937	"Hell Hound on My Trail"	Robert Johnson	Vo 03623	2:37

YEAR	TITLE	PERFORMER	LABEL / CATALOG NUMBER	RUNNING TIME
1937	"Devilment Blues"	Peetie Wheatstraw	De 7422	3:10
1937	"Done Sold My Soul to the Devil"	Dave Edwards & His Alabama Boys	De 5493-B	3:01
1937	"Sold My Soul to the Devil"	Casey Bill Weldon	Vo 03561	3:23
1937	"Sold It to the Devil"	John D. Twitty	BB B6995	3:07
1937	"Sold It to the Devil"	The Yas Yas Girl (Merline Johnson)	Vo 03599	3:03
1937	"Hospital, Heaven or Hell"	Roosevelt Sykes	De 7401	3:06
1937	"Me and the Devil Blues (Take 1)"	Robert Johnson	Vo 04108	2:36
1937	"Peetie Wheatstraw Stomp"	Peetie Wheatstraw	De 7292	2:31
1937	"Peetie Wheatstraw Stomp No. 2"	Peetie Wheatstraw	De 7391	2:38
1938	"You Got the Devil to Pay"	Harlem Hamfats	DOCD-5273	3:08
1938	"Devil's Got the Blues"	Lonnie Johnson	De 7487	2:57
1938	"Hellish Old Feeling"	Tampa Red	BB B8086	3:15
1938	"I Got Ways Like the Devil"	Blue Lu Barker	De 7560	2:54
1938	"Hell Ain't but a Mile and a Quarter"	Red Mike Bailey	BB B7744	2:56
1938	"Hell Ain't but a Mile and a Quarter"	Big Bill (Broonzy)	Vo 04532	2:56
1938	"War Broke Out in Hell"	Curtis Jones	Vo 04520	2:50
1938	"Deep Down in the Ground"	John Lee "Sonny Boy" Williamson	BB B7805	3:12
1938	"Old Devil"	Bo Carter	BB B8093	3:00
1939	"If I Was the Devil"	Leroy's Buddy (Bill Gaither)	De 7563	2:51
1939	"The Devil with the Devil"	Golden Gate Jubilee Quartet	BB B8594	3:04
1939	"Grief Will Kill You"	Little Buddy Doyle	Vo 05111	2:37
1939	"Hell Is So Low Down"	Ollie Shepard	De 7716	3:12
1939	"Mean Devil Blues"	Bill Gaither	De 7749	2:22

YEAR	TITLE	PERFORMER	LABEL / CATALOG NUMBER	RUNNING TIME
1940	"Crooked Woman Blues"	Blind Boy Fuller	Vo 05527	2:46
1940	"I Been Dealing with the Devil"	John Lee "Sonny Boy" Williamson	BB B8580	2:46
1940	"Dealing with the Devil"	Brownie McGhee	OK 06329	2:36
1940	"Don't Deal with the Devil"	Tampa Red	BB B8991	2:53
1941	"The Devil's Gonna Get You"	The Gospeleers	De 7851	2:48
1941	"She Belongs to the Devil"	Washboard Sam	BB B8937	3:04
1942	"The Devil's Woman"	Lonnie Johnson	BB B9022	3:18
1943	"The Devil Has Thrown Him Down"	Sister Rosetta Tharpe	De 48024	2:54
1947	"The Devil Blues"	Bill "Jazz" Gillum	Vi 20–3118	2:54
1949	"Burnin' Hell"	John Lee Hooker	Sensation 21	2:42
1949	"Devil's Jump"	John Lee Hooker	King 4315	2:54
1949	"Evil Blues"	Little Son Jackson	Gold Star 663	2:51
1950	"Crossroads"	"Texas" Alexander	Freedom 1538	2:42
1953	"Dealing with the Devil"	Eddie Burns	DeLuxe 6024	2:58
1954	"The Devil Is a Busy Man"	Sunnyland Slim	Blue Lake 105	2:49
1954	"Standing at the Crossroads"	Elmore James	Flare 1057	2:46
1956	"Devil or Angel"	The Clovers	Atlantic 1083	2:26
1956	"Little Demon"	Screamin Jay Hawkins	OK 58-4097	2:25
1957	"Crossroads"	Cousin Leroy (Rozier)	E2139	2:45
1960	"She Devil"	Lonnie Johnson	Bluesville BVLP 1007	2:57
1961	"Cross Road Blues" (alternate take)	Robert Johnson	CL 1654	2:29
1962	"Devil Is Watching You"	Lightnin' Hopkins	Bluesville BVLP 1057	4:01
1962	"The Devil Jumped the Black Man"	Lightnin' Hopkins	Veejay LP 1044	4:14
1963	"Must Have Been the Devil"	Otis Spann (w/ Lonnie Johnson, gtr.)	Storyville SLP 157	2:53
1964	"I'd Rather Be the Devil"	Otis Spann	DR 33245	2:42

YEAR	TITLE	PERFORMER	LABEL / CATALOG NUMBER	RUNNING TIME
1966	"Devil Got My Woman"	Skip James	Verve Folkways FTS-3010	5:15
1968	"My Home's in Hell"	Champion Jack Dupree	Blue Horizon LP BH7702	4:57
1970	"It Must Have Been the Devil"	Jack Owens and Bud Spires	Te T 2222	9:48
1972	"Everybody's Got a Little Devil in Their Soul"	Tommie Young	Soul Power SP-112	
1973	"Couldn't Find a Mule"	Sunnyland Slim	Sonet (UK) SNTF 671	5:05
1973	"Devil's Daughter"	Johnny Shines	Xtra (UK) 1142	3:15
1975	"Too Poor to Die"	Louisiana Red	Blue Labor BL 104	6:33
1981	"Devil Got My Man"	Rory Block	Dargil 3061	2:20
1982	"Devil's Hand"	Johnny Copeland	Rounder 2030	3:07
1984	"Me and the Devil"	Blind Will Dukes	JSP 1079	2:20
1985	"Flamin' Mamie"	Koko Taylor	Alligator AL 4740	3:32
1987	"The Devil's Gonna Have a Field Day"	Koko Taylor	Alligator AL 4754	5:30
1989	"Devil Child"	Kenny Neal	Alligator AL 4774	3:14
1991	"The Devil Made Me Do It"	George "Wild Child" Butler	Blue Horizon (UK)	3:13
1992	"Devil Got My Woman"	John Cephas and Phil Wiggins	Flying Fish FF 70580	3:19
1992	"Dream about the Devil"	Long John Hunter	Spindletop STP 1003	4:31
1993	"Hell Bound Man"	Big Wheeler	Delmark DE-661	5:50
1994	"Young Devil"	Phillip Walker and Otis Grand	JSP (UK) JSPCD 248	3:45
1995	"When the Devil Starts Crying"	John Mayall and the Bluesbreakers	Jive	4:14
1995	"Dealing with the Devil"	James Cotton	Verve 529 849	3:36
1996	"Devil in Disguise"	Little Joe Blue	Evijim	3:43

YEAR	TITLE	PERFORMER	LABEL / CATALOG NUMBER	RUNNING TIME
1996	"I Got the Power"	Guy Davis	Red House RHRCD 89	4:54
1998	"Nothing but the Devil"	Lazy Lester	Antone's ANT10042	3:11
1999	"I Thought I Heard the Devil"	Walter Trout	Ruf	4:36
2000	"My Deal at the Crossroads"	Jerry McCain	Sire	5:26
2001	"Devil at Your Doorstep"	Floyd Lee Band	Amogla	5:15
2001	"She's Got the Devil in Her"	Buddy Guy	Sweet Tea	5:11
2002	"Don't Let the Devil Ride"	Precious Bryant	Terminus	3:18
2002	"Stack and the Devil"	Cephas & Wiggins	Alligator	3:35
2002	"Mississippi KKKrosroads"	Chris Thomas King	21st Century Blues	3:46
2002	"Somebody Let the Devil Out"	Popa Chubby	DixieFrog	5:53
2004	"The Devil Gonna Drag You Down"	Popa Chubby	Blind Pig	4:14
2004	"She Wasn't Nothin' but a Devil"	John Lee Hooker Jr.	Kent	4:07
2005	"At da' Crossroads"	Billy Jones	Black and Tan	3:09
2005	"Deal wit' da' Devil"	Billy Jones	Black and Tan	3:53
2005	"Devil's Got to Burn"	James "Blood" Ulmer	Hyena	4:54
2005	"Take My Music Back to the Church"	James "Blood" Ulmer	Hyena	4:43
2006	"Devil Take My Soul"	Son of Dave	Kartel	4:16
2006	"I'd Rather Be the Devil"	Jimmy "Duck" Holmes	Broke & Hungry	4:30
2006	"Me and the Devil Blues"	Rory Block	Ryko/WEA	3:17
2006	"Devil's Cadillac"	Watermelon Slim and The Workers	Northern Blues	4:04
2006	"Slide Devil Man Slide"	Popa Chubby	Blind Pig	4:22
2006	"The Devil's Guitar'	Popa Chubby	Blind Pig	6:35
2007	"Hell Sent Me You"	Denise LaSalle	Ecko	4:00
2008	"Deal with the Devil"	Payne Brothers	Payne Brothers	2:56
2008	"Devil Blues"	Jimmy "Duck" Holmes	Fat Possum	3:43

YEAR	TITLE	PERFORMER	LABEL / CATALOG NUMBER	RUNNING TIME
2009	"Sounds Like the Devil"	Shemekia Copeland/ John Hahn	Telarc	3:34
2009	"Devil in Me"	Jim Suhler and Monkey Beat	Underworld	3:32
2009	"Walkin' with the Devil"	Seasick Steve and the Level Devils	Bronzerat	4:41
2009	"Done with the Devil"	Jason Ricci and New Blood	Eclecto Groove	5:11
2010	"The Devil Is an Angel"	Janiva Magness	Alligator	3:09
2011	"The Lord Is Waiting the Devil Is Too"	Johnny Sansone	CD Baby	4:52
2011	"Devil's Candy"	James Armstrong	Catfood	4:29
2011	"Devil Got My Woman"	Gregg Allman	New Rounder	4:52
2012	"The Devil Ain't Got No Music"	Lurrie Bell/Matthew Skoller	Aria BG	3:30
2012	"The Devil's Gonna Lie"	Otis Taylor	Telarc	3:57
2013	"The Devil's Daughter"	Buddy Guy	RCA	5:14
2014	"Speak of the Devil"	John Mayall	Forty Below	3:26
2014	"The Devil You Know"	Tommy Castro	Alligator	4:23
2015	"The Blues Ain't the Blues No More"	Anthony Gomes	Up 2 Zero Entertainment	2:38

Notes

INTRODUCTION

1. See the appendix for this list. All the lyrics cited in this study are my own transcriptions of the recordings in question. With a handful of better-known artists, including Bessie Smith, Ma Rainey, Peetie Wheatstraw, and Robert Johnson, I was assisted in this pursuit by one or more previously published versions of a particular lyric; in many other cases, I began with the lamentably error-filled versions found on lyricsfreak.com and similar user-generated websites, along with the somewhat more precise renderings offered by Harry's Blues Lyrics Online and Michael Taft's concordance/anthology of prewar blues lyrics. In all cases, these sources were merely the first step in the arduous process of playing, replaying, transcribing, deliberating, and adjudicating familiar to any blues researcher.

2. In a 2004 interview with Matt Lauer on *The Today Show*, for example, in which he was promoting his album *Me and Mr. Johnson*, Clapton said of Johnson, "Someone had his (first) album and played it to me and that was it. And I was I was completely bowled over." "Eric Clapton: Talkin' about His Inspiration." See also Bockris, *Keith Richards*, 43; and Dylan, *Chronicles*, 282.

3. Finn, *The Bluesman*, 215.

4. Floyd, *The Power of Black Music*, 73.

5. As I note below, Spencer harshly criticizes Oliver and Garon for their views. See notes 10, 11, and 12.

6. Evans, "Report on Adam Gussow, *Beyond the Crossroads*."

7. See, for example, "Willie Foster Sings Highway 61."

8. Quoted in Lomax, *The Land Where the Blues Began*, 460–61.

9. O'Neal, Wisner, and Nelson, "Snooky Pryor," 11.

10. Spencer, *Blues and Evil*, xii, xxi.

11. Oliver, *Blues Fell This Morning*, 117–18, 255.

12. Garon, *Blues and the Poetic Spirit*, 148.

13. J. T. "Funny Paper" Smith, "Fool's Blues" (1931).

14. Spencer, *Blues and Evil*, xxii.

15. Quoted in Alyn, *I Say Me for a Parable*, 52.

16. Young, *Woke Me Up This Morning*, 4.

17. Sarah Martin, "Death Sting Me Blues" (1928).

18. Sunnyland Slim, "The Devil Is a Busy Man" (1954).

19. Big Wheeler, "Hell Bound Man" (1993).

20. Humphrey, "Prodigal Sons," 168.

21. Bessie Smith, "Moan, You Moaners" (1930).

22. The claim I am making here for the importance of the devil in the blues tradition is a counterstatement to Evans's claim that "the devil and Mister Blues, and even the Christian God and Santa Claus who also make occasional appearances in traditional blues texts, are hinderers and helpers of the blues singer but are not the main subject of the songs." In certain specific songs, such as the Mississippi Sheiks' "I Am the Devil" (1934), Evans's assertion is literally untrue, but in many other songs, including Clara Smith's "Done Sold My Soul to the Devil" (1924), Lightnin' Hopkins's "The Devil Jumped the Black Man" (1962), and Chris Thomas King's "Mississippi KKKrossroads" (2002), the devil is the singer's principal antagonist and is in that sense clearly the main subject, or one of the two main subjects, of the song. See Evans, "Traditional Blues Lyric and Myth," 22–23.

23. Bessie Smith, "Black Mountain Blues" (1930).

24. In his otherwise cogent article, Evans errs when he characterizes the views of Spencer and Floyd as a form of romantic Afrocentrism that he calls "putting robes on the blues." African American intellectuals and musicologists, he argues, seek to "cast off the trappings of Western cultural influence" from blues singers and "counter the stereotyped images of 'naked' Africans found in Tarzan movies and *National Geographic* magazines." This romantic distortion of the blues' African inheritance, in Evans's view, occurs when scholars insist on comparing African American blues players to two heroic African figures: the robed *griot* "singing epic songs of ancient heroes and kings" and a robed "African priest of some 'crossroads' trickster deity such as Eshu or Legba":

> When a blues singer sings about "me and the devil," supposedly he or she is really singing about one of these African deities whose identity is disguised through syncretism with the devil of Christianity. The blues singer performing "the devil's music" is thus a cultural descendant of priests or worshippers of these African deities.

Although Spencer and Floyd do indeed argue for Legba's persistence on black southern terrain, neither scholar compares bluesmen with griots—Spencer doesn't even mention griots in the book cited by Evans—and neither scholar argues that blues singers are cultural descendants of African priests. Spencer argues, by contrast, that blues singers *incarnate* Legba, not worship him. See Evans, "African Elements in the Blues," 3–16.

25. Kubik, *Africa and the Blues*, 22.

26. Ibid., 22–23.

27. Cartwright, *Reading Africa into American Literature*, 10, 13–14.

28. Hazzard-Donald, *Mojo Workin'*, 45.

29. "The Southern Negro . . . gives the devil as a personage considerably more attention than is paid him by the present [southern] whites." See Puckett, *Folk Beliefs of the Southern Negro*, 548.

30. Herskovits, *The Myth of the Negro Past*, 252.

31. Kubik, *Africa and the Blues*, 13. See also Eltis, "The Diaspora of Yoruba Speakers," 35.

32. Lawal, "Reclaiming the Past," 293. Although the Bight of Benin's overall numerical contribution to America's African-born slave population was "minimal," according to historian Michael A. Gomez, at only 4.3 percent of the total, that area's "cultural

impact . . . especially in New Orleans and the lower Mississippi, was disproportionately enormous." See Gomez, *Exchanging Our Country Marks*, 31.

33. Hyatt, *Hoodoo—Conjuration—Witchcraft—Rootwork*; Puckett, *Folk Beliefs of the Southern Negro*.

34. Spencer, *Blues and Evil*, 10.

35. Pelton, *The Trickster in West Africa*, 163.

36. Garon, *The Devil's Son-in-Law*, 73.

CHAPTER 1

1. Pearson, *"Sounds So Good to Me,"* 153n19.

2. Quoted in ibid. See also Oakley, *The Devil's Music*, 47.

3. For more on Prohibition and bootlegging in Mississippi, see Calt, *I'd Rather Be the Devil*, 80–86.

4. O'Neal, Wisner, and Nelson, "Snooky Pryor," 11.

5. Quoted in Guralnick, *Searching for Robert Johnson*, 12.

6. Quoted in Richard, "The Crossroads and the Myth of the Mississippi Delta Bluesman," 23.

7. Morton is quoted in Giordano, *Satan in the Dance Hall*, 130. I discuss the artists listed in this paragraph in the remainder of the chapter, with the exception of the following. For John Cephas, see Pearson, *Jook Right On*, 107. For Nappy Brown, see ibid., 123. For Nat D. Williams, see Green, *Battling the Plantation Mentality*, 174. For Koko Taylor, see Aykroyd and Manilla, *Elwood's Blues*, 108–9. For Lonnie Pitchford, see Pearson, *Jook Right On*, 63. For Lillie Mae "Big Mama" Glover, see Scott, *Blues Empress in Black Chattanooga*, 106. Arvell Shaw, Louis Armstrong's longtime bassist, reported that his father, a Baptist preacher, condemned jazz as devil's music. See Barnhart, *The World of Jazz Trumpet*, 82.

8. Myrdal, *An American Dilemma*, 875.

9. Bebey, *African Music*, 26; Oliver, *Savannah Syncopators*, 98, 100; Oliver, "African Influence on the Blues," 13–17; Evans, "Africa and the Blues," 27–29; Cartwright, *Reading Africa into American Literature*, 9.

10. "In the wars over these issues in the early and mid-2000s," according to Tony Thomas, "it was established that very few if any griots/jales were ever enslaved in North America and there is no reliable record of a single one. West Africanists have long discredited Alex Haley's *Roots* as pure fiction on this issue." E-mail to Adam Gussow, January 9, 2015.

11. Duran, "POYI!," 232, 243n46.

12. Kubik, *Africa and the Blues*, 21.

13. Robert B. Winans's inventory of references to musical instruments in the WPA slave narratives found that "the most common instrument was clearly the fiddle, mentioned twice as often as the next instrument, the banjo." See Winans, "Black Instrumental Music Traditions in the Ex-slave Narratives," 43. See also Jenoure, "The Afro-American Fiddler," 68–81; DjeDje, *Fiddling in West Africa*; Wells, "Fiddling as an Avenue of Black-White Musical Interchange," 135–47.

14. Olofson, "Children of the Bowed Lute," 921–22.

15. Ames, "Igbo and Hausa Musicians," 250.

16. Gomez, "Muslims in Early America," 702.

17. Ames, "Igbo and Hausa Musicians," 272.

18. According to Mohammed Bashir Salau, author of *The West African Slave Plantation: A Case Study* (2011), the great majority of Hausa caught up in the slave trade ended up in Brazil, Cuba, or (when intercepted by the British Navy) Sierra Leone. "Overall, therefore," he concluded, "relatively few Hausa slaves would have made it to North America directly from Africa." E-mail to Adam Gussow, March 10, 2015.

19. Gomez, *Exchanging Our Country Marks*, 66.

20. Powell, *Three Richard Parkers of Va.*, 3–4. Also see Epstein, *Sinful Tunes and Spirituals*, 80. For an extended discussion of "devil's instruments," see Hinson, *Fire in My Bones*, 348–49.

21. Woods, *The Devil in Dog Form*, 66.

22. Rudwin, *The Devil in Legend and Literature*, 256.

23. Woods, *The Devil in Dog Form*, 66.

24. Swift, "Journal to Stella," 265.

25. Kawabata, "Virtuosity, the Violin, the Devil," 85–108, 189–90.

26. Epstein, *Sinful Tunes and Spirituals*, 100.

27. Jenoure, "The Afro-American Fiddler," 73.

28. Quoted in Epstein, *Sinful Tunes and Spirituals*, 207.

29. Quoted in Heyrman, *Southern Cross*, 56.

30. Quoted in Epstein, *Sinful Tunes and Spirituals*, 104.

31. Murphy, "The Survival of African Music in America," 662.

32. Quoted in Epstein, *Sinful Tunes and Spirituals*, 212.

33. Quoted in Clinkscales, *On the Old Plantation*, 8–12.

34. Epstein, *Sinful Tunes and Spirituals*, 114.

35. Northup, *Twelve Years a Slave*, 91.

36. Hazzard-Gordon, *Jookin'*, 78.

37. Quoted in Raboteau, *Slave Religion*, 222.

38. Quoted in Hazzard-Gordon, *Jookin'*, 78.

39. Genovese, *Roll, Jordan, Roll*, 218–19.

40. Quoted in Epstein, *Sinful Tunes and Spirituals*, 213.

41. Gomez, "Muslims in Early America," 261.

42. Bibb, *Narrative of the Life and Adventures of Henry Bibb*, 21, 23.

43. Allen, Ware, and Garrison, *Slave Songs of the United States*, x.

44. White southern fiddlers, like black southern fiddlers, generally found it easy to shake off evangelical disapproval and keep on playing. "In spite of the opposition to the 'Devil's Own Instrument,'" wrote one well-known fiddler of life the Ozarks in the 1970s, "fiddling has continued to flourish." Quoted in Halpert, "The Devil, the Fiddle, and Dancing," 46.

45. Cimbala, "Black Musicians from Slavery to Freedom," 15–29.

46. See Thomas, "Why Black Folks Don't Fiddle"; and Miller, *Segregating Sound*. Blues harmonica player Noah Lewis covered the traditional fiddler's reel, "Devil in the Woodpile" (1929), with his Memphis-based group, Cannon's Jug Stompers.

47. Lincoln and Mamiya, *The Black Church in the African American Experience*, 95.

48. Battle, *The Black Church in America*, 93.

49. Lincoln and Mamiya, *The Black Church in the African American Experience*, 28.

50. Sacré, "The Saints and the Sinners under the Swing of the Cross," 16.

51. Rev. Emmett Dickinson, "Is There Harm in Singing the Blues" (1930); "a Baptist preacher on Chicago's East Side": Wardlow, *Chasin' That Devil Music*, 157. Dickinson also recorded several other sermons that favorably reference a blues performer ("Death of Blind Lemon") and repurpose the title of a blues recording ("It Was Tight Like That"), but neither mentions blues music per se.

52. "The Sermon as Heard by Zora Neale Hurston from C. C. Lovelace, at Eau Gallie in Florida, May 3, 1929," 35.

53. Hughes, "My Adventures as a Social Poet," 217.

54. Handy, *Father of the Blues*, 15–16.

55. Robertson, *W. C. Handy*, 38–39. On Handy's father's AME affiliation and class ambitions, see Jackson, *Singing in My Soul*, 24.

56. Evans, "The Guitar in the Blues Music of the Deep South," 13.

57. Noonan, *The Guitar in America*, 11.

58. Abbott and Seroff, *Out of Sight*, 149, 186, 222, 223, 231–32, 254–55.

59. Broonzy, as told to Bruynoghe, *Big Bill Blues*, 35–36.

60. Lomax, *The Land Where the Blues Began*, 361.

61. Calt, *I'd Rather Be the Devil*, 168.

62. Gioia, *Delta Blues*, 165.

63. Wald, *Shout, Sister, Shout!*, 22–23.

64. Ferris, *The William R. Ferris Reader*, n.p.

65. Best, *Passionately Human, No Less Divine*, 114.

66. Jackson, *Singing in My Soul*, 24.

67. Pearson, *Jook Right On*, 120.

68. Collis, *The Story of Chess Records*, 53.

69. Gordon, *Can't Be Satisfied*, 16–17.

70. Ibid., 17.

71. Pearson, *"Sounds So Good to Me,"* 62.

72. Earl, "A Lifetime in the Blues," 6.

73. Lomax, *The Land Where the Blues Began*, 399.

74. Waters, as told to Duckett, "'Got a Right to Sing the Blues,'" 6.

75. O'Neal, "Jack Owens," 33.

76. Ibid., 33.

77. Smith, *"Let the Church Sing!,"* 34–35.

78. Alyn, *I Say Me for a Parable*, 52.

79. Quoted in Young, *Woke Me Up This Morning*, 234; "effectively ended her career as a blues performer": thanks to David Evans for this observation.

80. Quoted in Oliver, *Screening the Blues*, 46.

81. Tommy Johnson never recorded any songs invoking the devil; he merely told his brother LeDell—as LeDell recounts the story—that he had sold his soul to the devil.

82. Quoted in Pearson with Burns, "Cedell Davis," 34.

83. Franz, *The Amazing Secret History of Elmore James*, 24.

84. Moon, "Eddy Clearwater," 16.

85. Quoted in Tracy, *Going to Cincinnati*, 154–55.

86. On Goodson, see Davis, *Blues Legacies and Black Feminism*, 6–7. On Ellis, see Pearson, *"Sounds So Good to Me,"* 64. On Duskin, see notes 87–90, below. On Magee, see Gussow, *Mister Satan's Apprentice*, 207.

87. In Pearson, *Jook Right On*, 102–4.

88. Ibid., xii, 104.

89. Tracy, *Goin' to Cincinnati*, 104.

90. Ibid., 104–7.

91. Murray, *Boogie Man*, 25.

92. Sacré, "The Saints and Sinners under the Swing of the Cross," 16.

93. In Murray, *Boogie Man*, 28–28.

94. Ibid., 32–33.

95. Ibid.

96. Son House, "My Black Mama, Part I" (1930).

97. John Lee Hooker, "Burnin' Hell" (1949).

98. See Obrecht, "Eddie Guitar Burns," 29, 31.

99. Pareles, "From Cool to Exultant, with a Touch of Blue."

100. Murray, *Boogie Man*, 38.

101. Marcus, *Mystery Train*, 24.

102. Quoted in Pearson and McCulloch, *Robert Johnson: Lost and Found*, 22.

103. Spencer, *The Rhythms of Black Folk*, 159–60; Spencer, *Blues and Evil*, 10.

104. Wald, *Escaping the Delta*, 275.

105. Szwed, "Musical Adaptation among Afro-Americans," 118.

106. Sernett, *Bound for the Promised Land*, 76.

107. The Mississippi Sheiks, "He Calls That Religion" (1932).

108. Humphrey, "Prodigal Sons," 167. On the question of continuities between the performance practices and ritual roles of preachers and bluesmen, see Giggie, *After Redemption*, 54; Sacré, *Saints and Sinners*, ix–x, 14–16; and Lornell, "Barrelhouse Singers and Sanctified Preachers," 125–29.

109. Quoted in Otis, *Upside Your Head!*, 60. Also see Lipsitz, *Midnight at the Barrelhouse*, 109–15.

110. Quoted in Ferris, *Blues from the Delta*, 86.

111. Powdermaker, *After Freedom*, 269–70.

112. Johnson, *Growing Up in the Black Belt*, 164.

113. Walton, "The Preachers' Blues," 220.

114. The Gospeleers, "The Devil's Gonna Get You" (1941).

115. Harvey, *Redeeming the South*, 179.

116. Quoted in Anyabwile and Piper, *The Faithful Preacher*, 132.

117. Quoted in Harvey, *Redeeming the South*, 179. Bluesman Junior Wells complained in an interview about the fundraising imperative of the preacher's calling. See O'Neal, "Junior Wells," 12.

118. Montgomery, *Under Their Own Vine and Fig Tree*, 324.

119. Charles S. Johnson suggests that black southern preachers in the 1930s, rather than combining farming with ministry, "prefer to cover a circuit of churches and get the maximum out of each group," with the collection-plate process in rural churches lasting as long as two hours. "The average congregations of 75 or 100 will yield about

$3.00, except around [harvest] settlement time when there is more money in circulation." Johnson, *Growing Up in the Black Belt*, 145.

120. Edwards, as told to Martinson and Frank, *The World Don't Owe Me Nothing*, 73–74.

121. In Ferris, *Blues from the Delta*, 83.

122. Sernett, *Bound for the Promised Land*, 76.

123. Quoted in ibid., 76.

124. Marsh, "Superintendent's Report" (1923), n.p.

125. Clay, "Superintendent's Report" (1917), n.p. In the census of 1910, the "preacher/ district superintendent" Norman R. Clay lived in Holly Springs, Mississippi. In the census of 1920, the fifty-six-year-old Reverend N. R. Clay lived in Clarksdale. *Thirteenth Census of the United States, 1910—Clarksdale, Coahoma County, Mississippi; Fourteenth Census of the United States, 1920—Clarksdale, Coahoma County, Mississippi*.

126. Clay, "Superintendent's Report" (1919), n.p.

127. Clay, "Superintendent's Report" (1920), n.p.

128. Clay, "Superintendent's Report" (1921), n.p.

129. Edwards, as told to Martinson and Frank, *The World Don't Owe Me Nothing*, 212.

130. Handy, *Father of the Blues*, 78–79; "The New World," Mississippi Blues Trail.

131. Quoted in Calt and Wardlow, *King of the Delta Blues*, 59–63, esp. 63.

132. Marsh, "Superintendent's Report" (1923), n.p.

133. Myrdal, *An American Dilemma*, 939.

134. Quoted in Litwack, *Trouble in Mind*, 436–37.

135. In Lomax, *The Land Where the Blues Began*, 158.

136. Work, Jones, and Adams, *Lost Delta Found*, 34.

137. Ibid., 34. My discussion of the third and fourth black Delta generations—the blues generations—is indebted to Elijah Wald's discussion in *Escaping the Delta*, 86–92, esp. 90.

138. Work, Jones, and Adams, *Lost Delta Found*, 34–35.

139. Quoted in ibid., 279.

140. Quoted in ibid., 81–82.

141. Marcus, *Mystery Train*, 24.

142. Ibid., 24.

143. Powdermaker, *After Freedom*, 246, 284.

144. In Work, Jones, and Adams, *Lost Delta Found*, 83, 243.

145. Robert Johnson, "Me and the Devil Blues" (1937). This is take 1.

146. Marcus, *Mystery Train*, 24.

147. Banks, "The Devil and Robert Johnson," 27–31.

148. Wald, *Escaping the Delta*, 274.

149. See Michael Taft, "Pre-war Blues Lyrics: The Concordance," http://www.dylan61 .se/michael%20taft,%20blues%20anthology.txt.WebConcordance/c1.htm (accessed August 10, 2016).

150. Ted Gioia has made a similar claim. See Gioia, *Delta Blues*, 116.

151. See also Blind Will Dukes, "Me and the Devil" (1984), which rewrites Johnson's song in a way that configures the devil more explicitly as the singer's "mistreater" side: "I said that lowdown old devil . . . done run my baby 'way from home."

152. Work, Jones, and Adams, *Lost Delta Found*, 239. The phrase "pervasive skepticism

of the pretensiveness of the church" is credited in *Lost Delta Found*, n. 24, to sociologist Charles S. Johnson's study, *Shadow of the Plantation* (1934)

153. Memphis Jug Band, "Whitewash Station Blues" (1928).

154. Rev. David Hall makes this claim in the course of a longer statement about C. H. Mason. See Young, *Woke Me Up This Morning*, 223.

155. Butler, *Women in the Church of God in Christ*, 47.

156. Moore and Wright, *Children, Youth, and Spirituality in a Troubling World*, 202.

157. Spencer, *Rhythms of Black Folk*, 159–60.

CHAPTER 2

1. Quoted in Giordano, *Satan in the Dance Hall*, 129.

2. Smith was a special sort of southern migrant; for roughly a decade prior to her resettlement in New York, she had lived the highly mobile life of a vaudeville and tent show performer, most of it on the Theatre Owners' Booking Association (TOBA) circuit in the South and Midwest. See Harrison, *Black Pearls*, 240.

3. Ogren, *The Jazz Revolution*, 6.

4. Douglas, *Terrible Honesty*, 54.

5. For more on early blues singers touring the Mississippi Delta during the 1910s, see Abbott and Seroff, *Ragged but Right*, esp. 298–99.

6. Quoted in Dennison, *Scandalize My Name*, 460.

7. Paul Oliver argues that the satirized figure of the black preacher or deacon in blues song "follow[s] a tired formula which has long been a mainstay of vaudeville, minstrel-show and medicine-show humour" and is, in effect, a reconstituted and more socially acceptable version of the lustful, chicken-stealing "nigger" figure. Oliver, *Screening the Blues*, 75.

8. See, for example, "Why Mose Jackson Could Not Vote."

9. Sotiropoulos, *Staging Race*, 163.

10. DuBois, "The Problem of Amusement," 225–26.

11. Irving Berlin, "Pack Up Your Sins (and Go to the Devil)" (1922), in *America's Songs II*, 81–83.

12. Allen, *Only Yesterday*, 78.

13. Reed, *The Holy Profane*, 120.

14. Fats Waller, "There's Gonna Be the Devil to Pay" (1935).

15. Wald, *Escaping the Delta*, 59.

16. Dickerson, *Go, Girl, Go!*, 1–2.

17. In Armstrong, "Satchmo and Me," 108–10.

18. Hay, *Goin' Back to Sweet Memphis*, 29.

19. Harley, "'Working for Nothing but for a Living,'" 58–61.

20. Defaa, *Blue Rhythms*, 19–20.

21. Ward, *Just My Soul Responding*, 188.

22. Harrison, *Black Pearls*, 21–22.

23. Higginbotham, *Righteous Discontent*, 194–95.

24. Quoted in Wolcott, *Remaking Respectability*, 100.

25. Ibid.

26. Butler, *Women in the Church of God in Christ*, 77.

27. Quoted in Freeland, *Ladies of Soul*, 144.

28. Wolcott, *Remaking Respectability*, 110.

29. Butler, *Women in the Church of God in Christ*, 81.

30. Carby, "Policing the Black Woman's Body in an Urban Context," 739.

31. Quoted in Sernett, *Bound for the Promised Land*, 16.

32. Clement, *Love for Sale*, 202, 209.

33. Wolcott, *Remaking Respectability*, 110.

34. Baker, *Blues, Ideology, and Afro-American Literature*, 13.

35. Grainger accompanied Smith on piano as well as composing the song. Columbia matrix 140076. "Done Sold My Soul to the Devil (And My Heart's Done Turned to Stone)/ Clara Smith," Discography of American Historical Recordings.

Grainger filed copyright for the song on October 2, 1924; copyright was renewed by his daughter Portia on December 11, 1951. See http://composers-classical-music.com/g/ GraingerPorter.htm and https://archive.org/details/catalogofcopyrig355libr (accessed August 10, 2016).

36. Clara Smith, "Done Sold My Soul to the Devil" (1924).

37. Spencer, *Blues and Evil*, 33.

38. MacKell and Noel, *Brothels, Bordellos, and Bad Girls*, 287.

39. See, for example, Bobbie Cadillac, "Carbolic Acid Blues" (1928).

40. Cannon, "Sexing Black Women," 12.

41. Drowne, *Spirits of Defiance*, 24.

42. Wolcott, *Remaking Respectability*, 103.

43. Quoted in Drowne, *Spirits of Defiance*, 103.

44. Douglas, *Terrible Honesty*, 410.

45. Quoted in Giordano, *Satan in the Dance Hall*, 136.

46. Allen, *Only Yesterday*, 78.

47. Carby, "Policing the Black Woman's Body in an Urban Context," 754–55.

48. Conforth, *African American Folksong*, 48–49; Odum and Johnson, *Negro Workaday Songs*, 157–58.

49. Odum, *Wings on My Feet*, 29–30.

50. Dave Edwards was the ensemble's manager. See https://books.google.com/books?id =Artpinv44boC&pg=PA44&lpg=PA44&dq=dave+edwards+%22guy+cotton+thompson %22&source=bl&ots=yagoKMCDXt&sig=P_x-9bArndbDnCkkU3LvxuHAwEA&hl =en&sa=X&ved=0ahUKEwi9oczPn7fOAhVHbiYKHVkNDP4Q6AEIKTAD#v=one page&q=dave%20edwards%20%22guy%20cotton%20thompson%22&f=false (accessed August 10, 2016).

51. Dave Edwards and His Alabama Boys, "Done Sold My Soul to the Devil" (1937).

52. Casey Bill Weldon, "Sold My Soul to the Devil" (1937).

53. See O'Neal, "Unraveling Casey Bill," 72–77; Marshall, "Headstone Campaign Raising Funds for Casey Bill Weldon." See also "Will Weldon," in Eagle and LeBlanc, *Blues*, 218.

54. John D. Twitty (Black Spider Dumpling), "Sold It to the Devil" (1937).

55. Clement, *Love for Sale*.

56. The Yas Yas Girl (Merline Johnson), "Sold It to the Devil" (1937).

57. "Merline Johnson," Allmusic, http://www.allmusic.com/artist/merline-johnson -mn0000447148/biography (accessed August 10, 2016).

58. Hazzard-Gordon, *Jookin'*.

59. Quoted in Giordano, *Satan in the Dance Hall*, 53, 55–56.

60. Harrison, *Black Pearls*, 116.

61. Sippie Wallace, "Devil Dance Blues" (1925).

62. Odum, *Religious Folk-Songs of the Southern Negroes*, 21.

63. Quoted in Giordano, *Satan in the Dance Hall*, 177.

64. Quoted in Ogren, *The Jazz Revolution*, 84–85.

65. Cressey, *The Taxi-Dance Hall*, 222–23.

66. Quoted in Giordano, *Satan in the Dance Hall*, 55.

67. Hunter, "'Sexual Pantomimes,'" 150–51.

68. Quoted in Walser, *Keeping Time*, 32.

69. Quoted in Giordano, *Satan in the Dance Hall*, 48. Also see Hunter, *To 'Joy My Freedom*.

70. Quoted in Higginbotham, *Righteous Discontent*, 199.

71. Quoted in ibid., 199.

72. Quoted in Collier-Thomas, *Daughters of Thunder*, 191.

73. Quoted in ibid., 162.

74. Quoted in Drake and Cayton, *Black Metropolis*, 637.

75. Oliver, *Songsters and Saints*, 150.

76. Rev. A. W. Nix, "Black Diamond Express to Hell, Part 2" (1927).

77. Quoted in Giordano, *Satan in the Dance Hall*, xiii.

78. Quoted in ibid., xiii.

79. Quoted in ibid., 129.

80. Ibid., 173–74.

81. Fess Williams, "I'm Feelin' Devilish," words and music by Maceo Pinkhard (1930).

82. Gertrude "Ma" Rainey, "Hellish Rag" (1927).

83. Malone, *Steppin' on the Blues*, 31.

84. Hunter, "Sexual Pantomimes," 152.

85. Sotiropoulos, *Staging Race*, 9.

86. Quoted in Allen, *Only Yesterday*, 66.

CHAPTER 3

1. Haley, "Malcolm X to Alex Haley."

2. Walker, "David Walker's *Appeal*," 189.

3. Walker, "Walker's *Appeal*, with a Brief Sketch of His Life by Henry Highland Garnett."

4. Douglass, *Narrative of the Life of Frederick Douglass*, 310.

5. Ibid., 309.

6. Baker, *Turning South Again*, 93.

7. Cecil Brown, invoking the words of Ben Sidran, makes a similar claim, stressing the threatening badman side of the black devil rather than his shifty and uncontrollable trickster side. "Thus the black oral culture fused the two apparently contradictory no-

tions of the devil as a white man and the devil as a 'bad nigger,' the free and independent black man who brought fear to the white culture through threat of physical and/or psychological violence." Brown, *Staggolee Shot Billy*, 170.

8. Spencer, *Blues and Evil*, xiv.

9. Quoted in Cone, *The Spirituals and the Blues*, 73.

10. Dollard, *Caste and Class in a Southern Town*, 303–5. See Lott, *Love and Theft*.

11. Lightnin' Hopkins, "The Devil Jumped the Black Man" (1962).

12. Allen, Ware, and Garrison, *Slave Songs of the United States*, 40.

13. Wells-Barnett, The Project Gutenberg eBook of *The Red Record*; Tolnay and Beck, *A Festival of Violence*, 47.

14. Quoted in Carr, *Our Town*, 122.

15. Spencer, *Blues and Evil*, 119.

16. Lovell, "The Social Implications of the Negro Spiritual," 642.

17. Levine, *Black Culture and Black Consciousness*, 160. See also Genovese, *Roll, Jordan, Roll*, 219; Spencer, *Blues and Evil*, 91; and Boots, *Singing for Equality*, 173–74.

18. Lizzie McCloud, quoted in Escott, *Slavery Remembered*, 99; Callie Elder, quoted in Dunaway, *Women, Work, and Family in the Antebellum Mountain South*, 83; James Lucas, quoted in Barnwell, *A Place Called Mississippi*, 60.

19. Sunnyland Slim (Albert Luandrew), "Couldn't Find a Mule" (1973). Several verses in this song seem to have been adapted from "Texas" Alexander, "Levee Camp Moan" (1927).

20. Sunnyland Slim (Albert Luandrew), "The Devil Is a Busy Man" (1954).

21. Champion Jack Dupree, "My Home's in Hell" (1968), BH-7702. The last two verses of this song seem to gesture at a well-known black folktale in which God, at the dawn of creation, asks mankind to wash in the River of Life. Everybody promptly follows his order—except the Negroes (goes the story), who dally so long that when they arrive at the river, all the water is gone, the white people are *very* white, and all that's left for bathing in is mud. See Hughes, "No Color Line in Hell," 65–66; and Sam Chatmon, "God Don't Like Ugly" (1973).

22. Reid, "Champion Jack Dupree Remembered," http://www.elsewhere.co.nz/blues/4700/champion-jack-dupree-remembered-seconds-out-of-the-ring/ (accessed August 10, 2016).

23. Interview with Champion Jack Dupree, "Born under a Bad Sign."

24. Champion Jack Dupree, "I'm Going to Write the Governor of Georgia" (1946, unissued in Dupree's lifetime).

25. Van Rijn, *The Truman and Eisenhower Blues*, 53–55.

26. Cone, *The Spirituals and the Blues*, 72–73.

27. These verses are taken from Odum and Johnson, *The Negro and His Songs*, 23, 47, 77; and Levine, *Black Culture and Black Consciousness*, 40.

28. Hopkins, "Slave Theology in the 'Invisible Institution,'" 810.

29. Quoted in Botkin, *Lay My Burden Down*, 163.

30. Quoted in Blackmon, *Slavery by Another Name*, 134.

31. Quoted in Litwack, *Been in the Storm So Long*, 224.

32. Quoted in Raboteau, *Slave Religion*, 297.

33. Quoted in ibid.

34. Quoted in McMillen, *Dark Journey*, 127.

35. Quoted in Epstein, *Sinful Tunes and Spirituals*, 220.

36. Quoted in Gussow, *Seems Like Murder Here*, 6.

37. Quoted in Ortiz, *Emancipation Betrayed*, 61.

38. Oshinsky, *"Worse Than Slavery"*; Blackmon, *Slavery by Another Name*; Fierce, *Slavery Revisited*; McMillen, *Dark Journey*. Also see Childs, "'You Ain't Seen Nothin' Yet.'"

39. Baker, *Turning South Again*, 93.

40. Mancini, *One Dies, Get Another*, 121.

41. Holland, *From the Mississippi Delta*, 256.

42. Cone, *The Spirituals and the Blues*, 119.

43. King, with Ritz, *Blues All around Me*, 54. According to biographer Charles Sawyer, the young black man in question had actually been electrocuted by the state of Mississippi—victim of a so-called legal lynching—and then "placed out on the courthouse steps for public viewing." See Sawyer, *The Arrival of B. B. King*, 49.

44. Although Broonzy sang the song in public during the late 1940s, it remained unrecorded until 1951 and unreleased in the United States until just after his death in 1958. See van Rijn, *The Truman and Eisenhower Blues*, 166n14.

45. Quoted in liner notes (n.p.), *Blues in the Mississippi Night*.

46. Big Bill Broonzy, "Hell Ain't but a Mile and a Quarter" (1938).

47. Saxon, Dreyer, Tallent, *Gumbo Ya-Ya*, 273.

48. Broonzy, as told to Bruynoghe, *Big Bill Blues*, 108.

49. Information for the recording date that produced "Hell Ain't but a Mile and a Quarter" can be found in House, *Blue Smoke*, 173.

50. Dray, *At the Hands of Persons Unknown*, 359–61.

51. "Can the States Stop Lynching?," 9.

52. Broonzy, as told to Bruynoghe, *Big Bill Blues*, 88–89.

53. Riesman, *I Feel So Good*, 224.

54. Ibid., 35. See also Mikkelsen, "Coming from Battle to Face a War."

55. Congress, *Blues Mandolin Man*, 56.

56. Quoted in Alyn, *I Say Me for a Parable*, 111–12.

57. Quoted in Whiteis, "Club Dates."

58. As a focus of renegade black desire, the devil's daughter figure in "Hell Ain't but a Mile and a Quarter" is part of a cultural tradition with roots in the slavery era. Broonzy's persona in the song incorporates elements of High John the Conqueror, a black folk hero who is born in Africa but manages to thrive on the plantation, in part because he's brazen enough to claim the devil's daughter as his own. See Hurston, "High John de Conquer," 100; and Levine, *Black Culture and Black Consciousness*, 331, 403. High John also reappears in the form of Stagolee—the most charismatic and popular black southern badman of the post-Reconstruction period, one whose lyric incarnations are cousin to Broonzy's somewhat less violent bluesman. "Stackolee took his big pistol and put it on de shelf," goes one version, "Took de pitchfork from de devil an' say, 'I'm put in charge of hell myself.'" See Brown, *Stagolee Shot Billy*, 163. In "Hell Ain't but a Mile and a Quarter," Broonzy puts the devil's daughter on the shelf, not a handgun. This may be the song's way of signifying on the dangers posed by the white woman to an audience that would have been broadly familiar with Stagolee folklore.

59. Recording by Alan Lomax, c. May 1952, in Riesman, *I Feel So Good*, 177.

60. Broonzy, as told to Bruynoghe, *Big Bill Blues*, 89.

61. Spencer, *Blues and Evil*, 7.

62. Smith, "Blues, Criticism, and the Signifying Trickster," 182.

63. Richard, "The Crossroads and the Myth of the Mississippi Delta Bluesman," 23; Garon, *The Devil's Son-in-Law*, 115.

64. Spencer, *Blues and Evil*, 12.

65. Stovepipe Johnson, "Devilish Blues" (1928).

66. "County farm" is common vernacular for a certain kind of agriculture-based, self-supporting penal institution in the American South. See Little, "Prison Lingo," 206.

67. Edwards, as told to Martinson and Frank, *The World Don't Owe Me Nothing*, 47.

68. Mississippi Sheiks, "I Am the Devil" (1934).

69. Sylvester Weaver, "Devil Blues" (1927).

70. Sylvester Weaver, "Can't Be Trusted Blues" (1927).

71. Spencer, *Blues and Evil*, 12. (The phrase is Spencer's, not Oliver's.)

72. Dulaney, *Black Police in America*.

73. Johnny Copeland, "Devil's Hand" (1982).

74. Friesen, "The Rev. Frederick Douglass Kirkpatrick."

75. Baker, *Blues, Ideology, and Afro-American Literature*, 13.

76. Odum and Johnson, *The Negro and His Songs*, 41.

77. Lovell, *Black Song*, 304.

78. Gussow, *Seems Like Murder Here*, 17–65.

79. Lipscomb, quoted in Alyn, *I Say Me for a Parable*, 306; Rush, quoted in Obrecht, "*Been Some Powerful Stuff Happen to Me*," 21; Dixon, *I Am the Blues*, 20.

80. Garon, *The Devil's Son-in-Law*, 114.

81. Tracy, "The Devil's Son-in-Law and *Invisible Man*," 56.

82. Brownderville, *Deep down in the Delta*, 66.

83. Garon, *The Devil's Son-in-Law*, 9.

84. Townsend, as told to Greensmith, *A Blues Life*, 62.

85. Peetie Wheatstraw, "Drinking Man Blues" (1936).

86. Peetie Wheatstraw, "C and A Train Blues" (1934).

87. Garon, *Devil's Son-in-Law*, 115.

88. Spencer, *Blues and Evil*, 9.

89. Garon, *The Devil's Son-in-Law*, 114.

90. Quoted in ibid., 73.

91. Scott, *Domination and the Arts of Resistance*, 183–201, esp. 198.

92. Tracy, "The Devil's Son-in-Law and *Invisible Man*," 48.

93. Peetie Wheatstraw, "Devil's Son-in-Law" (1931).

94. Baker, *Blues, Ideology, and Afro-American Literature*, 5.

95. Peetie Wheatstraw, "Peetie Wheatstraw Stomp" (1937).

96. Peetie Wheatstraw, "Peetie Wheatstraw Stomp No. 2" (1937).

97. Himes, "Musician Willie King Mixes Politics with Blues."

98. *Straight outta Compton* was produced by Ruthless Records and distributed by Priority Records, which in 1996 was purchased by EMI.

99. Jones, *"Dutchman" and "The Slave*," 35.

100. For a notable exception, see Willie King, "Terrorized," http://www.amazon.com/Terrorized/dp/B001BJEGSG (accessed August 10, 2016).

101. King, "Mississippi KKKrossroads" (2002). Lyrics provided by King and used with his permission.

102. Howlin' Wolf, "Back Door Man"; Robert Johnson, "Cross Road Blues" (1936); John Lee Hooker, "I'm Bad Like Jesse James"; Nina Simone, "Mississippi Goddamn"; Marvin Gaye, "Let's Get It On"; George Thorogood, "Bad to the Bone."

103. Guy Davis, "I Got the Power" (1996).

104. Davis and Dee, *With Ossie and Ruby*, 8.

CHAPTER 4

1. Davis, *Blues Legacies and Black Feminism*, 4.

2. Hartman, *Scenes of Subjection*, 84.

3. Davis, *Blues Legacies and Black Feminism*, 8.

4. Quoted in Spencer, *Blues and Evil*, 57.

5. Quoted in Cone, *The Spirituals and the Blues*, 115.

6. Davis, *Blues Legacies and Black Feminism*, 9.

7. Bessie Smith, "You've Got to Give Me Some" (1929).

8. The phrase is Spencer's in *Blues and Evil*, 51.

9. "Young Devil" (1994) by Phillip Walker and Otis Grand is the exception that proves the rule: a blues song about a thoroughly satisfying devil-woman. "She just my type . . . just my speed / She always give me . . . anything I need."

10. Quoted in Beaumont, *Preachin' the Blues*, 174–75.

11. Spencer, *Blues and Evil*, 139.

12. Ibid., 126–27.

13. Ibid., 125.

14. Spencer, *Blues and Evil*, xxii–xxiii.

15. Blassingame, *The Slave Community*, 162.

16. Ibid., 165.

17. Foster, *'Til Death or Distance Do Us Part*, 22, 36.

18. Gutman, *The Black Family in Slavery and Freedom*, 455–56.

19. Johnson, *Growing Up in the Black Belt*, 73.

20. Edwards, as told to Martinson and Frank, *The World Don't Owe Me Nothing*, 121.

21. Bumble Bee Slim (Amos Easton), "Busy Devil" (1934).

22. Pelton, *The Trickster in West Africa*, 130.

23. Leroy's Buddy (Bill Gaither), "If I Was the Devil" (1939).

24. Edwards, as told to Martinson and Frank, *The World Don't Owe Me Nothing*, 121.

25. Powdermaker, *After Freedom*, 170.

26. Ibid., 193.

27. Lightnin' Hopkins, "Devil Is Watching You" (1962).

28. White, "'The Blues Ain't Nothin','" 1.

29. Ibid., 3.

30. Lonnie Johnson, "Sam, You're Just a Rat" (1932).

31. Robert Peeples, "Wicked Devil's Blues" (1929).

32. Peetie Wheatstraw, "Sweet Home Blues" (1936).

33. Spencer, *Blues and Evil*, 19–26.

34. Gruver, "The Blues as a Secular Religion," 229.

35. Blind Boy Fuller, "Crooked Woman Blues" (1940). For additional examples of the devil-or-angel conceit, see The Clovers, "Devil or Angel" (1956); Kenny Neal, "Devil Child" (1989); and Little Joe Blue, "Devil in Disguise" (1996).

36. Alger, *The Original Guitar Hero and the Power of Music*, 52–53.

37. Ibid., 66–69.

38. Davis, *The History of the Blues*, 146.

39. Pearson and McCulloch, *Robert Johnson: Lost and Found*, 66.

40. Lonnie Johnson, "She's Making Whoopee in Hell Tonight" (1930). See also King Solomon Hill, "Whoopee Blues" (1932).

41. Walter Donaldson/Gus Kahn, "Makin' Whoopee" (1928), http://lyrics.wikia.com/ Eddie_Cantor:Makin%27_Whoopee (accessed August 10, 2016).

42. Pearson, "Standing at the Crossroads," 222.

43. Lonnie Johnson, "The Devil's Woman" (1942).

44. Lonnie Johnson, "She Devil" (1960).

45. Washboard Sam, "She Belongs to the Devil" (1941).

46. Mississippi Sheiks, "Shake Hands and Tell Me Goodbye" (1931).

47. The Mississippi Moaner (Isaiah Nettles), "Mississippi Moan" (1935).

48. White, "'The Blues Ain't Nothin,'" 5.

49. Papa Charlie Jackson, "The Cat's Got the Measles" (1925).

50. "Texas" Alexander, "Blue Devil Blues" (1928).

51. Winborn, *Deep Blues*, 31–32.

52. John Lee "Sonny Boy" Williamson, "Deep Down in the Ground" (1938).

53. Sleepy John Estes, "Stack o' Dollars" (1930).

54. Cushing, *Blues before Sunrise*, 138. Kim Field claims that Gillum was killed in a shooting. Field, *Harmonicas, Harps, and Heavy Breathers*, 167–68.

55. Bloomfield with Summerville, *Me and Big Joe*, n.p.

56. Bill "Jazz" Gillum, "The Devil Blues" (1947).

57. Edwards, as told to Martinson and Frank, *The World Don't Owe Me Nothing*, 121.

58. Calt, *I'd Rather Be the Devil*, 107.

59. Ibid., 111.

60. Skip James, "Devil Got My Woman" (1931).

61. Skip James, "Devil Got My Woman" (1966).

62. Tommy McClennan, "Whiskey Headed Woman" (1939).

63. John Lee "Sonny Boy" Williamson, "I Been Dealing with the Devil" (1940).

64. Davis, *Blues Legacies and Black Feminism*, 15.

65. Hurston, "Characteristics of Negro Expression," 65.

66. Novelist and performance artist Sharon Bridgforth offers a notable exception in *Delta Dandi*, a "performance novel" that focuses on women of the black diaspora and features a character (or presence) named Seer, a spirit of the crossroads. See Lara, "'i think i might be broken.'"

67. Hurston, *Their Eyes Were Watching God*, 103.

68. Bessie Smith, "Devil's Gonna Get You" (1928).

69. See Chinn, "The Pulpit and the Pew," esp. 285–89. Of the principal African American denominations, only the AME Zion church was open to ordaining female preachers, doing so for the first time in the mid-1890s. The AME church, by contrast, refused women full ordination until 1948, and the CME church did not ordain them until 1954. COGIC, meanwhile, continued as late as the 1980s to have "a firm policy stand against the full ordination of women as clergy," although the widow of a minister was sometimes given tacit permission to complete, unordained, the ministry of her late husband.

70. Koko Taylor, "The Devil's Gonna Have a Field Day" (1987).

71. Delbanco, *The Death of Satan*, 26.

72. Spencer, *The Rhythms of Black Folk*, 163.

73. See Bob Groom, 4–5, in www.wirz.de/music/shortjd/grafik/groom1.pdf. Also see Ferris, *Blues from the Delta*, 77. Many hoodoo practitioners, of course, were women; the female equivalent to Short's sexual braggadocio in "Snake Doctor Blues" is Merline Johnson's "Black Gypsy Blues" (1940), which uses fortune-telling—a conjure woman who "know[s] what to do"—as a metaphor for sexual healing. More commonly, male and female blues singers (such as Memphis Minnie with "Hoodoo Lady Blues") sing songs about conjure women who throw sexual "fixes" on the unlucky, destroying their sexual potency. See "Show 41: Hoodoo Women," http://uncensoredhistoryoftheblues .purplebeech.com/2009/03/show-41-hoodoo-women.html (accessed August 10, 2016).

74. Jackson, *A Bad Woman Feeling Good*, 67.

75. Braziel, "'Bye, Bye Baby,'" 9–10.

76. Harrison, *Black Pearls*, 75–76.

77. Bessie Smith, "Black Mountain Blues" (1930).

78. Ralph Ellison, "Richard Wright's Blues," 104.

79. Bessie Smith, "Dyin' by the Hour" (1927).

80. Georgia White, "Your Hellish Ways" (1936).

81. Bessie Smith and Her Blue Boys, "Send Me to the 'Lectric Chair" (1927).

82. Gertrude "Ma" Rainey, "Rough and Tumble Blues" (1925). For Mo'Nique, see http:// www.youtube.com/watch?v=t1XO10Nx6eE (accessed August 10, 2016).

83. Denise LaSalle, "Hell Sent Me You" (2007).

84. http://www.indemandtalent.com/talent/artist.php?id=424 (accessed July 17, 2015).

85. Pinn, "When Demons Come Calling," 63–64.

86. Salaam, *What Is Life*, 14.

CHAPTER 5

1. "James Dean of the blues": DiGiacomo, "Searching for Robert Johnson," 206.

2. "Educated, secular Americans": Rothenbuhler, "The Myth of Robert Johnson"; "literacy skills": Copeland and Goering, "Blues You Can Use," 436; "simple reality": Pearson and McCulloch, *Robert Johnson: Lost and Found*, x–ix.

3. Cousin Leroy (Rozier), "Crossroads" (1957).

4. Tomko, "Look for Me and I'll Be Gone," 8–9.

5. For the sake of focus I have summarized a much more extensive scholarly debate about the cultural origins of the crossroads devil in the blues tradition. See Pelton, *The Trickster in West Africa*, 87–88, 127–30; Reed, *The Holy Profane*, 1–2; Thompson, *Flash*

of the Spirit, 19; Farrow, *Faith, Fancies, and Fetich or Yoruba Paganism*, 13, 23, 85–86; Messadié, *A History of the Devil*, 183–85; Kubik, *Africa and the Blues*, 21; Evans, "Demythologizing the Blues"; and Spencer, *Blues and Evil*, 26–30.

6. Brisbin, "Jimmy Rogers," 15.

7. Wardlow, *Chasin' That Devil Music*, 197.

8. Pearson and McCulloch, *Robert Johnson: Lost and Found*, 30–31; Welding, "Hell Hound on His Trail,"16.

9. Danaher, "Subculture and Myth," 300.

10. Welding, "Hell Hound on His Trail," 17.

11. Blesh, *Shining Trumpets*, 121–22; Charters, *The Country Bluesmen*, 210; Wald, *Escaping the Delta*, 266.

12. Pearson and McCulloch, *Robert Johnson: Lost and Found*, 4; Palmer, *Deep Blues*; Guralnick, *Searching for Robert Johnson*; Finn, *The Bluesman*.

13. Brackett, "Preaching Blues," 114.

14. Evans, *Tommy Johnson*, 22–23.

15. Wardlow, *Chasin' That Devil Music*, 197.

16. Evans, *Tommy Johnson*, 89.

17. Beaumont, *Preachin' the Blues*, 175.

18. Puckett, *Folk Beliefs of the Southern Negro*; Hyatt, *Hoodoo—Conjuration—Witchcraft—Rootwork*, esp. 97–111.

19. Puckett, *Folk Beliefs of the Southern Negro*, 550–51.

20. Hyatt, *Hoodoo—Conjuration—Witchcraft—Rootwork*, 104.

21. Ibid., 105.

22. Ibid., 100.

23. Quoted in Herskovits, *The Myth of the Negro Past*, 252.

24. Ibid., 252–53.

25. See Rudwin, *The Devil in Legend and Literature*, 169–70; Garry and El-Shamy, "Choice of Roads."

26. Floyd, *The Power of Black Music*, 73–74.

27. Marcus, *Mystery Train*, 24. For McCormick's "stated position," see Hunt, *The Search for Robert Johnson*.

28. Son House, interview with John Fahey. Quoted in Wald, *Escaping the Delta*, 110.

29. LaVere argues that Johnson didn't return to the Delta until "late 1933." I'll say more about this in part 3 of this chapter.

30. LaVere, "A Biography" (liner notes); Gioia, *Delta Blues*, 171.

31. Conforth, "Ike Zimmerman," 68–73. The quotes used here are taken from an earlier version of the essay downloaded from Academia.edu.

32. Maynard, "Bruce Conforth."

33. See The Delta Blues (website): http://www.tdblues.com/2011/10/ike-zimmerman-more-details-around-the-legend/ (accessed September 20, 2014).

34. Quoted in Conforth, "Ike Zimmerman," 6–7.

35. Ibid., 10.

36. Ibid., 9–10.

37. Hazzard-Donald, *Mojo Workin'*, 84, 92.

38. Powdermaker, *After Freedom*, 296.

39. Quoted in Pearson and McCulloch, *Robert Johnson: Lost and Found*, 101.

40. Finn, *The Bluesman*, 220.

41. Quoted in Conforth, "Ike Zimmerman," 8.

42. Goffman, *The Presentation of Self in Everyday Life*, 84–85.

43. Quoted in Becker, "The Professional Dance Musician and His Audience," 143–44.

44. Pearson and McCulloch, *Robert Johnson: Lost and Found*, 110.

45. Willie Coffee interview with Stephen LaVere, in *Hellhounds on My Trail* (documentary).

46. Alan Lomax, "Fisk, 3. 5. Dave Edwards."

47. Gioia, *Delta Blues*, 164.

48. Paul Trynka interview with Honeyboy Edwards, excerpted in e-mail to Adam Gussow, June 24, 2013. A lightly edited version of this interview can be found in Trynka, *Portrait of the Blues*, 38.

49. Quoted in Hunt, *The Search for Robert Johnson*.

50. Schroeder, *Robert Johnson*, 31–32.

51. Trynka, e-mail to Adam Gussow, June 24, 2013.

52. Quoted in Pearson and McCulloch, *Robert Johnson: Lost and Found*, 101.

53. King, *I'm Feeling the Blues Right Now*, 97.

54. Goffman, *The Presentation of Self in Everyday Life*, 85.

55. Quoted in Hunt, *The Search for Robert Johnson*.

56. Pearson and McCulloch, *Robert Johnson: Lost and Found*, 98.

57. O'Neal, "The Death of Robert Johnson," 24.

58. Pearson and McCulloch misidentify the location of the Leonard-Hearns encounter as Greenwood, Mississippi. See Pearson and McCulloch, *Robert Johnson: Lost and Found*, 97.

59. Interview with LaVere, in *Hellhounds on My Trail*.

60. Quoted in Guralnick, *Searching for Robert Johnson*, 59.

61. Karlos K. Hill has recently argued that "Hellhound on My Trail" "can be understood as a lynching ballad that describes grassroots responses to lynching, such as flight and the anxieties that arise from perpetually fleeing lynch mob violence. See Hill, "Robert Johnson's 'Hellhound on My Trail' as a Lynching Ballad."

62. Interview with LaVere, in *Hellhounds on My Trail*.

63. Quoted in Obrecht, *Blues Guitar*, 8.

64. Wald, *Escaping the Delta*, 131.

65. Pearson and McCulloch, *Robert Johnson: Lost and Found*, 27.

66. Ibid., 29.

67. Robert Johnson, "Cross Road Blues" (alternate take, 1961).

68. Robert Johnson, "Cross Road Blues" (1937).

69. Guralnick, *Searching for Robert Johnson*, 38.

70. DeSalvo, *The Language of the Blues*, 55; Evans, "Early Deep South and Mississippi Basin Blues," quoted in Rudinow, *Soul Music*, 40.

71. "Robert Johnson, Every Time He'd Get Drunk He'd Cuss God," 15.

72. Pearson, "Standing at the Crossroads," 222.

73. Evans, "Ramblin': Robert Johnson and the Supernatural, Part 3," 13.

74. Wald, *Escaping the Delta*, 152.

75. Gioia, *Delta Blues*, 179.

76. Robert Johnson, "They're Red Hot" (1937).

77. Gioia, *Delta Blues*, 179–80.

78. Robert Johnson, "From Four Until Late" (1937).

79. Wald, *Escaping the Delta*, 171.

80. Gioia, *Delta Blues*, 181.

81. Quoted in Earl, *Dark Symbols, Obscure Signs*, 59–60.

82. Gioia, "Did Robert Johnson Sell His Soul to the Devil?"

83. Hazzard-Donald, *Mojo Workin'*, 99.

84. Ibid., 98.

85. Robert Johnson, "Hell Hound on My Trail" (1937).

86. Kellett, "Fathers and Sons."

87. Quoted in Guralnick, *Searching for Robert Johnson*, 24.

88. Robert Johnson, "Malted Milk" (1937).

89. Kempley, "'Crossroads,'" 27; Salem, "Bluesy Superkid Leaves a Sync-ing Sensation."

90. Pearson and McCulloch, *Robert Johnson: Lost and Found*, 100; Lipsitz, *The Possessive Investment in Whiteness*, 120–21; Fitzsimmons, "'Hellhound on My Trail,'" 175; Schroeder, *Robert Johnson*, 95.

91. Schroeder, *Robert Johnson*, 98; Fitzsimmons, "'Hellhound on My Trail'": 181; Fusco, phone interview, July 22, 2013.

92. Roth, phone interview, July 15, 2013.

93. There was, of course, another American blues scene in existence at the time: the remnants of the so-called chitlin' circuit, in which African American performers such as Z. Z. Hill, Little Milton, Bobby Rush, and Denise LaSalle performed before black audiences and got airplay on black radio. This black blues scene, although unknown to most white blues fans (and especially to blues-rock fans), received significant coverage in *Living Blues*.

94. The prelude to all this was the notable expansion of the white rock-blues scene between 1965 and 1970: inaugurated by the British blues invasion, powered by the success of the Butterfield Blues Band and Cream, and culminating with a June 1969 show at Madison Square Garden featuring Janis Joplin, Paul Butterfield, and Johnny Winter—an apotheosis celebrated by Albert Goldman in a *New York Times* article titled "Why Do Whites Sing Black?" and excoriated by Black Arts spokesman Stephen C. Henderson. The crisis being explored here took a while to arrive. See Gussow, "'If Bessie Smith Had Killed Some White People,'" esp. 238–40.

95. O'Neal, "Muddy Waters," 10; Palmer, "Muddy Waters, Blues Performer, Dies," 44; "Thousand Fans Attend Rites for Muddy Waters," 15.

96. For comments on Stevie Ray Vaughan first meeting Albert King at Antone's at the age of nineteen, see Kot, "Jimmie Vaughan."

97. Aschoff and Aschoff, "1984 Delta Blues Festival," 43.

98. Miller, "Bad Luck Is Good Luck for Bluesman."

99. See, for example, Neal, "A Review-Essay," 43–47.

100. "Crossroads" (*Living Blues*). The tastes of Vaughan's fan base would have been prejudiced against heavy metal theatrics by the sort of coverage Vaughan's no-nonsense

stagecraft was receiving in the guitar magazines. "He has no light show to speak of, no dry ice, no fog, no lasers," wrote Bill Milkowski in *Guitar World*. "He doesn't go in for the leather-and-studs macho posturing of popular heavy metal bands." See Milkowski, "Stevie Ray Vaughan."

101. The Eighties Club website, http://eightiesclub.tripod.com/id137.htm (accessed August 10, 2016).

102. Browning, "Stevie Vuaghan's [*sic*] Awesome Bebut [*sic*]"; Niester, "Bluesman Impressive but Something Missing."

103. Kerrigan, "1984 W. C. Handy Blues Awards Show," 40.

104. O'Neal, "Handy Awards Forum," 14–15.

105. Varner, "*Living Blues* Interview," 25.

106. "Incredulity toward metanarratives": Lyotard, *The Postmodern Condition*. For two versions of the "blues is black music" argument, see Harris, "Can White People Play the Blues?," and Garon, "White Blues." For counterstatements to that view, see Leitch, "Blues Southwestern Style"; Bertrand, *Race, Rock, and Elvis*; Urban with Evdokimov, *Russia Gets the Blues*; and Gussow, "'If Bessie Smith Had Killed Some White People," 227–52. For the Blues Hall of Fame inductees list, see http://www.blues.org/hall-of-fame/performers-in-the-blues-hall-of-fame/.

107. Documentaries include *The Search for Robert Johnson* (1992), *Can't You Hear the Wind Howl* (1998), and *Hellhounds on My Trail: The Afterlife of Robert Johnson* (1999). Tribute albums include John Hammond Jr., *At the Crossroads* (2003); Eric Clapton, *Me and Mr. Johnson* (2004); and Rory Block, *The Lady and Mr. Johnson* (2006). The conference was held at Case Western Reserve University on September 26, 1998, and titled "Hellhound on My Trail: Robert Johnson and the Blues."

108. Graves, *Crossroads*, 83, 90; Johnson, phone interview, June 25, 2013.

109. The argument for Legba's survival within black southern culture through the process of religious syncretism traces back to Herskovits and Hurston and has recently become the focus of revisionist skepticism by Kubik and Evans. The debate has little relevance for the point made here, except for the fact that Palmer, the source Fusco drew on, helped popularize the Herskovits/Hurston position. See Herskovits, *The Myth of the Negro Past*, 252–53; Kubik, *Africa and the Blues*, 21; and Evans, "Demythologizing the Blues." On O'Neal's contribution to *Crossroads*: Johnson, phone interview, June 25, 2013; Fusco, phone interview, July 22, 2013; and Hyatt, *Hoodoo—Conjuration—Witchcraft—Rootwork*.

110. Guralnick, *Searching for Robert Johnson*, 5. Guralnick's book was originally published, without additional back matter, as "Searching for Robert Johnson," *Living Blues* 53 (Summer/Autumn 1982): 27–41.

111. Seneca as Cutler: "Crossroads: Production Information." Muddy Waters: Palmer, *Deep Blues*, 260.

112. Schroeder, *Robert Johnson*, 95; Fitzsimmons, "'Hellhound on My Trail,'"181; on the connection between lynching and the blues, see Gussow, *Seems Like Murder Here*, 17–65. "Big black man": Evans, *Tommy Johnson*, 20.

113. Schroeder, *Robert Johnson*, 95.

114. Quoted in Segrest and Hoffman, *Moanin' at Midnight*, 79–80.

115. For Glissant and Montgomery, see Cartwright, *Reading Africa into American Literature*, 16, 95.

116. Quoted in Wald, *Escaping the Delta*, 118.

117. Murray, *Stomping the Blues*, 69; Murray, *The Blue Devils of Nada*, 16.

118. McGinley, *Staging the Blues*, 197.

119. See, for example, http://www.youtube.com/watch?v=NeIOXKO_OzI and http://www.youtube.com/watch?v=lVgM8n8GlUM (accessed August 10, 2016).

120. Those who write of "two guitars" include veteran music journalist Robert Gordon ("36 Hours in Clarksdale, Miss."); cultural critic Stephen Asma ("Blues Man on a Mojo Mission"); and Scottish journalist Alistair McKay ("Play Me Your Delta Blues").

121. A notable exception to the dearth of coverage on Barbieri has been Jesse Wright, editor of the *Clarksdale Press-Register*. See Wright, "Creator Cleanses Crossroads."

122. Barretta, "The North Delta."

123. Neff, *Let the World Listen Right*, 23.

124. Ibid., 4; Barretta, "The North Delta," 32; Luther Brown, quoted in Stolle, *Hidden History of Mississippi Blues*, 59.

125. "Morgan Freeman's Dream for 'Birthplace of Blues.'"

126. King, *I'm Feeling the Blues Right Now*, 95. For Clarksdale Revitalization Inc., see http://www.revitalizeclarksdale.org/ (accessed August 10, 2016).

127. www.cityofclarksdale.org (accessed August 10, 2016).

128. *Clarksdale, Coahoma County Street Map and Resource Guide.*

129. http://www.deltabluesmuseum.org (accessed August 10, 2016). See House's actual statement as reported in Welding, "Hell Hound on His Trail," n. 10.

130. See Puckett, *Folk Beliefs of the Southern Negro*, 554; for the Delta Blues Museum, see http://www.deltabluesmuseum.org/follow_robert/start.html (accessed August 10, 2016).

131. Beaumont, *Preachin' the Blues*, 90; Pearson and McCullock, *Robert Johnson: Lost and Found.*

132. http://www.deltabluesmuseum.org/cart/default.asp (accessed August 10, 2016).

133. Quoted in Kitchen Sisters, "Kibbe at the Crossroads."

134. Quoted in King, *I'm Feeling the Blues Right Now*, 96.

135. LeBlanc, phone interview, June 27, 2013.

136. Quoted in Jacobson, "Down to the Crossroads."

137. House, as told to Lester, "I Can Make My Own Songs," 38–45; Welding, "Hell Hound on His Trail," 16–17.

138. Conforth, "Ike Zimmerman."

139. Lester, phone interview, September 7, 2014.

140. Palmer, *Deep Blues*, 113; LaVere, "A Biography" (liner notes). In an e-mail to the author dated September 10, 2014, LaVere wrote, "I found RJ in the 1930 Census in Bolivar County on the day following his first wife's death. It was probably shortly thereafter that he left for Hazlehurst and may have been around that time or maybe even before that he was sent packing."

141. Pearson and McCulloch, *Robert Johnson: Lost and Found*, 7.

142. Komara, *The Road to Robert Johnson*, 24.

143. Lester, phone interview, September 7, 2014; Welding, "Hell Hound on His Trail," 16–17.

144. Lester, phone interview, September 7, 2014.

145. Welding, "Hell Hound on His Trail," 17.

146. Komara, *The Road to Robert Johnson*, 24.

147. Beaumont, *Preachin' the Blues*, 90.

148. Conforth, Facebook post, September 14, 2014.

149. Graves, *Crossroads*, 27; LaVere, e-mail to Adam Gussow, September 10, 2014.

150. Komara, *The Road to Robert Johnson*, 32.

151. See Neff, *Let the World Listen Right*, 3–4, 22–24; Butler and Birdsong, personal interview, June 19, 2013; Grandt, *Shaping Words to Fit the Soul*, 76–77; Luther Brown, quoted in Stolle, *Hidden History of Mississippi Blues*, 59.

152. *Clarksdale, Coahoma County Street Map and Resource Guide.*

153. "Principal Traveled Highways."

154. Neff, *Let the World Listen Right*, 3–4.

155. Butler and Birdsong, personal interview, June 19, 2013.

156. Spencer, *Blues and Evil*, 135.

157. "Sanborn Fire Insurance Map" (1938).

158. "Sanborn Fire Insurance Map" (1929). The Mississippi State University Library does not permit visitors to photograph maps, which is why the photograph shows the intersection as rendered in 1918 and 1938 Sanborn maps. The intersection remained unchanged between 1918 and 1929, although Sycamore was extended another quarter of a mile to the east, dead-ending at Florida Avenue.

159. Quoted in an untitled item in the *New Orleans Times-Picayune*, October 1, 1928, 6.

160. Lesseig, "Automobility and Social Change," 125–26.

161. Ibid., 126–27.

162. "County Gives Its Approval of $200,000 Bond Project," 1.

163. "Highway Bids for Roads Are in Publication," 9.

164. "Road Map of Mississippi" (1932).

165. "Highway Work to Be Rushed in This Area," 8.

166. "Paul Claxton, Engineers Are to Make Route," 2.

167. "Highway Route Not Definite, Say Surveyors," 8.

168. "Linker's Plan for Road Here Is Presented," 8.

169. "Resolution to Leave Road up to Engineers," 9.

170. "Club Re-opens Road Fight," 1.

171. "We Back Rotary to the Limit," 4.

172. "Young Men's Business Club Gives Endorsement," 8; "New Hat in the Ring," 2; "A Final No?," 2.

173. "Withdrawal of Highway Funds Not Possible," 6.

174. "Commissioner of Roads Here for Gathering," 6.

175. This estimate is based on several sources. According to a "Road Map of Mississippi" published in the January 1935 issue of *Mississippi Highways*, both the northward stretch of Highway 61 from Clarksdale to the Tunica County line and the stretch of Highway 49 between Clarksdale and Tutwiler were completed and paved in their new locations. The portion of Highway 61 running south from Clarksdale to Cleveland, however, was still unpaved gravel. "Road Map of Mississippi" (1935). According to the *Biloxi Daily Herald* in the spring of 1935, "Construction of the new $80,000 bridge over the Sunflower River at 10th Street is almost completed, and construction of abutments and

paving of the new link on Highway No. 61 will begin soon. The project will be open in June or July." *Biloxi Daily Herald*, March 5, 1935, 2.

176. *Telephone Directory, Clarksdale, Miss.* (1936), 122.

177. Moss, *Barbecue*, 150.

178. From an untitled article in *Here's Clarksdale*, 11. Cited on the website Issaquena Avenue and Cotton—Family—Religion.

179. "Vacation Postcards: Cotton Boll Court, Clarksdale." In interviews, both Nell Smith and Pat Davis spoke of Cotton Boll Court. Smith remembered Kyle's involvement; Davis remembered the fire. Smith, phone interview, August 18, 2014; Davis, informal conversation, September 24, 2014.

180. Butler and Birdsong, personal interview, June 19, 2013.

181. *Telephone Directory, Clarksdale, Miss.* (May 1964).

182. Twiford, phone interview, July 17, 2013.

183. Smith, phone interview, August 18, 2014.

184. Barbieri, personal interview, July 16, 2013.

185. Ferris, phone interview, July 10, 2013.

186. Johnson, phone interview, June 25, 2013.

187. Palmer, *Deep Blues*, 126–27.

188. O'Neal, phone interview, July 23, 2014.

189. Titon, "The New Blues Tourism."

190. O'Neal, phone interview, July 23, 2014.

191. Ruskey, phone interview, May 20, 2014.

192. Johnson, phone interview, June 25, 2013.

193. LeBlanc, phone interview, June 27, 2013.

194. Johnson, phone interview, June 25, 2013.

195. Bynum, phone interview, June 24, 2013.

196. Ibid.

197. Baird, "Mississippi's Got the Blues."

198. Hamlin, *Crossroads at Clarksdale*, 254; Hyland, "Tourism in the Lower Mississippi Delta," 156–57; Nuwer, "Gambling in Mississippi."

199. Twiford, phone interview, July 17, 2013.

200. Ruskey, phone interview, May 20, 2014.

201. Fair, personal interview, July 29, 2014.

202. Johnson, phone interview, June 25, 2013. I was unable to locate Hood-Adams's article in the *Press-Register*.

203. Butler and Birdsong, personal interview, June 19, 2013; *Great Drives*.

204. *Great Drives*. Literature as well as popular culture had joined the chorus for Clarksdale's crossroads by that point. Although the novel doesn't specifically name Highways 49 and 61, Walter Mosley's *RL's Dream* (1995) has its fictionalized Robert Johnson tell narrator Atwater "Soupspoon" Wise that he had "made a blood sacrifice with a witch woman down Clarksdale . . . then goes out to the crossroads." See Mosley, *RL's Dream*,142.

205. "Every Crossroads . . . Has a Story," 130.

206. Warner, "On the Blues Highway."

207. Standish, "Highway to the Blues."

208. Butler and Birdsong, personal interview, June 19, 2013.

209. Ibid.; Smith, phone interview, August 18, 2014; Luckett, e-mail forwarded by Shelley Ritter, June 14, 2013.

210. Barbieri, personal interview, July 16, 2013. The narrative that follows, along with the interpolated quotations, are drawn largely from this interview.

211. Twiford, phone interview, July 17, 2013.

212. Butler and Birdsong, personal interview, June 19, 2013; Dickerson, phone interview, August 18, 2014. The conversation that follows is reconstructed from these two interviews.

213. Mayfield, "Crossroads Sign," 1.

214. Twiford, e-mail to Adam Gussow, October 30, 2014.

215. "Harlem Inn," Mississippi Blues Trail website.

216. Twiford, e-mail to Adam Gussow, October 30, 2014.

217. Twiford, phone interview, July 17, 2013.

218. "Minutes of the Meeting of the Board of Mayor and Commissioners."

219. Wardlow, *Chasin' That Devil Music*, 199.

220. Komara, *The Road to Robert Johnson*, 23.

221. O'Neal, "Delta Blues Map Kit."

222. Bynum, phone interview, June 24, 2013.

223. In an interview, Twiford mentioned the Tennessee Williams preference. Both Barbieri and Henderson mentioned the occasional objection to the monument raised by Christian townspeople, but both said that such objections were rare. Twiford, phone interview, July 17, 2013; Barbieri, personal interview, July 16, 2013; Henderson, phone interview, August 1, 2014.

224. Henderson, phone interview, August 1, 2014.

225. Twiford, e-mail to Adam Gussow, October 30, 2014; Mississippi Legislature, "House Bill No. 1745."

226. Mississippi Legislature, "House Bill 1749."

CONCLUSION

1. For Clapton's dismissal of the Johnson devil-legend, see Clapton, interview with Andrew Franklin, in Scherman, "The Hellhound's Trail," 50. For Clapton's awed testimonials, see Clapton, *Clapton: The Autobiography*, 39–40, 291–92; and Schumacher, *Crossroads*, 18–19. Clapton's recorded homages include *Me and Mr. Johnson* (2004) and the accompanying DVD, *Sessions for Robert J*. Clapton also founded and helps fund the Crossroads Centre Antigua, a drug and alcohol treatment facility.

2. "Racial and Ethnic Tensions in American Communities: Poverty, Inequality, and Discrimination—Volume VII: The Mississippi Delta Report," http://www.usccr.gov/pubs/msdelta/ch1.htm (accessed August 10, 2016).

3. On Clinton's visit to Clarksdale, see Babington, "Clinton Vows Help for Struggling Delta Region"; and Hamlin, *Crossroads at Clarksdale*, 245–46.

4. Quoted in Vulliamy, "The Unbeautiful South."

5. Twiford, phone interview, July 17, 2013; Strauss, "A Home of the Blues."

6. Quoted in Strauss, "A Home of the Blues."

7. Butler and Birdsong, personal interview, June 19, 2013.

8. King, *I'm Feeling the Blues Right Now*, 95–96.

9. Seratt, phone interview, July 11, 2013.

10. Klatzel's blues paintings can be viewed on his website, http://www.earlklatzel.com/gallery.htm (accessed August 10, 2016).

11. Ross, "Investors Plan New Entertainment Complex." See also "Robert Johnson Crossroads Blues Legends Park." Although plans for a park at Clarksdale's crossroads appear to have been scrapped, Klatzel is collaborating with the Robert Johnson Blues Foundation on a similarly ambitious park in Crystal Springs, Mississippi. See "Robert Johnson Blues Park – Proposal."

12. Klatzel, phone interview, July 22, 2014.

13. Ruskey, phone interview, May 20, 2014.

14. Klatzel, phone interview, July 22, 2014. All subsequent quotes from Klatzel come from this interview.

15. Fair, personal interview, July 29, 2014. All subsequent quotes from Fair come from this interview.

16. See appendix for a comprehensive list of blues recordings featuring the devil and hell.

17. Pearson and McCulloch, *Robert Johnson: Lost and Found*, 25.

18. "A 2004 Gallup Poll," according to sociologist Joseph Baker, "reported that belief in religious evil was rising. Where 56 percent of Americans believed in hell in 1997, 70 percent claimed belief in it in 2004. Similarly 55 percent believed in the devil in 1990, while 70 percent claimed belief in 2004. This rise of belief in religious evil may reflect a post-9/11 effect with the United States in a period of war, although there are likely other factors influencing this rise as well." See Baker, "Who Believes in Religious Evil?," 206.

19. "Text of President Bush's 2002 State of the Union Address"; Stout, "Chavez Calls Bush 'the Devil' in U.N. Speech."

20. "What Every Non-Muslim Needs to Know about Islam!"

21. Reed, *The Holy Profane*, 104.

22. See, for example, Palmer, "The Pop Life; Rock: No Longer 'Devil's Music.'"

23. "Tommie Young," Soulwalking.co.uk, http://www.soulwalking.co.uk/Tommie%20Young.html (accessed August 10, 2016).

24. Tommie Young, "Everybody's Got a Little Devil in Their Soul" (1972).

25. Quoted in Wald, *Escaping the Delta*, xvii.

26. Smith, *"Let the Church Sing!,"* 35.

27. Ibid., 36–37.

28. Quoted in Young, *Woke Me Up This Morning*, 174.

29. Quoted in Stolle, *Hidden History of Mississippi Blues*, 101–4.

30. See "Ten New Artists You Need to Know."

31. "Info," Leobudwelch.com.

Bibliography

Abbott, Lynn, and Doug Seroff. *Out of Sight: The Rise of African American Popular Music, 1889–1895*. Jackson: University Press of Mississippi, 2003.

———. *Ragged but Right: Black Traveling Shows, "Coon Songs," and the Dark Pathway to Blues and Jazz*. Jackson: University Press of Mississippi, 2007.

"A Final No?" *Clarksdale Daily Register*, November 16, 1931.

Alger, Dean. *The Original Guitar Hero and the Power of Music: Lonnie Johnson, Music, and Civil Rights*. Denton: University of North Texas Press, 2014.

Allen, Frederick Lewis. *Only Yesterday*. 1931. New York: Bantam, 1959.

Allen, William Francis, Charles Pickard Ware, and Lucy McKim Garrison. *Slave Songs of the United States*. 1867. Bedford, Mass.: Applewood, n.d.

Alyn, Glen, ed. *I Say Me for a Parable: The Oral Autobiography of Mance Lipscomb, Texas Bluesman*. New York: W. W. Norton, 1993.

Ames, David W. "Igbo and Hausa Musicians: A Comparative Examination." *Ethnomusicology* 17, no. 2 (May 1973): 250–78.

Anderson, Jeffrey E. *Conjure in African American Society*. Baton Rouge: Louisiana State University Press, 2005.

Anyabwile, Thabiti M., and John Piper, eds. *The Faithful Preacher: Recapturing the Vision of Three Pioneering African-American Pastors*. Wheaton, Ill.: Crossway, 2007.

Armstrong, Lil Hardin. "Satchmo and Me." *American Music* 25, no. 1 (Spring 2007): 106–18.

Armstrong, Mary Frances, Helen W. Ludlow, and Thomas P. Fenner. *Hampton and Its Students*. New York: G. P. Putnam's Sons, 1874.

Aschoff, Peter, and Patricia Aschoff. "1984 Delta Blues Festival: September 15, 1984—Freedom Village, Mississippi." *Living Blues*, no. 64 (March/April 1985): 41–44.

Asma, Stephen T. "Blues Man on a Mojo Mission." *Chronicle of Higher Education* 49, no. 11 (2002): B16–B17. https://works.bepress.com/stephen_asma/31/.

Aykroyd, Dan, and Ben Manilla. *Elwood's Blues: Interviews with the Blues Legends and Stars*. San Francisco: Backbeat, 2004.

Babington, Charles. "Clinton Vows Help for Struggling Delta Region." *Washington Post*, July 7, 1999. http://www.washingtonpost.com/wp-srv/politics/daily/july99/clinton7.htm.

Baird, Robert. "Mississippi's Got the Blues." *Historic Traveler* 3, no. 5 (May 1997): 37–44.

Baker, Houston A., Jr. *Blues, Ideology, and Afro-American Literature: A Vernacular Theory*. Chicago: University of Chicago Press, 1984.

———. *Turning South Again: Re-thinking Modernism/Re-reading Booker T.* Durham, N.C.: Duke University Press, 2001.

Baker, Joseph. "Who Believes in Religious Evil? An Investigation of Sociological Patterns of Belief in Satan, Hell, and Demons." *Review of Religious Research* 50, no. 2 (2008): 206–20.

The Baldwin and Register Clarksdale Mississippi ConSurvey Directory. Master ed. Hebron, Neb., and Clarksdale, Miss.: Baldwin ConSurvey Company and the Clarksdale Register, 1936.

Banks, Russell. "The Devil and Robert Johnson." *New Republic*, April 29, 1991, 27–31.

Barbieri, Vic. Personal interview with Adam Gussow, July 16, 2013.

Barnhart, Scotty. *The World of Jazz Trumpet*. Milwaukee: Hal Leonard, 2005.

Barnwell, Marion Barnwell, ed. *A Place Called Mississippi: Collected Narratives*. Jackson: University of Mississippi Press, 1967.

Barretta, Scott. "The North Delta." *Living Blues*, no. 233 (October 2014). http://digital .livingblues.com/article/The+North+Delta/1823589/226901/article.html.

Bastin, Bruce. *Never Sell a Copyright: Joe Davis and His Role in the New York Music Scene, 1916–1978*. Chigwell, U.K.: Storyville, 1990.

Battle, Michael. *The Black Church in America: African American Christian Spirituality*. Malden, Mass.: Blackwell, 2006.

Beaumont, Daniel. *Preachin' the Blues: The Life and Times of Son House*. New York: Oxford University Press, 2011.

Bebey, Francis. *African Music: A People's Art*. Translated by Josephine Bennett. Brooklyn, N.Y.: Lawrence Hill, 1975 [1969].

Becker, Howard S. "The Professional Dance Musician and His Audience." *American Journal of Sociology* 57, no. 2 (September 1951): 136–44.

Bertrand, Michael T. *Race, Rock, and Elvis*. Urbana: University of Illinois Press, 2000.

Best, Wallace D. *Passionately Human, No Less Divine: Religion and Culture in Black Chicago, 1915–1952*. Princeton, N.J.: Princeton University Press, 2005.

Bibb, Henry. *Narrative of the Life and Adventures of Henry Bibb, an American Slave, Written by Himself*. 1849. http://docsouth.unc.edu/neh/bibb/bibb.html.

Blackmon, Douglas A. *Slavery by Another Name: The Re-enslavement of Black Americans from the Civil War to World War II*. New York: Anchor, 2009.

Blassingame, John W. *The Slave Community: Plantation Life in the Antebellum South*. New York: Oxford University Press, 1979 [1972].

Blesh, Rudi. *Shining Trumpets: A History of Jazz*. Rev. ed. New York: Knopf, 1958 [1946].

Bloomfield, Michael, with S. Summerville. *Me and Big Joe*. San Francisco: RE/ SEARCH, 1980.

Blues in the Mississippi Night. Sound recording with liner notes by Alan Lomax. Ryko RCD 90155. 1990 [1957].

Bockris, Victor. *Keith Richards: The Biography*. New York: Da Capo, 2003 [1992].

Boots, Cheryl C. *Singing for Equality: Hymns in the American Antislavery and Indian Rights Movement, 1640–1855*. Jefferson, N.C.: McFarland, 2013.

Botkin, B. A., ed. *Lay My Burden Down: A Folk History of Slavery*. 1945. Chicago: University of Chicago Press, 1968.

Brackett, David. "Preaching Blues." *Black Music Research Journal* 32, no. 1 (Spring 2012): 113–36.

Bray, Colin J. *The Yas Yas Girl: Complete Recorded Works in Chronological Order*. Vol. 1, *4 May 1937 to 7 April 1938*. Vienna: Document DOCD-5292.

Braziel, Jana Evans. "'Bye, Bye Baby': Race, Bisexuality, and the Blues in the Music of Bessie Smith and Janis Joplin." *Popular Music and Society* 27, no. 1 (February 2004): 3–26.

Brisbin, John Anthony. "Jimmy Rogers: I'm Havin' Fun Right Today." *Living Blues*, no. 135 (September/October 1997): 13–27.

British Broadcasting Corporation. "Born under a Bad Sign." Interview with Champion Jack Dupree. First installment of *Blue Britannia: Can Blue Men Sing the Whites?* Originally aired May 1, 2009.

Broonzy, Big Bill. *Big Bill Blues: William Broonzy's Story*, as told to Yannick Bruynoghe. New York: Da Capo, 1992 [1972].

Brown, Cecil. *Stagolee Shot Billy*. Cambridge, Mass.: Harvard University Press, 2003.

Brown, Sterling A. "'The Devil and the Black Man' (Slim Greer in Hell)." Edited by B. A. Botkin. *Folk-Say* 4 (1932): 246–49.

Brownderville, Greg Alan. *Deep down in the Delta: Folktales and Poems*. Cotton Plant, Ark.: Doodlum Brothers, 2005.

Browning, Boo. "Stevie Vuaghan's [*sic*] Awesome Bebut [*sic*]. *Washington Post*, July 22, 1983. https://www.washingtonpost.com/archive/lifestyle/1983/07/22/stevie -vuaghans-awesome-bebut/8b4e2396-cbc4-494f-b41d-2190e0f77fd6/.

Butler, Anthea D. *Women in the Church of God in Christ: Making a Sanctified World*. Chapel Hill: University of North Carolina Press, 2007.

Butler, James, and Robert Birdsong. Personal interview with Adam Gussow, June 19, 2013.

Bynum, Sandy. Phone interview with Adam Gussow, June 24, 2013.

Calt, Stephen. *I'd Rather Be the Devil: Skip James and the Blues*. Chicago: Chicago Review Press, 2008 [1994].

Calt, Stephen, and Gayle Wardlow. *King of the Delta Blues: The Life and Music of Charlie Patton*. Newton, N.J.: Rock Chapel, 1988.

"Can the States Stop Lynching?" *The Crisis* 46, no. 1 (January 1939): 9.

Cannon, Katie Geneva. "Sexing Black Women: Liberation from the Prisonhouse of Anatomical Authority." In Pinn and Hopkins, *Loving the Body*, 11–30.

Carby, Hazel V. "Policing the Black Woman's Body in an Urban Context." *Critical Inquiry* 18, no. 4 (Summer 1992): 738–55.

Carr, Cynthia. *Our Town: A Heartland Lynching, a Haunted Town, and the Hidden History of White America*. New York: Crown, 2006.

Cartwright, Keith. *Reading Africa into American Literature: Ethics, Fables, and Gothic Tales*. 2002. Lexington: University Press of Kentucky, 2004.

Chambers, Erve, ed. *Tourism and Culture: An Applied Perspective*. Albany: State University of New York, 1997.

Charters, Samuel. *The Country Blues*. Rev. ed. New York: Da Capo, 1975 [1959].

Cheseborough, Steve. *Blues Traveling: The Holy Sites of Delta Blues*. Jackson: University Press of Mississippi, 2001.

Childs, Dennis. "'You Ain't Seen Nothin' Yet': *Beloved*, the American Chain Gang, and the Middle Passage Remix." *American Quarterly* 61, no. 2 (June 2009): 271–97.

Chinn, Charlotte B. "The Pulpit and the Pew: The Black Church and Women."
In Lincoln and Mamiya, *The Black Church in the African American Experience*,
274–308.

Cimbala, Paul A. "Black Musicians from Slavery to Freedom: An Exploration of
an African-American Folk Elite and Cultural Continuity in the Nineteenth-
Century Rural South." *Journal of Negro History* 80, no. 1 (Winter 1995): 15–29.

Clapton, Eric. *Clapton: The Autobiography*. New York: Broadway, 2007.

Clarksdale, Coahoma County Street Map and Resource Guide. Clarksdale/
Coahoma County Chamber of Commerce. Pinckneyville, Ill.:
CommunityLink, 2011.

Clay, N. R. "Superintendent's Report, Clarksdale District." In *Official Journal of
the Twenty-Seventh Annual Session of the Upper Mississippi Conference of the
Methodist Episcopal Church*, edited by B. F. Woolfolk. Grenada, Miss.: Sentinel,
1917. J. B. Cain Archives of Mississippi Methodism, Millsaps College.

———. "Superintendent's Report, Clarksdale District." In *Official Journal of
the Twenty-Ninth Annual Session of the Upper Mississippi Conference of the
Methodist Episcopal Church*, edited by B. F. Woolfolk. January 9–12, 1919. J. B.
Cain Archives of Mississippi Methodism, Millsaps College.

———. "Superintendent's Report, Clarksdale District." In *Official Journal of the
Thirtieth Annual Session of the Upper Mississippi Conference of the Methodist
Episcopal Church*, edited by B. F. Woolfolk. January 14–18, 1920. Jackson,
Tenn.: McCoway-Mercer, 1920. J. B. Cain Archives of Mississippi Methodism,
Millsaps College.

———. "Superintendent's Report, Clarksdale District." In *Official Journal of the
Thirty-First Annual Session of the Upper Mississippi Conference of the Methodist
Episcopal Church*, edited by B. F. Woolfolk. January 12–16, 1921. J. B. Cain
Archives of Mississippi Methodism, Millsaps College.

Clement, Elizabeth Alice. *Love for Sale: Courting, Treating, and Prostitution in
New York City, 1900–1945*. Chapel Hill: University of North Carolina Press, 2006.

Clinkscales, John George. *On the Old Plantation: Reminiscences of His Childhood*.
Spartanburg, S.C.: Band & White, 1916.

"Club Re-opens Road Fight." *Clarksdale Daily Register*, November 3, 1931.

Cobb, James C. *The Most Southern Place on Earth: The Mississippi Delta and the
Roots of Regional Identity*. New York: Oxford University Press, 1992.

Cohn, Lawrence, ed. *Nothing but the Blues: The Music and Musicians*. New York:
Abbeville, 1993.

Collier-Thomas, Bettye. *Daughters of Thunder: Black Women Preachers and Their
Sermons, 1850–1979*. San Francisco: Jossey-Bass, 1998.

Collis, John. *The Story of Chess Records*. New York: Bloomsbury, 1998.

"Commissioner of Roads Here for Gathering." *Clarksdale Daily Register*, February 26,
1932.

Cone, James H. *The Spirituals and the Blues: An Interpretation*. Maryknoll, N.Y.:
Orbis, 1992 [1972].

Conforth, Bruce M. *African American Folksong and American Cultural Politics:
The Lawrence Gellert Story*. Lanham, Md.: Scarecrow, 2013.

———. Facebook post. September 14, 2014. https://www.facebook.com/adam
.gussow/posts/10152374629513061.

———. "Ike Zimmerman: The X in Robert Johnson's Crossroads." *Academia.
edu*. https://www.academia.edu/2408177/_Ike_Zimmerman_The_X_in_Robert
_Johnson_s_Crossroads_Living_Blues_200819. Accessed August 14, 2016.

Congress, Richard. *Blues Mandolin Man: The Life and Music of Yank Rachell*. Jackson:
University Press of Mississippi, 2001.

Copeland, Matt, and Chris Goering. "Blues You Can Use: Teaching the Faust Theme
through Music, Literature, and Film." *Journal of Adolescent and Adult Literacy* 46,
no. 5 (February 2003): 436–41.

"County Gives Its Approval of $200,000 Bond Project." *Clarksdale Daily Register*,
November 22, 1930.

Cressey, Paul Goalby. *The Taxi-Dance Hall: A Sociological Study of Commercialized
Recreation and City Life*. 1932. Chicago: University of Chicago Press, 2008.

"Crossroads." *Living Blues*, no. 66 (July/August 1985): 24–25.

"*Crossroads*: A Mark Carliner Production. A Walter Hill Film." Columbia Pictures
press release. 1986. Film Treatments. *Crossroads*. Blues W-1. Blues Archive. J. D.
Williams Library. University of Mississippi.

"*Crossroads*: Production Information." Columbia Pictures press release. 1986.
Film Treatments. *Crossroads*. Blues W-1. Blues Archive. J. D. Williams Library.
University of Mississippi.

Cushing, Steve. *Blues before Sunrise: The Radio Interviews*. Urbana: University of
Illinois Press, 2010.

Danaher, William F. "Subculture and Myth: The Case of Robert Johnson in the
1920s–1930s US South." *Studies in Symbolic Interaction* 35 (2010): 285–307.

Davis, Angela Y. *Blues Legacies and Black Feminism: Gertrude "Ma" Rainey, Bessie
Smith, and Billie Holiday*. New York: Pantheon, 1998.

———. "I Used to Be Your Sweet Mama: Ideology, Sexuality, and Domesticity."
In Tracy, *Write Me a Few of Your Lines*, 470–501.

Davis, Francis. *The History of the Blues: The Roots, the Music, the People: From Charley
Patton to Robert Cray*. New York: Hyperion, 1995.

Davis, Ossie, and Ruby Dee. *With Ossie and Ruby: In This Life Together*. New York:
It, 2000 [1998].

Davis, Pat. Informal conversation with Adam Gussow. Coahoma Community College,
September 24, 2014.

Defaa, Chip. *Blue Rhythms: Six Lives in Rhythm and Blues*. Urbana: University of
Illinois Press, 1996.

Delbanco, Andrew. *The Death of Satan: How Americans Have Lost the Sense of Evil*.
New York: Farrar, Straus and Giroux, 1995.

Dennison, Sam. *Scandalize My Name: Black Imagery in American Popular Music*.
New York: Garland, 1982.

DeSalvo, Debra. *The Language of the Blues: From Alcorub to Zuzu*. New York:
Billboard, 2006.

Dickerson, James L. *Go, Girl, Go! The Women's Revolution in Music*. New York:
Schirmer Trade, 2005.

Dickerson, James, III. Phone interview with Adam Gussow, August 18, 2014.

DiGiacomo, Frank. "Searching for Robert Johnson." *Vanity Fair*, November 2008, 204–7, 251–55.

Dixon, Willie, with Don Snowden. *I Am the Blues: The Willie Dixon Story*. New York: Da Capo, 1990.

DjeDje, Jacqueline Cogdell. *Fiddling in West Africa: Touching the Spirit in Fulbe, Hausa, and Dagbamba Cultures*. Bloomington: Indiana University Press, 2008.

Dollard, John. *Caste and Class in a Southern Town*. Madison: University of Wisconsin Press, 1988 [1935].

Douglas, Ann. *Terrible Honesty: Mongrel Manhattan in the 1920s*. New York: Farrar, Straus and Giroux, 1992.

Douglass, Frederick. *Narrative of the Life of Frederick Douglass*. In *The Classic Slave Narratives*, edited by Henry Louis Gates Jr., 243–331. New York: New American Library, 1987 [1845].

Drake, St. Clair, and Horace R. Cayton. *Black Metropolis: A Study of Negro Life in a Northern City*. New York: Harcourt, Brace, 1945.

Drash, Wayne. "Barbecue, Bible, and Abe Chase Racism from Mississippi Rib Joint." *CNN.com/travel*. September 4, 2009. http://www.cnn.com/2009/TRAVEL/09/04/mississippi.lebanese/index.html?iref=nextin.

Dray, Philip. *At the Hands of Persons Unknown: The Lynching of Black America*. New York: Random House, 2002.

Drowne, Kathleen. *Spirits of Defiance: National Prohibition and Jazz Age Literature, 1920–1933*. Columbus: Ohio State University Press, 2005.

DuBois, W. E. B. "The Problem of Amusement" (1897). In *On Sociology and the Black Community*, edited by Dan S. Green and Edward Driver, 226–37. Chicago: University of Chicago Press, 1995.

Dulaney, W. Marvin. *Black Police in America*. Bloomington: Indiana University Press, 1996.

Dunaway, Wilma A. *Women, Work, and Family in the Antebellum Mountain South*. New York: Cambridge University Press, 2008.

Dundes, Alan, ed. *Mother Wit from the Laughing Barrel: Readings in the Interpretation of Afro-American Folklore*. Englewood Cliffs, N.J.: Prentice-Hall, 1973.

Duran, Lucy. "POYI! Bamana *Jeli* Music, Mali, and the Blues." *Journal of African Cultural Studies* 25, no. 2 (2013): 211–46.

Dylan, Bob. *Chronicles*. Vol. 1. New York: Simon & Schuster, 2004.

Eagle, Bob, and Eric S. LeBlanc. "Will Weldon." In *Blues: A Regional Experience, 218*. Santa Barbara, Calif.: Praeger, 2013.

Earl, John. "A Lifetime in the Blues: Johnny Shines." *Blues World* 46/49 (1973): 3–13, 20–22.

Earl, Riggins R., Jr. *Dark Symbols, Obscure Signs: God, Self, and Community in the Slave Mind*. Maryknoll, N.Y.: Orbis, 1993.

"Economic Development Update: A Weekly Report from the Mississippi Department of Economic Development." Signed by Jerry McDonald." March 8, 1985. Film Treatments. *Crossroads*. Blues W-1. Blues Archive. J. D. Williams Library. University of Mississippi.

Edwards, David Honeyboy, as told to Janis Martinson and Michael Robert Frank. *The World Don't Owe Me Nothing: The Life and Times of Delta Bluesman Honeyboy Edwards*. Chicago: Chicago Review Press, 1997.

Ellison, Ralph. "Richard Wright's Blues." In *Shadow and Act*, 89–104. New York: Signet, 1966 [1964].

Eltis, David. "The Diaspora of Yoruba Speakers, 1650–1865: Dimensions and Implications." In *The Yoruba Diaspora in the Atlantic World*, edited by Toyin Falola and Matt D. Childs, 17–39. Bloomington: University of Indiana Press, 2004.

Epstein, Dena J. *Sinful Tunes and Spirituals: Black Folk Music to the Civil War*. Urbana: University of Illinois Press, 2003 [1977].

"Eric Clapton: Talkin' about His Inspiration." *Today Show*, March 23, 2004. http://www.today.com/id/4584867/ns/today/t/eric-clapton-talkin-about-his-inspiration/.

Escott, Paul D. *Slavery Remembered: A Record of Twentieth-Century Slave Narratives*. Chapel Hill: University of North Carolina Press, 1979.

Evans, David. "Africa and the Blues." *Living Blues*, no. 10 (Autumn 1972): 27–29.

———. "African Elements in the Blues." In *L'oceano dei suoni: Migrazioni, musica e razze nella formazione della Società Euroatlantische*, edited by Pierangelo Castagneto, 3–16. Turin: Otto, 2007.

———. *Big Road Blues: Tradition and Creativity in the Folk Blues*. New York: Da Capo, 1986 [1982].

———. "Demythologizing the Blues." *ISAM Newsletter* 29, no. 1 (Fall 1999). http://www.crookedsaws.com/myths/.

———. "Early Deep South and Mississippi Basin Blues." Quoted in Rudinow, *Soul Music*.

———. "The Guitar in the Blues Music of the Deep South." In *Guitar Cultures*, edited by Andy Bennett and Kevin Dawe, 11–26. New York: Berg, 2001.

———. "Ramblin': Robert Johnson: Pact with the Devil?" *Blues Revue* 21 (February/March 1996): 12–13.

———. "Ramblin': Robert Johnson: Pact with the Devil? Part 2." *Blues Revue* 22 (April/May 1996): 12–13.

———. "Ramblin': Robert Johnson and the Supernatural, Part 3." *Blues Revue* 23 (June/July 1996): 12–13.

———. "Report on Adam Gussow, *Beyond the Crossroads: The Devil and the Blues Tradition*" (proposal and partial manuscript). Referee's report for the University Press of Mississippi, November 13, 2012.

———. *Tommy Johnson*. London: Studio Vista, 1971.

———. "Traditional Blues Lyric and Myth: Some Correspondences." In *The Lyrics in African American Popular Music: Proceedings of Metz*, 17–40. New York: Peter Lang, 2004.

"Every Crossroads . . . Has a Story." Advertisement. *Living Blues*, no. 130 (November/December 1996): 130.

Fair, Shirley. Personal interview with Adam Gussow, July 29, 2014.

Farrow, Stephan S. *Faith, Fancies, and Fetich or Yoruba Paganism: Being Some Account of the Religious Beliefs of the West African Negroes, Particularly of the Yoruba Tribe*. Brooklyn, N.Y.: Athelia Henrietta, 1996 [1926].

Ferris, William R. *Blues from the Delta.* 1978. New introduction by Billy Taylor. New York: Da Capo, 1984.

———. "Interview: The Devil and His Blues: James 'Son Ford' Thomas." *Southern Cultures* 15, no. 3 (Fall 2009): 5–20.

———. Phone interview with Adam Gussow, July 10, 2013.

———. "Racial Repertoires among Blues Performers." *Ethnomusicology* 14, no. 3 (September 1970): 439–49.

———. *The William R. Ferris Reader, Omnibus E-book: Collected Essays from the Pages of "Southern Cultures," 1995–2013.* Chapel Hill: University of North Carolina Press, 2014.

Field, Kim. *Harmonicas, Harps, and Heavy Breathers: The Evolution of the People's Instrument.* New York: Simon & Schuster, 1993.

Fierce, Milfred C. *Slavery Revisited: Blacks and the Southern Convict Leasing System.* Brooklyn, N.Y.: Africana Studies Research Center, City University of New York, 1994.

Finn, Julio. *The Bluesman: The Musical Heritage of Black Men and Women in the Americas.* London: Quartet, 1986.

Fitzsimmons, Lorna. "'Hellhound on My Trail': *Crossroads* and the Racist Ravishment." *European Journal of American Culture* 20, no. 3 (2001): 164–82.

Floyd, Samuel A., Jr. *The Power of Black Music: Interpreting Its History from Africa to the United States.* New York: Oxford University Press, 1995.

Foster, Frances Smith. *'Til Death or Distance Do Us Part: Love and Marriage in African America.* New York: Oxford University Press, 2010.

Franz, Steve. *The Amazing Secret History of Elmore James.* St. Louis: BlueSource, 2003.

Freeland, David. *Ladies of Soul.* American Made Music Series. Jackson: University Press of Mississippi, 2001.

Friesen, Gordon. "The Rev. Frederick Douglass Kirkpatrick." *Broadside,* no. 96 (January–February 1969). http://singout.org/downloads/broadside/b096.pdf.

Fusco, John. E-mail to Adam Gussow, July 22, 2013.

———. Phone interview with Adam Gussow, July 22, 2013.

Garon, Paul. *Blues and the Poetic Spirit.* San Francisco: City Lights, 1996 [1975].

———. *The Devil's Son-in-Law: The Story of Peetie Wheatstraw & His Songs.* Chicago: Charles H. Kerr, 2003 [1971].

———. "The Police and the Church." In Tracy, *Write Me a Few of Your Lines,* 252–57.

———. "White Blues." Summer 1993. http://racetraitor.org/blues.html.

Garon, Paul, and Beth Garon. *Woman with Guitar: Memphis Minnie's Blues.* New York: Da Capo, 1992.

Garry, Jane, and Hasan El-Shamy. "Choice of Roads, Motif N122.0.1 and Crossroads, Various Motifs." In *Archetypes and Motifs in Folklore and Literature.* New York: Routledge, 2004.

Genovese, Eugene D. *Roll, Jordan, Roll: The World the Slaves Made.* 1972. New York: Vintage, 1976.

Giggie, John M. *After Redemption: Jim Crow and the Transformation of African American Religion in the Delta, 1875–1915.* New York: Oxford University Press, 2008.

Gioia, Ted. *Delta Blues: The Life and Times of the Mississippi Masters Who Revolutionized American Music.* New York: W. W. Norton, 2008.

———. "Did Robert Johnson Sell His Soul to the Devil?" *Alibi*, August 2011. http://alibimagazine.com/pages/did-robert-johnson-sell-his-soul-to-the-devil.

Giordano, Ralph G. *Satan in the Dance Hall: Rev. John Roach Straton, Social Dancing, and Morality in 1920's New York City.* Lanham, Md.: Scarecrow, 2008.

Goffman, Erving. *The Presentation of Self in Everyday Life.* New York: Doubleday, 1959.

Gomez, Michael A. *Exchanging Our Country Marks: The Transformation of African Identities in the Colonial and Antebellum South.* Chapel Hill: University of North Carolina Press, 1998.

———. "Muslims in Early America." *Journal of Southern History* 60, no. 4 (November 1994): 671–710.

Goodman, Walter. "The Screen: Walter Hill's *Crossroads.*" *New York Times*, March 14, 1986. http://www.nytimes.com/movie/review?res=9A0DEEDD103FF937A25750C0A960948260.

Gordon, Robert. *Can't Be Satisfied: The Life and Times of Muddy Waters.* Boston: Little, Brown, 2002.

———. "36 Hours in Clarksdale, Miss." *New York Times.* June 16, 2006. http://www.nytimes.com/2006/06/16/travel/escapes/16hour.html?_r=0.

"Governor Has Blues Bill on Desk." *Clarksdale Press-Register*, April 8, 1999.

Grandt, Jurgen E. *Shaping Words to Fit the Soul: The Southern Ritual Grounds of Afro-Modernism.* Columbus: Ohio State University Press, 2009.

Graves, Tom. *Crossroads: The Life and Afterlife of Blues Legend Robert Johnson.* Spokane, Wash.: Demers, 2008.

Great Drives. Performed by Levon Helm and Robert Townsend. PBS/Four Point Entertainment, 1997. Videocassette.

Green, Laurie Boush. *Battling the Plantation Mentality: Memphis and the Black Freedom Struggle.* Chapel Hill: University of North Carolina Press, 2007.

Gruver, Rod. "The Blues as a Secular Religion" (1970). In Tracy, *Write Me a Few of Your Lines*, 222–30.

Guralnick, Peter. *Searching for Robert Johnson.* New York: Plume, 1992 [1989].

Gussow, Adam. "'If Bessie Smith Had Killed Some White People': Racial Legacies, the Blues Revival, and the Black Arts Movement." In *New Thoughts on the Black Arts Movement*, edited by Lisa Gail Collins and Margo Natalie Crawford, 227–52. New Brunswick, N.J.: Rutgers University Press, 2006.

———. *Mister Satan's Apprentice: A Blues Memoir.* New York: Pantheon, 1998.

———. *Seems Like Murder Here: Southern Violence and the Blues Tradition.* Chicago: University of Chicago Press, 2002.

Gutman, Herbert G. *The Black Family in Slavery and Freedom, 1750–1925.* 1976. New York: Vintage, 1977.

Haley, Alex. "Malcolm X to Alex Haley: The Playboy Interview." *Playboy Magazine*, May 1963. http://www.malcolm-x.org/docs/int_playb.htm.

Halpert, Herbert. "The Devil, the Fiddle, and Dancing." *Fields of Folklore: Essays in Honor of Kenneth S. Goldstein*, edited by Roger D. Abrahams et al., 44–54. Bloomington, Ind.: Trickster, 1995.

Hamlin, Francoise N. *Crossroads at Clarksdale: The Black Freedom Struggle in the Mississippi Delta after World War II*. Chapel Hill: University of North Carolina Press, 2012.

Handy, W. C. *Father of the Blues: An Autobiography*. New York: Da Capo, 1991 [1941].

Haralambos, Michael. *Soul Music: The Birth of a Sound in Black America*. New York: Da Capo, 1985 [1974].

"Harlem Inn." Mississippi Blues Trail. http://www.msbluestrail.org/blues-trail-markers/harlem-inn. Accessed August 10, 2016.

Harley, Sharon. "'Working for Nothing but for a Living': Black Women in the Underground Economy." In *Sister Circle: Black Women and Work*, edited by Sharon Harley and the Black Women and Work Collective, 48–66. New Brunswick, N.J.: Rutgers University Press, 2002.

Harris, Corey. "Can White People Play the Blues?" *Blues Is Black Music!* blog. May 10, 2015. http://bluesisblackmusic.blogspot.com/2015/05/can-white-people-play-blues.html.

Harrison, Daphne Duval. *Black Pearls: Blues Queens of the 1920s*. New Brunswick, N.J.: Rutgers University Press, 1993 [1988].

Hartman, Saidiya V. *Scenes of Subjection: Terror, Slavery, and Self-Making in Nineteenth-Century America*. New York: Oxford University Press, 1997.

Harvey, Paul. *Redeeming the South: Religious Cultures and Racial Identities among Southern Baptists, 1865–1925*. Chapel Hill: University of North Carolina Press, 1997.

Hay, Fred J. *Goin' Back to Sweet Memphis: Conversations with the Blues*. Athens: University of Georgia Press, 2005.

Hazzard-Donald, Katrina. *Mojo Workin': The Old African American Hoodoo System*. Urbana: University of Illinois Press, 2013.

Hazzard-Gordon, Katrina. *Jookin': The Rise of Social Dance Formations in African-American Culture*. Philadelphia: Temple University Press, 1990.

Hellhounds on My Trail: The Afterlife of Robert Johnson. Documentary directed by Robert Mugge. Nonfiction Films and Mug-Shot Productions, 1999.

Henderson, Leonard. Phone interview with Adam Gussow, August 1, 2014.

Herskovits, Melville J. *The Myth of the Negro Past*. Boston: Beacon, 1990 [1958].

Heyrman, Christine Leigh. *Southern Cross: The Beginnings of the Bible Belt*. Chapel Hill: University of North Carolina Press, 1997.

Higginbotham, Evelyn Brooks. "Rethinking Vernacular Culture: Black Religion and Race Records in the 1920s and 1930s." In West and Glaude, *African American Religious Thought*, 978–95.

———. *Righteous Discontent: The Women's Movement in the Black Baptist Church, 1880–1920*. Cambridge, Mass.: Harvard University Press, 1997 [1993].

"Highway Bids for Roads Are in Publication." *Clarksdale Daily Register*, February 25, 1931.

"Highway Route Not Definite, Say Surveyors." *Clarksdale Daily Register*, June 5, 1931.

"Highway Work to Be Rushed in This Area." *Clarksdale Daily Register*, May 5, 1932.

Hill, Karlos K. "Robert Johnson's 'Hellhound on My Trail' as a Lynching Ballad." *Study the South*, May 11, 2015. http://southernstudies.olemiss.edu/study-the-south/.

Himes, Geoffrey. "Musician Willie King Mixes Politics with Blues." *Chicago Tribune*, June 21, 2002. http://articles.chicagotribune.com/2002-06-21/features/0206210328_1_blues-juke-joint-protest.

———. "Vaughan: Good Pickin'." *Washington Post*, July 28, 1983.

Hinson, Glenn. *Fire in My Bones: Transcendence and the Holy Spirit in African American Gospel*. Philadelphia: University of Pennsylvania Press, 2000.

Holland, Endesha Ida Mae. *From the Mississippi Delta: A Memoir*. New York: Simon & Schuster, 1997.

Hopkins, Dwight N. "Slave Theology in the 'Invisible Institution.'" In West and Glaude, *African American Religious Thought*, 790–830.

House, Roger. *Blue Smoke: The Recorded Journey of Big Bill Broonzy*. Baton Rouge: Louisiana State University Press, 2010.

House, Son, as told to Julius Lester. "I Can Make My Own Songs." *Sing Out!* 15, no. 3 (July 1965): 38–45.

Hughes, Langston. "My Adventures as a Social Poet" (1947). In Tracy, *Write Me a Few of Your Lines: A Blues Reader*, 217.

———. "No Color Line in Hell: Jokes Negroes Tell on Themselves." *Negro Digest*, 1951 (rpt. July 1962), 63–67.

Hughes, Langston, and Arna Bontemps, eds. *The Book of Negro Folklore*. New York: Dodd, Mead, 1983 [1958].

Humphrey, Mark A. "Holy Blues: The Gospel Tradition." In Cohn, *Nothing but the Blues*, 107–49.

———. "Prodigal Sons: Son House and Robert Wilkins." In Sacré, *Saints and Sinners*, 167–94.

"'Hunchback of Notre Dame' at Grand; Clara Smith Heads Show at Monogram; '7–11' Turns Them Away at Olympic." *Chicago Defender*, February 7, 1925.

Hunt, Chris, dir. *The Search for Robert Johnson*. Narrated by John Hammond. Video tape recording. Sony, 1992.

Hunter, Tera W. "'Sexual Pantomimes,' the Blues Aesthetic, and Black Women in the New South." In Radano and Bohlman, *Music and the Racial Imagination*, 145–64.

———. *To 'Joy My Freedom: Southern Black Women's Lives and Labors after the Civil War*. Cambridge, Mass.: Harvard University Press, 1997.

Hurston, Zora Neale. "High John de Conquer." In Hughes and Bontemps, *The Book of Negro Folklore*, 93–102.

———. "Characteristics of Negro Expression." In *The Sanctified Church: The Folklore Writings*, 49–68. Berkeley, Calif.: Turtle Island, 1981.

———. *Their Eyes Were Watching God*. New York: Perennial Library, 1990 [1937].

Hyatt, Harry Middleton. *Hoodoo—Conjuration—Witchcraft—Rootwork: Beliefs Accepted by Many Negroes and White Persons[,] These Being Orally Recorded among Blacks and Whites*. Vol. 1. Hannibal, Mo.: Western Pub., 1970.

Hyland, Stanley E. "Tourism in the Lower Mississippi Delta: Whose Field of Dreams? The Struggle among the Landed Aristocracy, the Grass-Roots Indigenous and the

Gaming Industry." In *Tourism and Culture: An Applied Perspective*, edited by Erve
    Chambers, 147–62. Albany: State University of New York Press, 1997.
"Info." Leobudwelch.com/about. Accessed November 19, 2016.
Jackson, Buzzy. *A Bad Woman Feeling Good: Blues and the Women Who Sing Them.*
    New York: W. W. Norton, 2005.
Jackson, Jerma A. *Singing in My Soul: Black Gospel Music in a Secular Age.* Chapel Hill:
    University of North Carolina Press, 2003.
Jacobson, Mark. "Down to the Crossroads." *Natural History* 105, no. 9 (September
    1996): 48–55.
Jasen, David A. *Tin Pan Alley: An Encyclopedia of the Golden Age of American Popular
    Song.* New York: Routledge, 2003.
"Jason." "Ike Zinnerman and His Graveyard." *Delta Blues.* http://www.tdblues
    .com/2009/05/ike-zinnerman-and-his-graveyard/. Accessed July 14, 2014.
Jenoure, Theresa. "The Afro-American Fiddler." *Contributions in Black Studies* 5,
    no. 6 (1981): 68–81. Special joint issue with *New England Journal of Black Studies.*
    Berkeley Electronic Press.
"Joe Morton: Biography." Columbia Pictures press release. 1986. Film Treatments.
    Crossroads. Blues W-1. Blues Archive. J. D. Williams Library. University of
    Mississippi.
Johnson, Charles S. *Growing Up in the Black Belt: Negro Youth in the Rural South.*
    New York: Schocken, 1967 [1941].
Johnson, Guy B. "Double Meaning in the Popular Negro Blues" (1927). In Dundes,
    Mother Wit from the Laughing Barrel: 258–66.
Johnson, Patty. Phone interview with Adam Gussow, June 25, 2013.
Jones, Carolyn M. Review of *Blues and Evil*, by Jon Michael Spencer. *Journal of the
    American Academy of Religion* 64, no.1 (Spring 1996): 181–85. http://www.jstor.org/
    stable/1465255.
Jones, LeRoi. *"Dutchman" and "The Slave": Two Plays by Leroi Jones.* New York:
    Perennial, 2001 [1964].
Joyner, Charles Joyner. *Down by the Riverside: A South Carolina Slave Community.*
    Urbana: University of Illinois Press, 2009.
Kawabata, Maiko. "Virtuosity, the Violin, the Devil . . .: What Really Made Paganini
    'Demonic'"? *Current Musicology* 83 (Spring 2007): 85–108, 189–90.
Kellett, Andrew James. "Fathers and Sons: American Blues and British Rock Music,
    1960–1970." PhD diss. University of Maryland, College Park, 2008.
Kempley, Rita. "'Crossroads': Muddled Directions." *Washington Post*, March 14,
    1986. https://www.washingtonpost.com/archive/lifestyle/1986/03/14/
    crossroads-muddled-directions/27e5621b-d0b5-425c-bec5-5e800f49450b/.
Kerrigan, David. "1984 W. C. Handy Blues Awards Show." *Living Blues*, no. 63
    (January/February 1985): 38–41.
King, B. B., with David Ritz. *Blues All around Me: The Autobiography of B. B. King.*
    New York: Avon, 1996.
King, Stephen A. *I'm Feeling the Blues Right Now: Blues Tourism and the Mississippi
    Delta.* Jackson: University Press of Mississippi, 2011.

———. "Race and Blues Tourism: A Comparison of Two Lodging Alternatives in Clarksdale, Mississippi." *Arkansas Review* 36, no. 1 (April 2005): 26–42.

Kitchen Sisters. "Kibbe at the Crossroads: A Lebanese Kitchen Story." January 31, 2008. http://www.npr.org/2008/01/31/18547399/kibbe-at-the-crossroads-a-lebanese-kitchen-story.

Klatzel, Earl. Phone interview with Adam Gussow, July 22, 2014.

Komara, Edward. E-mail to Adam Gussow, May 15, 2014.

———. *The Road to Robert Johnson.* Milwaukee: Hal Leonard, 2007.

Kot, Greg. "Jimmie Vaughan a Terrific Team Player." *Chicago Tribune*, August 14, 2011. http://articles.chicagotribune.com/2011-08-14/entertainment/chi-jimmie-vaughan-interview-guitarist-profiled-20110814_1_jimmie-vaughan-stevie-ray-vaughan-webb-pierce.

Kubik, Gerhard. *Africa and the Blues.* Jackson: University Press of Mississippi, 1999.

Laird, Ross. *Moanin' Low: A Discography of Female Popular Vocal Recordings, 1920–1933.* Westport, Conn.: Greenwood, 1996.

Lara, Ana-Maurine. "'i think i might be broken': The Reconstitution of Black Atlantic Bodies and Memories in Sharon Bridgforth's *Delta Dandi*." In *Diasporic Women's Writing of the Black Atlantic: (En)Gendering Literature and Performance*, edited by Emilia María Durán-Almarza and Esther Alvarez-López, 34–51. New York: Routledge, 2014.

Lasser, Michael. *America's Songs II: Songs from the 1890s to the Post-war Years.* New York: Routledge, 2014.

LaVere, Stephen C. "A Biography Reassessed and Amended upon the 100th Anniversary of His Birth." Liner notes. *The Centennial Collection: The Complete Recordings [of] Robert Johnson.* Columbia/Legacy CK 88697/85907 2.

———. E-mail to Adam Gussow, September 10, 2014.

Lawal, Babatunde. "Reclaiming the Past: Yoruba Elements in African American Arts." In *The Yoruba Diaspora in the Atlantic World*, edited by Toyin Falola and Matt D. Childs, 291–324. Bloomington: University of Indiana Press, 2004.

LeBlanc, Pat. Phone interview with Adam Gussow, June 27, 2013.

Leitch, Vincent B. "Blues Southwestern Style." In *Theory Matters*, 137–64. New York: Routledge, 2003.

Lesseig, Corey Todd. "Automobility and Social Change: Mississippi, 1909–1939." PhD diss. University of Mississippi, 1997.

Lester, Bill. Phone interview with Adam Gussow. September 7, 2014.

Levine, Lawrence W. *Black Culture and Black Consciousness: Afro-American Folk Thought from Slavery to Freedom.* New York: Oxford University Press, 1978 [1977].

Lincoln, C. Eric, and Lawrence H. Mamiya. *The Black Church in the African American Experience.* Durham, N.C.: Duke University Press, 1990.

"Linker's Plan for Road Here Is Presented." *Clarksdale Daily Register*, August 5, 1931.

Lipsitz, George. *Midnight at the Barrelhouse: The Johnny Otis Story.* Minneapolis: University of Minnesota Press, 2010.

———. *The Possessive Investment in Whiteness: How White People Profit from Identity Politics.* Revised and expanded edition. Philadelphia: Temple University Press, 2006.

Little, Bert. "Prison Lingo: A Style of American English Slang." *Anthropological Linguistics* 24, no. 2 (Summer 1982). https://www.jstor.org/stable/30027838.

Litwack, Leon F. *Been in the Storm So Long: The Aftermath of Slavery.* New York: Vintage, 1980 [1979].

————. *Trouble in Mind: Black Southerners in the Age of Jim Crow.* New York: Alfred A. Knopf, 1998.

Lomax, Alan. "Fisk, 3. 5. Dave Edwards." [1942]. Alan Lomax Collection (AFC 2004/004, folder 09.04.07 9/9. America Folklife Center, Library of Congress.

————. *The Land Where the Blues Began.* New York: Pantheon, 1993.

Lornell, Christopher. "Barrelhouse Singers and Sanctified Preachers." In Sacré, *Saints and Sinners*, 37–49.

Lott, Eric. *Love and Theft: Blackface Minstrelsy and the American Working Class.* Oxford: Oxford University Press, 1993.

Lovell, John, Jr. *Black Song: The Forge and the Flame: The Story of How the Afro-American Spiritual Was Hammered Out.* New York: Paragon, 1986 [1972].

————. "The Social Implications of the Negro Spiritual." *Journal of Negro Education* 8, no. 4 (October 1939): 634–43.

Luckett, Bill. E-mail forwarded by Shelley Ritter, June 14, 2013.

Lyotard, Jean-Francois. *The Postmodern Condition: A Report on Knowledge.* Translated from the French by Geoff Bennington and Brian Massumi. Minneapolis: University of Minnesota Press, 1003. http://faculty.georgetown.edu/irvinem/theory/Lyotard-PostModernCondition1-5.html. Accessed November 20, 2016.

MacKell, Jan, and Thomas J. Noel. *Brothels, Bordellos, and Bad Girls: Prostitution in Colorado, 1860–1930.* Albuquerque: University of New Mexico Press, 2007.

Malone, Jacqui. *Steppin' on the Blues: The Visible Rhythms of African American Dance.* Urbana: University of Illinois Press, 1996.

Mancini, Matthew. *One Dies, Get Another: Convict Leasing in the American South, 1866–1928.* Columbia: University of South Carolina Press, 1996.

Marcus, Greil. *Mystery Train: Images of American in Rock 'n' Roll Music.* 2nd ed. New York: E. P. Dutton, 1982.

"Marking the Spot." *Clarksdale Press-Register*, May 11, 1999. Photo by Carol Knight.

Marsh, J. M. "Superintendent's Report, Clarksdale District." In *Official Journal of the Thirty-Third Annual Session of the Upper Mississippi Conference of the Methodist Episcopal Church*, edited by B. F. Woolfolk. January 31–February 4, 1923. J. B. Cain Archives of Mississippi Methodism, Millsaps College.

Marshall, Matt. "Headstone Campaign Raising Funds for Casey Bill Weldon, Kansas City's Blues Mystery Man." *American Blues Scene*, March 18, 2014. https://www.americanbluesscene.com/2014/03/headstone-campaign-raising-funds-for-casey-bill-weldon-kansas-citys-blues-mystery-man/.

Mayfield, Panny. "Crossroads Sign Runs into State Roadblock." *Clarksdale Press-Register*, March 16, 1999.

————. "Delta Blues Museum Turns 20." *Clarksdale Press-Register*, March 22, 1999.

Maynard, Mark. "Bruce Conforth on the Real Life of Robert Johnson, the Real Hell of the Rock and Roll Hall of Fame, and What It Was Like Coming of Age Inside Izzy's Young's Folklore Center as the Young Bobby Zimmerman Hammered Out Songs

on the Typewriter in the Back Room . . . on Episode 44 of the Saturday Six Pack."
http://markmaynard.com/2016/07/bruce-conforth-on-the-real-life-of-robert-
johnson-the-real-hell-of-the-rock-and-roll-hall-of-fame-and-what-it-was-like-
coming-of-age-inside-izzys-youngs-folklore-center-as-the-young-bobby-zimmer/
. Accessed August 14, 2016.

McGinley, Paige A. *Staging the Blues: From Tent Shows to Tourism*. Durham, N.C.:
Duke University Press, 2014.

McKay, Alastair. "Play Me Your Delta Blues." *Scotsman*, March 20, 2004. https://www
.highbeam.com/doc/1P2-13043323.html.

McMahon, John R. "Unspeakable Jazz Must Go!" *Ladies Home Journal*, December
1921.

McMillen, Neil R. *Dark Journey: Black Mississippians in the Age of Jim Crow*. Urbana:
University of Illinois Press, 1990.

Mencken, H. L. *The American Language, Supplement One*. New York: Alfred A. Knopf,
1956.

Merryweather, L. W. "*Hell* in American Speech." *American Speech* 6, no. 6 (August
1931). www.jstor.org/stable/452398.

Messadié, Gérald. *A History of the Devil*. Translated by Marc Romano. New York:
Kodansha International, 1996 [1993].

Mikkelsen, Vincent P. "Coming from Battle to Face a War: The Lynching of Black
Soldiers in the World War I Era." PhD diss., Florida State University, 2007.
https://fsu.digital.flvc.org/islandora/object/fsu:180643/datastream/PDF/view.

Milkowski, Bill. "Stevie Ray Vaughan: Hendrix' White Knight." *Guitar World*, May
1984. http://www.guitarworld.com/stevie-ray-vaughan-opens-his-first-guitar
-world-interview-1984.

Miller, Karl Hagstrom. *Segregating Sound: Inventing Folk and Pop Music in the Age of
Jim Crow*. Durham, N.C.: Duke University Press, 2010.

Miller, Mark. "Bad Luck Is Good Luck for Bluesman." *Globe and Mail*, April 2, 1985.

"Minutes of the Meeting of the Board of Mayor and Commissioners of the City of
Clarksdale." March 15, 1999. E-mail to Adam Gussow from Cathy Clark, June 11,
2013.

Mississippi Legislature. "House Bill No. 1745." 1999. http://billstatus.ls.state.ms.us/
documents/1999%5Cpdf%5CHB/1700–1799/HB1745PS.pdf. Mississippi Legislature. "House Bill 1749." 1999. http://billstatus.ls.state.ms.us/documents/1999
%5Chtml%5CHB/1700–1799/HB1749SG.htm.

Montgomery, William E. *Under Their Own Vine and Fig Tree: The African-American
Church in the South, 1865–1900*. Baton Rouge: Louisiana State University Press,
1993.

Moon, D. Thomas. "Eddy Clearwater: It's a Hard Way to Make an Easy Living." *Living
Blues*, no. 127 (May/June 1996): 14–27.

Moore, Mary Elizabeth, and Almeda M. Wright. *Children, Youth, and Spirituality in a
Troubling World*. Atlanta: Chalice, 2008.

"Morgan Freeman Revives 'Birthplace of Blues.'" Robin Meade interviews Morgan
Freeman and Bill Luckett. *Morning Express* on HLN, September 5, 2013. http://www
.hlntv.com/video/2013/09/03/morgan-freeman-bill-luckett-clarksdale-mississippi.

Mosley, Walter. *RL's Dream*. New York: Pocket, 1996.

Moss, Robert F. *Barbecue: The History of an American Institution*. Tuscaloosa: University of Alabama Press, 2010.

Muchembled, Robert. *A History of the Devil: From the Middle Ages to the Present*. Translated by Jean Birrell. Cambridge, U.K.: Polity, 2003 [2000].

Murphy, Jeannette Robinson. "The Survival of African Music in America." *Popular Science Monthly* 55, no. 41 (September 1899): 662.

Murray, Albert. *The Blue Devils of Nada: A Contemporary American Approach to Aesthetic Statement*. New York: Pantheon, 1996.

———. *Stomping the Blues*. New York: Da Capo, 1987 [1976].

Murray, Charles Shaar. *Boogie Man: The Adventures of John Lee Hooker in the American Twentieth Century*. New York: St. Martin's, 2000.

Myrdal, Gunnar. *An American Dilemma: The Negro Problem and Modern Democracy*. Vol. 2. New York: Harper Torchbooks, 1969 [1944].

National Public Radio. "Interview: Singer Chris Thomas King Discusses His Unique Style of Blues Music and His Role in the New Film *O Brother, Where Art Thou?*" *Weekend All Things Considered*, January 6, 2001.

———. "Profile: Church Remembrance of Blues Legend Robert Johnson." *Morning Edition*, August 17, 2001.

Neal, Larry. "A Review-Essay: *The Sound of Soul*, by Phyl Garland." *Black World/Negro Digest*, January 1970, 43–47.

Neff, Ali Colleen. *Let the World Listen Right: The Mississippi Delta Hip-Hop Story*. Jackson: University Press of Mississippi, 2009.

"Negro Superstition Concerning the Violin." *Journal of American Folklore* 5, no. 19 (October–December 1892): 329–30. www.jstor.org/stable/533246.

"New Hat in the Ring." *Clarksdale Daily Register*, November 6, 1931.

"The New World." Mississippi Blues Trail. http://www.msbluestrail.org/blues-trail-markers/the-new-world. Accessed November 18, 2016.

Niester, Alan. "Bluesman Impressive but Something Missing: Vaughan More Smoke Than Fire." *Globe and Mail*, March 30, 1985.

Noonan, Jeffrey J. *The Guitar in America: Victorian Era to Jazz Age*. Jackson: University Press of Mississippi, 2008.

Northup, Solomon. *Twelve Years a Slave*. Radford, Va.: Wilder, 2008 [1853].

Nuwer, Deanne S. "Gambling in Mississippi: Its Early History." *Mississippi Now*. http://mshistorynow.mdah.state.ms.us/articles/80/gambling-in-mississippi-its-early-history.

Nye, Russel B. "Saturday Night at the Paradise Ballroom; or, Dance Halls in the Twenties." *Journal of Popular Culture* 7, no. 1 (Summer 1973): 14–22.

Oakley, Giles. *The Devil's Music: A History of the Blues*. New York: Da Capo, 1997 [1976].

Obrecht, Jas. "Been Some Powerful Stuff Happen to Me." *Living Blues*, no. 142 (November/December 1998): 18–31.

———. *Blues Guitar: The Men Who Made the Music*. San Francisco: GPI, 1993.

———. "Eddie Guitar Burns: Inside Detroit Blues." *Living Blues*, no. 156 (March/April 2001): 28–39.

Odum, Howard W. "Folk-Song and Folk-Poetry as Found in the Secular Songs of the Southern Negroes." *Journal of American Folklore* 24 (July–September 1911): 255–94. In Tracy, *Write Me a Few of Your Lines*, 133–71.

———. *Religious Folk-Songs of the Southern Negroes*. Rpt., *American Journal of Religious Psychology and Education* 3 (July 1909): 265–365.

———. *Wings on My Feet: Black Ulysses at the Wars*. Indianapolis: Bobbs-Merrill, 1929.

Odum, Howard W., and Guy B. Johnson. *The Negro and His Songs: A Study of Typical Negro Songs of the South*. Chapel Hill: University of North Carolina Press, 1925.

———. *Negro Workaday Songs*. New York: Negro Universities Press, 1977 [1926].

Ogren, Kathy J. *The Jazz Revolution: Twenties America and the Meaning of Jazz*. New York: Oxford University Press, 1992 [1989].

Oliver, Paul. "African Influence on the Blues." *Living Blues*, no. 8 (Spring 1972): 13–17.

———. *Blues Fell This Morning: Meaning in the Blues*. New York: Cambridge University Press, 1990 [1960].

———. *Conversation with the Blues*. New York: Horizon, 1965.

———. *Savannah Syncopators: African Retentions in the Blues*. London: Studio Vista, 1970.

———. *Screening the Blues: Aspects of the Blues Tradition*. New York: Da Capo, 1968.

———. *Songsters and Saints: Vocal Traditions on Race Records*. New York: Cambridge University Press, 1984.

Olofson, Harold. "Children of the Bowed Lute: Social Organization and Expressive Culture of Hausa Urban Itinerant Entertainers." *Anthropos* 75, nos. 5/6 (1980): 920–29.

O'Neal, Jim. "The Crossroads." *Living Blues*, no. 172 (March/April 2004): 27.

———. "The Death of Robert Johnson." *Living Blues*, no. 94 (November/December 1990): 8–24.

———. "Delta Blues Map Kit." 1994. Self-published.

———. E-mail to Adam Gussow, July 22, 2008.

———. "Handy Awards Forum." *Living Blues*, no. 73 (January/February 1987): 14–15.

———. "Jack Owens: A Remembrance." *Living Blues*, no. 137 (January/February 1998): 30–37.

———. "Junior Wells." *Living Blues*, no. 119 (January/February 1995): 8–29.

———. "Muddy Waters." *Living Blues*, no. 57 (Autumn 1983): 10.

———. Phone interview with Adam Gussow, July 23, 2014.

———. "A Traveler's Guide to the Crossroads." *Living Blues*, no. 94 (November/December 1990): 21–24.

———. "Unraveling Casey Bill: The Hawaiian Guitar Wizard." *Living Blues*, no. 228 (November/December 2013): 72–77.

O'Neal, Jim, and Amy van Singel, eds. *The Voice of the Blues: Classic Interviews from "Living Blues" Magazine*. New York: Routledge, 2002.

O'Neal, Jim, Steve Wisner, and David Nelson. "Snooky Prior: I Started the Big Noise around Chicago." *Living Blues*, no. 123 (September/October 1995): 8–21.

"One of Longest Straightest Paved Roads in the World—It's in Coahoma County, Mississippi." *Mississippi Highways* 4, no. 4 (July 1935): 10.

Ortiz, Paul. *Emancipation Betrayed: The Hidden History of Black Organizing and White Violence in Florida from Reconstruction to the Bloody Election of 1920*. Berkeley: University of California Press, 2005.

Oshinsky, David M. *"Worse Than Slavery": Parchman Farm and the Ordeal of Jim Crow Justice*. New York: Free Press, 1996.

Otis, Johnny. *Upside Your Head! Rhythm and Blues on Central Avenue*. Hanover, N.H.: University Press of New England, 1993.

Palmer, Robert. *Deep Blues: A Musical and Cultural History of the Mississippi Delta*. New York: Viking, 1981.

———. "Muddy Waters, Blues Performer, Dies." *New York Times*, May 1, 1983. http://www.nytimes.com/learning/general/onthisday/bday/0404.html.

———. "The Pop Life; Rock: No Longer 'Devil's Music.'" *New York Times*, September 16, 1981. http://www.nytimes.com/1981/09/16/arts/the-pop-life-rock-no-longer-devil-s-music.html.

Pareles, Jon. "From Cool to Exultant, with a Touch of Blue; Lincoln Center Mixes Blues, Gospel and Folk." *New York Times*, August 26, 1988. http://www.nytimes.com/1988/08/26/arts/cool-exultant-with-touch-blue-lincoln-center-mixes-blues-gospel-folk.html.

"Paul Claxton, Engineers Are to Make Route." *Clarksdale Daily Register*, June 1, 1931.

Pearson, Barry Lee. *Jook Right On: Blues Stories and Blues Storytellers*. Knoxville: University of Tennessee Press, 2005.

———. *"Sounds So Good to Me": The Bluesman's Story*. Philadelphia: University of Pennsylvania Press, 1984.

———. "Standing at the Crossroads between Vinyl and Compact Discs: Reissue Blues Recordings in the 1990s." *Journal of American Folklore* 105, no. 416 (Spring 1992): 215–26.

Pearson, Barry Lee, and Bill McCulloch. *Robert Johnson: Lost and Found*. Urbana: University of Illinois Press, 2003.

Pearson, Barry Lee, with the assistance of Rich Burns. "Cedell Davis: Pine Bluff Blues." *Living Blues*, no. 166 (November/December 2002): 30–37.

Pelton, Robert D. *The Trickster in West Africa: A Study of Mythic Irony and Sacred Delight*. Berkeley: University of California Press, 1980.

Pinn, Anthony B. *Terror and Triumph: The Nature of Black Religion*. Minneapolis: Fortress, 2003.

———. "When Demons Come Calling: Dealing with the Devil and Paradigms of Life in African American Music." In *The Lure of the Dark Side: Satan and Western Demonology in Popular Culture*, edited by Christopher Partridge and Eric Christianson, 60–73. London: Equinox, 2009.

Pinn, Anthony B., and Dwight N. Hopkins. *Loving the Body: Black Religious Studies and the Erotic*. New York: Palgrave Macmillan, 2004.

Powdermaker, Hortense. *After Freedom: A Cultural Study in the Deep South*. With a new introduction by Brackette F. Williams and Drexel G. Woodson. Madison: University of Wisconsin Press, 1993 [1939].

Powell, Carry Craig. "Talkin' Blues at the 'Living Blues' Symposium." *Arkansas Review: A Journal of Delta Studies* 35, no. 2 (August 2004): 121.

Powell, Waunita, ed. *Three Richard Parkers of Va*. http://www.nhn.ou.edu/~parker/
Genealogy/Ancestors/Books/ThreeRichardParkers.pdf, September 23, 2009, 3–4.

"Principal Traveled Highways." *Mississippi Highways* (December 1931): 18–19.

"Proclamation and Resolution." Board of Mayor and Commissioners of the City of
Clarksdale, May 24, 1999. E-mail from Cathy Clark, June 11, 2013.

"Pros Say It's Easy to Sell the Mississippi Delta Blues." Special publication of the
Mississippi Business Journal, May 22, 2006. http://www.allbusiness.com/north
-america/united-states-mississippi/4097107-1.html.

Puckett, Newbell Niles. *Folk Beliefs of the Southern Negro*. Montclair, N.J.: Patterson
Smith, 1968 [1926].

Raboteau, Albert J. *Slave Religion: The "Invisible Institution" in the Antebellum South*.
New York: Oxford University Press, 1980 [1978].

Radano, Ronald. *Lying up a Nation: Race and Black Music*. Chicago: University of
Chicago Press, 2003.

Radano, Ronald, and Philip V. Bohlman, eds. *Music and the Racial Imagination*.
Chicago: University of Chicago Press, 2000.

Rawick, George P., ed. *The American Slave: A Composite Autobiography*, vol. 19,
God Struck Me Dead (Fisk University). Westport, Conn.: Greenwood, 1972.

Reed, Teresa L. *The Holy Profane: Religion in Black Popular Music*. Lexington:
University Press of Kentucky, 2003.

Reid, Graham. "Champion Jack Dupree Remembered: Seconds Out of the Ring . . ."
Elsewhere. http://www.elsewhere.co.nz/blues/4700/champion-jack-dupree-
remembered-seconds-out-of-the-ring/. Accessed August 10, 2016.

"Resolution to Leave Road Up to Engineers." *Clarksdale Daily Register*, August 12,
1931.

Richard, Melissa J. "The Crossroads and the Myth of the Mississippi Delta Bluesman."
Interdisciplinary Humanities 23, no. 2 (Fall 2006): 19–26.

Richter, Simon. "Help from the Devil in Boosting Course Enrollments." *Chronicle of
Higher Education* 46, no. 45 (2000): A56.

Riesman, Bob. *I Feel So Good: The Life and Times of Big Bill Broonzy*. Chicago:
University of Chicago Press, 2011.

"Road Map of Mississippi." *Mississippi Highways*, October 1932, 18–19.

"Road Map of Mississippi." *Mississippi Highways*, January 1935, 2.

"Robert Johnson." http://en.wikipedia.org/wiki/Robert_Johnson. Accessed July 2,
2013.

"The Robert Johnson Blues Park—Proposal." http://www.robertjohnsonblues
foundation.org/photos/robert-johnson-blues-park-proposal/. Accessed
November 19, 2016.

"Robert Johnson Crossroads Blues Legends Park." https://web.archive.org/web/
20090202200646/http://www.crossroadshotel.tv/. Accessed November 19, 2016.

"Robert Johnson, Every Time He'd Get Drunk He'd Cuss God." Interview with
Memphis Slim. *Living Blues*, no. 94 (November/December 1990): 15.

"Robert Johnson: The Legend behind *Crossroads*." Columbia Pictures press release.
1986. Film Treatments. *Crossroads*. Blues W-1. Blues Archive. J. D. Williams
Library. University of Mississippi.

Roberts, John W. *From Trickster to Badman: The Black Folk Hero in Slavery and Freedom*. Philadelphia: University of Pennsylvania Press, 1989.

Robertson, David. *W. C. Handy: The Life and Times of the Man Who Made the Blues*. New York: Alfred A. Knopf, 2009.

Rose, Joel. "Robert Johnson at 100, Still Dispelling Myths." Weekend Edition Saturday, May 6, 2011. http://www.npr.org/2011/05/07/136063911/robert-johnson-at-100 -still-dispelling-myths.

Ross, Andy. "Investors Plan New Entertainment Complex." *Clarksdale Press-Register*, September 17, 2008.

Roth, Arlen. "Crossroads." http://arlenroth.com/html/crossroads.shtml. Accessed August 10, 2016.

———. E-mail to Adam Gussow, March 10, 2014.

———. Phone interview with Adam Gussow, July 15, 2013.

Rothenbuhler, Eric. "The Myth of Robert Johnson." Paper presented at the annual meeting of the International Communication Association, Dresden International Congress Centre, Dresden, Germany, June 16, 2006. http://www.allacademic.com/ meta/p91612_index.html.

Rudinow, Joel. *Soul Music: Tracking the Spiritual Roots of Pop from Plato to Motown*. Ann Arbor: University of Michigan Press, 2010.

Rudwin, Maximilian. *The Devil in Legend and Literature*. Lasalle, Ill.: Open Court, 1973 [1931].

Ruskey, John. "Deep down in the Delta: Confusion at the Crossroads." *Blues Revue* 52 (November 1999): 62–63.

———. "Deep down in the Delta: Mario Meets the Devil." *Blues Revue* 53 (December 1999): 70–72.

———. Phone interview with Adam Gussow, May 20, 2014.

Russell, Tony. *The Blues: From Robert Johnson to Robert Cray*. London: Aurum, 1997.

Sacré, Robert, ed. *Saints and Sinners: Religion, Blues, and (D)evil in African-American Music and Literature*. Proceedings of the Conference Held at the Université de Liège, October 1991. Liège, Belgium: Société Liégeoise de Musicologie, 1996.

———. "Saints and Sinners Under the Swing of the Cross." In Sacré, *Saints and Sinners*, 3–36.

Salaam, Kalamu ya. *What Is Life? Reclaiming the Black Blues Self*. Chicago: Third World, 1994.

Salau, Mohammed Bashir. E-mail to Adam Gussow, March 10, 2015.

Salem, James M. *The Late Great Johnny Ace and the Transition from R&B to Rock 'n' Roll*. Urbana: University of Illinois Press, 1999.

Salem, Rob. "Bluesy Superkid Leaves a Sync-ing Sensation." *Toronto Star*, March 14, 1986.

"Sanborn Fire Insurance Map from Clarksdale, Coahoma County, Mississippi." New York: Sanborn Map Company, June 1929. Mississippiana. Special Collections. Mississippi State University Library.

"Sanborn Fire Insurance Map from Clarksdale, Coahoma County, Mississippi." New York: Sanborn Map Company, 1938. Carnegie Public Library. Clarksdale, Mississippi.

Sanders, Cheryl J. *The Holiness-Pentecostal Experience in African American Religion and Culture*. New York: Oxford University Press, 1996.

Sawyer, Charles. *The Arrival of B. B. King: The Authorized Biography*. New York: Da Capo, 1982 [1980].

Saxon, Lyle, Edward Dreyer, and Robert Tallent, eds. *Gumbo Ya-Ya: Folk Tales of Louisiana*. Gretna, La.: Pelican, 1987 [1945].

Scherman, Tony. "The Hellhound's Trail: Following Robert Johnson." *Musician* 147 (January 1991): 31–48.

Schroeder, Patricia R. *Robert Johnson, Mythmaking, and Contemporary American Culture*. Urbana: University of Illinois Press, 2004.

Schumacher, Michael. *Crossroads: The Life and Music of Eric Clapton*. New York: Hyperion, 1995.

"Scores of Men Get Jobs Here on Road Work." *Clarksdale Daily Register*, March 26, 1931.

Scott, James C. *Domination and the Arts of Resistance: Hidden Transcripts*. New Haven, Conn.: Yale University Press, 1990.

Scott, Michelle R. *Blues Empress in Black Chattanooga: Bessie Smith and the Emerging Urban South*. Urbana: University of Illinois Press, 2008.

Segrest, James, and Mark Hoffman. *Moanin' at Midnight: The Life and Times of Howlin' Wolf*. New York: Pantheon, 2004.

Seratt, Bill. Phone interview with Adam Gussow, July 11, 2013.

"The Sermon as Heard by Zora Neale Hurston from C. C. Lovelace, at Eau Gallie in Florida, May 3, 1929." *Negro: An Anthology*, edited by Nancy Cunard and Hugh D. Ford, 35–39. New York: Continuum, 1996 [1934].

Sernett, Milton C. *Bound for the Promised Land: African American Religion and the Great Migration*. Durham, N.C.: Duke University Press, 1997.

"*Show 41: Hoodoo Women*." *Uncensored History of the Blues*. March 18, 2009. http://uncensoredhistoryoftheblues.purplebeech.com/2009/03/show-41-hoodoo-women .html.

Smith, Ayana. "Blues, Criticism, and the Signifying Trickster." *Popular Music* 24, no. 2 (2005): 179–91.

Smith, Nell. Phone interview with Adam Gussow, August 18, 2014.

Smith, Therese. *"Let the Church Sing!" Music and Worship in a Black Mississippi Community*. Rochester, N.Y.: University of Rochester Press, 2004.

Sotiropoulos, Karen. *Staging Race: Black Performers in Turn of the Century America*. Cambridge, Mass.: Harvard University Press, 2006.

Spencer, Jon Michael. *Blues and Evil*. Knoxville: University of Tennessee Press, 1993.

———. *The Rhythms of Black Folk: Race, Religion, and Pan-Africanism*. Trenton, N.J.: Africa World, 1995.

Standish, David. "Highway to the Blues: Highway 61, Known as Blues Alley, Takes You along the Mississippi River Delta through an Unrelentingly Flat Landscape That Has Nurtured the Blues as Lovingly as It Has Cotton." *Vancouver Sun*, August 1, 1998.

Stolle, Roger. *Hidden History of Mississippi Blues*. Charleston, S.C.: History Press, 2011.

Stout, David. "Chavez Calls Bush 'the Devil' in U.N. Speech." *New York Times*,

September 20, 2006. http://www.nytimes.com/2006/09/20/world/americas
/20cnd-chavez.html.

Strauss, Neil. "A Home of the Blues, Singing a New Tune." *New York Times*,
October 26, 1999.

Stuckey, Sterling. *Slave Culture: Nationalist Theory and the Foundations of Black
America*. New York: Oxford University Press, 1987.

Swift, Jonathan. "Journal to Stella." *The Works of the Rev. Jonathan Swift*. Edited by
Thomas Sheridan and John Nichols. London: J. Johnson, 1808.

Szwed, John F. "Musical Adaptation among Afro-Americans." *Journal of American
Folklore* 82, no. 324 (April–June 1969): 112–21.

Telephone Directory, Clarksdale, Miss. 1936. Mississippi Collection, Carnegie Public
Library, Clarksdale.

Telephone Directory, Clarksdale, Miss. 1941. Mississippi Collection, Carnegie Public
Library, Clarksdale.

Telephone Directory, Clarksdale, Miss. May 1964. Mississippi Collection, Carnegie
Public Library, Clarksdale.

"Ten New Artists You Need to Know: Leo 'Bud' Welch." *Rolling Stone*, February 2015.
http://www.rollingstone.com/music/pictures/10-new-artists-you-need-to-know
-february-2015–20150219.

"Text of President Bush's 2002 State of the Union Address." *Washington Post*,
January 29, 2002. http://www.washingtonpost.com/wp-srv/onpolitics/transcripts/
sou012902.htm.

Thomas, Tony. "Why Black Folks Don't Fiddle." *BlueGrass West*. http://www
.bluegrasswest.com/ideas/why_black.htm. Accessed August 10, 2016.

———. E-mail to Adam Gussow, January 9, 2015.

Thompson, Robert Farris. *Flash of the Spirit: African and Afro-American Art &
Philosophy*. New York: Vintage, 1984 [1983].

"Thousand Fans Attend Rites for Muddy Waters," *New York Times*, May 6, 1983. http://
www.nytimes.com/1983/05/06/arts/thousand-fans-attend-rites-for-muddy-waters
.html.

Titon, Jeff Todd. *Early Downhome Blues: A Musical and Cultural Analysis*. 2nd ed.
Chapel Hill: University of North Carolina Press, 1994.

———. "The New Blues Tourism." *Arkansas Review: A Journal of Delta Studies* 29,
no. 1 (1998): 5–10.

Tolnay, Stewart E., and E. F. Beck. *A Festival of Violence: An Analysis of Southern
Lynchings, 1882–1930*. Urbana: University of Illinois Press, 1995.

Tomko, Gene. "Look for Me and I'll Be Gone: The Mysterious Life of Cousin Leroy."
Living Blues, no. 217 (January/February 2012): 8–9.

Townsend, Henry, as told to Bill Greensmith. *A Blues Life*. Urbana: University of
Illinois Press, 1999.

Tracy, Steven C. "The Devil's Son-in-Law and *Invisible Man*." *MELUS* 15, no. 3
(Autumn 1988): 47–64.

———. *Going to Cincinnati: A History of the Blues in the Queen City*. Urbana:
University of Illinois Press, 1993.

————, ed. *Write Me a Few of Your Lines: A Blues Reader*. Amherst: University of Massachusetts Press, 1999.

Tramontana, Gianluca. "David 'Honeyboy' Edwards: Traveling Up and Down the Road." *Dirty Linen* 87 (April–May 2000): 34–35, 37.

Trynka, Paul. E-mail to Adam Gussow, June 24, 2013.

————. Interview with Honeyboy Edwards, December 9, 1994. Excerpted in e-mail to Adam Gussow, June 24, 2013.

————. Phone interview with Adam Gussow, July 17, 2013.

————. *Portrait of the Blues*. Photographs by Val Wilmer. New York: Da Capo, 1997 [1996].

Twiford, Hunter H. E-mail to Adam Gussow, June 21, 2013.

————. E-mail to Adam Gussow, October 30, 2014.

————. Phone interview with Adam Gussow, July 17, 2013.

Urban, Michael, with Andrei Evdokimov. *Russia Gets the Blues: Music, Culture, and Community in Unsettled Times*. Ithaca, N.Y.: Cornell University Press, 2004.

"Vacation Postcards: Cotton Boll Court, Clarksdale." Preservation in Mississippi: It Ain't All Moonlight and Moonlight and Magnolias website, https://misspreservation.com/2010/10/11/vacation-postcards-cotton-boll-court%C2%A0clarksdale/.

van Rijn, Guido. *The Truman and Eisenhower Blues: African-American Blues and Gospel Songs, 1945–1960*. New York: Continuum, 2004.

Varner, Roy. "*Living Blues* Interview: Robert Cray Doesn't Hitchhike to Gigs Anymore." *Living Blues*, no. 73 (January/February 1987): 22–27.

"The Viper Label Online Store—Up Jumped the Devil: American Devil Songs 1920s to 1950s." http://www.viper-store.co.ukshop.php/cd-albums/up-jumped-the-devil/p_54.html. Accessed September 10, 2008.

Vulliamy, Ed. "The Unbeautiful South." *The Observer*. October 21, 2000. http://www.theguardian.com/world/2000/oct/22/uselections2000.usa1.

Wald, Elijah. *Escaping the Delta: Robert Johnson and the Invention of the Blues*. New York: HarperCollins, 2004.

Wald, Gayle F. *Shout, Sister, Shout! The Untold Story of Rock-and-Roll Trailblazer Sister Rosetta Tharpe*. Boston: Beacon, 2007.

Walker, David. "David Walker's *Appeal*" (1829). In *The Norton Anthology of African American Literature*, edited by Henry Louis Gates Jr. and Nellie Y. McKay, 179–90. New York: W. W. Norton, 1997.

————. "Walker's *Appeal*, with a Brief Sketch of His Life by Henry Highland Garnett" (1848). http://www.gutenberg.org/files/16516/16516-h/16516-h.htm.

Walser, Robert, ed. *Keeping Time: Readings in Jazz History*. New York: Oxford University Press, 1999.

"Walter Hill: Biography." Columbia Pictures press release. 1986. Film Treatments. *Crossroads*. Blues W-1. Blues Archive. J. D. Williams Library. University of Mississippi.

Walton, Jonathan L. "The Preachers' Blues: Religious Race Records and Claims of Authority on Wax." *Religion and American Culture* 20, no. 2 (Summer 2010): 205–32.

Ward, Brian. *Just My Soul Responding: Rhythm and Blues, Black Consciousness, and Race.* London: University College London, 2003.

Wardlow, Gayle Dean. *Chasin' That Devil Music: Searching for the Blues.* San Francisco: Backbeat, 1998.

Warner, Gary A. "On the Blues Highway: A Trip to the Delta's Musical Heartland." *Toronto Star*, May 30, 1998.

"Was His Greatness Due to Satan?" *USA Today*, October 11, 1990.

Waters, Muddy, as told to Alfred Duckett. "'Got a Right to Sing the Blues'—Muddy Waters." *Chicago Defender*, March 26, 1955.

"We Back Rotary to the Limit." *Clarksdale Daily Register*, November 4, 1931.

"Welcome to Clarksdale Station." *Clarksdale Press-Register*, March 13, 1999. Photo by Panny Mayfield.

Welding, Pete. "Hell Hound on His Trail: Robert Johnson." *Blues Unlimited*, no. 83 (July 1971): 16–17. Reprinted from Down Beat's Music '66. Chicago: Maher, 1966.

Wells, Paul F. "Fiddling as an Avenue of Black-White Musical Interchange." *Black Music Research Journal* 23, nos. 1–2 (Spring–Autumn 2003): 135–47.

Wells-Barnett, Ida B. The Project Gutenberg eBook edition of *The Red Record* (1895). http://www.gutenberg.org/files/14977/14977-h/14977-h.htm.

West, Cornell, and Eddie S. Glaude Jr., eds. *African American Religious Thought: An Anthology.* Louisville, Ky.: Westminster John Knox Press, 2003.

"What Every Non-Muslim Needs to Know about Islam!" http://www.bible.ca/islam/islam-encyclopedia-westerners-need-to-know-list.htm. Accessed November 19, 2016.

White, Matthew B. "'The Blues Ain't Nothin' but a Woman Want to Be a Man': Male Control in Early Twentieth Century Blues Music." *Canadian Review of American Studies* 24, no. 1 (Winter 1994): 19, 22.

Whiteis, David. "Club Dates: Johnny Shines Brings His Blues Back Home." *Chicago Reader*, May 10, 1990. http://www.chicagoreader.com/chicago/club-dates-johnny-shines-brings-his-blues-back-home/Content?oid=875656.

"Why Mose Jackson Could Not Vote." *New York Times*, February 9, 1908.

"Will Renovated Depot Fuel Downtown Resurgence?" *Clarksdale Press-Register*, March 13, 1999.

"Willie Foster Sings 'Highway 61.'" December 9, 2014. https://www.youtube.com/watch?v=jKPFGlpL2gI.

Winans, Robert B. "Black Instrumental Music Traditions in the Ex-slave Narratives." *Black Music Research Journal* 10, no. 1 (Spring 1990): 43–53.

Winborn, Mark. *Deep Blues: Human Soundscapes for the Archetypal Journey.* Cheyenne, Wyo.: Fisher King, 2011.

"Withdrawal of Highway Funds Not Possible." *Clarksdale Daily Register*, December 2, 1931.

Wolcott, Victoria W. *Remaking Respectability: African American Women in Interwar Detroit.* Chapel Hill: University of North Carolina Press, 2001.

Woods, Barbara Allen. *The Devil in Dog Form: A Partial Type-Index of Devil Legends.* Folklore Studies 11. Berkeley: University of California Press, 1959.

Work, John W., Lewis Wade Jones, and Samuel C. Adams Jr. *Lost Delta Found: Rediscovering the Fisk University–Library of Congress Coahoma County Study, 1941–1942*. Edited by Robert Gordon and Bruce Nemerov. Nashville, Tenn.: Vanderbilt University Press, 2005.

"Work on Highway 61." *Biloxi Daily Herald*, June 21, 1932.

Wright, Jesse. "Creator Cleanses Crossroads." *Clarksdale Press-Register*, November 1, 2012.

Young, Alan. *Woke Me Up This Morning: Black Gospel Singers and the Gospel Life*. Jackson: University Press of Mississippi, 1997.

"Young Men's Business Club Gives Endorsement of Western Route for Highway, Approves Rotary's Efforts." *Clarksdale Daily Register*, November 5, 1931.

Yronwode, Catherine. "The Crossroads in Hoodoo Magic and the Ritual of Selling Yourself to the Devil." http://www.luckymojo.com/crossroads.html. Accessed October 12, 2016.

Song Credits

Grateful acknowledgment is made to the following for permission to reprint copyrighted compositions.

"Devil's Got the Blues," by Lonnie Johnson. Published by Lonesome Ghost Blues (SOCAN). Administered by Wixen Music Publishing Inc. All rights reserved. Used by permission.

"Mississippi KKKrossroads," by Chris Thomas King. Published by Young Blues Rebel Music, LLC. All rights reserved. Used by permission.

"I Got the Power." Words and music by Guy Davis. © Medicine Hand Music, Administered by Records on the Wall. All rights reserved. Used by permission.

"Devil's Cadillac," by William P. Homans III. William P. Homans Music (ASCAP). Administered by Chris Hardwick / Southern Artist Management. All rights reserved. Used by permission.

"Somebody Let the Devil Out," by Popa Chubby (Theodore Joseph Horowitz). Dutchdaddy Music (ASCAP) c/o Burton Goldstein & Co LLC. All rights reserved. Used by permission.

"Sounds Like the Devil." Words and music by Charon Shemekia Copeland, John Patrick Hahn, and Kevin So. Published by Shemekia Music, Avarice and Greed Publishing, and Wing Bone Music. All rights reserved. Used by permission.

"I Thought I Heard the Devil," by Walter C. Trout. Published by Yakkabiz Music (ASCAP). Administered by Little Bad Ruf Music. All rights reserved. Used by permission.

"Done with the Devil." Words by Jason Ricci, music by Shawn Dustin Stachurski. All rights reserved. Used by permission.

"She Wasn't Nothin' but a Devil." Words and music by John Lee Hooker Jr. © 2004 John Lee Hooker Jr. and On the Hook Blues Music (BMI). Administered by BMG Rights Management US, LLC, d.b.a. BMG Bumblebee. All rights reserved. Used by permission. Reprinted with permission of Hal Leonard Corporation.

Index

Abjection, 15, 151, 189, 222–23, 227, 236
Ace, Johnny, 21
Africa. *See* Blues: African cultural origins of; Crossroads: in African cosmology; Devil: as African cultural inheritance; Devil's music: African origins of
African Americans. *See* Black man; Black woman
African Methodist Episcopal (AME) Church: condemnation of dance by, 100; ministers, 33, 35
Alabama, 33, 43, 94, 101, 120, 208
Alexander, "Texas," 175, 347n19
"All in My Mind" (M. Brown), 84
"Another Woman Booked Out and Bound to Go" (Johnson), 172
Arkansas, 19, 41, 57, 82, 123, 124, 128, 142, 144, 217, 266, 288
Armstrong, Louis, 81, 339n7
Arnold, Eddy, 293
"At da' Crossroads" (Jones), 313

Bailey, Red Mike, 126
Baker, Houston A., 86, 96, 108, 123, 139, 146, 149
Banjo, 23, 31, 39, 42, 204–5, 339n13
Baptist(s), 35, 41, 60, 81; blues musician as, 7, 21, 47; church-building, 32, 64; condemnation of the blues, 47, 72; conversion, 28; distinction between "good music" and "devil's music," 320; dress code, 37, 84; founding of Church of God in Christ, 37; and guitar, 36, 37; and "Heaven and Hell" party, 67–68, 106; and Robert Johnson, 319; and migration, 90; minister/ preacher, 32, 33, 38, 43, 45, 48, 50, 55, 74, 80, 83, 97, 102, 179, 185, 320, 321–322, 339n7, 341n51; and morals,

61, 100; National Baptist Convention, 100–101; National Baptist Women's Convention, 84; and respectability, 81, 83
Barbieri, Vic, 15–16, 255–60, 273, 281, 291–97, 300, 303, 305–6, 307, 311, 325, 357n121, 360n223
Berlin, Irving, 78
Big Bill (Broonzy), 5–6, 13, 36, 96, 124–31, 135, 144, 149, 153, 348n44, 348n58
Big Wheeler, 8
"Black, Brown, and White" (Broonzy), 6, 124–25, 131
Black Diamond Express to Hell (Nix), 90, 101–2, 104
Black man: association with devil's daughter, 109; as authenticator of younger white blues musician, 235; black woman's criticism of, 159; in Clarksdale, Miss., 310; complaints about black woman, 183; control over black woman, 164; as creative artist, 17, 53; in *Crossroads*, 233; and cross-roads mythology, 17, 203, 204, 250; as devil figure, 17, 113; in folklore, 111; impact of southern penal system on, 122–23; and Jim Crow, 139; perception of southern white man as devil, 129; as pimp, 85, 95, 105; as preacher, 53; resistance to white authority, 111, 125, 136, 144–45, 347; as superior blues singer, 231, 249; as subject of white violence, 112, 118, 124, 125, 126, 127–28, 138, 141, 151, 164, 178, 348; and white man's sexual predation, 163, 164; and white woman, 130, 144–45, 164, 178, 250. *See also* Bluesman; "Devil Jumped the Black Man"

"Black Mountain Blues" (Smith), 9–10, 188–89

Black woman: black man's complaints about, 183; black man's control over, 163; bluesman's troubled relationship with, 47; as "fallen woman," 88; lyric use of devil by, 188; as migrant, 74; National League for the Protection of Colored Women, 85, 87; and politics of respectability, 96; and prostitution, 84–85, 95; relationship with black man, 164, 188; and sexual freedom, 154; temptation of, 83; as urban worker, 83; and white bossman, 134; white man's sexual exploitation of, 163, 164, 178

Black Spider Dumpling. See Twitty, John D.

Blind Boy Fuller, 170

Blind Lemon Jefferson, 8, 46

Bloomfield, Michael, 177, 238, 242

"Blue Devil Blues" (Alexander), 175

Blues, 108; and addiction, 181; African cultural origins of, 10–13, 22–25, 132–33, 186, 338n24; association with jazz, 75, 84, 97, 105, 248; association with migration and prostitution, 83–86; audience, 2, 13, 53, 67, 81, 88, 90, 105, 116, 124, 129, 140, 146, 166, 220, 223, 225, 228, 233–34, 237, 239, 240, 253, 287, 308, 315–16, 348n58; awards, 15, 235, 237, 241–42, 243–44, 248, 283; as "bad behavior," 135; "battle" in *Crossroads*, 234; black familial condemnation of, 64, 72–73, 82–83, 142; and black masculinity, 152, 163, 168, 173, 180; black ministerial condemnation of, 21–22, 23, 33, 38, 44–46, 51, 53, 60, 72–73, 82–83, 142; black ministerial defense of, 22, 32–33, 48, 321, 341n51; "blues matrix," 86; British, 246, 355n94; community condemnation of, 83, 148, 200, 213, 318, 320; as confessional mode, 111, 157; in contemporary period, 150–53, 193–94, 199, 214, 235–49, 254, 312–22, 355n93; culture, 1, 13, 18–19, 38, 60, 61, 231, 244, 306, 313; and dancing, 49, 81, 97, 99, 105; Delta, 20, 67–68, 195, 201, 223, 232, 236, 241, 252, 290, 296, 304, 320, 344n5; demimonde, 87, 160–61, 248; demonization of, 25, 32, 36–37, 64, 199; development of, 3, 140, 207; as devil's music, 22–25, 33, 37–38, 42, 46, 50, 52–53, 59, 64, 72, 84, 327, 338n24; dream narratives in, 98; embrace of by 1920s urbanites, 62; ethos, 148–49; as "evil," 3, 6, 7, 56; fans/aficionados, 2, 16, 128, 181, 194, 200, 202, 229, 231–32, 235, 236, 237, 239, 241, 243, 262–63, 277, 281, 285, 288, 298, 307, 308, 312, 321, 355n93, 355n95; and Faustian storyline, 34; favorable invocations of the devil in, 78; and fiddle, 31, 36, 52; in film, 2; as forbidden fruit, 43; as form of devil worship, 83; as form of preaching, 5, 52, 56, 64, 185–86; future of, 232, 235, 242, 244, 248–49, 252; as gateway to hell, 38, 41; grooves, 50; Ground Zero Blues Club, 16; and guitar, 16, 36–39, 52, 75, 177, 195, 204, 234, 238–39, 242, 243, 244, 251–53, 307; and harmonica, 5, 340n46; highways, 260, 268, 270, 277; "hokum," 174; interview, 17–18, 33; jump, 142; as locus of romantic ambivalence, 175, 178–79, 184, 192; lore, 3, 169, 308; lyric tradition, 2, 75, 86, 108–9, 122, 155, 158, 194, 249, 271; market for, 174, 220, 258, 262, 279, 281; "ministerial blues," 21, 51, 57–58; Mr. Blues, 10, 140, 141; mixed with sacred material, 8; as "moving spirit," 59–60; mythology, 3, 14, 17, 49, 62, 86, 150, 231, 232, 246, 247, 309; and paternal disappearance, 135; and piano, 42–43, 75, 126, 143; postmodernity, 244–45, 247, 249–50, 356n106; in post-Reconstruction period, 8; as protest, 124, 135; rap and, 150, 269; "real," 238, 245, 246, 288, 289; refutation of devil's music charge by performers of, 18–19, 39–42, 47–48, 67–68; rise of, 21, 64, 122, 247; romance, 154–92; as

Brown, Willie, 2, 64, 201–2, 214, 218, 221, 222–23, 231, 233–34, 240, 243, 245, 247–48, 250, 253–54. *See also* Johnson, Robert; Seneca, Joe
Bryant, Precious, 8
Bumble Bee Slim. *See* Easton, Amos
Bunch, William. *See* Wheatstraw, Peetie
"Burnin' Hell" (Hooker), 47–48, 50, 70, 73
Burns, Eddie, 21, 48, 182
"Busy Devil" (Easton), 162–63, 168

"C and A Train Blues" (Wheatstraw), 143
"Can't Be Trusted Blues" (Weaver), 10, 132, 136–37
Carter, Bo, 52–53
Cartwright, Keith, 11, 22, 151, 252
Castro, Tommy, 316
"Cat's Got the Measles, The" (Jackson), 174
Cephas, John, 21, 314, 339n7
Chatmon, Bo, 10, 51, 132
Chicago, 33, 38–39, 57, 59, 62, 64, 75, 82, 83, 94, 96, 97, 101, 103, 112, 117, 125, 126, 129, 130, 132, 141–42, 144, 155, 162, 177, 211, 232, 236, 240, 245, 270–71, 281, 293, 341n51. *See also* "Sweet Home Chicago"
Church of God in Christ (COGIC), 352n69; acceptance of guitar by, 37; condemnation of blues by, 37, 72; dress code of, 37, 72, 84; emphasis on respectability, 81
Civil rights movement, 6, 149, 250, 297, 300
Clapton, Eric, 2, 193, 242, 246, 304, 316, 337n2, 360n1
Clarksdale, Miss., 20, 21, 38, 42, 45, 47, 48, 50, 54, 56, 57, 59, 60–61, 65, 67–68, 80, 106, 193–95, 212, 217, 246–47, 259–60, 263, 264, 265, 266, 269, 298, 321, 358n175, 361n11; Bill Clinton's visit to, 305; blues tourism in, 247, 255, 288, 297–303; City Beautification Commission, 278, 280, 291, 295–96, 299, 305, 309; conflict with state (1930s), 257, 262; conflict with state (1990s), 262, 295–96; Morgan

Freeman and, 281, 306; Ground Zero Blues Club, 16, 281; "new" crossroads, 1, 15–16, 193, 255, 257–58, 261–62, 267–303, 304–11, 359n204; "old" crossroads, 257, 268–72, 278, 305, 311. *See also* Blues tourism/tourists; Crossroads; Delta Blues Museum; Delta, the; Luckett, Bill
Clearwater, Eddy "The Chief," 21, 42
Collins, Sam, 137
Conforth, Bruce, 14, 209, 266–67
Conversion, 103; antebellum era, 26, 28–30, 98, 113, 169, 227; by blues musician, 7, 40, 203–4; to devil, 91; to Pentecostalism, 100
Cooke, Sam, 21, 257, 287, 290
Copeland, Johnny, 138–40, 244
Copeland, Shemekia, 314–15
Cotton, James, 182, 236
"Couldn't Find a Mule" (Sunnyland Slim), 114–15
"Crawling Kingsnake" (Hollins), 46
"Crooked Woman Blues" (Fuller), 170
"Cross Road Blues" (Johnson), 14, 19, 193, 197, 198, 202, 214, 219–22, 223, 225, 226, 229–30, 249, 257–58, 260, 282, 290–92, 299, 304, 327
Crossroads: in African cosmology, 3, 12–13, 23, 75, 132–33, 143–44, 156–57, 197, 199, 206–7, 210, 246, 247, 251, 338n24, 352–53n5; in American folklore, 2, 23, 113, 199–200, 204–6, 211–12, 217, 247, 250; in blues mythologies, 3, 10, 12, 16, 17, 20, 74, 156–57, 193, 195–96, 197–98, 200, 201, 202–4, 207, 208, 210–17, 219–30, 231–32, 233, 246, 247, 251, 262–71, 279–92, 297–299, 301, 306–11, 312–13, 319–20; in European folklore, 12, 23, 197, 199, 206, 210; Guitar Festival, 193; and Robert Johnson, 2, 14, 16, 17, 74, 193, 195–96, 197–98, 201, 204, 207, 208–17, 219–30, 231, 246, 247, 257, 258–59, 263–71, 279–92, 295, 297–299, 301, 304, 306–11, 312–13, 319–20; and Tommy Johnson, 202–4; in other Mississippi locations, 262, 285–86,

and women, 169; Robert Johnson and, 14, 195, 210

bluesman's identification with, 68, 133, 163, 168; bluesman's refutation of imputed, 52; devil as, 109, 113, 132, 152, 156, 183, 187, 199; good and, 10, 40, 175, 192; and jazz, 100; in Jazz Age, 100; Robert Johnson as, 50, 68, 70; slaveholding South as, 119, 120; spirits, 22, 209; "strong sense" of, 113; terrorism as, 314; whiteness as, 3, 8, 109, 111, 114, 153; white southern lawman as, 150; woman as, 129, 169

"Evil Blues" (Jackson), 17

Father of the Blues (Handy), 33–34

Faustian bargain. *See* Crossroads

Ferguson, H. Bomb, 21, 42–43, 45

Ferris, William, 37, 26, 281

Fiddle, 26–31, 33, 36, 42, 92, 204; demonization of, 25, 50, 63, 340n44; as devil's instrument, 28, 31, 45; slave musician's use of, 20, 24, 51–52, 339n13

Finn, Julio, 3, 75, 202, 210

"First Time I Met You, The" (Montgomery), 141

Floyd, Samuel, 3, 75, 207, 338n24

Folklorist, 12, 14, 31, 37, 38, 56, 62, 91, 113, 125, 213, 247, 281

"Fool's Blues" (Smith), 7

Foster, Willie, 4

"From Four Until Late" (Johnson), 225–26

Fusco, John, 15, 234, 236, 244, 247–48, 282, 285

Gaither, Bill, 10, 132, 163

Garon, Paul, 3, 6–7, 132, 142–44

Gates, Henry Louis, 10–11

Georgia, 30, 83, 102, 106, 117–18, 127, 153, 197, 198

Georgia Tom, 133

Gillum, Bill "Jazz," 177–78

Glover, Lillie Mae "Big Mama," 21, 82, 84

Gomes, Anthony, 313

Goodson, Ida, 21, 43

Gospeleers, The, 55, 59

Gospel music, 18, 32, 36–37, 43, 45, 51, 191, 307–8, 319–21, 327

Grainger, Porter, 13, 86, 91, 185

Gray, Harold. *See* Grainger, Porter

Great Awakening, 26, 27, 32, 45, 67, 107

Great Migration, 22, 51, 57, 59, 62, 64, 68

Great Revival, 169

Greeley, Andrew, 7

Griot, 22–23, 338n24, 339n10

Ground Zero Blues Club, 16, 281. *See also* Clarksdale, Miss.

Guitar, 14–16, 17, 22, 23, 32, 35–39, 42, 48, 49, 51–52, 56, 62, 64, 75, 82, 93, 141–42, 161, 170, 177, 193, 195–96, 199, 201, 203–4, 205–6, 208–12, 214, 218, 221, 223–24, 229, 231, 233–34, 236–38, 239–46, 249, 251, 252–53, 254, 255, 257, 258, 260–61, 253–67, 270, 284, 288–89, 290, 291, 292, 294, 297, 299, 306, 307, 309, 311, 321; as devil's instrument, 20, 34, 36, 38–39, 41, 46; steel-string, 15, 20, 35–37, 42, 293. *See also* Blues; Bluesman; Crossroads

Guy, Buddy, 238, 241, 316

Handy, W. C., 21, 33–36, 38, 46, 60, 71, 76, 77, 80, 81–82; Blues Awards (Handys), 235, 237, 241–42, 243–44, 248

Hardin, Lil, 81–82, 84

Harlem, 37, 62, 75, 80, 87, 88, 100–101, 103, 108, 297

Harmonica, 5, 19, 35, 38, 48, 64, 177, 231, 239, 252, 292

Hazzard-Donald, Katrina, 11, 97, 210, 228

"Heaven and Hell" party, 73, 106

"He Calls That Religion" (Mississippi Sheiks), 51–53, 54, 68, 72

Hell, 56, 92, 105, 177; black romantic relationships as, 155, 163, 167, 183, 184, 190–92; blues association with, 5, 18–19, 22, 38, 41, 43; bluesman as ruler of, 136, 153, 167; bluesman's skepticism about, 47–49, 72–73; in blues recordings, 2, 122, 151; as code for Jim Crow South, 5, 109, 112–13, 116–18, 122–31, 153, 194; and "Cross Road Blues," 221–23; in *Crossroads*, 233; dance association with, 28, 38, 80, 90, 97, 99, 102, 103; as devil's residence,

Johnson, Mary, 21, 41, 170

Johnson, Merline, 13, 34, 95–96, 352n73

Johnson, Robert, 59, 96, 151, 237, 294, 353n29; association with Faust, 34, 202; and Willie Brown, 201, 208, 223, 264–66, 282; Clarksdale, Mississippi's claim on, 1, 15–16, 193–95, 255, 257–63, 266–71, 277–92, 295–311; *Complete Recordings* of, 2, 15, 17, 194, 199, 214, 246, 283, 313, 320; "Cross Road Blues," 14, 19, 197–98, 202, 219–23, 226, 229, 249, 257–58, 260, 282, 290, 292, 304; crossroads mythology and, 1–3, 14–16, 17, 74, 193–205, 207–8, 210–17, 221–22, 230, 249, 255, 257–67, 269–71, 277–79, 281–86, 288–90, 295–99, 301, 304, 306–9, 311, 313, 320; as "early influence" in Rock and Roll Hall of Fame, 246; and Honeyboy Edwards, 213–16, 225, 229, 263, 307; grave site of, 319–20; as haunted figure, 67; "Hell Hound on My Trail," 14, 50, 197, 219–21, 225–28, 229–30; identification with the devil, 10, 20, 41, 49–50, 68–70, 72, 132, 207, 212–13; *King of the Delta Blues Singers*, 199, 220, 246, 304; "Me and the Devil Blues," 14, 22, 49, 68–70, 80, 106, 132, 197, 202, 220–21, 227, 229–30, 262; performing repertoire of, 253; pop-cultural investments in, 193–94, 246, 312–13; pseudonyms of, 217–18; representation in *Crossroads* (1986), 1–2, 14, 199, 231–33, 246, 248–50, 252, 282, 313; scholarship on, 193, 195, 202, 219–21, 224–26, 232–33, 247, 249, 259, 264–67, 299; and Johnny Shines, 215, 218, 223, 263; and Son House, 201, 203–4, 208, 223, 263–67, 278, 289; "They're Red Hot," 224; and Virginia Travis, 208, 212; women and, 218–19, 222, 226–29, 259; as "young modern," 64, 69–71, 74, 197, 210, 228; and Ike Zimmerman, 1, 14, 196, 209–11, 217, 222, 226, 229, 263–64, 267, 276. *See also* "Cross Road Blues;" Crossroads; Devil; "Devilish Blues;" Devil-lore; "Devil's Got the Blues"; "Devil's Woman, The"; Evil; "From Four Until Late"; "Hell Hound on My Trail"; "Rambling on my Mind"; "Sweet Home Chicago"

Johnson, Stovepipe, 10, 132, 133–34, 136–38

Johnson, Tommy, 41, 64, 150, 202–5, 207, 221, 341n81

Jones, Billy, 313

Jones, Deacon, 48–49, 51–53, 57, 67, 68, 79

Jones, Lewis Wade, 62–63, 64

Jones, Maggie, 5

Jordan, Louis, 62, 78–79, 142

Judd, Robert, 15, 232–34, 240, 247–49

Juke joint, 19–20, 24, 36–37, 47, 49, 53, 60, 64, 65, 75, 97, 99, 132, 140, 146, 150, 165, 176–77, 181, 191, 200–201, 203, 211, 221–22, 229, 239, 249–50, 252, 263–67, 271, 278, 297, 306, 310

King, Albert, 236, 237–38, 240–42, 244

King, B. B., 36–37, 46, 64, 124, 236, 289, 321

King, Chris Thomas, 150–52, 194

King, Willie, 149, 198, 236

King and Anderson Plantation, 65, 71, 284

Kubik, Gerhard, 10–12, 24–25, 356n109

Ku Klux Klan (KKK), 112, 113, 117, 141, 153

Lacy, Rev. Rube, 8

LaSalle, Denise, 190–92, 355n93

Legba. *See* Eshu-Elegbara/Eshu/Esu

Leroy's Buddy. *See* Gaither, Bill

Lewis, Noah, 340n46

"Lick It before You Stick It" (LaSalle), 191

Lipscomb, Mance, 7, 21, 40, 128–29, 141

Lomax, Alan, 21, 36, 38, 62–63, 80, 125, 127, 129–30, 135, 213–14, 218

Louisiana, 12, 29–30, 116, 123, 127, 139, 150, 155. *See also* New Orleans

Louisiana Red, 98

Luckett, Bill, 16, 257–59, 267, 276, 281, 291–92, 294, 301, 306

Lynching, 45, 58, 110, 112, 117–18, 122, 131,

Printed in Great Britain
by Amazon